Adam Smith's Theory of Society

Vernon L. Smith

Adam Smith's Theory of Society

Social Rules for Order in Society and Economy

palgrave
macmillan

Vernon L. Smith
Economic Science Institute
Chapman University
Orange, CA, USA

ISBN 978-3-031-68493-7 ISBN 978-3-031-68494-4 (eBook)
https://doi.org/10.1007/978-3-031-68494-4

Cover credit: Adam Smith Business School, CC BY-SA 4.0, via Wikimedia Commons

Acquiring editor: Bronwyn Geyer
Production: Susan Westendorf, Melvin Thomas, Geetha Chockalingam

This Palgrave Macmillan imprint is published by the registered company Springer Nature Switzerland AG
The registered company address is: Gewerbestrasse 11, 6330 Cham, Switzerland

If disposing of this product, please recycle the paper.

Preface

Because it defines the tone and substance of Smith's works, I want to call attention to his first notable composition, which was not published until after his death: Smith, Adam (1982) Essays on Philosophical Subjects including *History of Astronomy*; hereafter, HA) Ed. W.P.D. Wightman and J.C. Bryce. Indianapolis: Liberty Press. The passage from it below nicely illustrates the long influential shadow that Sir Isaac Newton's work had cast into and across the eighteenth century. Newton was the scientific author of the idea that visible motion could be described by invisible forces of nature whose mysteries had remained hidden in the night until he exposed them to the light of his equations of motion. Smith, a deep admirer of Newton was destined to extend this theme and discoveries to a comparably grand theory of morality, society, jurisprudence, and economy. Only ill health and death could interfere with this lifelong intention to write a comprehensive theory of jurisprudence. Smith used the metaphor of the "invisible hand" to describe the attainment of ends that were not part of the intentions of the actors in society.

In Smith's discussion of Newton, he notes that Newton's followers used his equations to predict the arrival of a particular comet in 1757: Comets were objects in the sky that had attracted the least attention from astronomers. The rarity and inconstancy of their appearance, seemed to define them in a separate category not plainly part of the more constant, regular, uniform heavenly objects, but rather that of the inconstant, transitory, and accidental that suddenly appeared in the earth's neighborhood.

Using his principles, Newton's followers ventured to predict the returns of several of these comets, especially one which is expected to appear in 1758. Smith and Hume before him had championed the "method of experimental reasoning" in which theory had to pass tests in a form represented by "experiments," by which they meant cases, where if a theory failed to account for case examples it must be reexamined and perhaps relegated to the dump heap.[1] Hence the significance of comets in HA. The comet Smith refers to is the one famously discovered by Edmund Halley, that returns about every 76 years. Its last appearances were in 1910 and 1986 (which I observed) and its next is scheduled for July 28, 2061. The 1758 sighting must have been truly astounding to Smith's eighteenth-century contemporaries. Newton had died only 31 years earlier, in 1727, and is here dominating the news with a confirmed prediction of a rare once-in-a-lifetime heavenly event.

Orange, USA Vernon L. Smith

[1] Without pursuing the details here, I should note that Newton and his followers saw theory as being deduced directly from the observational evidence, a proposition subsequently found to be flawed. See: Smith, Vernon L. (2008) *Rationality in Economics*. Cambridge: Cambridge University Press, pp. 283–311.

A Note from the Author

This book is a consequence of my personal interest in persuading contemporary intellectuals, writers, and academics to directly study the contributions of Adam Smith, especially his lesser-known book from 1759, *The Theory of Moral Sentiments and on the Origins of Languages* (*hereafter TMS*). The version referenced in this book is the Stewart edition, published by Henry G. Bohn in 1853.

This interest grew with the gradual deepening of my study of *TMS* and the intellectual rewards of learning from its unique and penetrating contribution to an understanding of the individual human's experience of others, its immediate and refreshing relevance to our contemporary world, and for the lives of all ordinary people.

On his deathbed in 1790 Adam Smith famously insisted that his friends—Joseph Black (Chemist) and David Hutton (Geologist)—burn all his papers. Previously he had left the same instructions to his philosopher friend David Hume, but Hume died in 1776. Smith was thus not deranged, but rather consciously concerned throughout his life, as a careful and scholarly writer, that his works which had not been completed to his satisfaction would be misinterpreted. What he did not understand nor anticipate was that his finished and published work, though completed to his satisfaction, would be misinterpreted anyway. Fortunately, he gave his friends discretion in including or not his "juvenal" *History of Astronomy*. But they burned his other papers and denied us knowledge of his working progress on a lifelong project to write a comprehensive theory of jurisprudence.

It is a rare scholar who can competently anticipate how posterity will judge his or her work. Smith overvalued the importance of published finished work and undervalued the impact of his scholarship on subsequent generations. It is better perhaps to let the chips fall where they may, which for most scholars means historical oblivion however much recognized and admired by one's contemporaries.

These characteristics apply most especially to *TMS* which was well received at the time of its publication then later—certainly by the twentieth century—was more commonly ignored, if not misunderstood, but is today being seen in a new appreciative light as a profound contribution.[1] In *TMS*, we find a systematic model of human sociability that views society as an emergent creation of ordinary people like you, me, and our neighbors whenever and wherever we grew up and wherever we might have moved about—a process that would have begun by its nature well before our first ancestors walked out of Africa. The theory constitutes a narrative-model about us as social creatures and why and how this collective of people we call "us" came to exist entirely without any intention or awareness—we did it unknowingly because we could not prevent its natural emergence and evolution governed by the "Great Author of Nature."

Subpopulations of us like the ancient Jews, aware that they were rule-followers but seemingly *unaware that they were rule-creators*, attributed this trait to their God having given the rules—in a form emphasizing the great "shalt not's"—to their leader Moses on a mountain top etched in stone tablets. These humans, curious like all peoples, had a deep need to explain and not yet having conceived of a natural science, or of nature's explanation, interpreted the essence of their rule-following society as a covenant from God.

In defense of the open mind, who's to say it was not?

[1] See Horn, Karen (2024) "Challenging the clichés: How recent scholarship refreshes the interpretation of Adam Smith's oeuvre." *Perspektiven der Wirtschaftspolitik*, January 10, online. https://www.degruyter.com/document/doi/10.1515/pwp-2023-0055/html.

Contents

CHAPTER 1

Introduction

Smith sought to explore the origins of culture and society in the propensity of all people everywhere to follow and fashion rules out of their day-to-day experience of living with each other—rules that enhance their happiness through beneficence and diminish their unhappiness through justice. The process was a consequence of a slow and gradual development by "nature," Smith's metaphor for how we learn God's will through our on-the-ground experience of each other.

And hence my design for a titled series of entries, at paragraph levels, to be part of, and to learn from, Adam Smith's articulation of a theory of society. These titles provide a detailed sketch of his model, unique manner of thought, and its implications for our loves and lives.

You may find it difficult to believe that Adam Smith's primary insights and understandings are not thoroughly incorporated into modern literature. But modern literature, including economics, has been, I believe, a distraction, a diversion from the roots of our intellectual social development. A clue signaling some of the evidence for this cultural separation is that many of the eighteenth-century key words that Smith used have fallen into disuse or have changed in their meaning, revealing changes in how we think, believe, and act. Thus, in *TMS*, we do not just approve, or disapprove, of some person's action in a particular circumstance; rather,

Vernon L. Smith, *Adam Smith's Theory of Society*,
https://doi.org/10.1007/978-3-031-68494-4_1

the person's action meets with our approbation or disapprobation.[1] As an alternative to "approbation" Smith sometimes uses "merits applause." The word "applause" captures the sentiment of simultaneous and spontaneous fellow-feeling, its recognition, and expression. Context specific rules emerging in practice are screened, selected, and adopted or rejected by community consent via their approbation or disapprobation. This concept of a community-based consensus on judgments of right and wrong action was implicit in the thinking and, therefore, in the words people used.

A key word whose meaning and significance has changed categorically is "fair," which meant "fair-play," or equality of application and enforcement of the rules that govern human action—not equality of outcomes—and whose opposite was "foul," not "unfair." Indeed, as demonstrated by the great linguist, Anna Wierzbicka, "fair" was a unique English word untranslatable into any other language.[2] Adam Smith had observed that people often find differential outcomes disagreeable, not least because of envy, but also because of superficial reputational attainments and pursuits failing to meaningfully satisfy, but there was no suggestion that this was an unfair undeserved state. (*TMS*, pp. 55–58, 61–78.)

"Awful" has reversed its meaning since Smith's time. In Samuel Johnson (1755, Aa), we have:

> A'wful. adj. [from awe and full.]... That which strikes with awe, or fills with reverence.

[1] From Johnson, Samuel (1755). *A Dictionary of the English Language*. Printed by W. Strahan (London), for J. and P. Knapton; T. and T. Longman; C. Hitch and L. Hawes; A. Millar; and R. and J. Dodsley. 2021. https://johnsonsdictionaryonline.com.

"Approba'tion. n.s. [approbatio, Lat.].

1. The act of approving, or expressing himself pleased.

That not past me, but.

By learned approbation of my judges.

Shakesp. Henry VIII.

2. The liking of any thing.

There is no positive law of men, whether received by formal consent, as in councils, or by secret approbation, as in customs, but may be taken away.

Hooker, b. iv. § 14.".

[2] Wierzbicka, Anna (2006) *English: Meaning and Culture*. Oxford: Oxford University Press, Chap. 5.

And here is how Smith uses the word:

> the great, the awful, and respectable, the virtues of self-denial, of self-government, of that command of the passions which subjects all the movements of our nature to what our own dignity and honour, and the propriety of our own conduct, require... (*TMS*, p. 26)

It was late in my professional career as an economist when I first read, and, out of fascination, began revisiting *TMS* the better to comprehend Smith's model of society, but also his precise and powerful methodological style. I first cited *TMS* in 1998,[3] I cannot, however, pretend to have approached any very deep comprehension of it, for I was not yet able to enter his thought patterns or to see and think about human social experiences as I came to believe that Adam Smith did. In the subsequent 25-year interval I have come to appreciate *TMS* as one of the great intellectual triumphs in the human career. Yet *TMS* is little known to economists and social scientists and has often been unfavorably compared with his better-known subsequent work, *The Wealth of Nations* (1776; hereafter, *WN*), by distinguished scholars whose ignorance of *TMS* is breathtaking but reflects a reality I would hope to help change.

It is noteworthy, however, that all of Smith's biographers report his own opinion that *TMS* was his best work.

I know of no other work comparable to its deep examination of the origins and foundations of society. What most uniquely matters is that Smith's model of community and society grows naturally out of our learning to follow rules of beneficent and just conduct based in family, extended family, neighbors, community, and nation. It is a rich narrative. It is yours. It is mine. It is that of others, and of a natural spontaneous diversity, and we are all well advised to know it. Generally, in conveying and elaborating upon his message in this book, I follow the text sequentially in *TMS*, with only occasional deviations. Also, where relevant I introduce passages from some of his other works.

My comments explicate his propositional predictive scientific style of thought, offering modern interpretations, and examples, but I cannot resist replicating the exquisite charm of his eighteenth-century King's English for want of anything comparable in our contemporary world.

[3] Smith, Vernon L. (1998) "The Two Faces of Adam Smith," Southern Economic Association Distinguished Guest Lecture. *Southern Economic Journal*, 65 (1), pp. 1–19.

Reminiscent of a prominent market theme in *WN*, which echoes Newton's account of invisible forces producing visible motion, in *TMS*, people intending only to better "get along with" their neighbors, achieve robust societal rules of order that are no part of their original design.

Smith's theory of society culminates in detailed formal propositions that are testable and there are cases everywhere, including laboratory decision experiments, that are consistent with his primary predictions, although the departures from expectations are easily as important as the confirmations. This is because Smith's propositions have many component moving parts, and the parts can be varied in saliency depending upon the relative payoffs to the actors, thus suggesting tests of their relative importance. A few of these experimental explorations have been reported but more will depend on a greater familiarity with *TMS*.[4]

Although this book was motivated by the theory and the theorizing process in *TMS*, that turned into an unanticipated pathway to a pleasant and delightful bonus: The rules for an orderly society emerge from rules that better people's lives, and this book has potential for helping you live a better life. Try it, I think you will like it as I did. Its propositions apply to you, your associates, your friends, family, and loved ones.

There is no other window on your own life, and that of an orderly society, quite like this one.

TMS is a difficult challenging study that constitutes a beautiful but rigorous treatment of why, how, and to what purpose we humankind are social and have created orderly communities that scale up to large societies. It scales down smoothly in helping us to simultaneously think and act morally within the limits of our vulnerability. It was there in antiquity—as today in you, in me, in our neighbor—when The Great Author of Nature prepared us for community, society, and nation. No more superior mansions could ever be built.

Why and how are we social?.

In *TMS* Adam Smith answers the implicit question of why and how we humans are social by supposing that a human being is born and grows to maturity in complete isolation from any other member of the species.

[4] Refer to Chaps. 8–13 in Smith, Vernon L. and Bart J. Wilson, 2019, *Humanomics*. Cambridge: Cambridge University Press.

Such a person:

> could not know any more about what it might mean for their mind to be deformed than for their face to be deformed. They could no more think of their own character, of the propriety or demerit of their own sentiments and conduct, of the beauty or deformity of their own mind, than of the beauty or deformity of their own face. All these are objects not part of their awareness, which naturally they do not look at, and about which they are supplied with no mirror which can present them to their view. Bring that person into society, however, and they are immediately provided with the mirror which they were lacking before. The mirror is placed in the countenance and behavior of all those that the person lives with, and who always mark when they enter into, and when they disapprove of the person's sentiments. It is here that the person first views the propriety and impropriety of their own passions, the beauty and deformity of their own mind, or their own face. To a person who from birth was a stranger to society, the objects of his passions, the external bodies which either pleased or hurt them, would occupy their entire attention. The passions themselves, the desires or aversions, the joys or sorrows, which those objects excited, though all are most immediate, cannot ever be the objects of their thoughts. The objects cannot interest the person's attentive consideration. The consideration of their joy could in them excite no new joy, nor that of their sorrow any new sorrow, though the consideration of the causes of those passions might often excite both. Bring the person into society, and all their own passions will immediately become the causes of new passions. They will observe that humankind approves of some of them and are disgusted by others. They will be elevated in the one case and cast down in the other; their desires and aversions, their joys and sorrows, will now often become the causes of new desires and new aversions, new joys and new sorrows: these will now, therefore, interest him deeply, and often call upon their most attentive consideration. (*TMS*, pp. 162–163)

We become social through others in relating to them.

The three-step process of socialization

We first learn what another person must feel by changing places with them in our imagination when we recall what we feel when we have been in situations like they now experience. The process is imperfect and deepens with practice and repetition. The exact context and circumstances of this other are important because these are what excite our imagination and remembered experiences. Second, we become aware that others are engaged in the same process of learning about us by changing places with us and imagining what we must feel. It is this foundation that gives rise to an ability to see ourselves as others see us. And third, we begin to take account of how others perceive and judge us when we choose our own actions.

When does it begin in our experience?

Smith's narrative begins with the observation that the very young child has no self-command. A child's parents, nurse, and protectors attend to its needs taking care to protect it from hazards in its environment. Learning about what others must feel begins later as it grows among family, friends, and intimates. It begins in the community with our playmates about the time the child is old enough to go to school, or to mix with its equals, as it soon finds that they have no such indulgent partiality as our parents. The child naturally wishes to gain their favor, acceptance, and to avoid their hatred or contempt. Regard even to its own safety teaches it to do so; and it soon finds that it can do so in no other way than by moderating, not only its anger, but all its other passions, to the degree which its playfellows and companions are likely to be pleased with.

The great school of self command

> Thus does the child enter, and embark upon, the great school of self-command. It studies to be more and more the Master of Itself; and begins to exercise over its own feelings a discipline which the practice of the longest life is very seldom sufficient to bring to complete perfection. (*TMS*, pp. 203–204)

PART I

Of the sense of propriety

This part concerns "Propriety," or the appropriateness of actions of a beneficial tendency, and the inappropriateness of actions of a hurtful tendency that we seek to limit. These two sets of conceptually distinct actions both express and define our sociability, or humanness, the first to increase our happiness, the second to reduce our unhappiness. Smith creates a grand theory of society unparalleled in its relevance for the contemporary understanding of the society in which we live.

I believe that the truth of this evaluation can only be grasped by a careful and systematic reading of Adam Smith's works beginning with *TMS*. Accordingly, what follows are a great many separately titled entries largely from *TMS* followed by my comments, explanations, elaborations, digressions, and references where appropriate.

CHAPTER 2

Of sympathy

Humankind's motivating principles include their deep interest in the happiness of others.

> How selfish soever man may be supposed, there are evidently some principles in his nature, which interest him in the fortune of others, and render their happiness necessary to him, though he derives nothing from it, except the pleasure of seeing it. (*TMS*, p. 3)

The key modeling concepts expressed here are conveyed in the words "principles" and "nature." Principles as revealed in the form of the rules we follow in our interactive relations with others and are what cause strictly self-interested people to be other-regarding in the actions they take toward others. We are rightly, naturally, and essentially, self-interested, for as Smith observes, no one is better positioned than you are for taking care of yourself, and others in taking care of themselves.

Smith's methodology—foreign to the contemporary modeling of human action—is founded on his fundamental distinction between people being self-interested and acting in their self-interest. In this, Smith stood unique among his Scotch contemporaries and, with equal force, among modern theorists of socio-economic action who predominantly explain such actions as attributable to "social" or "altruistic" preferences which, unlike Smith's model, fail to make general circumstance-specific predictions of the form: Z given circumstances Y implies X. Rather, the modern

Vernon L. Smith, *Adam Smith's Theory of Society*,
https://doi.org/10.1007/978-3-031-68494-4_2

methodology is to backward induct from discovered empirical regularities in choice to infer what particular utility preference function might be consistent with the discovered regularity.

Many of Smith's propositions are crisply stated, rigorous and falsifiable:

> Actions of a beneficent tendency, which proceed from proper motives, seem alone to require a reward; because such alone are the approved objects of gratitude, or excite the sympathetic gratitude of the spectator. (*TMS*, p. 112)

Other propositions are more conjectural inviting exploration and further consideration:

> Love is an agreeable, resentment a disagreeable passion and accordingly we are not half so anxious that our friends should adopt our friendships, as that they should enter into our resentments. (*TMS*, p. 12)

Thus, for Smith the glue that binds friends may be much more concerned with sharing "enemies" in common than the sharing of other friends. Imagine making many acquaintances, some of them become friends. Then you discover that in matters of politics you and your friend are opposites. Your friend does not share your taste either in political parties or candidates.

This is more likely to be a strain on your relationship than would otherwise occur. You and your friend drift apart. Similarly with others, so that your friends predominantly are characterized by sharing a common dislike for the same politicians. Hence, Smith's proposition.

In my discussion of the entries from *TMS*, I will often cite modern discoveries and learning, showing how they are predicted in *TMS*; some scholars say they are "anticipated" in *TMS* which is merely a euphemistic form of admitting that we were not aware of the modernity of Smith's contributions and out of ignorance failed to cite him. Also, they sometimes presume that recent contributions are superior to those of Smith two hundred and sixty-five years earlier, a largely uniformed claim without merit.

Sociability and what others might feel

Our sociability begins with knowing what others might feel.

> As we have no immediate experience of what other men feel, we can form no idea of the manner in which they are affected, but by conceiving what we ourselves should feel in the like situation. (*TMS*, p. 3)

All knowledge of others, which is the driving source of order in human society, originates in our experience of ourselves and, in this knowledge, inferring via our imagination what others must feel and experience when in situations like, or analogous to, those that we have experienced.

Fellow-feeling accounts for our joy and grief in the experiences of others.

> Whatever is the passion which arises from any object in the person principally concerned, an analogous emotion springs up, at the thought of his situation, in the breast of every attentive spectator. Our joy for the deliverance of those heroes of tragedy or romance who interest us, is as sincere as our grief for their distress, and our fellow-feeling with their misery is not more real than that with their happiness. (*TMS*, p. 5)

Consider the popularity of modern movies created by our favorite performers—John Wayne, Katherine Hepburn, Spencer Tracey, Clint Eastwood, Ingrid Bergman, and Glenda Jackson. We fellow feel their sorrows, their joys, their distress, and their perplexities as if we were in their scenes. We also chuckle at their aphorisms, as when John Wayne declares: "No one can own a cat." Smiith's knowledge of English, Roman, and Greek plays was an immense source of information to discipline and inform his theory.

Sympathy will be used to denote our fellow-feeling with any passion.

> Pity and compassion are words appropriated to signify our fellow-feeling with the sorrow of others. Sympathy, though its meaning was, perhaps, originally the same, may now, however, without much impropriety, be made use of to denote our fellow-feeling with any passion whatever. (*TMS*, p. 5)

Smith didn't have the word "empathy," which entered common English use only in the twentieth century. By "sympathy" he will include fellow-feeling with any passion that invokes it. But his conception of mutual reciprocal fellow-feeling was stronger than mere empathy in conveying the idea of bidirectionality and simultaneity at the roots of human emotions and human sociability. Because third-party observers concur and consent in sympathy with principals, bilateral social interactions meet with the approbation (or disapprobation) of others, become multilateral, and characterize community. Hence, simply modernizing Smith's "sympathy" with "empathy" is neither satisfactory nor complete.

Not knowing their provocation, the angry person invokes no sympathy.

> There are some passions of which the expressions excite no sort of sympathy, but, before we are acquainted with what gave occasion to them, serve rather to disgust and provoke us against them. The furious behaviour of an angry man is more likely to exasperate us against himself than against his enemies. As we are unacquainted with his provocation, we cannot bring his case home to ourselves. (*TMS*, p. 6)

Smith's style is to give illustrative examples and often to give or imply contrary examples demonstrating the important conditionals of a proposition. It is thus true that excesses in the expressed emotion of anger are more difficult for an observer to bring home to their inner world, that is, until and unless they are acquainted with the exact provocative circumstances of the angry person.

Sympathetic fellow-feeling requires a context.

> Sympathy ... does not arise so much from the view of the passion, as from that of the situation which excites it. (*TMS*, p. 7)

The sympathy we feel for another tends to be specifically bound to the situation experienced because emotions are nuanced in the context associated with them. If we know nothing of the situation in which another experiences pain or elation, our capacity for fellow-feeling with these emotions is muted or even distorted.

Our imagined dread of death serves society by restraining injustice.

> It is from this very illusion of the imagination, that the foresight of our own dissolution is so terrible to us, and that the idea of those circumstances, which undoubtedly can give us no pain when we are dead, makes us miserable while we are alive. And from thence arises one of the most important

> principles in human nature, the dread of death—the great poison to the happiness, but the great restraint upon the injustice of mankind; which, while it afflicts and mortifies the individual, guards and protects the society. (*TMS*, p. 9)

Smith's dreary discussion of death, which I have here shortened, seems to have the intention of explaining why that anxious human dread serves to restrain actions that might lead to a person's death in this life, and why people everywhere have supported capital punishment to deter murder. As we shall see, however, Smith was aware of the widespread early historical use of victim compensation as a punishment for murder that attempted to help restore the wholeness of the victim.

Fellow-feeling is the source of our greatest pleasure.

> But whatever may be the cause of sympathy, or however it may be excited, nothing pleases us more than to observe in other men a fellow-feeling with all the emotions of our own breast; nor are we ever so much shocked as by the appearance of the contrary. (*TMS*, p. 10)

Smith believes that there is a pleasure in fellow-feeling that lives in a different space from that which we find in the calculus of utilitarianism, wherein: Action-for-Own implies Own-Outcome implies Actor-Own-Pleasure. Perhaps Smith's proposition can be depicted more precisely as Action-for-Own-Other implies Joint Own-Other-Outcome implies Own-Other-Fellow-Feeling. Fellow-feeling enhances whatever other benefits are felt and diminishes any costs felt. But each step, so written, has an internal structure, and it is necessary that there be common knowledge that each is strictly self-interested with more of a good thing being better; otherwise, Smith's propositions are incoherent. The propriety of the action and the response must also satisfy the approbation of the community of observers. Indeed, Smith was adamant in rejecting utilitarian explanations of why we are social and have created society and often offers evidence against any such hypothesis.

Action responses that are too instantaneous to be merely utilitarian.

> Those who are fond of deducing all our sentiments from certain refinements of self-love ... [are] at no loss to account...both for this pleasure and this pain. Man...conscious of his own weakness, and of the need...for the assistance of others, rejoices whenever...he is...assured of that assistance...-grieves whenever he observes the contrary, because he is then assured of their opposition. But both the pleasure and the pain are always felt so instantaneously, and often upon such frivolous occasions, that it seems evident that neither of them can be derived from any such self-interested consideration. A man is mortified when, after having endeavoured to divert the company, he looks round and sees that nobody laughs at his jests but himself. On the contrary, the mirth of the company is highly agreeable to him, and he regards this correspondence of their sentiments with his own as the greatest applause. (*TMS*, p. 10)

In *TMS*, Smith models individuals in their relations with others, focusing on the rules we learn to follow ("norms"), or not, that yield, or not, stable communities, based on moral sentiments. We are motivated to create and follow these rules in order that we "go along with" others (i.e., each other) because we experience the pleasures of mutual fellow-feeling. But in this, we must restrain our self-interest which yields greater immediate benefit. The 10 Commandments would be an example of the emergent process Smith is modeling, a process which in his view originated in antiquity. People are aware of this rule-based order that surrounds them but they are unaware of their part in creating and following it. Hume had emphasized that "the rules of morality are not the result of reason." Of course, these rules are efficient in enabling order, but Smith understood that this is not why we create and follow them.

Smith saw the origins of human action as distinct from their consequences, a strictly non-utilitarian methodological proposition.

His critique in the paragraph above is of those who argue that all sentiments derive from (utilitarian) refinements of self-love. He sees rule-following actions as being much too automatic, spontaneous, and quick to be utilitarian, which he associates with more deliberative and slow action choices.

Thus, very early in *TMS*, Smith hypothesizes that spontaneous actions that convey good, or bad, consequences for another are associated with the socio-psychological rules that we learn to follow automatically, while slow response actions are linked with current outcome utility in which we are more deliberative. This juxtaposition, and its predictive and explanatory content in *TMS*, seems not to have been identified, as such, in the modern psychology and economics of decision behavior. Thus, Daniel Kahneman has written insightfully on the empirical concept of two mental systems—fast and automatic, slow and deliberate:

> System 1 operates automatically and quickly, with little or no effort and no sense of voluntary control. System 2 allocates attention to the effortful mental activities that demand it, including complex computations. The operations of System 2 are often associated with the subjective experience of agency, choice, and concentration. (*Thinking, Fast and Slow*, 2011)

TMS elaborates a social-psychological theory of human sociality and community governed by an order of rule-following behavior, which we learn without conscious awareness, and follow automatically, exactly as described by Kahneman as "System 1." Alternatively, the class of slow action responses is categorized as self-interested (utilitarian) actions, as in "System 2."

Hence, *TMS* offers a theory, summarized in predictive propositions, antecedent to the many modern empirical discoveries in behavioral psychology, including those associated with the two fast vs slow systems.

Fellow-feeling arises in response to our direct interaction with the pleasure or distress felt by another.

> Neither does his pleasure [of fellow-feeling] seem to arise...from the additional vivacity which his mirth may receive from sympathy with theirs, nor his pain from the disappointment he meets with when he misses this pleasure...When we have read a book or poem so often that we can no longer find any amusement in reading it by ourselves, we can still take pleasure in reading it to a companion. To him it has all the graces of novelty; we enter into the surprise and admiration which it naturally excites in him, but which it is no longer capable of exciting in us; we consider all the ideas which it presents, rather in the light in which they appear to him, than in that in which they appear to ourselves, and we are amused by sympathy with his amusement, which thus enlivens our own. (*TMS*, pp. 10–11)

Why do we find pleasure in reading a text to another which is so familiar that we would not find pleasure in reading to ourselves? We often read to a friend or spouse a text we, or someone, has written that was meaningful, or "enlivening" to us, but is no longer surprising or informative. We do this to verify our expectation that they will be enlivened as we were, and we find that shared experience itself pleasurable. Yet "fellow feeling" is already long an unconscious part of the rules we follow. Smith, as often is his wont, turns this common-place event around, citing it as evidence of fellow-feeling—a source of pleasure quite distinct from any personal utilitarian pleasure from things or choices. Smith models relationships, individuals as an integral part of their connectedness with others, not isolated individuals making choices pleasurable only to themselves, which he does not disapprove of, but recognizes as incomplete in accounting for the whole person. Smith is here sharply distinguishable from the neoclassical program concerned and directed to displace him and his followers with the narrower utilitarian consequentialist model he found inadequate.

Sympathy enlivens joy and alleviates grief.

> The sympathy which my friends express with my joy, might indeed give me pleasure by enlivening that joy; but that which they express with my grief could give me none, if it served only to enliven that grief. Sympathy, however, enlivens joy and alleviates grief. It enlivens joy by presenting another source of satisfaction; and it alleviates grief by insinuating into the heart almost the only agreeable sensation which it is at that time capable of receiving. (*TMS*, p. 11)
>
> Because sympathy is the emotion whereby Nature links us with others through fellow-feeling it must be sensitive to what others feel in states of joy and of grief. Joy has its own ebullient reward while grief incurs only a dispiriting cost which may be alleviated, not enlivened, by others. If it is in their power, neighborly others will want to soften or alleviate that grief, as they know from experience how disagreeable and distressful that feels. Friends become brothers and sisters in the sharing of the mind-burdens of grief.

We especially wish to convey to our friends our disagreeable passions.

> [W]e are still more anxious to communicate to our friends our disagreeable, than our agreeable passions; that we derive still more satisfaction from their sympathy with the former, than from that with the latter, and that we are still more shocked by the want of it. (*TMS*, p. 11)

Thus is made coherent in a single-sentence proposition, a corollary application of Smith's fundamental asymmetry between our sorrows and our joys, a phenomenon rediscovered empirically by behavioral psychologists and experimental economists, in the downstream decision context of loss versus gain in decision under probabilistic risk. Curiously, this modern research has been uninformed by the testable propositions implied by Smith's social-psychological theory of society, which he controlled by testing against observations from culture, history, and literature.

Relief from distress is disburdened by sharing in conversation.

> How are the unfortunate relieved when they have found out a person to whom they can communicate the cause of their sorrow! Upon his sympathy they seem to disburden themselves of a part of their distress: he is not improperly said to share it with them. He not only feels a sorrow of the same kind with that which they feel, but, as if he had derived a part of it to himself; what he feels seems to alleviate the weight of what they feel. Yet, by relating their misfortunes, they in some measure renew their grief. They awaken in their memory the remembrance of those circumstances which occasion their affliction. Their tears accordingly flow faster than before, and they are apt to abandon themselves to all the weakness of sorrow. They take pleasure, however, in all this, and it is evident are sensibly relieved by it; because the sweetness of his sympathy more than compensates the bitterness of that sorrow, which, in order to excite this sympathy, they had thus enlivened and renewed. The cruelest insult, on the contrary, which can be offered to the unfortunate, is to appear to make light of their calamities. To seem not to be affected with the joy of our companions, is but want of politeness; but not to wear a serious countenance when they tell us their afflictions, is real and gross inhumanity. (*TMS*, p. 12)

For Smith to say "found out" suggests that one actively searches and discovers someone who can enter one's grief felt and play a positive role in helping to alleviate the resulting pain. Of course, it is often a close friend that one particularly trusts in sharing intimate personal experiences with. Talking about your distress with such a friend was the way to relieve it in Smith's time. Today, many rely on a professional therapist as markets have enormously expanded the availability of personal service specializations—a realization of Smith's later work showing that the division of labor is limited by the extent of the market. But we also still strongly rely on voluntary group associations and the therapeutic sharing of distress as a source of mental "unburdening" as a supplementary treatment for alcohol and drug addiction, depression, and other mental and emotional disorders.

And this very observation serves to demonstrate the contemporary relevance of Smith's propositional theory of society.

We are more anxious that our friends share our enemies than that they share our other friends.

> Love is an me agreeable; resentment, a disagreeable passion; and accordingly we are not half so anxious that our friends should adopt our friendships, as that they should enter into our resentments...They can easily avoid being friends to our friends, but can hardly avoid being enemies to...our enemies. (*TMS*, p. 12)

So far as I have been able to determine the idea that bonds of friendship might depend more on the sharing of common enemies than on the sharing of other friends, has not been examined in the modern decision behavior literature. For Smith, it is one of many natural consequences of the asymmetry in experienced joy and sorrow. Such studies might include the circumstances that cause friends to break up. In a long lifetime the turnover of friends may relate directly and causally to the turnover of what constitutes controversial opinion and the impulse to identify with others who share the same antagonists. The young, just emerging from the caring and sharing culture of family associations, are more likely to sympathize with, and embrace, socialist views, which may change with new experiences and friendships.

CHAPTER 3

Of the pleasure of mutual sympathy

To entirely sympathize, or not, with the passions of another is to approve of them, or not, and is achieved by imagining ourselves in their situation.

> When the original passions of the person principally concerned are in perfect concord with the sympathetic emotions of the spectator, they necessarily appear to this last just and proper, and suitable to their objects; and, on the contrary, when, upon bringing the case home to himself, he finds that they do not coincide with what he feels, they necessarily appear to him unjust and improper, and unsuitable to the causes which excite them. To approve of the passions of another, therefore, as suitable to their objects, is the same thing as to observe that we entirely sympathize with them; and not to approve of them as such, is the same thing as to observe that we do not entirely sympathize with them. (*TMS*, p. 14)

Sympathy, a characteristic identified with the capacity for human feeling, is what enables us to speak of the approval or the disapproval of a passion originating in another—a social and socializing phenomenon—and experienced by means of the human ability to effectively change places with another in their imagination. Smith intends to treat this process as definitionally equivalent to the more familiar concept of approval, or not, of a passion in another. Hence, the origin of the concept

Vernon L. Smith, *Adam Smith's Theory of Society*,
https://doi.org/10.1007/978-3-031-68494-4_3

of approval is social, and founded in intersubjective experience. But none of this process need be part of our self-aware understanding.

To approve or disapprove the opinions of another is to adopt them, or not, and this applies equally to the approbation or disapprobation of the sentiments of others.

> To approve of another man's opinions is to adopt those opinions, and to adopt them is to approve of them. If the same arguments which convince you, convince me likewise, I necessarily approve of your conviction; and if they do not, I necessarily disapprove of it; neither can I possibly conceive that I should do the one without the other. To approve or disapprove, therefore, of the opinions of others is acknowledged, by every body, to mean no more than to observe their agreement or disagreement with our own. But this is equally the case with regard to our approbation or disapprobation of the sentiments or passions of others. (*TMS*, p. 15)

The concept of individual approval, arising from the experience of imagining changing places with another, is extended conceptually from individual bilateral interactions to all third-party observers. Bidirectional approval is now extended socially to all relevant observers as a collective and is said to meet with the approbation of any such set of observers. Symmetrically, disapproval is extended to the social concept of disapprobation. Approbation and disapprobation involve experienced-based consensus agreement in the relevant group. Approbation is especially well defined by the shared experience when an audience bursts into applause. I feel it, you feel it, we all feel it. Smith is systematically building a theory of community from individual human sympathy, which, given this capacity, develops because we are brought up with family, and playfellows. Juvenile playtime is developmental in all mammals. In humans, witness the arrested development in children caused by their relative isolation due to the behavioral responses and policies stemming from the Covid-19 pandemic. Policy tends to not take account of individual and social incentives and their opportunity costs.

Because the general rules emerging from Smith's theory of society are composed of many moving parts, each subject to error, we are positioned to think through cases that test them in social science research.

Maxims, like loving your neighbor as yourself [or, since knowledge of ourselves is so dependent on others, loving yourself as your neighbor loves you], are already an implicit part of human experience, with origins not consciously part of our reason, that give bedrock voice to community.

CHAPTER 4

Of the manner in which we judge of the propriety or impropriety of the affections of other men, by their concord or dissonance with our own

Distinguishing the origins of human action from the consequences of human action.

> The sentiment or affection of the heart, from which any action proceeds, and upon which its whole virtue or vice must ultimately depend, may be considered under two different…relations; first, in relation to the cause which excites it, or the motive which gives occasion to it; and, secondly, in relation to the end which it proposes, or the effect which it tends to produce.
> In the suitableness or unsuitableness, in the proportion or disproportion, which the affection seems to bear to the cause or object which excites it, consists the propriety or impropriety, the decency or ungracefulness, of the consequent action.
> In the beneficial or hurtful nature of the effects which the affection aims at, or tends to produce, consists the merit or demerit of the action, the qualities by which it is entitled to reward, or is deserving of punishment. (*TMS*, p. 17)

Passion is an affection of the breast and, therefore, related to action—either an action we take or see taken by another. So far, Smith has been preparing us to understand human action, which is central to his theory

Vernon L. Smith, *Adam Smith's Theory of Society*,
https://doi.org/10.1007/978-3-031-68494-4_4

of society. Thus, in this passage, Smith explicitly proposes to examine human action first from the perspective of its origins, and secondly from the perspective of its consequences thereby allowing them to be entirely independent, or not, as seems appropriate. This methodological perspective occurs in the other works of Adam Smith and serves sharply to distinguish classical from neoclassical and modern economics, and Smith from modern behavioral psychology and economics, in which optimal action is modeled almost exclusively as utility maximization over outcome consequences. Today, if forms of other-regarding action are observed, the payoffs of others are included in the actor's utility function, ex post hoc. Adam Smith does not commit this error and often is impelled to criticize such explanations.

Judging others can only be based on judging ourselves in a like situation.

> When we judge…any affection, as proportioned[1] or disproportioned to the cause which excites it, it is scarce possible that we should make use of any other rule or canon but the correspondent affection in ourselves. If, upon bringing the case home to our own breast, we find that the sentiments which it gives occasion to coincide and tally with our own, we necessarily approve of them, as proportioned and suitable to their objects; if otherwise, we necessarily disapprove of them, as extravagant and out of proportion. Every faculty in one man is the measure by which he judges of the like faculty in another. I judge of your sight by my sight, of your ear by my ear, of your reason by my reason, of your resentment by my resentment, of your love by my love. I neither have, nor can have, any other way of judging about them. (*TMS*, pp. 17–18)

Thus, Smith grounds all judgment of others in our own experience, and in reasonable extensions of that experience, such as fellow-feeling, in which we find others involved in the same process. He explicitly rules out any a' priori knowledge, or inborn sense of sympathetic fellow-feeling, which would undermine the challenge of relating it to experience and articulating its function. Of course, this sympathetic capacity for learning from own and other experience may be inborn. As a cultural evolutionist,

[1] In Smith, I interpret Y proportioned to X as meaning generally that Y Is positively related to X, which includes strict proportionality, but might simply mean that Y is increasing in X.

Smith pushed the roots of action to phenomena that are conceptually part of our experience in life. We are not born social. Rather, we are born with characteristics that allow us to learn to be social. This allows for diversity of form that Smith observes across English, French, Russian, etc., realizations.

CHAPTER 5

The same subject continued

Sympathy, involving an imaginary change of places with another person, does not enter our evaluation of beauty, art, and science, where, if another's sentiments correspond to our own, we ascribe to them the qualities of taste and good judgment.

> With regard to those objects which are considered without any peculiar relation either to ourselves or to the person whose sentiments we judge of; wherever his sentiments entirely correspond with our own, we ascribe to him the qualities of taste and good judgment. The beauty of a plain, the greatness of a mountain, the ornaments of a building, the expression of a picture, the composition of a discourse, the conduct of a third person, the proportions of different quantities and numbers, the various appearances which the great machine of the universe is perpetually exhibiting, with the secret wheels and springs which produce them; all the general subjects of science and taste, are what we and our companions regard as having no peculiar relation to either of us. We both look at them from the same point of view, and we have no occasion for sympathy, or for that imaginary change of situations from which it arises, in order to produce, with regard to these, the most perfect harmony of sentiments and affections. If, notwithstanding, we are often differently affected, it arises either from the different degrees of attention which our different habits of life allow us to give easily to the several parts of those complex objects, or from the different degrees of natural acuteness in the faculty of the mind to which they are addressed. (*TMS*, pp. 19–20)

Vernon L. Smith, *Adam Smith's Theory of Society*,
https://doi.org/10.1007/978-3-031-68494-4_5

Smith here identifies sympathy [which implements fellow-feeling] with what enables different individual perspectives to interact compatibly, enrich each other, and that render us social creatures even though we might disagree in some of our tastes and opinions. Because matters of beauty, art, and science exist as phenomena viewed in common outside of each of us, they do not concern sympathy in the above sense, and constitute matters that need examination distinct from those that make us social. In this accommodation we become peaceful beneficiaries of our tolerance for each other's differences.

Smith is preparing us for the next entry, which concerns the intellectual virtues, functionally distinct presumably from what drives personal social virtues.

Intellectual virtues arise from our agreement with others on art, science, and curiosity-inspired sources of order in the universe. That these qualities have utility is an afterthought, not their origin.

> When the sentiments of our companion coincide with our own in matters of beauty and order in the universe...though we, no doubt, must approve of them, yet he seems to deserve no praise or admiration on account of them. But when they not only coincide with our own, but lead and direct our own; when, in forming them, he appears to have attended to many things which we had overlooked, and to have adjusted them to all the various circumstances of their objects; we not only approve of them, but wonder and are surprised at their uncommon and unexpected acuteness and comprehensiveness, and he appears to deserve a very high degree of admiration and applause...and upon this foundation is grounded the greater part of the praise which is bestowed upon what are called the intellectual virtues.[1]
>
> The utility of these qualities, it may be thought, is what first recommends them to us; and, no doubt, the consideration of this, when we come to attend to it, gives them a new value. Originally, however, we approve of another man's judgment, not as something useful, but as right, as accurate,

[1] In his History of Astronomy, included in Smith, Adam (1982) written as a young scholar but posthumously published, Smith uses "sentiments" in connection with commonly viewed extraordinary objects: "What is new and singular, excites that sentiment which, in strict propriety, is called Wonder; what is unexpected, Surprise; and what is great or beautiful, Admiration" (Smith, 1982, p. 33). Here, he argues that those whose insight and depth go much beyond our own in comprehending beauty and order in the universe become the standard setters who define the "intellectual virtues.".

as agreeable to truth and reality; and it is evident we attribute those qualities to it for no other reason but because we find that it agrees with our own. Taste, in the same manner, is originally approved of, not as useful, but as just, as delicate, and as precisely suited to its object. The idea of the utility of all qualities of this kind is plainly an afterthought, and not what first recommends them to our approbation. (*TMS*, pp. 20–21)

Ordinarily, where our sentiments agree with others, on beauty, art, or science, no praise or admiration seems appropriate or expected. But when we learn from others new features that we overlooked, finding unexpected agreement, these deserve praise and admiration. Smith is defining opinion-setting leaders, or experts, and their emergence as people who are acclaimed in defining standards in art, literature, or science. So, our sentiments in the intellectual virtues involve agreement, and the enhancement of agreement on abstract enduring values, in contrast with the virtues of magnanimity and tolerance that make us social and enable and support a neighborly stable community among people who are otherwise very diverse in opinion, and who may have little interest or expertise in the intellectual virtues defined by contemplative specialists. Thus, social norms are the dominion of all ordinary people. Smith warns us not to view our approval of the judgments of others as utilitarian, or useful, but rather as right and fit. Utilitarian usefulness, and the efficiency of outcomes, is an afterthought, not the origin of our experience and sense of that which is right. If the afterthoughts constitute the theory, there is no forethought to explain why.

Companions easily differ in opinion in art, literature, or science, but in matters of personal distress, our affections are nearly the same.

With regard to those objects, which affect in a particular manner either ourselves or the person whose sentiments we judge of, it is at once more difficult to preserve this harmony and correspondence, and, at the same time, vastly more important. My companion does not naturally look upon the misfortune that has befallen me, or the injury that has been done me, from the same point of view in which I consider them. They affect me much more nearly. We do not view them from the same station, as we do a picture, or a poem, or a system of philosophy; and are therefore apt to be very differently affected by them. But I can much more easily overlook the want of this correspondence of sentiments with regard to such indifferent objects as concern neither me nor my companion, than with regard to

> what interests me so much as the misfortune that has befallen me, or the injury that has been done me. Though you despise that picture, or that poem, or even that system of philosophy which I admire, there is little danger of our quarrelling upon that account. Neither of us can reasonably be much interested about them. They ought all of them to be matters of great indifference to us both; so that, though our opinions may be opposite, our affections may still be very nearly the same. (*TMS*, p. 21)

We are companions who "get along with" each other because of the rules we have learned to follow that make us sympathetically compassionate toward the hurts and misfortunes that befall us. To achieve this does not require us to have the same tastes in beauty, art, and science, which might be quite different.

But sometimes people do converge in accepting new standards of beauty and art, for example in accepting modern art at one time thought outrageous. I wonder, however, if this acceptance state does not involve forms of fellow-feeling or fellow-understanding in which people enter each other's experience of intellectual virtues via their imagination. Relativity theory (RT) is an example of an intellectual virtue in which opinions have converged to the point of having achieved final-or-ultimate-truth status, once attributed to Newtonian theory before Einstein, and to Ptolemaic theory before Newton. The axiom that nothing can exceed the velocity of light implies a compression of measures of length and time that logically imply "twin paradoxes," where imagined twins travel at different velocities and return of differing ages because they age at different rates. The famous limerick, which I recall reading in one of Bertrand Russell's books, states an implication of the violation of this axiom. It went something like this:

> *There once was a lady named Bright,*
> *who could exceed the velocity of light.*
> *She went out one day,*
> *in a Relative way,*
> *And returned on the preceding night.*

But why have theorists imposed a maximum velocity, that of light, on RT? Observations appearing to falsify it leads to new theory explaining the theory in terms of short-cuts between regions of space–time. Why not just drop the axiom, deduce its implications, and see if that contradicts other observations regarding RT?[2]

Although I can easily overlook your opinion in matters of taste, if you have no fellow-felling with my misfortunes, our conversation is at an end.

> Though your judgments in matters of speculation, though your sentiments in matters of taste, are quite opposite to mine, I can easily overlook this opposition; and if I have any degree of temper, I may still find some entertainment in your conversation, even upon those very subjects. But if you have either no fellow-feeling for the misfortunes I have met with, or none that bears any proportion to the grief which distracts me; or if you have either no indignation at the injuries I have suffered, or none that bears any proportion to the resentment which transports me, we can no longer converse upon these subjects. We become intolerable to one another. I can neither support your company, nor you mine. You are confounded at my violence and passion, and I am enraged at your cold insensibility and want of feeling. (*TMS*, p. 22)

What is different about matters specifically affecting you and me, versus those that do not, comes down to Smith's presumed greater role of experienced fellow-feeling in the former. In matters of science, agreement may lead to much satisfaction, but it is not a fellow-feeling with the joy or distress of another who has received a promotion, lost a friend, or fallen into ill health. Smith has in mind professional communities of independent scientists.

However, today I believe there is greater scope for place-changing in matters of professional interactions than allowed for by Smith in his expression of a truth about our emotional experiences. In such an exercise a scientist imagines taking the place of another to better understand how they think about and understand their data and reach a different conclusion than the first. But scientists today commonly live in their world of

[2] As you might suppose this has been done in Ramzi, Suleiman (2019) Relativizing Newton. New York: Nova Science Publishers. It was my pleasure to write the Foreword emphasizing the methodological importance of having at least one alternative to the standard theory against which one can construct empirical tests. Because of his work challenging RT, Suleiman is viewed with great disdain by conventional scientists. Welcome to the world of science.

scientific experience as they live in their own bodies of social experience. Hence, the process of changing or interchanging places has the potential for better understanding the sources of error that account for the different conclusions. I am thinking of astronomers who contract to schedule telescope time and live in associated astronomical communities for extended periods. Less intensively this process is approximated at week-long conferences with presentations, commentaries, and informal work sessions that blend into the peer-review of journal submissions. More intensely, but usually smaller, are the multiple author research programs that engage in continuous place-changing while conducting joint research and reporting it. In Smith's time and for long after, scholarship was considered the hunting territory of a lone wolf.

To have and to hold a companion, our spectator must strive to place our self with entre sympathy into their situation.

> [T]hat there may be some correspondence of sentiments between the spectator and the person principally concerned, the spectator must, first of all, endeavour as much as he can to put himself in the situation of the other, and to bring home to himself every little circumstance of distress which can possibly occur to the sufferer. He must adopt the whole case of his companion, with all its minutest incidents; and strive to render as perfect as possible that imaginary change of situation upon which his sympathy is founded. (*TMS*, p. 22)

Sympathy with our most intimate companions requires us to change places with them in our imagination in minute detail if we are thereby to approach completeness in feeling what they feel. Smith is here associating intimacy of companionship with greater attention to the details of the companion's experiences of the actions of others and the effects of those experiences on the actions of the companion. In this sense, one adopts the "whole case" of the companion.

For social concord, nature teaches us to see ourselves as others see us, and to judge our own action in the light of how others judge us.

> In order to produce...concord [of fellow feeling], as nature teaches the spectators to assume the circumstances of the person principally concerned, so she teaches this last in some measure to assume those of the spectators. As they are continually placing themselves in his situation, and thence

> conceiving emotions similar to what he feels; so he is as constantly placing himself in theirs, and thence conceiving some degree of that coolness about his own fortune, with which he is sensible that they will view it. As they are constantly considering what they themselves would feel, if they actually were the sufferers, so he is constantly led to imagine in what manner he would be affected if he was only one of the spectators of his own situation. As their sympathy makes them look at it in some measure with his eyes, so his sympathy makes him look at it, in some measure, with theirs, especially when in their presence, and acting under their observation: and, as the reflected passion which he thus conceives is much weaker than the original one, it necessarily abates the violence of what he felt before he came into their presence, before he began to recollect in what manner they would be affected by it, and to view his situation in this candid and impartial light. (*TMS*, pp. 23–24)

For social harmony, we first learn to know what another must feel, by, in our imagination, changing paces with them in context-specific situations. Symmetrically, others are learning of our feelings in the same manner. In this we are each better able to see ourselves as another sees us. Although what we each feel may be weaker than what the principal feels, our experience abates the extremes of what we each felt in the absence of each other's presence. In this we each come to see our own and other conduct in a more candid and impartial light.

In this, companions tend to bring us more satisfaction and tranquility than acquaintances or strangers. And thereby do companions embrace more powerful forms of mutual simultaneous fellow-feeling.

The company of a friend, being sympathetic, brings shared tranquility and sedateness to our breast. An acquaintance is less sympathetic and therefore in their presence we assume more tranquility on our own. In the presence of a stranger, we assume still more tranquility.

> The mind…is rarely so disturbed, but that the company of a friend will restore it to some degree of tranquillity and sedateness. The breast is…calmed and composed the moment we come into his presence. We are immediately put in mind of the light in which he will view our situation, and we begin to view it ourselves in the same light; for the effect of sympathy is instantaneous. We expect less sympathy from a common acquaintance than from a friend; we cannot open to the former all those

> little circumstances which we can unfold to the latter; we assume, therefore, more tranquillity before him, and endeavour to fix our thoughts upon those general outlines of our situation which he is willing to consider. We expect still less sympathy from an assembly of strangers, and we assume, therefore, still more tranquillity before them, and always endeavour to bring down our passion to that pitch, which the particular company we are in may be expected to go along with. Nor is this only an assumed appearance for if we are at all masters of ourselves, the presence of a mere acquaintance will really compose us, still more that of a friend; and that of an assembly of strangers still more than that of an acquaintance. (*TMS*, pp. 24–25)

Our interaction with a friend brings us tranquility and sedateness under extreme duress; an acquaintance brings less, and strangers still less. This reflects their relative influence in removing us from self-indulgent thoughts concerning our misfortune. Smith says that the moment we are in the presence of the friend our thoughts turn to the friend's views of us, which transports us from preoccupation with ourselves and into thoughts of the light with which the friend is likely to view us. We expect no comparable sympathy from a mere acquaintance because we are not open to them as we are to a friend. Consequently, we are diverted from any self-indulgence with our grief to consider the variety of ways the acquaintance might view us. Still less will a stranger be able to sympathize with us, and correspondingly is our own tranquility still more boosted by our efforts to lower the pitch of our passions to a level with which we can expect the stranger to go along.

Society and conversation are powerful means for restoring our lost sense of peace in mind.

> Society and conversation...are the most powerful remedies for restoring the mind to its tranquillity, if, at any time, it has unfortunately lost it; as well as the best preservatives of that equal and happy temper, which is so necessary to self-satisfaction and enjoyment. Men of retirement and speculation, who are apt to sit brooding at home over either grief or resentment, though they may often have more humanity, more generosity, and a nicer sense of honour, yet seldom possess that equality of temper which is so common among men of the world. (*TMS*, p. 25)

The restoration as well as the preservation of peace of mind is best achieved by society and conversation with others—friends, acquaintances, and strangers. Introverts, if tending to brood over their griefs and resentments, and others poor in spirit, may not possess the temper of the plain and ordinary people that contribute so much to the creation of our social world.

CHAPTER 6

Of the amiable and respectable virtues

The foundation of the control of passions is self-government which emerges in part from our conduct being judged by others, and in part from our sense of being judged of.

> Upon these two different efforts, upon that of the spectator to enter into the sentiments of the person principally concerned, and upon that of the person principally concerned, to bring down his emotions to what the [fair, cool, and impartial] spectator can go along with, are founded two different sets of virtues. The soft, the gentle, the amiable virtues...of candid condescension[1] and indulgent humanity, are founded upon the one: the great, the awful, and respectable, the virtues of self-denial, of self-government, of that command of the passions which subjects all the movements of our nature to what our own dignity and honour, and the propriety of our own conduct, require, take their origin from the other. (*TMS*, p. 26)

[1] In Samuel Johnson, eighteenth-century dictionary of English, we have:
Condescension. n.s. [from condescend.] *Voluntary humiliation; descent from superiority; voluntary submission to equality with inferiors.*
It forbids pride and ambition, and vain glory; and commands humility and modesty, and condescension to others.
Today it means the opposite, to show feelings of superiority; to be patronizing.

Vernon L. Smith, *Adam Smith's Theory of Society*,
https://doi.org/10.1007/978-3-031-68494-4_6

Two different sets of virtues are founded on two different judgments: First, those of the "spectator," i.e., those socially involved others—family, friends, neighbors, and acquaintances—who judge our conduct. Second, those of the person whose action is judged of, in terms of bringing down their emotions to what others can go along with. The first constitutes the set of soft, gentile, and amiable humanitarian virtues, while the second constitutes the great, "awe-filled," and respectable virtues of appropriate self-denial, self-government, or self-command.

The impartial spectator permits no vengeance beyond fair-play rules, requires indignation, not rage, and that the punishment always fit the crime.

> The insolence and brutality of anger…when we indulge its fury without check or restraint, is, of all objects, the most detestable. But we admire that noble and generous resentment which governs its pursuit of the greatest injuries, not by the rage which they are apt to excite in the breast of the sufferer, but by the indignation which they naturally call forth in that of the impartial spectator; which allows no word, no gesture, to escape it beyond what this more equitable sentiment would dictate; which never, even in thought, attempts any greater vengeance, nor desires to inflict any greater punishment, than what every indifferent person would rejoice to see executed. (*TMS*, p. 27)

The fury of unrestrained anger is detestable. Resentment for injuries suffered is admired when it motivates the justified redress of those injuries driven by the indignation felt by the victim and by every impartial spectator. Nor can any vengeance or punishment be tolerated than what every indifferent spectator would consider fit and appropriate to the original injury inflicted.

It is often said that humanness comes down to listening to one's inner consciousness. But the metaphor of the "fair and impartial spectator" articulates the process of social rule making that makes an inner consciousness possible, for it cannot be full born in a vacuum without experience.

Perfection in human nature is to feel little for ourselves, much for others, resulting in humankind's harmony of sentiments.

> [T]hat to feel much for others, and little for ourselves, to restrain our selfish, and to indulge our benevolent, affections, constitutes the perfection of human nature; and can alone produce among mankind that harmony of sentiments and passions in which consists their whole grace and propriety. (*TMS*, pp. 27–28)

Smith, a person of deep but questioning faith, asks how nature implements the will of an all-powerful God for the objects of His creation, who practice free will. Nature is God's on-the-ground means of communication, guidance, caution, and warning. Our perceived circumstances are always subject to deliberate modification in fear, in joy, in distress, and in our aspirations. Nothing is final, written in stone, as learning in the Great School of Self-Command is nature's lifelong project. Smith's sociology is one of dynamic hope and optimism, not despair and defeat. If perfection is to feel much for others and little for ourselves, that implies a commitment to contribute to the happiness in others, as others join in contributing to our happiness.

Christianity calls us to love our neighbor as ourselves. Nature calls us to love ourselves only as our neighbor is capable of loving us.

> As to love our neighbour as we love ourselves is the great law of Christianity, so it is the great precept of nature to love ourselves only as we love our neighbour, or, what comes to the same thing, as our neighbour is capable of loving us. (*TMS*, p. 28)

In *TMS*, the overarching question in our existence is how we mortals come to know morality. The answer is that we can only know through others, mirror-like, who we are. But that process operates without our conscious awareness. Hence, the proposition that in learning of ourselves through others we come to love ourselves as we love them. We know well, however, our self-love and practice it with hardly a thought; hence, the Christian moral that we love others as we love ourselves builds on that conscious truth to a larger morality. Christians, if not corrupted by the ever-presence of temptation, essentially seek to practice what nature teaches as the foundation of harmony.

We discover virtue not in the common degree of the moral, but in the uncommonly great and beautiful, and by an astonishing self-command of the ungovernable passions of human nature.

> As taste and good judgment, when they are considered as qualities which deserve praise and admiration, are supposed to imply a delicacy of sentiment and an acuteness of understanding not commonly to be met with; so the virtues of sensibility and self-command are not apprehended to consist in the ordinary, but in the uncommon degrees of those qualities….As in the common degree of the intellectual qualities, there are no abilities; so in the in the common degree of the moral, there is no virtue. Virtue is excellence, something uncommonly great and beautiful, which rises far above what is vulgar and ordinary. The amiable virtues consist in that degree of sensibility which surprises by its exquisite and unexpected delicacy and tenderness. The awful [that is, "awe-filled"] and respectable, in that degree of self-command which astonishes by its amazing superiority over the most ungovernable passions of human nature. (*TMS*, p. 28)

We create virtues out of the whole cloth of interactive experience as iconic signs of the ideal. We live up to these ideals only in proportion to our self-command. If there is no self-command, there is no practiced morality. Thus *TMS* defines a self-ordering, bottom-up, internally generated process for free peoples, their neighborhoods, communities, and nations. Without self-command it all crumbles into nothing, the easy prey of the tyrant among or in us, and of our own potentially destructive capability; with self-command comes a resilience that survives the insults of civil strife, civil war, populist excesses and violence, and the evil self-corruption found in all top-down processes that centralize the power that always must be decentralized and self-commanded if order is to overcome strife.

Virtue is propriety celebrated, not merely approved.

> There is ... a considerable difference between virtue and mere propriety; between those qualities and actions which deserve to be admired and celebrated, and those which simply deserve to be approved of. Upon many occasions, to act with the most perfect propriety, requires no more than that common and ordinary degree of sensibility or self-command which the most worthless of mankind are possessed of, and sometimes even that degree is not necessary. (*TMS*, p. 28)

Propriety is the stuff that emerges from mutually reinforced neighborly good conduct, and by which neighborly bad conduct is deterred. Ideals emerge from propriety only if applauded, and thus celebrated, by all.

Standards of perfect versus practical perfection in moral judgment.

> [W]hen we are determining the degree of blame or applause which seems due to any action, we very frequently make use of two different standards. The first is the idea of complete propriety and perfection, which, in those difficult situations, no human conduct ever did, or ever can, come up to; and in comparison with which the actions of all men must forever appear blamable and imperfect. The second is the idea of that degree of proximity or distance from this complete perfection, which the actions of the greater part of men commonly arrive at. Whatever goes beyond this degree, how far soever it may be removed from absolute perfection, seems

> to deserve applause; and whatever falls short of it, to deserve blame. (*TMS*, pp. 29–30)

The standard of complete propriety and perfection we use to define the ideal which we do not expect any human to live up to. Abstract theories in music, art, performance, mathematics, and science often express these ideal states achievable by no mortal. It is from our applause for the outsized practical attainments by imperfect humans that we arrive at the possibilities for the morally unusual.

PART II

Of the degrees of the different passions which are consistent with propriety

Section I: Of the sense of merit and demerit

> It has already· been observed, that the sentiment or affection of the heart from which any action proceeds, and upon which its whole virtue or vice depends, may be considered under two different aspects, or in two different relations; first, in relation to the cause or object which excites it; and, secondly, in relation to the end which it proposes, or to the effect which it tends to produce: that upon the suitableness or unsuitableness, upon the proportion or disproportion; which the affection seems to bear to the cause or object which excites it; depends the propriety or impropriety, the decency or ungracefulness, of the consequent action; and that upon the beneficial or hurtful effects which the affection proposes or tends to produce depends the merit or demerit, the good or ‘ill desert, of the action to which it gives occasion. Wherein consists our sense of the propriety or impropriety of actions, has been explained in the former part of this discourse. We come now to consider, wherein consists that of their good or ill desert. (*TMS*, p. 91)

Propriety or impropriety is qualitative judgment of social appropriateness or inappropriateness. To also judge their merit or demerit requires an examination of the degree of benefit or hurt caused by an action. All such judgements are reached by a consent process in the relevant group. Orderly community is created out of both the qualitative judgements, and the judgements of degree. One category of human action concerns the good things we do for each other, Beneficence; the other is concerned with limiting the bad things we do to each other, Justice.

CHAPTER 7

Of the passions which take their origin from the body

The indecent passions of the body, such as hunger and sex.

> It is indecent to express any strong degree of those passions which arise from a certain situation or disposition of the body; because the company, not being in the same disposition, cannot be expected to sympathize with them. Violent hunger, for example, though upon many occasions not only natural, but unavoidable, is always indecent; and to eat voraciously is universally regarded as a piece of ill manners... It is the same case with the passion by which nature unites the two sexes. Though naturally the most furious of all the passions, all strong expressions of it are upon every occasion indecent, even between persons in whom its most complete indulgence is acknowledged by all laws, both human and divine, to be perfectly innocent. There seems, however, to be some degree of sympathy even with this passion. To talk to a woman as we should to a man is improper: it is expected that their company should inspire us with more gaiety, more pleasantry, and more attention; and an entire insensibility to the fair sex renders a man contemptible in some measure even to the men. (*TMS*, pp. 33–34)

Hunger, as an indecent passion, is perhaps as strong today as in Smith's time. Charles Laughton's portrayal of the screen's most disgusting table manners of all time in Henry the 8th (1933) became a cult classic.[1]

[1] https://youtu.be/v4tOb9J7W2k.

Vernon L. Smith, *Adam Smith's Theory of Society*,
https://doi.org/10.1007/978-3-031-68494-4_7

The portrayal of sexual passions has varied from Hollywood's censorship of Mae West's delightfully impromptu, but considered outrageous at the time, comic lines beginning in the 1920s and early 1930s—"Officer, are you glad to see me or is that a gun in your pocket"[2]—to letting it all hang out in the 1950–60s, then backing away from its boring over-indulgence.

Aversion to passions is due to our inability to enter into them in others.

> Such is our aversion for all the appetites which take their origin from the body ... [that] all strong expressions of them are loathsome and disagreeable. According to some ancient philosophers, these are the passions which we share in common with the brutes, and which having no connection with the characteristical qualities of human nature, are upon that account beneath its dignity. But there are many other passions which we share in common with the brutes, such as resentment, natural affection, even gratitude, which do not, upon that account, appear to be so brutal. The true cause of the peculiar disgust which we conceive for the appetites of the body when we see them in other men, is, that we cannot enter into them. To the person himself who feels them, as soon as they are gratified, the object that excited them ceases to be agreeable: even its presence often becomes offensive to him; he looks round to no purpose for the charm which transported him the moment before, and he can now as little enter into his own passion as another person. When we have dined, we order the covers to be removed; and we should treat in the same manner the objects of the most ardent and passionate desires, if they were the objects of no other passions but those which take their origin from the body. (*TMS*, p. 34)

[2] For those unfamiliar with West, here are some classics:
When I'm good, I'm very good. But when I'm bad I'm better.
I generally avoid temptation unless I can't resist it.
When choosing between two evils, I always like to try the one I've never tried before.
I used to be Snow White, but I drifted.
A man has one hundred dollars and you leave him with two dollars, that's subtraction.
A hard man is good to find.
Don't keep a man guessing too long - he's sure to find the answer somewhere else.
I only like two kinds of men, domestic and imported.
Those who are easily shocked should be shocked more often.
Read more at https://www.brainyquote.com/authors/mae-west-quotes.

What does Smith mean in saying that the true cause of our disgust concerning matters of the body is our inability to enter into them? He is saying that we cannot enter them via shared public experiences as with our learning of social norms. The general abstract rules we learn to follow are excited by the particular circumstances we observe in others and can thereby relate to our own imagined similar experiences. Private experiences that are not observed in, or by, others leave still more to the imagination. Hence, we cannot enter into them in a comparable way.

The genius of Smith was his insight in seeing what mattered to people, to ask why, and through careful observation and contemplation to explain why. Inadvertently, out of that inquiry, emerged a theory of liberal society relevant to all peoples and times. "Liberal" meant that society is founded on principles of inherently diverse voluntary participation, with control dispersed among multiple actors each choosing in their own way disciplined by their own rules of justice.

For example, contemporary liberal society has expanded its choice tolerance to include same-sex attraction. Such phenomena are not easily entered into by changing places in one's imagination with them by others who have entirely different experiential sexual orientations. Hence, this liberating tolerance accepts the right of free social choice as a principle applied to all actions that are deemed desirable by the individual without being edited by what others might not go along with in their own experience. This movement has graduated into the LBGT + form which is open for innovation. This form is already colliding with female sports in which people identifying as "women in men's bodies" are entering such sports with "unfair" advantages. Hence, are we discovering the flaws in male–female human categorization in sports. The phenomenon appeared long ago in horse races and was solved not by gender identification but by handicapping weights for superior ability. If ability is measured in units per kg, then racing authorities just add artificial kilograms to the jockey's weight to equalize the chances of any given horse winning a race. These handicaps are market-based because they are determined by the wager market in horse racing.

The same market-based solution would solve the problem created by male vs women sports. Horse races involve both male and female participants. If horse races are liberal, why not all human races?

Prudence restrains while the virtue of temperance commands the appetites of the body.

> In the command of...(the)...appetites of the body consists that virtue which is properly called temperance. To restrain them within those bounds...is the part of prudence. But to confine them within those limits, which grace, which propriety, which delicacy, and modesty, require, is the office of temperance. (*TMS*, pp. 34–35)

Prudence describes a person's ability to control the public expression of their bodily appetites, like hunger and sex. Temperance requires a person to be in self-command of those appetites and not merely their expression.

Unlike the passions of the imagination, those of body excite either no, or disproportionately too much, sympathy. we more easily enter into the passions of the imagination because we naturally relate to the imagined social consequences to the sufferer, including loss of dignity, friends, and reputation.

> [Concerning] all the passions which take their origin from the body: they excite either no sympathy at all, or such a degree of it, as is altogether disproportioned to the violence of what is felt by the sufferer. It is quite otherwise with those passions which take their origin from the imagination. The frame of my body can be but little affected by the alterations which are brought about upon that of my companion; but my imagination is more ductile, and more readily assumes...the shape and configuration of the imaginations of those with whom I am familiar. A disappointment in love, or ambition, will, upon this account, call forth more sympathy than the greatest bodily evil. Those passions arise altogether from the imagination. The person who has lost his whole fortune, if he is in health, feels nothing in his body. What he suffers is from the imagination only, which represents to him the loss of his dignity, neglect from his friends, contempt from his enemies, dependence, want, and misery, coming fast upon him; and we sympathize with him more strongly upon this account, because our imaginations can more readily mould themselves upon his imagination, than our bodies can mould themselves upon his body. (*TMS*, pp. 35–36)

As we have indicated, an example of "too much" is memorably well-illustrated by Charles Laughton's Henry the 8th (1933) gorging on food and drink in the famous Banquet Scene. The scene leaves nothing to the imagination and is more jarring as a result. It is the opposite with those feelings that find their origin in the imagination. A job loss, a bad educational test score, or a failed expected promotion, ignite the imagination to conjure thoughts that we will lose reputation, suffer a crescendo of decline, inspire nightmares, and blunt our self-confidence. But that same imagination can mount techniques that reduce the risk of a failed performance. I remember greatly overpreparing for public speaking events, relying often on well-polished text to be read aloud at a podium, which was not the practiced tradition in economics. I observed, however, that philosophers seemed always to present papers orally from text. I attended a lecture by Bertrand Russell at Caltech in 1945, which he carefully and skillfully read in a conversational manner. With maturity and increased knowledge, I came to eschew that delivery format because I wanted the freedom to free-associate, in effect think out loud, which brought a form of satisfaction and comfort, perhaps even sometimes some creativity. These presentations became papers, edited from typescripts of the oral presentations. Instead of "giving" a paper at a lecture, I produced a paper from a lecture. One of my models was Kenneth Boulding who stammered badly but was an engaging speaker, not least because he made his stammer work elegantly for him and his audience. Similarly, Stephen Hawking turned a handicap into an engagement with his mind that defined his style.

The unintended benefit from losing a mistress—many get a finer one.

> The loss of a leg may generally be regarded as a more real calamity than the loss of a mistress. It would be a ridiculous tragedy, however, of which the catastrophe was to turn upon a loss of that kind. A misfortune of the other kind, how frivolous soever it may appear to be, has given occasion to many a fine one. (*TMS*, p. 36)

Thus, we have Adam Smith's own special style of British humor. It is sometimes advertised when he states the usual proffered explanatory defense of a practice then adds "The real reason is...."

Physical pain is quickly forgotten, but not emotional pain.

> Nothing is so soon forgot as pain. The moment it is gone, the whole agony of it is over, and the thought of it can no longer give us any sort of disturbance. We ourselves cannot then enter into the anxiety and anguish which we had before conceived. An unguarded word from a friend will occasion a more durable uneasiness. The agony which this creates is by no means over with the word. What at first disturbs us is not the object

> of the senses, but the idea of the imagination. As it is an idea, therefore, which occasions our uneasiness, till time and other accidents have in some measure effaced it from our memory, the imagination continues to fret and rankle within, from the thought of it. (*TMS*, p. 36)

Physical pain loses its sting immediately on our no longer suffering it, but this is not so for emotional pain. That the latter involves the active and sometimes uncontrollable seizing of the imagination is the key to understanding why the emotional pain of a witless remark by a friend is more lasting than physical pain.

We not only have the satisfaction that "time heals all wounds" but also that "in time, all heals are wounded."

Fear derives from the imagination, invoking our sympathy.

> Pain never calls forth any very lively sympathy, unless it is accompanied with danger. We sympathize with the fear, though not with the agony, of the sufferer. Fear, however, is a passion derived altogether from the imagination, which represents, with an uncertainty and fluctuation that increases our anxiety, not what we really feel, but what we may hereafter possibly suffer. The gout or the toothache, though exquisitely painful, excite very little sympathy; more dangerous diseases, though accompanied with very little pain, excite the highest. (*TMS*, p. 36)

Smith's identification of the role of the imagination as the source of all our fears, anxieties, and systemic discomfort is insightful and therapeutic. We can seek better control of our imagination and better recognize that such control may be part of our lifelong discipline in the Great School of Self-command.

Admiration for pain endurance derives naturally from its failure to invoke sympathy.

> The little sympathy which we feel with bodily pain is the foundation of the propriety of constancy and patience in enduring it. The man who under the severest tortures, allows no weakness to escape him, vents no groan, gives way to no passion which we do not entirely enter into, commands our highest admiration. His firmness enables him to keep time with our indifference and insensibility. We admire and entirely go along with the magnanimous effort which he makes for this purpose. We approve of his behaviour, and from our experience of the common weakness of human

> nature, we are surprised, and wonder how he should be able to act so as to deserve approbation. Approbation mixed and animated by wonder and surprise, constitutes the sentiment which is properly called admiration, of which applause is the natural expression...(*TMS*, p. 38)

The general principle in this proposition is that we admire a person's self-commanding tolerance for emotional circumstances that they quietly and stoically avoid advertising. Examples include extreme hunger, the ecstasy of one in love, and the experiences of a war veteran too horrible to share. The war veteran is the more admired that he does not share his dreaded experiences.

CHAPTER 8

Of those passions which take their origin from a particular turn or habit of the imagination

A lover may be good company to his mistress, but he is so to no other.

> Even of the passions derived from the imagination, those which take their origin from a peculiar turn or habit it has acquired…are…but little sympathized with. The imaginations of mankind, not having acquired that particular turn, cannot enter into them; and such passions, though they may be allowed to be almost unavoidable in some part of life, are always in some measure ridiculous. This is the case with that strong attachment which naturally grows up between two persons of different sexes, who have long fixed their thoughts upon one another. Our imagination not having run in the same channel with that of the lover, we cannot enter into the eagerness of his emotions. If our friend has been injured, we readily sympathize with his resentment, and grow angry with the very person with whom he is angry. If he has received a benefit, we readily enter into his gratitude, and have a very high sense of the merit of his benefactor. But if he is in love, though we may think his passion just as reasonable as any of the kind, yet we never think ourselves bound to conceive a passion of the same kind, and for the same person for whom he has conceived it. The passion appears to every body, but the man who feels it, entirely disproportioned to the value of the object; and love, though it is pardoned in a certain age, because we know it is natural, is always laughed at, because we cannot enter into it. All serious and strong expressions of it appear ridiculous to

Vernon L. Smith, *Adam Smith's Theory of Society*,
https://doi.org/10.1007/978-3-031-68494-4_8

> a third person; and though a lover may be good company to his mistress, he is so to nobody else. He himself is sensible of this; and as long as he continues in his sober senses, endeavours to treat his own passion with raillery and ridicule. It is the only style in which we care to hear of it; because it is the only style in which we ourselves are disposed to talk of it. (*TMS*, pp. 39–40)

Raillery, an uncommonly used word today, is also the perfect word for how Smith discusses the traditional attitude of men toward their intimacy with women. "It is the only style in which we care to hear of it." In this context, the loss of a mistress cannot be considered a tragedy like the loss of a leg, especially as noted by Smith it may lead to a better one. A lover may be good company to his mistress, but in such matters, he is to no other.

We do, however, embrace the high hope of happiness in lovers.

> But though we feel no proper sympathy with an attachment of this kind, though we never approach even in imagination towards conceiving a passion for that particular person, yet as we either have conceived, or may be disposed to conceive, passions of the same kind, we readily enter into those high hopes of happiness which are proposed from its gratification, as well as into that exquisite distress which is feared from its disappointment. It interests us not as a passion, but as a situation that gives occasion to other passions which interest us; to hope, to fear, and to distress of every kind: in the same manner as in a description of a sea voyage, it is not the hunger which interests us, but the distress which that hunger occasions. Though we do not properly enter into the attachment of the lover, we readily go along with those expectations of romantic happiness which he derives from it. (*TMS*, p. 40)

More seriously (and rising above the raillery), we all enter into the aspirations for happiness in lovers looking forward to their shared romantic embrace, though we fear its distress if love turns to disappointment. Young people today expect and cultivate sexual relations separate from marriage, but this need not avoid distress where expectations diverge leaving scope for much disappointment.

Addendum: women, disadvantaged under the law in adultery, has been justified by men's uncertainty as to the paternity of their children. But the real reason is that men make the laws and indulge themselves.

In *LJ*, Adam Smith summarizes the account usually given as to the punishment of adultery committed by women, which is much greater than the same offense if committed by men, namely that it prevents "spurious offspring" from being imposed on a husband (*LJ*, p. 147). Although this might appear reasonable, Smith argues that such cases are actually fraught with expressions of jealousy arising from the passions of love. It seems that the public tends to go along with the more injured party whether husband or wife because the cases show alienation from affection as much by husband as by wife. Smith wryly adds that the real reason for this asymmetry is that it is the men who make these laws and are inclined to curb the women in such matters and indulge themselves.

Smith takes advantage of the fact that the real reason for anything is sometimes the most straight forward, transparent, and obvious reason. If men make the laws, the law will everywhere embody their perspective with little reason to change. Hence, the origins of the disadvantageous treatment of women before the law is that their voice is not represented. He notes that the reason we have protection for property in all liberal nation states is because the rich have it, the poor do not, and the rich want to defend against the poor taking it. But the protection of property has unintended benefits for the poor and for society. The origins of an action routinely differ from the consequences of actions, which is why it is so important to keep them separate in all investigations as Smith carefully and steadfastly does.

His style was to think through such deep questions as, why society? Why economy? Or here why women are so treated? With little restraint imposed by what others might have said. Thus, Part VII, Of Systems of Moral Philosophy, was added in the 6th and final edition of *TMS* in 1790, the year of Smith's death. There, he examined deeply what others had done only after finishing what he had done. Of course, he had been much influenced by his friend David Hume, but Smith went far deeper than Hume into the theory of morals as the foundation for a theory of society and rejected Hume's reliance on utilitarian explanations.

That society treats women unequally in matters of love makes it the more interesting.

> The reserve which the laws of society impose upon the fair sex, with regard to (the passions of love)...renders it more peculiarly distressful in them, and, upon that very account, more deeply interesting. We are charmed with the love of Phædra, as it is expressed in the French tragedy of that name, notwithstanding all the extravagance and guilt which attend it. That very extravagance and guilt may be said, in some measure, to recommend it to us. Her fear, her shame, her remorse, her horror, her despair, become thereby more natural and interesting. All the secondary passions...which arise from the situation of love, become necessarily more furious and violent; and it is with these secondary passions only that we can properly be said to sympathize. (*TMS*, pp. 41–42)

Smith has a generalizable insight arising from his thoughts on the unequal treatment of women in his society: Knowing little about a matter that is of great universal interest surrounds it with an aura of secrecy that can only sharpen our interest and desire for revelation. Thus, both men and women are interested in fallen women, but also those women who excel in management, organization, war, and beauty, precisely for the reasons that they stand apart, with the unexpected yielding the enhanced attractions of novelty.

Love, however much exaggerated, is graceful or agreeable, mixed with humanity, generosity, kindness, friendship, esteem, and is not naturally odious, or intentionally mischievous.

> Of all the passions, however, which are so extravagantly disproportioned to the value of their objects, love [contrasted, say, with anger or hatred] is the only one that appears...to have any thing in it that is either graceful or agreeable. In itself, first of all, though it may be ridiculous, it is not naturally odious; and though its consequences are often fatal and dreadful, its intentions are seldom mischievous. And then, though there is little propriety in the passion itself, there is a good deal in some of those which always accompany it. There is in love a strong mixture of humanity, generosity, kindness, friendship, esteem; passions with which...we have the greatest propensity to sympathize, even notwithstanding we are sensible that they are, in some measure, excessive. The sympathy which we feel with them, renders the passion which they accompany less disagreeable, and supports it in our imagination, notwithstanding all the vices which

> commonly go along with it; though in the one sex it necessarily leads to the last ruin and infamy; and though in the other, where it is apprehended to be least fatal, it is almost always attended with an incapacity for labour, a neglect of duty, a contempt of fame, and even of common reputation.[1] Notwithstanding all this, the degree of sensibility and generosity with which it is supposed to be accompanied, renders it to many the object of vanity; and they are fond of appearing capable of feeling what would do them no honour if they had really felt it. (*TMS*, pp. 42–43)

Hence, does Smith see the passion of love surviving its more extreme manifestations in the smitten, and all the high school level raillery, to account for its associated lasting values of humanity, generosity, kindness, friendship, and esteem, in which we universally sympathize. Love's substance emerges from the triviality and becomes part of the enduring pleasantries of society.

The reserve with which we speak of the love affairs of friends also applies to coworkers and professionals.

> It is for a reason of the same kind, that a certain reserve is necessary when we talk of our own friends, our own studies, our own professions. All these are objects which we cannot expect should interest our companions in the same degree in which they interest us. And it is for want of this reserve, that the one half of mankind make bad company to the other. A philosopher is company to a philosopher only; the member of a club to his own little knot of companions. (*TMS*, p. 43)

Smith, ever alert to correspondences, sees similarity in the reserve with which people talk about sexual partners, and their reserve in speaking of close friends, or our professions. Most other people do not share our knowledge of close friends, nor do they know of our professional expertise in a specialty, or that of our professional cohorts. Neither should we expect them to much care, except in broad outline.

Hence, the propositional truth is that specialists are good company to each other but to no other.

[1] Thus, in the twentieth century, the Duke of Winsor famously gave up his birthright to the throne for the love of the divorced American woman he married. To many that seemed ridiculous but there seems little doubt of the Duke's complete sincerity of feelings.

CHAPTER 9

Of the unsocial passions

The pitch of the passions of hatred and resentment must be dampened to lower their intensity felt if others are to accept them gracefully.

> There is another set of passions, which, though derived from the imagination, yet before we can enter into them, or regard them as graceful or becoming, must always be brought down to a pitch much lower than that to which undisciplined nature would raise them. These are hatred and resentment, with all their different modifications. With regard to all such passions, our sympathy is divided between the person who feels them and the person who is the object of them. The interests of these two are directly opposite. What our sympathy with the person who feels them would prompt us to wish for, our fellow-feeling with the other would lead us to fear. As they are both men [valued persons], we are naturally concerned for both; and our fear for what the one may suffer, damps our resentment for what the other has suffered. Our sympathy, therefore, with the man who has received the provocation, necessarily falls short of the passion which naturally animates him, not only upon account of those general causes which render all sympathetic passions inferior to the original ones, but upon account of that particular cause which is peculiar to itself, our opposite sympathy with another person. Before resentment, therefore, can become graceful and agreeable, it must be more humbled, and brought down below that pitch to which it would naturally rise, than almost any other passion. (*TMS*, p. 44)

Vernon L. Smith, *Adam Smith's Theory of Society*,
https://doi.org/10.1007/978-3-031-68494-4_9

We fellow feel with both the person who feels resentment and the person whose action gave cause for the provocation resented. When a person's resentment is tinged with hatred, our sympathy may be conflicted between the one who feels the hatred and the one to whom it is directed. Out of respect our concern may naturally involve both parties. Before people can find such resentment graceful, the sense of the pitch of they who feel the hatred must be reduced to a level that others can go along with.

Strong is our natural sympathy for the victims of injury and against those who inflict it, but our sense felt is diminished relative to that of the principals and enhanced by their forbearance.

> [Humankind] ... have a very strong sense of the injuries that are done to another. The villain in a tragedy or romance, is as much the object of our indignation as the hero is that of our sympathy and affection. We detest Iago as much as we esteem Othello; and delight as much in the punishment of the one, as we are grieved at the distress of the other. But though mankind have so strong a fellow-feeling with the injuries that are done to their brethren, they do not always resent them the more that the sufferer appears to resent them. Upon most occasions, the greater his patience, his mildness, his humanity, provided it does not appear that he wants spirit, or that fear was the motive of his forbearance, the higher the resentment against the person who injured him. The amiableness of the character exasperates their sense of the atrocity of the injury. (*TMS*, p. 44)

As revealed in our identification with the heroes and against the villains of stage and screen, we naturally are drawn to sympathy for the victims of harm, and against those inflicting harm. What we feel is a weakened reflection of what the principals feel but our feelings may be enhanced where the principal shows patient forbearance, a feature that we admire.

Sympathy for wrongs done others are essential features of human nature but they who fail to defend themselves are contemptable.

> These passions, however, are regarded as necessary parts of the character of human nature. A person becomes contemptible who tamely sits still and submits to insults, without attempting either to repel or to revenge them. We cannot enter into his indifference and insensibility: we call his behaviour mean-spiritedness, and are as really provoked by it as by the insolence of

> his adversary. Even the mob are enraged to see any man submit patiently to affronts and ill usage. They desire to see this insolence resented, and resented by the person who suffers from it. They cry to him with fury to defend, or to revenge himself. If his indignation rouses at last, they heartily applaud and sympathize with it. It enlivens their own indignation against his enemy, whom they rejoice to see him attack in turn, and are as really gratified by his revenge, provided it is not immoderate, as if the injury had been done to themselves. (*TMS*, p. 45)

We support those who defend themselves against unjustified injury, and not only expect and applaud their defense but despise them if they do not.

This proposition powerfully underlies and explains the spontaneous expressions of emotions by collections and "mobs" of people. We experience spontaneity of pleasantry most often at a play or musical event in which the sitting audience bursts into applause by a signal performance of a skit or aria that triggers simultaneous feelings of great intensity. The phenomena usually depend on common experience peculiar to a group confined in space and time.

It rarely if ever happens nationally and internationally.

Vividly do I remember the solemnity of the Pearl Harbor attack in 1941, now 83 years ago. Everyone felt unbounded outrage, but there was no explosive marching in the streets; only a silent determination to right a wrong that was thought neither justified nor anticipated, though much later we learned that it had been unambiguously signaled by the withdrawal of Japanese envoys from negotiations over the American trade embargo. Yes, pain is more pungent than joy, but when felt universally the pain implied an enormous task to be done, whereas Victory in Europe (VE) and later in Japan (VJ) each meant that the job had been accomplished and with it came a pent-up release of emotions and dancing in the streets that words cannot capture.

Nor was there marching when Army Lt Colonel Jimmy Doolittle commanded the unusually daring takeoff of 16 one-way B-25 bombers from an aircraft carrier to bomb Tokyo less than four months after Pearl Harbor. One B-25 crash-landed in China, one in Russia, after the raid on their military and industrial targets. All the others landed in China and were returned to the US. I recall how our spirits were so greatly lifted by Doolittle and his air command company in their astonishing escapade. A great American hero, Doolittle lived to the age of 96.

Utilitarianism inadequately captures passion-driven actions.

> [T]hough the utility of those passions [of hatred and resentment] to the individual, by rendering it dangerous to insult or injure him, be acknowledged; and though their utility to the public, as the guardians of justice, and of the equality of its administration, be not less considerable...yet there is still something disagreeable in the passions themselves, which makes the appearance of them in other men the natural object of our aversion. The expression of anger towards any body present, if it exceeds a bare intimation that we are sensible of his ill usage, is regarded not only as an insult to that particular person, but as a rudeness to the whole company. Respect for them ought to have restrained us from giving way to so boisterous and offensive an emotion. It is the remote effects of these passions [the countervailing responses from the offended] which are agreeable; the immediate effects are mischief to the person against whom they are directed. But it is the immediate, and not the remote, effects of objects which render them agreeable or disagreeable to the imagination...(*TMS*, pp. 45–46)

The passions of hatred and resentment have utility value to society in discouraging the extreme unjustified injuries that invoke them. Such passions, however, are inherently disagreeable and rude when we see them in others, which accounts for our aversion toward their appearance, outbursts that perhaps exceed the restraints of self-command. That is the process, based on its emotional origins that Smith models and that determine the rules that emerge, not the utilitarian consequence. Thus we have utility considerations appearing as an afterthought.

Similar elements apply to qualities of mind and to conceptions of God.

> It is the same case with the qualities of the mind. The ancient stoics were of opinion, that as the world was governed by the all-ruling providence of a wise, powerful, and good God, every single event ought to be regarded as making a necessary part of the plan of the universe, and as tending to promote the general order and happiness of the whole: that the vices and follies of mankind, therefore, made as necessary a part of this plan as their wisdom or their virtue; and by that eternal art which reduces good from ill, were made to tend equally to the prosperity and perfection of the great system of nature. No speculation of this kind, however, how deeply soever it might be rooted in the mind, could diminish our natural abhorrence for

> vice, whose immediate effects are so destructive, and whose remote ones are too distant to be traced by the imagination. (*TMS*, p. 47)

Vice as well as virtue was a necessary part of the stoical conception of the plan of an all-powerful God, which included the operations of nature. Yet such speculation has not prevented nature from deeply implanting in the human breast an abhorrence for the destructive short- and long-term effects of vice. We are conceived with an abhorrence for vice and a love of virtue, aspiring to avoid the one and embrace the other.

A witty popular counterview before Smith was written by Bernard Mandeville Originally published in 1705, I have always read it as one of the finest in delightful satire. For example, in a key stanza:

> *Thus every Part was full of Vice,*
> *Yet the whole Mass a Paradise;...*
> *And Virtue, who from Politicks*
> *Had learn'd a Thousand Cunning Tricks,*
> *Was, by their happy Influence,*
> *Made Friends with Vice: And ever since,*
> *The worst of all the Multitude*
> *Did something for the Common Good.*
> (*The Fable of the Bees*, Vol. 2, p. 24)

And the moral of the poem included:

> *So Vice is beneficial found,*
> *When it's by Justice lopt and bound.*
> (*The Fable of the Bees*, referenced in a two-volume resource by F.B. Kaye in 1988: Vol. 2, p. 37)

Adam Smith, however, did not believe that Mandeville's humor compensated for its flawed analysis:

> There is, however, another system which seems to take away altogether the distinction between vice and virtue, and of which the tendency is, upon that account, wholly pernicious; I mean the system of Dr Mandeville. Though the notions of this author are in almost every respect erroneous, there are, however, some appearances in human nature, which, when viewed in a certain manner, seem at first sight to favour them. These, described and exaggerated by the lively and humorous, though coarse and rustic eloquence of Dr Mandeville, have thrown upon his doctrines an air

> of truth and probability which is very apt to impose upon the unskilful. (*TMS*, p. 451)

Hatred and anger are the only passions so disgusting as to deserve suppression while a smiling countenance elevates us into a gay sympathy.

> [The] immediate effects [of the passions of hatred and resentment] are so disagreeable, that even when they are most justly provoked, there is still something about them which disgusts us. These, therefore, are the only passions of which the expressions...do not dispose and prepare us to sympathize with them, before we are informed of the cause which excites them. The plaintive voice of misery, when heard at a distance, will not allow us to be indifferent about the person from whom it comes. As soon as it strikes our ear, it interests us in his fortune, and, if continued, forces us almost involuntarily to fly to his assistance. The sight of a smiling countenance, in the same manner, elevates even the pensive into that gay and airy mood, which disposes him to sympathize with, and share, the joy which it expresses; and he feels his heart, which with thought and care was before that shrunk and depressed, instantly expanded and elated. But it is quite otherwise with the expressions of hatred and resentment. The hoarse, boisterous, and discordant voice of anger, when heard at a distance, inspires us either with fear or aversion. We do not fly towards it, as to one who cries out with pain and agony. Women, and men of weak nerves, tremble and are overcome with fear, though sensible that themselves are not the objects of the anger. They conceive fear, however, by putting themselves in the situation of the person who is so. Even those of stouter hearts are disturbed: not indeed enough to make them afraid, but enough to make them angry; for anger is the passion which they would feel in the situation of the other person. It is the same case with hatred. Mere expressions of spite inspire it against nobody, but the man who uses them. Both these passions are by nature the objects of our aversion. Their disagreeable and boisterous appearance never excites, never prepares, and often disturbs, our sympathy. Grief does not more powerfully engage and attract us to the person in whom we observe it, than these, while we are ignorant of their cause, disgust and detach us from him. It was, it seems, the intention of nature, that those rougher and more unamiable emotions, which drive men from one another, should be less easily and more rarely communicated. (*TMS*, pp. 47–49)

Anger and hatred are the only passions in which nature does not prepare us with sympathy, we are slow to support them unless informed of their justification, whereas misery always calls our sympathy as does a smiling countenance. Thus, does nature seek to dampen the unamiable emotions that drive people apart, and to enlarge the amiable emotions that draw them together.

Music imitates all passions; most powerfully the social and agreeable—joy, grief, love, admiration, devotion; the harsh tones of anger are discordant.

> When music imitates the modulations of grief or joy, it either actually inspires us with those passions, or at least puts us in the mood which disposes us to conceive them. But when it imitates the notes of anger, it inspires us with fear. Joy, grief, love, admiration, devotion, are all of them passions which are naturally musical. Their natural tones are all soft, clear, and melodious; and they naturally express themselves in periods which are distinguished by regular pauses, and which upon that account are easily adapted to the regular returns of the correspondent airs of a tune. The voice of anger, on the contrary, and of all the passions which are akin to it, is harsh and discordant. Its periods too are all irregular, sometimes very long, and sometimes very short, and distinguished by no regular pauses. It is with difficulty, therefore, that music can imitate any of those passions; and the music which does imitate them is not the most agreeable. A whole entertainment may consist, without any impropriety, of the imitation of the social and agreeable passions. It would be a strange entertainment which consisted altogether of the imitations of hatred and resentment. (*TMS*, p. 49)

Smith's reliance on the mood-power of musical metaphors to express human relationships is revealed in the frequency of his use of the word "harmony," forty-two times, "concord," fifteen times, "discord" four times, "pitch," ten times, and such like-meaning phrases as "keep time to" or "beat time with." His use of words like discord and discordant are the antithesis of anything musical. These features underscore his perspective in which action comes from relationships between fundamentally self-interested individuals who modify their actions in the interest of strengthening those concordant relationships, rather than only to pursue independent one-dimensional personal utilitarian gain. Hence the experiences of musical entertainment are appropriate in capturing amiable virtues, not the anger inherent in vice. The musical tones of anger are harsh, discordant, and disagreeable. When we hear them, they grate on our sensibility.

Mind is poisoned by hatred and anger, which are destructive of happiness, but countered by love and gratitude.

> If [the discordant] ... passions are disagreeable to the spectator, they are not less so to the person who feels them. Hatred and anger are the greatest poison to the happiness of a good mind. There is, in the very feeling of those passions, something harsh, jarring, and convulsive, something that tears and distracts the breast, and is altogether destructive of that composure and tranquillity of mind which is so necessary to happiness, and which is best promoted by the contrary passions of gratitude and love. It is not the value of what they lose by the perfidy and ingratitude of those they live with, which the generous and humane are most apt to regret. Whatever they may have lost, they can generally be very happy without it. What most disturbs them is the idea of perfidy and ingratitude exercised towards themselves; and the discordant and disagreeable passions which this excites, constitute, in their own opinion, the chief part of the injury which they suffer. (*TMS*, pp. 49–50)

The passions of love and gratitude offset the harsh, jarring passions of hate-inspired resentment, the latter distinct from the natural impulse to resent inappropriately hurtful action concerning which there is universal third-party sympathy for the victim. Nor does the ingratitude of others toward the generous and humane disturb them so much as that which exists among themselves and the disagreeable passions that it excites. Smith seems to suggest that those who are the most generous and humane tend to fall short in their support of each other, perhaps taking each other too much for granted, and underestimating our mutual need for reinforcement from praise and recognition coupled with solace in times of distress. We also may wish to avoid any implication of neediness because that is despised if it is not justified.

Great offenses give occasion to the cool and impartial spectator, smaller ones merit neglect in the interest of unruffled composure.

> How many things are requisite to render the gratification of resentment completely agreeable, and to make the spectator thoroughly sympathize with our revenge? The provocation must first of all be such that we should

> become contemptible, and be exposed to perpetual insults, if we did not, in some measure, resent it. Smaller offences are always better neglected; nor is there any thing more despicable than that forward and captious humour which takes fire upon every slight occasion of quarrel. We should resent more from a sense of the propriety of resentment, from a sense that mankind expect and require it of us, than because we feel in ourselves the furies of that disagreeable passion. There is no passion, of which the human mind is capable, concerning whose justness we ought to be so doubtful, concerning whose indulgence we ought so carefully to consult our natural sense of propriety, or so diligently to consider what will be the sentiments of the cool and impartial spectator. Magnanimity, or a regard to maintain our own rank and dignity in society, is the only motive which can ennoble the expressions of this disagreeable passion. This motive must characterize our whole style and deportment. These must be plain, open, and direct; determined without positiveness, and elevated without insolence; not only free from petulance and low scurrility, but generous, candid, and full of all proper regards, even for the person who has offended us. It must appear, in short, from our whole manner, without our labouring affectedly to express it, that passion has not extinguished our humanity; and that if we yield to the dictates of revenge, it is with reluctance, from necessity, and in consequence of great and repeated provocations. When resentment is guarded and qualified in this manner, it may be admitted to be even generous and noble. (*TMS*, pp. 50–51)

What is the level of resentment that is balanced and justified in the eyes of the cool, fair, and impartial spectator? A level whereby we would appear contemptible if it did not engender strong resentment. A major insult must be insulting. Humankind accepts the principle that each of us is born with a right to defend ourselves, not from every careless and witless minor indignity, but from recognizably deliberate injury. (That an insult should be settled by a duel is surely a masculine overreaction, a cultural aberration. But we will comment below on a proposition that relates to it. Smith will also comment below on dueling.) Hence, the great crimes are murder, theft, and robbery, with guilt established by due process, and which, if not sufficiently controlled or deterred, render the existence of society impossible. All small trespasses can be left to neighborly peaceful negotiation and sometimes to good humor.

CHAPTER 10

Of the social passions

All the social and benevolent passions—generosity, kindness, compassion, mutual friendship and esteem—invariably please the unbiased spectator.

> As it is a divided sympathy which renders the whole set of [unsocial] passions [hatred, anger, and resentment:] … so ungraceful and disagreeable; so there is another set opposite to these which a redoubled sympathy renders almost always peculiarly agreeable and becoming. Generosity, humanity, kindness, compassion, mutual friendship and esteem, all the social and benevolent affections, when expressed in the countenance or behaviour, even towards those who are not peculiarly connected with ourselves, please the indifferent spectator upon almost every occasion. His sympathy with the person who feels those passions exactly coincides with his concern for the person who is the object of them. The interest, which, as a man, he is obliged to take in the happiness of this last, enlivens his fellow-feeling with the sentiments of the other, whose emotions are employed about the same object. We have always, therefore, the strongest disposition to sympathize with the benevolent affections. They appear in every respect agreeable to us. We enter into the satisfaction both of the person who feels them, and of the person who is the object of them. For as to be the object of hatred and indignation gives more pain than all the

Vernon L. Smith, *Adam Smith's Theory of Society*,
https://doi.org/10.1007/978-3-031-68494-4_10

> evil which a brave man can fear from his enemies; so there is a satisfaction in the consciousness of being beloved, which, to a person of delicacy and sensibility, is of more importance to happiness than all the advantage which he can expect to derive from it. What character is so detestable as that of one who takes pleasure in sowing dissension among friends, and turning their most tender love into mortal hatred? Yet wherein does the atrocity of this so much abhorred injury consist? Is it in depriving them of the frivolous good offices which, had their friendship continued, they might have expected from one another? It is in depriving them of that friendship itself, in robbing them of each other's affections, from which both derived so much satisfaction; it is in disturbing the harmony of their hearts, and putting an end to that happy commerce which had before subsisted between them. These affections, that harmony, this commerce, are felt, not only by the tender and the delicate, but by the rudest vulgar of mankind, to be of more importance to happiness than all the little services which could be expected to flow from them. (*TMS*, pp. 52–53)

Benevolent affections support a systemic state of wellbeing that results in the observed day-to-day good favors exchanged in a reciprocal manner by the citizens of a friendly community. The services are a consequence of the beneficial relational system supported by sympathy and fellow-feeling. For Smith the weakness of utilitarian explanations of society resides in the lack of an articulated social structure for sustaining them; the observed services are evidence of the structure to be accounted for, not the structure itself. Attaching other-regarding utility functions to the services explains and predicts nothing and cannot be a path to understanding. What Smith brilliantly and insightfully models is not reciprocity, per se, but the social and socializing process that identifies the functional forms of positive and negative reciprocity that creates an orderly society.

Love is the sentiment of peace for individual and community and is set asunder by its opposite.

> The sentiment of love is, in itself, agreeable to the person who feels it. It soothes and composes the breast, seems to favour the vital motions, and to promote the healthful state of the human constitution; and it is rendered still more delightful by the consciousness of the gratitude and satisfaction which it must excite in him who is the object of it. Their mutual regard renders them happy in one another, and sympathy with this mutual regard, makes them agreeable to every other person. With what pleasure do we look upon a family, through the whole of which reign mutual love and

> esteem, where the parents and children are companions for one another, without any other difference than what is made by respectful affection on the one side, and kind indulgence on the other; where freedom and fondness, mutual railery and mutual kindness, shew that no opposition of interest divides the brothers, nor any rivalship of favours sets the sisters at variance, and where every thing presents us with the idea of peace, cheerfulness, harmony, and contentment? On the contrary, how uneasy are we made when we go into a house in which jarring contention sets one half of those who dwell in it against the other; where, amidst affected smoothness and complaisance, suspicious looks and sudden starts of passion betray the mutual jealousies which burn within them, and which are every moment ready to burst out through all the restraints which the presence of the company imposes? (*TMS*, pp. 53–54)

To love and be loved, the two sides of a single sentiment, is the great aspiration of humankind and the enduring source of happiness that all desire. Its value is nowhere made plainer than in the house divided. By that contrast we are assured of the truth content of these ancient virtues. They are inherently decentralized values that filter up into public norms. They are nurtured by social, political, and economic freedom, which is antithetical to concentrations of power that enable hatred to prevail as a justification for suppressing greater imagined evils.

Bertrand Russell once said that men seek power because they don't trust others with it. Thus, power corrupts in the name of the failure of others to be trusting! Hence, to love, and be loved, becomes to hate, and be hated. This is what set the stage for the great prophets of religion, such as Jesus, whose popularity led to opposition from the authorities who could wash their hands of guilt both then and in the continuance of such offenses twenty centuries later.

Love's excesses of tenderness, indulgence, and friendship are never aversive.

> Those amiable passions, even when they are acknowledged to be excessive, are never regarded with aversion. There is something agreeable even in the weakness of friendship and humanity. The too tender mother and the too indulgent father, the too generous and affectionate friend, may sometimes, perhaps, on account of the softness of their natures, be looked upon with a species of pity, in which, however, there is a mixture of love, but can never be regarded with hatred and aversion, nor even with contempt, unless

> by the most brutal and worthless of mankind. It is always with concern, with sympathy, and kindness, that we blame them for the extravagance of their attachment. There is a helplessness in the character of extreme humanity which more than any thing interests our pity. There is nothing in itself which renders it either ungraceful or disagreeable. We only regret that it is unfit for the world, because the world is unworthy of it, and because it must expose the person who is endowed with it as a prey to the perfidy and ingratitude of insinuating falsehood, and to a thousand pains and uneasinesses, which, of all men, he the least deserves to feel, and which generally too he is, of all men, the least capable of supporting. It is quite otherwise with hatred and resentment. Too violent a propensity to those detestable passions, renders a person the object of universal dread and abhorrence, who, like a wild beast, ought, we think, to be hunted out of all civil society. (*TMS*, p. 54)

Love in excess may be boring, perhaps pedantically serving to advertise its presence and shore up self-doubt, but it is not offensive, odious, or hurtful. It may merely be a deficiency in the individual's ability to see themselves as others see them. But excessive resentment supports hatred, the great poison of order in community and society. Self-command in control of resentment is our most important virtue, for if it fails, all the amiable virtues are crowded out.

CHAPTER 11

Of the selfish passions

Grief and joy are a third set of passions that reside between the social and unsocial passions. In these we are more disposed to sympathize with small joys and great sorrows.

> Besides those two opposite sets of passions, the social [generosity, humanity, kindness, compassion, mutual friendship, and esteem] and unsocial [hatred and excessive resentment], there is another which holds a sort of middle place between them; is never either so graceful as is sometimes the one set, nor is ever so odious as is sometimes the other. Grief and joy, when conceived upon account of our own private good or bad fortune, constitute this third set of passions. Even when excessive, they are never so disagreeable as excessive resentment, because no opposite sympathy can ever interest us against them; and when most suitable to their objects, they are never so agreeable as impartial humanity and just benevolence; because no double sympathy can ever interest us for them. There is, however, this difference between grief and joy, that we are generally most disposed to sympathize with small joys and great sorrows. The man who, by some sudden revolution of fortune, is lifted up all at once into a condition of life greatly above what he had formerly lived in, may be assured that the congratulations of his best friends are not all of them perfectly sincere. An upstart…is generally disagreeable, and a sentiment of envy commonly prevents us from heartily sympathizing with his joy. If he…is sensible of this, and instead of appearing to be elated with his good fortune, he endeavours, as much as he can, to smother his joy, and keep down

Vernon L. Smith, *Adam Smith's Theory of Society*,
https://doi.org/10.1007/978-3-031-68494-4_11

> that elevation of mind with which his new circumstances naturally inspire him….He redoubles his attention to his old friends, and endeavours more than ever to be humble, assiduous, and complaisant…behaviour which in his situation we most approve of; because we expect…that he should have more sympathy with our envy and aversion to his happiness, than we have to his happiness. It is seldom that with all this he succeeds. We suspect the sincerity of his humility, and he grows weary of this constraint. In a little time, therefore, he generally leaves all his old friends behind him, some of the meanest of them excepted, who may, perhaps, condescend to become his dependants: nor does he always acquire any new ones; the pride of his new connections is as much affronted at finding him their equal, as that of his old ones had been by his becoming their superior: and it requires the most obstinate and persevering modesty to atone for this mortification to either. He generally grows weary too soon, and is provoked, by the sullen and suspicious pride of the one, and by the saucy contempt of the other, to treat the first with neglect, and the second with petulance, till at last he grows habitually insolent, and forfeits the esteem of all. If the chief part of human happiness arises from the consciousness of being beloved…those sudden changes of fortune seldom contribute much to happiness. He is happiest who advances more gradually to greatness, whom the public destines to every step of his preferment long before he arrives at it…(and) when it comes, it can excite no extravagant joy, and with regard to whom it cannot reasonably create either any jealousy in those he overtakes, or any envy in those he leaves behind. (*TMS*, pp. 55–56)

Grief is associated with private misfortune, joy with private good fortune. These reside between the uplifting beneficent-social, and the destructive-unsocial, passions. We sympathize with small joys but large sorrows. Why? Of course, joy has its own reward whatever the response of friends. But Smith believes there is necessarily an element of envy when a friend experiences unusual fortune in recognition and attainment, which sentiment is hidden not least because who wants to admit, if capable of recognizing, their own enviousness? The upstart, or precocious, recipient of unusual recognition and fortune is well advised to suppress their elation. If not, it will only exacerbate the person's tendency to drift away from their friends. That prophets might feel like strangers in their hometown expresses an analogous message of great insight. Any humility will be suspect, so even more important that it be genuine, not a sudden discovery. For ideal social graciousness, a person's progression to greatness will be gradual, with public acceptance well ahead of the person's private perceptions. An advantage to anyone in being of modest original means, or "lowborn," is that you do not expect unusual success, nor are attuned to see yourself as others see you in this regard.

I do not naturally relate to Smith's idea of "a tendency to drift away from friends"; rather, I have simply outlived them which is more saddening than regretful. I am grateful to have acquired friends across the spectrum of age, making it quite impossible to outlive them all.

Humans sympathize with small joys that sparkle in the young remembering their agreeableness with abandon as they age.

> Mankind, however, more readily sympathizes with those smaller joys which flow from less important causes. It is decent to be humble amidst great prosperity; but we can scarce express too much satisfaction in all the little occurrences of common life, in the company with which we spent the evening last night, in the entertainment that was set before us, in what was said, and what was done, in all the little incidents of the present conversation, and in all those frivolous nothings which fill up the void of human life. Nothing is more graceful than habitual cheerfulness, which is always founded upon a peculiar relish for all the little pleasures which common occurrences afford. We readily sympathize with it: it inspires us with the same joy, and makes every trifle turn up to us in the same agreeable aspect in which it presents itself to the person endowed with this happy disposition. Hence it is that youth, the season of gaiety, so easily engages our affections. That propensity to joy which seems even to animate the bloom, and to sparkle from the eyes of youth and beauty, though in a person of the same sex, exalts, even the aged, to a more joyous mood than ordinary. They forget, for a time, their infirmities, and abandon themselves to those agreeable ideas and emotions to which they have long been strangers, but which, when the presence of so much happiness recalls them to their breast, take their place there, like old acquaintance, from whom they are sorry to have ever been parted, and whom they embrace more heartily upon account of this long separation. (*TMS*, pp. 56–57)

Small joys sparkle with freshness in the young and so exalts in the aged that it helps compensate for their aches and pains. In this, the aged are fortunate indeed to have young friends who keep that sparkle alive and invigorated though they outlive their contemporaries. But the small joys are also ephemeral and ought to inspire the discovery of more lasting values. Satisfaction wherever it occurs is more fulfilling and greater than joy.

Though we are naturally averse to it, our greatest sympathy is with the deep affliction of grief.

> Small vexations excite no sympathy, but deep affliction calls forth the greatest. The man who is made uneasy by every little disagreeable incident; who is hurt if either the cook or the butler have failed in the least article of their duty; who feels every defect in the highest ceremonial of politeness, whether it be shewn to himself or to any other person … who is put out of humour by the badness of the weather when in the country, by the badness of the roads when upon a journey, and by the want of company, and dulness of all public diversions, when in town; such a person ... will seldom meet with much sympathy. Joy is a pleasant emotion, and we gladly abandon ourselves to it upon the slightest occasion. We readily, therefore, sympathize with it in others, whenever we are not prejudiced by envy. But grief is painful, and the mind, even when it is our own misfortune, naturally resists and recoils from it. We would endeavour either not to conceive it at all, or to shake it off as soon as we have conceived it. Our aversion to grief will not, indeed, always hinder us from conceiving it in our own case upon very trifling occasions, but it constantly prevents us from sympathizing with it in others when excited by the like frivolous causes: for our sympathetic passions are always less irresistible than our original ones. There is, besides, a malice in mankind, which not only prevents all sympathy with little uneasinesses, but renders them in some measure diverting. Hence the delight which we all take in railery, and in the small vexation which we observe in our companion, when he is pushed, and urged, and teased upon all sides. Men of the most ordinary good breeding dissemble the pain which any little incident may give them; and those who are more thoroughly formed to society, turn, of their own accord, all such incidents into railery, as they know their companions will do for them. The habit which a man, who lives in the world, has acquired of considering how every thing that concerns himself will appear to others, makes those frivolous calamities turn up in the same ridiculous light to him, in which he knows they will certainly be considered by them. (*TMS*, pp. 57–58)

Smith's list of the complaints of the naysayers of his day—the weather, roads, lack of company, and the dullness of public entertainment—are the great constants in life that ring with popular fresh truth even with our modern cars, endless gadgets, and abundant means of communication. In opposition to such trivia, I find much to enter sympathetically into in some of the modern, and a precious few contemporary, movies and TV shows, from the *Maltese Falcon* (1941), *Casablanca* (1943),

The Treasure of Sierra Madre (1848), to *1923* (2023)! What I do not like in the contemporary movie and TV shows is seeing and hearing people talking as they walk up or down stairs, or hallways, in homes or offices, in the Whitehouse or on the street, joined occasionally by one or two interlopers who peel off, in an apparent attempt to instill a fake dynamic sense of interaction that is not part of the script but an artificial independent add-on related to nothing. What you do not observe is spontaneous reactions, inspired in the moment by context, that become famous: "Police badge? I don' need no damn police badge" in *The Treasure of Sierra Madre* (1848); or "I'll have what she's having," in *When Harry Met Sally* (1989). Directors let these eruptions stand to everyone's merriment. What made Charlie Chaplin movies both competent and astonishing is that he let the camera run on long episodes, eschewing the focus on short episodes to be pasted together into a whole not experienced wherein the actors have to see the final film clip to have any idea what they produced. The exquisite final scene in *City Lights* was repeated in its entirety countless times by Chaplin until it was just-right and became a classic. Remarkably, he wrote, directed, produced, performed-in, choreographed, and composed the theme songs in his own movies.

Our deepest sympathy is reserved for our friends' deepest sorrow, our shallowest for raillery.

> Our sympathy…with deep distress, is very strong and very sincere…We weep even at the feigned representation of a tragedy. If you labour…under any signal calamity; if by some extraordinary misfortune you are fallen into poverty, into diseases, into disgrace and disappointment; even though your own fault may have been in part, the occasion, yet you may generally depend upon the sincerest sympathy of all your friends, and, as far as interest and honour will permit, upon their kindest assistance too. But if your misfortune is not of this dreadful kind, if you have only been a little baulked in your ambition, if you have only been jilted by your mistress, or are only henpecked by your wife, lay your account with the raillery of all your acquaintance. (*TMS*, pp. 58–59)

We have the strongest and most heartfelt sympathy for deep distress. Our friends are always ready to soften our pain when we encounter distress. But if you are merely being henpecked by your wife, disappointed in a love affair, or outmaneuvered in your competitive ambitions, expect only raillery, that great masculine exercise in ego leveling.

PART III

Of the effects of prosperity and adversity upon the judgment of mankind' with regard to the propriety of action; and why it is more easy to obtain their approbation in the one state than in the other

CHAPTER 12

That though our sympathy with sorrow is generally a more lively sensation than our sympathy with joy, it commonly falls much more short of the violence of what is naturally felt by the person principally concerned

We applaud sympathy with sorrow and tolerate its excess, but we do not tolerate an excess of joy.

> Our sympathy with sorrow…has been more taken notice of than our sympathy with joy. The word sympathy, in its most proper and primitive signification, denotes our fellow-feeling with the sufferings, not that with the enjoyments, of others… [Consequently] our sympathy with sorrow is…more universal, than that with joy. Though sorrow is excessive, we may still have some fellow-feeling with it. What we feel does not…amount to that complete sympathy, to that perfect harmony and correspondence of sentiments which constitutes approbation. We do not weep, and exclaim, and lament, with the sufferer. We are sensible, on the contrary, of his weakness, and of the extravagance of his passion, and yet often feel a very sensible concern upon his account. But if we do not entirely enter into, and go along with, the joy of another, we have no sort of regard or fellow-feeling for it. The man who skips and dances about with that intemperate

Vernon L. Smith, *Adam Smith's Theory of Society*,
https://doi.org/10.1007/978-3-031-68494-4_12

> and senseless joy which we cannot accompany him in, is the object of our contempt and indignation. (*TMS*, pp. 60–61)

I found lasting solace in my mother's reaction to distress—"this will pass," or, with deep distress, "this, even this, will pass" (See, 2 Corinthians 4: 17–18). She turned up the blank backside of her therapeutic wood-plaque handicraft, with its markings for mindless engraving, to expose its plain side and engraved on that blank slate the words: "Give me Courage and Gaiety and the Quiet Mind." From her Faith she received much gaiety, a little of the quiet mind, and in the end courage that surpassed understanding. Such expressions acknowledge both the cultural universality of distress, and a pungency of feelings that most commonly peaks-out, or more appropriately, troughs-out, afterwards. Sorrow draws universal sympathy while joy normally seems to not draw any comparable such sympathy. But I believe, because I have experienced it, that there is an exception to the latter, where people feel an intense comradery, an emergent sense of purpose, and mission, who join to celebrate every milestone, and to counter the envious naysayers whose experiential knowledge is nothing, which fact is so obviously revealed in their malicious gossip. I am just so sorry that my mother was challenged in finding that solace in her final days. But she did what was necessary and required given that she was due to be committed to a Cuckoo's Nest from which there can be no voluntary return after being stripped of all self-command.

Sympathy with pain is more pungently felt, even when suppressed, than sympathy with joy even if there is no envy in the latter case.

> Pain, besides, whether of mind or body, is a more pungent sensation than pleasure, and our sympathy with pain, though it falls greatly short of what is naturally felt by the sufferer, is generally a more lively and distinct perception than our sympathy with pleasure, though this last often approaches more nearly…to the natural vivacity of the original passion. Over and above all this, we often struggle to keep down our sympathy with the sorrow of others. Whenever we are not under the observation of the sufferer, we endeavour, for our own sake, to suppress it as much as we can, and we are not always successful. The opposition which we make to it, and the reluctance with which we yield to it, necessarily oblige us to take more particular notice of it. But we never have occasion to make this opposition to our sympathy with joy. If there is any envy in the case, we never feel the least propensity towards it; and if there is none, we give way to it without

> any reluctance. On the contrary, as we are always ashamed of our own envy, we often pretend, and sometimes really wish, to sympathize with the joy of others, when by that disagreeable sentiment we are disqualified from doing so. We are glad, we say, on account of our neighbour's good fortune, when in our hearts, perhaps, we are really sorry. We often feel a sympathy with sorrow when we would wish to be rid of it; and we often miss that with joy when we would be glad to have it. The obvious observation…to make, is, that our propensity to sympathize with sorrow must be very strong, and our inclination to sympathize with joy very weak. Notwithstanding this prejudice, however, I will venture to affirm, that, when there is no envy in the case, our propensity to sympathize with joy is much stronger than our propensity to sympathize with sorrow; and that our fellow-feeling for the agreeable emotion approaches much more nearly to the vivacity of what is naturally felt by the persons principally concerned, than that which we conceive for the painful one. (*TMS*, pp. 61–62)

We take notice of our sympathy with the sorrow of another, because, with mixed success, we struggle to suppress it when not in the presence of the sufferer. But in our sympathy with joy, we never experience such opposition and reluctance. If there is envy in our feelings then we are without sympathy, if none then there is no reluctance that opposes it. Smith, unlike most modern behavioral scholars, believes that envy plays a decisive role in explaining the far greater sympathy felt and expressed for sorrow than for joy. We are never envious of our friend's sorrow and always, in Smith's view, envious of their joys. Is this because envy has no role in modern behavioral economic studies? There is a large and persistent literature on attitudes toward differential payoffs in two person games, referred to neutrally as inequality aversion, less neutrally as due to unfairness, but almost never as enviousness.[1] We wish neither to admit of enviousness nor accuse others of it.

[1] In Humanomics, Cambridge, 2019, pp. 50–55, Smith and Wilson show that a model of enviousness is consistent with ultimatum game behavior in which unequal offers by Player 1 are rejected by Player2, whereas the results seem to have been near universally rationalized by behavioral and experimental economists as due to "unfairness." The subjects in ultimatum games also have explained their rejection of unequal outcomes as due to "unfairness." Given Smith's hypothesis that "we are always ashamed of our own envy," then in confirmation, both scientist and subject would naturally choose to attribute action in rejecting unequal offers to unfairness by others, not the enviousness of themselves. H. Bortof (1996, p. 17), The wholeness of Nature. Edinburgh: Floris, notes that scientists believe themselves to be objective but are actually subjective because the witness is compelled to answer the questions that the scientist asks, believing that nature answers,

We pardon display of excessive grief, but we never pardon intemperance of joy.

> We have some indulgence for that excessive grief which we cannot entirely go along with. We know what a prodigious effort is requisite before the sufferer can bring down his emotions to complete harmony and concord with those of the spectator. Though he fails, therefore, we easily pardon him. But we have no such indulgence for the intemperance of joy; because we are not conscious that any such vast effort is requisite to bring it down to what we can entirely enter into. The man who, under the greatest calamities, can command his sorrow, seems worthy of the highest admiration; but he who, in the fulness of prosperity, can in the same manner master his joy, seems hardly to deserve any praise. We are sensible that there is a much wider interval in the one case than in the other, between what is naturally felt by the person principally concerned, and what the spectator can entirely go along with. (*TMS*, pp. 61–62)

Because we so easily enter into the sorrow of another, we are more tolerant of the expressions of that excess. And it is precisely because we do not so readily enter into another's joy, we are less tolerant of any exuberant expressions of that joy. We admire, even marvel, at the person who is in control and command of their composure under great sorrow. But they who enjoy great prosperity, yet master their elation, hardly deserve any comparable admiration. We expect people to suppress excessive expression of delight at their own accomplishments. That is a good occasion for the beneficiary to shut up, sit down, and let others offer their commentaries and congratulations.

The fundamental asymmetry between sorrow and joy: adversity depresses the mind much further below its natural state than ever prosperity can elevate it above that state.

> What can be added to the happiness of the man who is in health, who is out of debt, and has a clear conscience? To one in this situation all accessions of fortune may properly be said to be superfluous; and if he is much elevated upon account of them, it must be the effect of the most frivolous levity. This situation, however, may very well be called the natural

whereas it is "the transposed echo of their own voice." So, is "unfairness of other" simply a euphemism for one's "own enviousness?" If so, how could you know and measure it?.

and ordinary state of mankind. Notwithstanding the present misery and depravity of the world, so justly lamented, this really is the state of the greater part of men. The greater part of men, therefore, cannot find any great difficulty in elevating themselves to all the joy which any accession to this situation can well excite in their companion. But though little can be added to this state, much may be taken from it. Though between this condition and the highest pitch of human prosperity, the interval is but a trifle; between it and the lowest depth of misery, the distance is immense and prodigious. Adversity, on this account, necessarily depresses the mind of the sufferer much more below its natural state, than prosperity can elevate him above it. The spectator, therefore, must find it much more difficult to sympathize entirely, and keep perfect time, with his sorrow, than thoroughly to enter into his joy, and must depart much further from his own natural and ordinary temper of mind in the one case than in the other. It is on this account, that though our sympathy with sorrow is often a more pungent sensation than our sympathy with joy, it always falls much short of the violence of what is naturally felt by the person principally concerned. (*TMS*, pp. 62–63)

In *TMS*, the fundamental asymmetry between joy and sorrow felt by people is due to Smith's hypothesis that the amount by which we can rise from a given state is most commonly small relative to the prodigious amount by which we can fall. Consequently, this root psychological asymmetry between joy and sorrow implies a derivative asymmetry between gain and loss in human action studied today in decision making. It is in this gain/loss form that it was discovered by D. Kahneman and A. Tversky (1979) "Prospect Theory: An Analysis of Decision under Risk" *Econometrica*, 47(2), March pp. 263–292, https://doi.org/https://doi.org/10.2307/1914185, as an empirical property of individual decision making under probabilistic risk. Smith's contrasting predictive theory of the phenomenon seems never to have been rediscovered or recognized in this modern literature although it has been extensively studied empirically by experimental psychologists and economists.

In the literature of modern behavioral economics and psychology, it is routinely referred to as "loss aversion" in preferences. But that designation is an artifact of a theory wherein all action is attributed to preference or dis-preference.

In *TMS*, on the contrary, all preferences are strictly selfish, but the psychological state of being self-interested is distinguished from that of acting in one's self-interest, allowing action to be modeled in terms of creating and following social and socializing rules that enable us to get along with others, the rules being highly context dependent because their nuances of meaning can only be conveyed by context. Consequently, in *TMS*, predictions are more precise in being contingent on circumstances such as in-context intentionality. Where a utilitarian experimentalist finds that intentions matter in experiments, they then include intentions in subjects' utility functions, as part of their ex post hoc theory of "social preferences." By definition the theory is correct, and always corroborated.

In *TMS*, are people loss averse? Well, obviously they are, because more is always better and less is always worse! But people, or subjects, are predicted to choose less if they want to reward another, as we say in English, out of the "debt of gratitude" that they feel due to another's good favor. Hence, transferring money to another is said not to be due to out-of-the-blue "altruistic"-utility, but is a consequence of social approbation which rewards properly motivated "actions of a beneficent tendency." In *TMS*, both the theory and its predictive consequences are richer in articulating the effect of circumstances as well as the emotions felt, than in utilitarianism today.

We enter another's grief with pain and reluctance, hiding our tears, but enter more smoothly into another's joy provided that our envy can be overcome.

> It is agreeable to sympathize with joy; and wherever envy does not oppose it, our heart abandons itself with satisfaction to the highest transports of that delightful sentiment. But it is painful to go along with grief, and we always enter into it with reluctance. When we attend to the representation of a tragedy, we struggle against that sympathetic sorrow which the entertainment inspires as long as we can, and we give way to it at last only when we can no longer avoid it: we even then endeavour to cover our concern from the company. If we shed any tears, we carefully conceal them, and are afraid lest the spectators, not entering into this excessive tenderness, should regard it as effeminacy and weakness. The wretch whose misfortunes call upon our compassion feels with what reluctance we are likely to enter into his sorrow, and therefore proposes his grief to us with fear and hesitation: he even smothers the half of it, and is ashamed, upon account of this hard-heartedness of mankind, to give vent to the fulness of his affliction. It is otherwise with the man who riots in joy and success. Wherever envy does not interest us against him, he expects our completest sympathy. He

> does not fear, therefore, to announce himself with shouts of exultation, in full confidence that we are heartily disposed to go along with him. (*TMS*, pp. 63–64)

Except for the shadow of envy cast upon it, the joy experienced by another is agreeable to our sensibility and they expect our sympathy. It is otherwise with grief for we never envy it and are reluctant to enter its painfulness. The sufferer, aware of our reluctance, is hesitant even to inform us of their situation, and tends to smother its full disclosure.

Both that which is observed and that which is not observed are part of the evidence to be explained and understood in a system of community thought and action as developed in *TMS*. Smith's reference to the literature of tragedy suggests that he was made acutely aware of his own feelings when in attendance to a tragedy, asked why this might be, and out of that private exploration offered an explanation. All such self-examination, and other examinations, seems to have been a source of evidence, or of cases, that potentially contradict our sociability if not resolved. These careful and close observations are a source of insight in *TMS*, and he tapped into a vast and rich data set for checking their truth content in English, Roman, and Greek literature in addition to the world about him to check the generalizability of his propositions.

We are more likely to laugh than weep in company, because others are more likely to go along with our agreeable than with our painful emotions.

> Why should we be more ashamed to weep than to laugh before company? We may often have as real occasion to do the one as to do the other: but we always feel that the spectators are more likely to go along with us in the agreeable than in the painful emotion. It is always miserable to complain, even when we are oppressed by the most dreadful calamities. But the triumph of victory is not always ungraceful. Prudence, indeed, would often advise us to bear our prosperity with more moderation; because prudence would teach us to avoid that envy which this very triumph is, more than any thing, apt to excite. (*TMS*, pp. 64–65)

To laugh is to outwardly express our joy, to weep is to similarly express our sorrow. The former is common, the latter less common. Smith sees in this anomalous observation evidence of our eagerness to embrace the psychological prosperity of joy and reluctance to enter into the sorrows of others. Because of our capacity for seeing ourselves as others see us, to complain is ungraceful even if our grief is sharply felt. And our recognition of envy may lower the pitch of our expressions of joy. Thus, prudence teaches us to moderate our celebration of joy, letting such sleeping dogs lie. Sympathy with sorrow is a private, not a public, sentiment, while joy is the opposite.

To admire is to not envy or at least to overcome it. Smith saw envy as likely reducing our admiration for the joy of prosperity in others. We avoid such explanations today, perhaps because they appear accusative, but Smith let the chips fall where they may. Asymmetries of action are sources of testable hypotheses to be explained by hidden inferred forces. Interestingly, however, the words "envy" and "admire" were used at compatible frequencies from 1600 until about 1825, at rates five times more frequently than in the twentieth century. Do we do any better in hiding our emotions today? For Smith emotions were a means of self-discovery, accounting for the rules of order in community, and an important invisible force or gravity or repulsion to be understood in human sociality.

Mirth is heartfelt at public celebrations as our friends' joy becomes our joy for the moment to advertise.

> How hearty are the acclamations of the mob, who never bear any envy to their superiors, at a triumph or a public entry? And how sedate and moderate is commonly their grief at an execution? Our sorrow at a funeral generally amounts to no more than an affected gravity: but our mirth at a christening or a marriage is always from the heart and without any affectation. Upon these, and all such joyous occasions, our satisfaction, though not so durable, is often as lively as that of the persons principally concerned. Whenever we cordially congratulate our friends, which, however, to the disgrace of human nature, we do but seldom, their joy literally becomes our joy: we are, for the moment, as happy as they are: our heart swells and overflows with real pleasure: joy and complacency sparkle from our eyes, and animate every feature of our countenance and every gesture of our body. (*TMS*, p. 65)

It is psychologically liberating to recognize and applaud the social and professional accomplishments of our friends. We adopt their victory as ours and claim it will likely bring reciprocity to strengthen our commitment to our own enterprises. Good friends make better friends. I recall with great satisfaction the announcement that Elinor Ostrom had been awarded the Nobel Prize in Economics, 2019. I felt even more vindicated when the message reverberating on the internet was "Elinor who?" which reflected ignorance of her contributions that I knew were now destined to change dramatically as economists became more widely informed of the significance and priority of her work. Implicitly, my feelings reflected knowledge of Smith's theorem that "the mob…never bear any envy to their superiors, at a triumph or a public entry." Indeed, many will rush to appear first on the bandwagon. In this case, any who might think that her award was because she was a woman, merely revealed their own ignorance. I was honored to be asked to write of her award for *Forbes*.[2]

The much we might feel of a friend's affliction is little compared with what they feel, but our heartfelt sympathy consoles them.

> [W]hen we condole with our friends in their afflictions, how little do we feel in comparison of what they feel? We sit down by them, we look at them, and while they relate to us the circumstances of their misfortune, we listen to them with gravity and attention. But while their narration is every moment interrupted by those natural bursts of passion which often seem almost to choke them in the midst of it, how far are the languid emotions of our hearts from keeping time to the transports of theirs? We may be sensible, at the same time, that their passion is natural, and no greater than what we ourselves might feel upon the like occasion. We may even inwardly reproach ourselves with our own want of sensibility, and perhaps, on that account, work ourselves up into an artificial sympathy, which, however, when it is raised, is always the slightest and most transitory imaginable; and generally, as soon as we have left the room, vanishes, and is gone for ever. Nature, it seems, when she loaded us with our own sorrows, thought that they were enough, and therefore did not command us to take any further share in those of others, than what was necessary to prompt us to relieve them. (*TMS* pp. 65–66)

Though what we feel for a friend's affliction may pale in comparison with what they feel, it is quite enough to trigger our sympathy and to want to console them. In this spontaneous response we are sufficiently

[2] See Smith, Vernon L (2009) "Governing the Commons." *Forbes*, October 12. https://www.forbes.com/2009/10/12/elinor-ostrom-commons-nobel-economics-opinions-contributors-vernon-l-smith.html?sh=543249175c35.

motivated to supply what they need. Our feelings may be only a shadow of what our companion feels, but it is quite enough to spur the necessary social and socializing action.

We have great admiration for those whose self-command endures the most dreadful of calamities.

> His behaviour is genteel and agreeable who can maintain his cheerfulness amidst a number of frivolous disasters. But he appears to be more than mortal who can support, in the same manner, the most dreadful calamities. We feel what an immense effort is requisite to silence those violent emotions which naturally agitate and distract those in his situation. We are amazed to find that he can command himself so entirely. His firmness, at the same time, perfectly coincides with our insensibility. He makes no demand upon us for that more exquisite degree of sensibility which we find, and which we are mortified to find, that we do not possess. There is the most perfect correspondence between his sentiments and ours, and on that account the most perfect propriety in his behaviour. It is a propriety, too, which, from our experience of the usual weakness of human nature, we could not reasonably have expected he should be able to maintain. We wonder with surprise and astonishment at that strength of mind which is capable of so noble and generous an effort. The sentiment of complete sympathy and approbation, mixed and animated with wonder and surprise, constitutes what is properly called admiration. (*TMS*, p. 66)

Small disasters, suffered cheerfully, require little self-command, and invite little corresponding admiration. We know with what difficulty we control our emotional feelings under dreadful sorrows. Consequently, their self-command enables them to weather severe calamity drawing our strongest sympathy, approbation, surprise, and admiration.

We singularly admire self-command in the outward expression of grief.

> Whenever we meet, in common life, with any examples of…heroic magnanimity, we are always extremely affected. We are more apt to weep and shed tears for such as, in this manner, seem to feel nothing for themselves, than for those who give way to all the weakness of sorrow: and in this particular case the sympathetic grief of the spectator appears to go beyond the original passion in the person principally concerned. The friends of Socrates all wept when he drank the last potion, while he himself

> expressed the gayest and most cheerful tranquillity. Upon all such occasions the spectator makes no effort, and has no occasion to make any, in order to conquer his sympathetic sorrow. He is under no fear that it will transport him to any thing that is extravagant and improper; he is rather pleased with the sensibility of his own heart, and gives way to it with complaisance and self-approbation. He gladly indulges, therefore, the most melancholy views which can naturally occur to him concerning the calamity of his friend, for whom, perhaps, he never felt so exquisitely before the tender and tearful passion of love. But it is quite otherwise with the person principally concerned. He is obliged, as much as possible, to turn away his eyes from whatever is either naturally terrible or disagreeable in his situation. Too serious an attention to those circumstances, he fears, might make so violent an impression upon him, that he could no longer keep within the bounds of moderation, or render himself the object of the complete sympathy and approbation of the spectators. He fixes his thoughts, therefore, upon those only which are agreeable, the applause and admiration which he is about to deserve by the heroic magnanimity of his behaviour. (*TMS*, p. 67)

Those who become resigned to great disaster may achieve a gay tranquility not imaginable by friends enwrapped in the deep sorrow occasioned by the disaster. In suicide, the sufferer's intensity of pain may not be known or even knowable to associates and friends. The event, so incomprehensible, may cause friends much more difficulty in finding resignation and closure than the person affected, who may have found relief and comfort from pain, a pain not otherwise endurable.

Sympathy is reduced when a person's distress is of their own making.

> On the contrary, he always appears, in some measure, mean and despicable, who is sunk in sorrow and dejection upon account of any calamity of his own. We cannot bring ourselves to feel for him what he feels for himself, and what, perhaps, we should feel for ourselves if in his situation. We therefore despise him; unjustly, perhaps, if any sentiment could be regarded as unjust, to which we are by nature irresistibly determined. The weakness of sorrow never appears in any respect agreeable, except when it arises from what we feel for others more than from what we feel for ourselves. A son, upon the death of an indulgent and respectable father, may give way to it without much blame. His sorrow is chiefly founded upon a sort of sympathy with his departed parent; and we readily enter into this humane emotion. But if he should indulge the same weakness upon account of any

> misfortune which affected himself only, he would no longer meet with any such indulgence. (*TMS*, pp. 67–68)

When our own situation is disagreeable but can be blamed on no other, we endure a deficit in sympathy from others, and, feeling this to be not undeserved, must redouble our efforts to adapt and find a path to a better state.

CHAPTER 13

Of the origin of ambition, and of the distinction of ranks

The social and existential implications of humankind's disposition to sympathize more with our joy than with sorrow.

> It is because mankind are disposed to sympathize more entirely with our joy than with our sorrow, that we make parade of our riches, and conceal our poverty. Nothing is so mortifying as to be obliged to expose our distress to the view of the public, and to feel, that though our situation is open to the eyes of all mankind, no mortal conceives for us the half of what we suffer. Nay, it is chiefly from this regard to the sentiments of mankind, that we pursue riches and avoid poverty. For to what purpose is all the toil and bustle of this world? what is the end of avarice and ambition, of the pursuit of wealth, of power, and pre-eminence? Is it to supply the necessities of nature? The wages of the meanest labourer can supply them. We see that they afford him food and clothing, the comfort of a house, and of a family. If we examine his economy with rigour, we should find that he spends a great part of them upon conveniences, which may be regarded as superfluities, and that, upon extraordinary occasions, he can give something even to vanity and distinction. What then is the cause of our aversion to his situation, and why should those who have been educated in the higher ranks of life, regard it as worse than death, to be reduced to live, even without labour, upon the same simple fare with him, to dwell under the same lowly roof, and to be clothed in the same humble attire? Do they imagine that their stomach is better, or their sleep sounder, in a palace than in a cottage? ... From whence, then, arises that

Vernon L. Smith, *Adam Smith's Theory of Society*,
https://doi.org/10.1007/978-3-031-68494-4_13

> emulation which runs through all the different ranks of men, and what are the advantages which we propose by that great purpose of human life which we call bettering our condition? To be observed, to be attended to, to be taken notice of with sympathy, complacency, and approbation, are all the advantages which we can propose to derive from it. It is the vanity, not the ease, or the pleasure, which interests us. But vanity is always founded upon the belief of our being the object of attention and approbation. The rich man glories in his riches, because he feels that they naturally draw upon him the attention of the world, and that mankind are disposed to go along with him in all those agreeable emotions with which the advantages of his situation so readily inspire him...The poor man, on the contrary, is ashamed of his poverty. He feels that it either places him out of the sight of mankind, or, that if they take any notice of him, they have, however, scarce any fellow-feeling with the misery and distress which he suffers. He is mortified upon both accounts...The poor man goes out and comes in unheeded, and when in the midst of a crowd is in the same obscurity as if shut up in his own hovel.... The fortunate and the proud wonder at the insolence of human wretchedness, that it should dare to present itself before them, and with the loathsome aspect of its misery presume to disturb the serenity of their happiness. The man of rank and distinction, on the contrary, is observed by all the world. Every body is eager to look at him, and to conceive, at least by sympathy, that joy and exultation with which his circumstances naturally inspire him...In a great assembly he is the person upon whom all direct their eyes; it is upon him that their passions seem all to wait with expectation, in order to receive that movement and direction which he shall impress upon them...he has, every moment, an opportunity of interesting mankind, and of rendering himself the object of the observation and fellow-feeling of every body about him. It is this, which, notwithstanding the restraint it imposes, notwithstanding the loss of liberty with which it is attended, renders greatness the object of envy, and compensates, in the opinion of mankind, all that toil, all that anxiety, all those mortifications, which must be undergone in the pursuit of it; and what is of yet more consequence, all that leisure, all that ease, all that careless security, which are forfeited for ever by the acquisition. (*TMS*, pp. 70–72)

The rich person often glories and makes parade of their riches because it draws the world's attention. The poor person goes out and returns unheeded, obscure even in crowds. It is not because we are attracted to greater comfort that we pursue our ambition to prosper but from the vanity of being recognized, and acclaimed, for having performed a task well done, even if it requires a sacrifice of the free spirit of choice.

And when our friends wish to see us recognized, we feel an even greater responsibility to not let them down. We spend our wealth on conveniences and superfluities, but is this the purpose of our toil and trouble? Let what we do and pursue be what we most desire and enjoy, not what we youthfully might imagine the rich find in their gadgetry.

Well, I do recall that when the Nobel Committee, on a speakerphone, called to read me their citation of recognition. They then asked, "How do you feel?" I replied that I felt much relieved, as my friends had been predicting this for some time, but I now would no longer feel that I was letting them down.

The illusions of rank and the pursuit of riches and greatness.

> When we consider the condition of the great, in those delusive colours in which the imagination is apt to paint it, it seems to be almost the abstract idea of a perfect and happy state...We feel, therefore, a peculiar sympathy with the satisfaction of those who are in it. We favour all their inclinations, and forward all their wishes. What pity, we think, that any thing should spoil and corrupt so agreeable a situation!...Great king, live for ever! is the compliment, which, after the manner of eastern adulation, we should readily make them, if experience did not teach us its absurdity. Every calamity that befalls them, every injury that is done them, excites in the breast of the spectator ten times more compassion and resentment than he would have felt, had the same things happened to other men. It is the misfortunes of kings only which afford the proper subjects for tragedy...To disturb, or to put an end to, such perfect enjoyment, seems to be the most atrocious of all injuries. The traitor who conspires against the life of his monarch, is thought a greater monster than any other murderer. All the innocent blood that was shed in the civil wars, provoked less indignation than the death of Charles I. A stranger to human nature, who saw the indifference of men about the misery of their inferiors, and the regret and indignation which they feel for the misfortunes and sufferings of those above them, would be apt to imagine, that pain must be more agonizing, and the convulsions of death more terrible, to persons of higher rank than to those of meaner stations. (*TMS*, pp. 72–73)

"Long live the king" expresses our wish for the success of the authoritatively great, and their imagined long and enjoyable lives. The higher ranked command higher expectations and their joys and misfortunes we imagine to be more pleasant and painful than the lower ranked. The rich and the influential stars of the popular screen are everywhere newsworthy, their afflictions, divorces, and sufferings excite our sensibilities. Marilyn Monroe's death is more tragic and subject to speculation about foul play than even a neighbor. Surely this is because on screen they have inspired our fellow-feeling for them in the roles they have played, and these sentiments follow them into life. The same for popular presidents like Eisenhower and Kennedy, hero-types that we could identify with.

So, kings have embodied our sense of the grandeur of a life well lived and enjoyed, however illusory is our imagination here revealed. Today, it is not kings, but great scholars, or heroes of wars in defense of freedom that command our most heartfelt sympathy, or an Ellsberg who saw his duty to the constitution as one of exposing high level misbehavior and lying about the misguided unholy Vietnam War, or a Jimmy Li freedom lover, champion of Hong Kong civil liberty, jailed for his activism in support of that liberty, and who refused to take flight because he was a Hongkonger.

The distinction of ranks in society is founded on our disposition to emulate the rich, fortunate, and powerful.

> Upon this disposition of mankind to go along with all the passions of the rich and the powerful, is founded the distinction of ranks and the order of society. Our obsequiousness to our superiors more frequently arises from our admiration for the advantages of their situation, than from any private expectations of benefit from their good-will. Their benefits can extend but to a few; but their fortunes interest almost every body. We are eager to assist them in completing a system of happiness that approaches so near to perfection; and we desire to serve them for their own sake, without any other recompence but the vanity or the honour of obliging them. Neither is our deference to their inclinations founded chiefly, or altogether, upon a regard to the utility of such submission, and to the order of society, which is best supported by it. Even when the order of society seems to require that we should oppose them, we can hardly bring ourselves to do it. That kings are the servants of the people, to be obeyed, resisted, deposed, or punished, as the public conveniency may require, is the doctrine of reason and philosophy; but it is not the doctrine of nature. Nature would teach us to submit to them for their own sake, to tremble and bow down before their exalted station, to regard their smile as a reward sufficient to compensate any services, and to dread their displeasure, though no other evil were to follow from it, as the severest of all mortifications. To treat them in any respect as men, to reason and dispute with them

> upon ordinary occasions, requires such resolution, that there are few men whose magnanimity can support them in it, unless they are likewise assisted by familiarity and acquaintance. The strongest motives, the most furious passions, fear, hatred, and resentment, are scarce sufficient to balance this natural disposition to respect them: and their conduct must, either justly or unjustly, have excited the highest degree of all those passions, before the bulk of the people can be brought to oppose them with violence, or to desire to see them either punished or deposed. Even when the people have been brought this length, they are apt to relent every moment, and easily relapse into their habitual state of deference to those to whom they have been accustomed to look up as their natural superiors. They cannot stand the mortification of their monarch. Compassion soon takes the place of resentment, they forget all past provocations, their old principles of loyalty revive, and run to re-establish the ruined authority of their old masters, with the same violence with which they had opposed it. (*TMS*, pp. 73–75)

For Smith, reason and philosophy ought to inform an order in society in which the authorities serve the public conveniency. That aspiration triumphed eventually in the constitutions of western nations. But in Smith's view, our natural tendency is to go along with the rich and powerful on whom is founded a hierarchical distinction of ranks. And that we are subservient to our superiors out of our respect and admiration for their achievements and vainly seek their recognition. Even when their conduct requires our opposition, we are reluctant to punish or depose them and too easily return to the old principles and revive that deposed authority. This is indeed evident in our daily politics, but it does not explain the power of our fifth amendment rights of dissent, as with Martin Luther King, to expand freedom and prosperity to the ranks of the disadvantaged.

The rich noblemen dutifully, if not by knowledge, industry, and virtue, pay an easy price in assuming the air of superiority expected of them.

> Do the great seem insensible of the easy price at which they may acquire the public admiration; or do they seem to imagine that to them, as to other men, it must be the purchase either of sweat or of blood? By what important accomplishments is the young nobleman instructed to support the dignity of his rank, and to render himself worthy of that superiority over his fellow-citizens, to which the virtue of his ancestors had raised

> them? Is it by knowledge, by industry, by patience, by self-denial, or by virtue of any kind? As all his words, as all his motions are attended to, he learns an habitual regard to every circumstance of ordinary behaviour, and studies to perform all those small duties with the most exact propriety. As he is conscious how much he is observed, and how much mankind are disposed to favour all his inclinations, he acts, upon the most indifferent occasions, with that freedom and elevation which the thought of this naturally inspires. His air, his manner, his deportment, all mark that elegant and graceful sense of his own superiority, which those who are born to inferior stations can hardly ever arrive at. These are the arts by which he proposes to make mankind more easily submit to his authority, and to govern their inclinations according to his own pleasure; and in this he is seldom disappointed ... supported by rank and pre-eminence ... [that] are ... sufficient to govern the world. (*TMS*, p. 75)

With an elegant sense of their externally recognized superiority of rank, young nobles are instructed in their demeanor and deportment to play the role into which they are born. Their actions, always attended to, do not require knowledge, industry, or any accomplished virtue to attain their administrative position, and need only to be instructed in the duties of their station which they tend to learn and execute well.

The inferior ranks must fund—with labor and mind—their knowledge and skill accomplishments.

> [I]t is not by accomplishments [of the rich, powerful, and great] ... that the man of inferior rank must hope to distinguish himself... it must be by more important virtues. He must acquire dependants to balance the dependants of the great, and he has no other fund to pay them from but the labour of his body and the activity of his mind. He must cultivate these therefore: he must acquire superior knowledge in his profession, and superior industry in the exercise of it. He must be patient in labour, resolute in danger, and firm in distress. These talents he must bring into public view, by the difficulty, importance, and, at the same time, good judgment of his undertakings, and by the severe and unrelenting application with which he pursues them. Probity and prudence, generosity and frankness, must characterize his behaviour upon all ordinary occasions; and he must ... engage in all those situations, in which it requires the greatest talents and virtues to act with propriety, but in which the greatest applause is to be acquired by those who can acquit themselves with honour. With what impatience does the man of spirit and ambition, who is depressed by his situation,

> look round for some great opportunity to distinguish himself? No circumstances, which can afford this, appear to him undesirable. He even looks forward with satisfaction to the prospect of foreign war, or civil dissension, and, with secret transport and delight, sees through all the confusion and bloodshed which attend them, the probability of those wished-for occasions presenting themselves, in which he may draw upon himself the attention and admiration of mankind … These virtues are hardly ever to be met with in men who are born to those high stations. In all governments accordingly, even in monarchies, the highest offices are generally possessed, and the whole detail of the administration conducted, by men who were educated in the middle and inferior ranks of life, who have been carried forward by their own industry and abilities, though loaded with the jealousy, and opposed by the resentment, of all those who were born their superiors, and to whom the great, after having regarded them, first with contempt and afterwards with envy, are at last contented to truckle with the same abject meanness with which they desire that the rest of mankind should behave to themselves. (*TMS*, pp. 76–78)

If a person of inferior social ranking is to accomplish distinction, they must purchase it by the labor of their body and the education of their mind to the professions, bringing superior knowledge, industry, and patience in applying these skills to society. Their greatest accomplishments must endure first the contempt of those who are born their superiors and later their envy.

Love is commonly succeeded by ambition, but ambition is hardly ever succeeded by love.

> Who hopes to "Love," says my Lord Rochefoucault, "is commonly succeeded by ambition, but ambition is hardly ever succeeded by love." That passion, when once it has got entire possession of the breast, will admit neither a rival nor a successor. To those who have been accustomed to the possession, or even to the hope, of public admiration, all other pleasures sicken and decay. Of all the discarded statesmen who, for their own ease, have studied to get the better of ambition, and to despise those honours which they could no longer arrive at, how few have been able to succeed? The greater part have spent their time in the most listless and insipid indolence, chagrined at the thoughts of their own insignificancy, incapable of being interested in the occupations of private life, without enjoyment, except when they talked of their former greatness, and without satisfaction, except when they were employed in some vain project

> to recover it. Are you in earnest resolved never to barter your liberty for the lordly servitude of a court, but to live free, fearless, and independent? There seems to be one way to continue in that virtuous resolution; and perhaps but one. Never enter the place from whence so few have been able to return; never come within the circle of ambition; nor ever bring yourself into comparison with those masters of the earth who have already engrossed the attention of half mankind before you. (*TMS*, p. 80)

Ambition seeks neither rivals, nor successors, and easily crowds out love of humanity. When ambition has acquired professional skills it may abandon all other pleasures to those of public administration. It then too easily seeks listless and insipid indolence in servitude to the court, abandoning all liberty and fearless independence, paying homage to committees and Deans. Never enter that place from whence so few have been able to return. Never come within the swallowing circle of ambition to emulate superficial accomplishment. Nor ought you ever bring yourself into comparison with these masters of the earth who have already engrossed the attention of half of humankind before you.

Place of rank and distinction is despised when founded on the superficial but admired when it reflects good propriety and the approbation of humankind.

> Of such mighty importance does it appear to be, in the imaginations of men, to stand in that situation which sets them most in the view of general sympathy and attention. And thus, place, that great object which divides the wives of aldermen, is the end of half the labours of human life; and is the cause of all the tumult and bustle, all the rapine and injustice, which avarice and ambition have introduced into this world. People of sense, it is said, indeed despise place; that is, they despise sitting at the head of the table, and are indifferent who it is that is pointed out to the company by that frivolous circumstance, which the smallest advantage is capable of overbalancing. But rank, distinction, preeminence, no man despises, unless he is either raised very much above, or sunk very much below, the ordinary standard of human nature; unless he is either so confirmed in wisdom and real philosophy, as to be satisfied that, while the propriety of his conduct renders him the just object of approbation, it is of little consequence though he may be neither attended to, nor approved of; or so habituated to the idea of his own meanness, so sunk in slothful and sottish indifference, as entirely to have forgot the desire, and almost the very wish, for superiority. (*TMS*, pp. 80–81)

That which is thought the great object of position or "place" in life, exhausts half the labors of human life, and is the root of all the hustle and bustle, the rapine injustice and avarice in this sorry world. People of sense despise place—to sit at the head of the table—and they care not a wit, who does. But rank, as distinction and pre-eminence, no person despises, unless they are raised very much above, or sunk very much below, the ordinary standard of human nature. They must either be confirmed in wisdom and philosophy and show that their conduct merits the approbation of professional peers, or be so thoroughly sunk in slothful indifference, as have entirely lost the desire and very wish for superiority of accomplishment.

When in China I learned that, because I was the oldest person at the table, I commanded rank and was to be served first. I remember how strange it seemed to acquire such distinctions merely by having lived longer than the others who happened to be at the table.

Honor is the greatest achievement, contempt the greatest failure.

> As to become the natural object of the joyous congratulations and sympathetic attentions of mankind is, in this manner, the circumstance which gives to prosperity all its dazzling splendour; so nothing darkens so much the gloom of adversity as to feel that our misfortunes are the objects, not of the fellow-feeling but of the contempt and aversion of our brethren. It is upon this account that the most dreadful calamities are not always those which it is most difficult to support. It is often more mortifying to appear in public under small disasters, than under great misfortunes. The first excite no sympathy; but the second, though they may excite none that approaches to the anguish of the sufferer, call forth, however, a very lively compassion. The sentiments of the spectators are, in this last case, less wide of those of the sufferer, and their imperfect fellow-feeling lends him some assistance in supporting his misery. Before a gay assembly, a gentleman would be more mortified to appear covered with filth and rags than with blood and wounds. This last situation would interest their pity; the other would provoke their laughter. The judge who orders a criminal to be set in the pillory, dishonours him more than if he had condemned him to the scaffold. The great prince, who, some years ago, caned a general officer at the head of his army, disgraced him irrecoverably. The punishment would have been much less, had he shot him through the body. By the laws of honour, to strike with a cane dishonours, to strike with a sword does not, for an obvious reason. Those slighter punishments, when inflicted on a gentleman, to whom dishonour is the greatest of all evils, come to be

> regarded among a humane and generous people as the most dreadful of any. With regard to persons of that rank, therefore, they are universally laid aside; and the law, while it takes their life upon many occasions, respects their honour upon almost all. To scourge a person of quality, or to set him in the pillory, upon account of any crime whatever, is a brutality of which no European government, except that of Russia, is capable. (*TMS*, pp. 81–82)

There is no greater honor than to be the natural object of the joyous congratulations and sympathetic attentions of humankind, nor more dishonor than to suffer the contempt and aversion of our brethren. Better for a gentleman to be covered in public with blood and wounds than rags and filth. The prince who caned his general disgraced him more than if he had simply had him shot him dead.

Honor prefers the scaffold to the pillory.

> A brave man is not rendered contemptible by being brought to the scaffold; he is, by being set in the pillory. His behaviour in the one situation may gain him universal esteem and admiration. No behaviour in the other can render him agreeable. The sympathy of the spectators supports him in the one case, and saves him from that shame, that consciousness, that his misery is felt by himself only, which is of all sentiments the most insupportable. There is no sympathy in the other; or, if there is any, it is not with his pain, which is a trifle, but with his consciousness of the want of sympathy with which this pain is attended. It is with his shame, not with his sorrow…The man, on the contrary, who dies with resolution, as he is naturally regarded with the erect aspect of esteem and approbation, so he wears himself the same undaunted countenance; and, if the crime does not deprive him of the respect of others, the punishment never will. He has no suspicion that his situation is the object of contempt or derision to any body, and he can, with propriety, assume the air, not only of perfect serenity, but of triumph and exultation. (*TMS*, pp. 82–83)

Historically, a brave person was never made contemptible by being brought to the scaffold and might have commanded esteem and admiration. But if confined to the pillory, he never gained such respect; only their sorrow may command sympathy, not their pain. Spectators might sympathize with a person's gallows end, but not their pillory end. Today it is a mark of humane progress that capital punishment has ended, and the worst criminals retain their lives provided they serve it in the "pillory" but the modern prison is one of relative comfort a place with free room and board and a warm place to sleep. This may seem inefficient and call for prisoners to work in the production of products for consumers and producers, except that is judged unfair competition for those who are free and so prison becomes enforced retirement.

We are presented with two different pathways to respect and respectability: the wise and virtuous; the rich and great.

> We desire both to be respectable and to be respected. We dread both to be contemptible and to be contemned. But, upon coming into the world, we soon find that wisdom and virtue are by no means the sole objects of respect; nor vice and folly, of contempt. We frequently see the respectful attentions of the world more strongly directed towards the rich and the great, than towards the wise and the virtuous. We see frequently the vices and follies of the powerful much less despised than the poverty and weakness of the innocent. To deserve, to acquire, and to enjoy, the respect and admiration of mankind, are the great objects of ambition and emulation. Two different roads are presented to us, equally leading to the attainment of this so much desired object; the one, by the study of wisdom and the practice of virtue; the other, by the acquisition of wealth and greatness. Two different characters are presented to our emulation; the one of proud ambition and ostentatious avidity; the other, of humble modesty and equitable justice. Two different models, two different pictures, are held out to us, according to which we may fashion our own character and behaviour; the one more gaudy and glittering in its colouring; the other more correct and more exquisitely beautiful in its outline; the one forcing itself upon the notice of every wandering eye; the other attracting the attention of scarce any body but the most studious and careful observer. They are the wise and the virtuous chiefly, a select, though, I am afraid, but a small party, who are the real and steady admirers of wisdom and virtue. The great mob of mankind are the admirers and worshippers, and, what may seem more extraordinary, most frequently the disinterested admirers and worshippers, of wealth and greatness...Human virtue is superior to pain, to poverty, to danger, and to death; nor does it even require its utmost efforts to despise them. But to have its misery exposed to insult and derision, to be led in triumph, to be set up for the hand of scorn to point at, is a situation in which its constancy is much more apt to fail. Compared with the contempt of mankind, all other external evils are easily supported. (*TMS*, pp. 84–85)

Moral rules teach us to strive for respect and respectability and to avoid the contemptible and the contemned. But the world drumbeat is for the vice and folly of the powerful which is much less despised than poverty or the weakness of the innocent. Take the credit of the philosophers of wisdom, let the cash of vice and folly go, and always heed the call of that distant drum.

Scarce any person does not respect more the rich and great than the poor and humble, but vice and folly rarely degrade wealth and greatness enough to change that ordering.

> The respect which we feel for wisdom and virtue is…different from that which we conceive for wealth and greatness…But, notwithstanding this difference, those sentiments bear a very considerable resemblance to one another. In some particular features they are no doubt different, but, in the general air of the countenance, they seem to be…the same…In equal degrees of merit there is scarce any man who does not respect more the rich and the great than the poor and the humble. With most men the presumption and vanity of the former are much more admired than the real and solid merit of the latter…that mere wealth and greatness, abstracted from merit and virtue, deserve our respect. We must acknowledge, however, that they almost constantly obtain it; and they may, therefore, be considered as, in some respects, the natural objects of it. Those exalted stations may, no doubt, be completely degraded by vice and folly. But the vice and folly must be very great, before they can operate this complete degradation. The profligacy of a man of fashion is looked upon with much less contempt and aversion than that of a man of meaner condition. In the latter, a single transgression of the rules of temperance and propriety is commonly more resented than the constant and avowed contempt of them ever is in the former. (*TMS*, pp. 85–86)

The profligacy of a person of fashion is viewed with much less contempt than one of lesser attainment. But the latter is held to a stricter standard of temperance and propriety. A single transgression is more resented than the constant and avowed contempt of them ever is in the former.

Success seldom fails, when the bottom half of life's stations join professional ability with prudent, temperate conduct.

> In the middling and inferior stations of life, the road to virtue and that to fortune....are, happily, in most cases very nearly the same. In all the middling and inferior professions, real and solid professional abilities, joined to prudent, just, firm, and temperate conduct, can very seldom fail of success. Abilities will even sometimes prevail where the conduct is by no means correct. Either habitual imprudence, however, or injustice, or weakness, or profligacy, will always cloud, and sometimes depress altogether, the most splendid professional abilities. Men in the inferior and middling stations of life, besides, can never be great enough to be above the law, which must generally overawe them into some sort of respect for, at least, the more important rules of justice. The success of such people...depends upon the favour and good opinion of their neighbours and equals; and without a tolerably regular conduct, these can very seldom be obtained. The good old proverb... honesty is the best policy, holds, in such situations, almost always perfectly true. In such situations, therefore, we may generally expect a considerable degree of virtue; and, fortunately for the good morals of society, these are the situations of by far the greater part of mankind. (*TMS*, pp. 86–87)

In America, premium examples of people from modest to middle backgrounds who became prominent leaders include George Washington and Benjamin Franklin. Washington, a model of good manners, commanded and also gave great respect. Franklin, one of the greatest scientists and statesmen of his time, became a symbol of American liberty, independence, and land of opportunity. Such was he acclaimed when he visited France and London, traveling to Edinburgh in 1759 when Smith and Franklin met at a dinner hosted by Dr. Robertson (John Rae, *Life of Adam Smith*. 1895: Ch. VIII, pp. 150–151).

And, in case you have not noticed, Adam Smith is in my view—and I have so represented him in this book—a super Ben Franklin. Ben was too busy being our hero and prime American representative, as well as scientist, to pursue his considerable philosophical accomplishments. We are surely the richer, more comforted, and freer as a result.

Flattery and falsehood often prevail over merit and ability in the drawing-rooms of the high-born.

> In the superior stations of life the case is unhappily not always the same [as in the middling and inferior]. In the courts of princes, in the drawing-rooms of the great, where success and preferment depend, not upon the esteem of intelligent and well-informed equals, but upon the fanciful and

> foolish favour of ignorant, presumptuous, and proud superiors; flattery and falsehood too often prevail over merit and abilities. In such societies, the abilities to please are more regarded than the abilities to serve. In quiet and peaceable times, when the storm is at a distance, the prince, or great man, wishes only to be amused, and is even apt to fancy that he has scarce any occasion for the service of any body, or that those who amuse him are sufficiently able to serve him. The external graces, the frivolous accomplishments, of that impertinent and foolish thing called a man of fashion, are commonly more admired than the solid and masculine virtues of a warrior, a statesman, a philosopher, or a legislator. All the great and awful [awe-filled] virtues, all the virtues which can fit, either for the council, the senate, or the field, are, by the insolent and insignificant flatterers, who commonly figure the most in such corrupted societies, held in the utmost contempt and derision. When the Duke of Sully was called upon by Louis XIII. to give his advice in some great emergency, he observed the favourites and courtiers whispering to one another, and smiling at his unfashionable appearance.—"Whenever your Majesty's father," said the old warrior and statesman, "did me the honour to consult me, he ordered the buffoons of the court to retire into the antechamber." (*TMS*, p. 87)

Better to nurture an ability to serve than to nurture an ability to please. Be pleasant in serving and render advice only in private.

Fashion produces admiration and imitation of the rich and great

> It is from our disposition to admire, and consequently to imitate, the rich and the great, that they are enabled to set, or to lead, what is called the fashion. Their dress is the fashionable dress; the language of their conversation, the fashionable style; their air and deportment, the fashionable behaviour. Even their vices and follies are fashionable; and the greater part of men are proud to imitate and resemble them in the very qualities which dishonour and degrade them. Vain men often give themselves airs of a fashionable profligacy, which, in their hearts, they do not approve of, and of which, perhaps, they are really not guilty. They desire to be praised for what they themselves do not think praiseworthy, and are ashamed of unfashionable virtues, which they sometimes practise in secret, and for which they have secretly some degree of real veneration. (*TMS*, pp. 87–88)

Vain people, embarrassed by unfashionable moral virtues, seek praise for what they do not believe in their hearts to be praiseworthy, and are ashamed of unfashionable virtues though such may be secretly admired.

Hypocrisy is not confined to the pursuit of wealth even finding its way into religion and virtue.

> There are hypocrites of wealth and greatness, as well as of religion and virtue and a vain man is as apt to pretend to be what he is not, in the one way, as a cunning man is in the other. He assumes the equipage and splendid way of living of his superiors, without considering, that whatever may be praiseworthy in any of these derives its whole merit and propriety from its suitableness to that situation and fortune which both require, and can easily support the expense. Many a poor man places his glory in being thought rich, without considering that the duties (if one may call such follies by so very venerable a name) which that reputation imposes upon him, must soon reduce him to beggary, and render his situation still more unlike that of those whom he admires and imitates, than it had been originally. (*TMS*, p. 88)

The spend thriftiness of a poor man, who expects glory in being thought rich, soon reduces himself to beggary, becoming even less like what he would wish for, than had he only accepted what he was. Even among the virtuous are to be found hypocrites.

The paths to virtue and to fortune lie sometimes in opposite directions.

> To attain to this envied situation, the candidates for fortune too frequently abandon the paths of virtue; for unhappily, the road which leads to the one and that which leads to the other, lie sometimes in very opposite directions. But the ambitious man flatters himself that, in the splendid situation to which he advances, he will have so many means of commanding the respect and admiration of mankind, and will be enabled to act with such superior propriety and grace, that the lustre of his future conduct will entirely cover, or efface, the foulness of the steps by which he arrived at that elevation. In many governments the candidates for the highest stations are above the law; and, if they can attain the object of their ambition, they have no fear of being called to account for the means by which they acquired it. They often endeavour…not only by fraud and falsehood, the ordinary and vulgar arts of intrigue and cabal, but sometimes by the perpetration of the most enormous crimes, by murder and assassination, by rebellion and civil war, to supplant and destroy those who oppose or stand in the way of their greatness. They more frequently miscarry than succeed; and commonly gain nothing but the disgraceful punishment which is due to their crimes.

> But, though they should be so lucky as to attain that wished-for greatness, they are always most miserably disappointed in the happiness which they expect to enjoy in it. It is not ease or pleasure, but always honour, of one kind or another, though frequently an honour very ill understood, that the ambitious man really pursues. But the honour of his exalted station appears, both in his own eyes and in those of other people, polluted and defiled by the baseness of the means through which he rose to it. Though by the profusion of every liberal expense; though by excessive indulgence in every profligate pleasure, the wretched, but usual, resource of ruined characters; though by the hurry of public business, or by the prouder and more dazzling tumult of war, he may endeavour to efface, both from his own memory and from that of other people, the remembrance of what he has done; that remembrance never fails to pursue him. He invokes in vain the dark and dismal powers of forgetfulness and oblivion. He remembers himself what he has done, and that remembrance tells him that other people must likewise remember it. Amidst all the gaudy pomp of the most ostentatious greatness; amidst the venal and vile adulation of the great and of the learned; amidst the more innocent, though more foolish, acclamations of the common people; amidst all the pride of conquest and the triumph of successful war, he is still secretly pursued by the avenging furies of shame and remorse; and, while glory seems to surround him on all sides, he himself, in his own imagination, sees black and foul infamy fast pursuing him, and every moment ready to overtake him from behind. Even the great Cæsar, though he had the magnanimity to dismiss his guards, could not dismiss his suspicions… (*TMS*, pp. 89–90)

Those who seek public recognition for greatness by methods vile and vulgar, full of intrigue and cabal, will find only misery, disappointment, and unhappiness, the victims of their own baseness with spots that cannot be erased. They remember their evil deeds and thereby know that others will remember them also. Recall the plaintive public pleading of an American President, "I am not a crook," but, consumed by his own machinations, his vain recording tapes suggested otherwise. He declared what no one would have believed if he had not known it, lived it, and revealed it.

PART IV

Of merit and demerit; or of the objects of reward and punishment consisting of three sections—Section I: Of the sense of merit and demerit

CHAPTER 14

That whatsoever appears to be the proper object of gratitude, appears to deserve reward; and that, in the same manner, whatever appears to be the proper object of resentment, appears to deserve punishment

The merit or demerit of an action deserving of reward or punishment, depends upon the proportionate benefit or hurt consequent to the propriety or impropriety of a person's action toward another.

> There is another set of qualities ascribed to the actions and conduct of mankind, distinct from their propriety or impropriety, their decency or ungracefulness, and which are the objects of a distinct species of approbation and disapprobation. These are Merit and Demerit, the qualities of deserving reward, and of deserving punishment...considered under...-first...the cause or object which excites it; and, secondly, in relation to the end which it proposes, or to the effect which it tends to produce: that upon the suitableness or unsuitableness, upon the proportion or disproportion, which the affection seems to bear to the cause or object which excites it, depends the propriety or impropriety, the decency or ungracefulness, of the consequent action; and that upon the beneficial or hurtful effects which the affection proposes or tends to produce depends the merit

Vernon L. Smith, *Adam Smith's Theory of Society*,
https://doi.org/10.1007/978-3-031-68494-4_14

> or demerit, the good or ill desert, of the action to which it gives occasion. (*TMS*, p. 93)

A beneficial action that excites the sense of a required reward is judged so by its social propriety or approbation. The degree of reward for the action is an increasing function of its merit, a judgement distinct from its propriety. Symmetrically, a harmful action that excites the sense of a deserved punishment is judged so by its social impropriety or disapprobation. The degree of punishment for the hurtful action is an increasing function of its demerit, a judgement distinct from its impropriety.

Characteristics of actions that appear to deserve reward or appear to deserve punishment.

> To us, therefore, that action must appear to deserve reward, which appears to be the proper and approved object of that sentiment which most immediately and directly prompts us to reward, or to do good to, another. And in the same manner, that action must appear to deserve punishment, which appears to be the proper and approved object of that sentiment which most immediately and directly prompts us to punish, or to inflict evil upon, another. (*TMS*, p. 94)

An action that appears to require reward is an action that is the proper and approved object of the sentiment that immediately and directly prompts us to reward the actor by doing good for them. An action that appears to deserve punishment is an action that immediately and directly prompts us to punish the actor by inflicting evil upon them. Whether an original action be beneficial or hurtful to another person, all third-party observers (the meaning of "us") agree that the action requires reward, or deserves punishment, by the person acted upon.

Gratitude and resentment constitute the origins in feelings of the rules governing our sense of the need to reward or punish an action.

> The sentiment which most immediately and directly prompts us to reward, is gratitude; that which most immediately and directly prompts us to punish, is resentment. To us, therefore, that action must appear to deserve reward, which appears to be the proper and approved object of gratitude; as, on the other hand, that action must appear to deserve punishment,

> which appears to be the proper and approved object of resentment. (*TMS*, p. 94)

To all attentive observers, that action must appear to deserve reward which appears to be the proper and approved object of gratitude. That action must appear to deserve punishment, which appears to be the proper and approved object of resentment.

Meaning of reward, of punishment.

> To reward, is to recompence, to remunerate, to return good for good received. To punish, too, is to recompence, to remunerate, though in a different manner; it is to return evil for evil that has been done. (*TMS*, p. 94)

Person A takes an action that directly and intentionally benefits another person B. For B to reward A is to recompense or remunerate A by returning good for good received. If A takes an action that directly hurts B, then for B to punish A is to return evil for that evil which was done to them.

Gratitude and resentment are passions that require us to act instrumentally.

> There are some other passions, besides gratitude and resentment, which interest us in the happiness or misery of others; but there are none which so directly excite us to be the instruments of either. The love and esteem which grow up upon acquaintance and habitual approbation, necessarily lead us to be pleased with the good fortune of the man who is the object of such agreeable emotions, and, consequently, to be willing to lend a hand to promote it. Our love, however, is fully satisfied, though his good fortune should be brought about without our assistance. All that this passion desires, is to see him happy, without regarding who was the author of his prosperity. But gratitude is not to be satisfied in this manner. If the person to whom we owe many obligations is made happy without our assistance, though it pleases our love, it does not content our gratitude. Till we have recompensed him, till we ourselves have been instrumental in promoting his happiness, we feel ourselves still loaded with that debt which his past services have laid upon us. (*TMS*, pp. 94–95)

We often delight in seeing a person benefit from good fortune, but if that person has directly acted to benefit us then our gratitude is not to be satisfied by any such external source of good fortune. In all such actions invoking gratitude, we must be the instrument of the good done for that person in response to their good action toward us. There is no other way for us to pay for and discharge our debt of gratitude. Thus, Smith clearly distinguishes our love for a friend and our gratitude for a particular favor our friend has done us. The latter requires us to be the instrument of a beneficial response for the friend.

Resentment seeks satisfaction that specific wrongs be avenged and recognized, that the offender feels the evil they have caused another. This natural gratification of resentment serves political ends, by correcting the criminal, and serves the public by example of actions to be avoided.

> The [passions of] hatred and dislike ... [if they] grew upon habitual disapprobation, would often lead us to take a malicious pleasure in the misfortune of the man whose conduct and character excite so painful a passion. But though dislike and hatred harden us against all sympathy, and sometimes dispose us even to rejoice at the distress of another, yet, if there is no resentment in the case, if neither we nor our friends have received any great personal provocation, these passions would not naturally lead us to wish to be instrumental in bringing it about. Though we could fear no punishment in consequence of our having had some hand in it, we would rather that it should happen by other means. To one under the dominion of violent hatred it would be agreeable, perhaps, to hear, that the person whom he abhorred and detested was killed by some accident. But if he had the least spark of justice, which, though this passion is not very favourable to virtue, he might still have, it would hurt him excessively to have been himself, even without design, the occasion of this misfortune. Much more would the very thought of voluntarily contributing to it shock him beyond all measure. He would reject with horror even the imagination of so execrable a design; and if he could imagine himself capable of such an enormity, he would begin to regard himself in the same odious light in which he had considered the person who was the object of his dislike. But it is quite otherwise with resentment: if the person who had done us some great injury, who had murdered our father or our brother, for example, should soon afterwards die of a fever, or even be brought to the scaffold upon account of some other crime, though it might soothe our hatred, it would not fully gratify our resentment. Resentment would

> prompt us to desire, not only that he should be punished, but that he should be punished by our means, and upon account of that particular injury which he had done to us. Resentment cannot be fully gratified, unless the offender is not only made to grieve in his turn, but to grieve for that particular wrong which we have suffered from him. He must be made to repent and be sorry for this very action, that others, through fear of the like punishment, may be terrified from being guilty of the like offence. The natural gratification of this passion tends, of its own accord, to produce all the political ends of punishment; the correction of the criminal, and the example to the public. (*TMS*, pp. 95–96)

The resentment of a person on whom evil has been inflicted by the direct action of another is not to be satisfied merely because that other person has suffered some independent external calamity. Whatever delight the harmed person may feel due to the other's bad fortune, the resentment felt, and caused by this other's harmful action, is not to be satisfied in this manner. Such resentment can only be avenged if the person who was the victim of the hurtful action takes avenging action to punish the offender for the harm done to them. That avengement may begin by calling the police and filing a report but is incomplete if the scoundrel is not apprehended.

That such avenging action can draw a sympathy-driven community response is evident in the "posse," which we Americans associate with a US territorial community of men, ready to ride in support of the Marshall's or Sheriff's request to pursue and "possess" an outlaw but with more ancient origins in the UK and elsewhere.

For society this natural gratification of resentment, through retaliatory punishment of criminal acts, serves of its own accord, the political ends of deterrence via punishment and criminal correction. It intends to make the offender repent and be sorry for their hurtful action taken if they are apprehended and found guilty. Others may thus be deterred in fear of being guilty of the same offense. The modern centralized state has adopted the concept that crimes against the public, established by due process, are to be suitably punished to deter their occurrence.

This philosophy recognizes no formal linking of punishment with victim compensation which, as we will learn from Smith, characterized early weak-government regimes in the natural history of jurisprudence.

The circumstances of action drive gratitude and resentment.

> Gratitude and resentment...are the sentiments which most immediately and directly prompt to reward and to punish. To us, therefore, he must appear to deserve reward, who appears to be the proper and approved object of gratitude; and he to deserve punishment, who appears to be that of resentment. (*TMS*, p. 96)

"To us" implies a community consensus: they who deserve reward are they who appear to be the proper and approved object of gratitude, and they who deserve punishment, the appropriate object of resentment. For Smith, it is community all the way down to bilateral interactions meeting with third-party approbation.

CHAPTER 15

Of the proper objects of gratitude and resentment

An impartial sympathetic social consensus justifies gratitude and resentment and the actions motivated by these feelings.

> To be the proper and approved object either of gratitude or resentment, can mean nothing but to be the object of that gratitude, and of that resentment, which naturally seems proper, and is approved of. But these, as well as all the other passions of human nature, seem proper and are approved of, when the heart of every impartial spectator entirely sympathizes with them, when every indifferent bystander entirely enters into, and goes along with, them. He, therefore, appears to deserve reward, who, to some person or persons, is the natural object of a gratitude which every human heart is disposed to beat time to, and thereby applaud: and he, on the other hand, appears to deserve punishment, who, in the same manner, is to some person or persons the natural object of a resentment which the breast of every reasonable man is ready to adopt and sympathize with. To us, surely, that action must appear to deserve reward which every body who knows of it would wish to reward, and therefore delights to see rewarded: and that action must as surely appear to deserve punishment which every body who hears of it is angry with, and upon that account rejoices to see punished. (*TMS*, p. 97)

This is Smith's strongest expression in the idea of community consensus on reward and punishment: To be the proper and approved object of gratitude or resentment means that the heart of every impartial

Vernon L. Smith, *Adam Smith's Theory of Society*,
https://doi.org/10.1007/978-3-031-68494-4_15

spectator, of every indifferent bystander, and of every reasonable person, beats time with, or goes along with, the reward or the punishment of the beneficial or hurtful action.

We join in sympathetic approbation for the gratitude of they who benefit from another's action and in their action to recompense that good favor.

> As we sympathize with the joy of our companions when in prosperity, so we join with them in the complacency and satisfaction with which they naturally regard whatever is the cause of their good fortune. We enter into the love and affection which they conceive for it, and begin to love it too. We should be sorry for their sakes if it was destroyed, or even if it was placed at too great a distance from them, and out of the reach of their care and protection, though they should lose nothing by its absence except the pleasure of seeing it. If it is man who has thus been the fortunate instrument of the happiness of his brethren, this is still more peculiarly the case. When we see one man assisted, protected, relieved, by another, our sympathy with the joy of the person who receives the benefit serves only to animate our fellow-feeling with his gratitude towards him who bestows it. When we look upon the person who is the cause of his pleasure with the eyes with which we imagine he must look upon him, his benefactor seems to stand before us in the most engaging and amiable light. We readily, therefore, sympathize with the grateful affection which he conceives for a person to whom he has been so much obliged; and consequently applaud the returns which he is disposed to make for the good offices conferred upon him. As we entirely enter into the affection from which these returns proceed, they necessarily seem every way proper and suitable to their object. (*TMS*, pp. 97–98)

Our natural sympathy with the joy of a companion who prospers from the action taken by another is further animated by our fellow-feeling with the gratitude our companion feels toward the person who took the beneficial action. By entirely entering into each other's grateful response to the good offices of others, there emerges the mutually beneficial and stable communities and societies that we live in.

We join in disapprobation for the conduct of they who inflict injury and in sympathy with they who resent the harm done to them; and rejoice in a fit retaliation to avenge the victim's offense.

> In the same manner, as we sympathize with the sorrow of our fellow-creature whenever we see his distress, so we likewise enter into his abhorrence and aversion for whatever has given occasion to it. Our heart, as it adopts and beats time to his grief, so is it likewise animated with that spirit by which he endeavours to drive away or destroy the cause of it. The indolent and passive fellow-feeling by which we accompany him in his sufferings, readily gives way to that more vigorous and active sentiment by which we go along with him in the effort he makes, either to repel them, or to gratify his aversion to what has given occasion to them. This is still more peculiarly the case, when it is man who has caused them. When we see one man oppressed or injured by another, the sympathy which we feel with the distress of the sufferer seems to serve only to animate our fellow-feeling with his resentment against the offender. We are rejoiced to see him attack his adversary in his turn, and are eager and ready to assist him whenever he exerts himself for defence, or even for vengeance, within a certain degree...we put ourselves in his situation, as we enter, as it were, into his body, and in our imaginations, in some measure...bring home in this manner his case to our own bosoms...The injury which he has suffered demands, we think, a principal part of our attention. We feel that resentment which we imagine he ought to feel, and which he would feel if in his cold and lifeless body there remained any consciousness of what passes upon earth. His blood, we think, calls aloud for vengeance...The horrors which are supposed to haunt the bed of the murderer, the ghosts which, superstition imagines, rise from their graves to demand vengeance upon those who brought them to an untimely end, all take their origin from this natural sympathy with the imaginary resentment of the slain. And with regard, at least, to this most dreadful of all crimes, nature, antecedent to all reflections upon the utility of punishment, has in this manner stamped upon the human heart, in the strongest and most indelible characters, an immediate and instinctive approbation of the sacred and necessary law of retaliation. (*TMS*, pp. 98–99)

Justice is baked into our nature as a law of retaliation that they who do evil will learn from the experience of punishment for the evil they have done another. That other is due life and liberty as are you. Community sympathy with the victim assures the approbation of a consensus on the propriety of what constitutes right and wrong action and the suitableness of the retaliation. This strong sentiment motivates even our desire to see the murdered victim avenged in his grave.

CHAPTER 16

That where there is no approbation of the conduct of the person who confers the benefit, there is little sympathy with the gratitude of him who receives it: and that, on the contrary, where there is no disapprobation of the motives of the person who does the mischief, there is no sort of sympathy with the resentment of him who suffers it

However beneficial or harmful an action, if we can find no propriety or impropriety in the action's motives, then there can be no sympathetic approbation for the gratitude or resentment felt.

> It is to be observed…that, how beneficial soever on the one hand, or how hurtful soever on the other, the actions or intentions of the person who acts may have been to the person who is…acted upon, yet if in the one case there appears to have been no propriety in the motives of the agent, if we cannot enter into the affections which influenced his conduct, we have little sympathy with the gratitude of the person who receives the benefit: or if, in the other case, there appears to have been no impropriety in the motives of the agent, if, on the contrary, the affections which influenced

Vernon L. Smith, *Adam Smith's Theory of Society*,
https://doi.org/10.1007/978-3-031-68494-4_16

> his conduct are such as we must necessarily enter into, we can have no sort of sympathy with the resentment of the person who suffers. Little gratitude seems due in the one case, and all sort of resentment seems unjust in the other. The one action seems to merit little reward, the other to deserve no punishment. (*TMS*, p. 100)

Whatever the attitude and motivation of the actor, who is the cause of benefit or hurt in another, if there is no socially recognized and affirmed propriety or impropriety in their action, then people cannot enter into sympathy with the gratitude or the resentment felt by they who receive the benefit or harm. There is approbation or disapprobation of human action by the community if and only if there is community embrace of the propriety or impropriety of the action.

If we entirely approve of the actions of the agent, we cannot sympathize with any resentment felt by the target sufferer.

> [W]herever the conduct of the agent appears to have been entirely directed by motives and affections which we thoroughly enter into and approve of, we can have no sort of sympathy with the resentment of the sufferer, how great soever the mischief which may have been done to him. When two people quarrel, if we take part with, and entirely adopt, the resentment of one of them, it is impossible that we should enter into that of the other. Our sympathy with the person whose motives we go along with, and whom, therefore, we look upon as in the right, cannot but harden us against all fellow-feeling with the other, whom we necessarily regard as in the wrong. Whatever this last, therefore, may have suffered, while it is no more than what we ourselves should have wished him to suffer, while it is no more than what our own sympathetic indignation would have prompted us to inflict upon him, it cannot either displease or provoke us. When an inhuman murderer is brought to the scaffold, though we have some compassion for his misery, we can have no sort of fellow-feeling with his resentment, if he should be so absurd as to express any against either his prosecutor or his judge. The natural tendency of their just indignation against so vile a criminal is indeed the most fatal and ruinous to him. But it is impossible that we should be displeased with the tendency of a sentiment, which, when we bring the case home to ourselves, we feel that we cannot avoid adopting. (*TMS*, pp. 101–102)

Wherever we can heartily go along with and approve the motives and affections of an agent who brings harm to another, then we can have no sort of sympathy with the resentment of the sufferer. If a murderer is executed, we can have no sympathy for their suffering if it is no more than what we would wish for as just punishment for their criminal action.

CHAPTER 17

Recapitulation of the foregoing chapters

Smith now pauses for a review of previous chapters. He wants the reader to not fail in grasping these fundamentals. Accordingly, we accept Smith's sense of their importance, and the next five entries offer his repetitions in modified forms of language as Smith endeavors to vary his descriptions to comprehensively convey his thought process and its generality.

We must entirely sympathize with the motives of an agent as a cause of the good fortune of another in order to go along with the gratitude felt by the beneficiary.

> We do not…thoroughly and heartily sympathize with the gratitude of one man towards another, merely because this other has been the cause of his good fortune, unless he has been the cause of it from motives which we entirely go along with. Our heart must adopt the principles of the agent, and go along with all the affections which influenced his conduct, before it can entirely sympathize with, and beat time to, the gratitude of the person who has been benefited by his actions. If in the conduct of the benefactor there appears to have been no propriety, how beneficial soever its effects, it does not seem to demand, or necessarily to require, any proportionable recompence. (*TMS*, p. 103)

We must adopt as our own and entirely go along with the heartfelt affections which influenced the conduct of an agent, before we can

Vernon L. Smith, *Adam Smith's Theory of Society*,
https://doi.org/10.1007/978-3-031-68494-4_17

entirely sympathize with, and beat time in harmony with the gratitude of the person who has benefited from the agent's actions. As I see it, Smith is here further articulating necessary and sufficient conditions for the rules that people create, follow, and embed in their communities, and thereby are resilient in the face of extreme insults and disruptions occasioned by populist movements that are without such bottom-up sustaining forces and tend to fade away with time. In this examination, a proposition might be of the form if–then, only if–then, or if-and only if–then.

When a beneficent action is joined with propriety, we entirely accept that the beneficiary is a proper object of the affection, and it calls-aloud for a proportional recompense.

> [W]hen to the beneficent tendency of the action is joined the propriety of the affection from which it proceeds, when we entirely sympathize and go along with the motives of the agent, the love which we conceive for him upon his own account, enhances and enlivens our fellow-feeling with the gratitude of those who owe their prosperity to his good conduct. His actions seem then to demand, and, if I may say so, to call aloud for a proportionable recompence. We then entirely enter into that gratitude which prompts to bestow it. The benefactor seems then to be the proper object of reward, when we thus entirely sympathize with, and approve of, that sentiment which prompts to reward him. When we approve of, and go along with, the affection from which the action proceeds, we must necessarily approve of the action, and regard the person towards whom it is directed as its proper and suitable object. (*TMS*, p. 103)

When the propriety of an action that benefits another brings social approval to the action, it enlivens and reinforces our sympathy with the gratitude felt by the beneficiary of the action, and with their desire to reward the kind-hearted action of the agent. Also, Smith now explicates his use of proportionable recompense. Propriety, which is only a qualitative rule, becomes quantitative proportionable recompense under the condition that it be joined with the love we feel toward someone on their own account, independent of this specifically favourable action.

We cannot abide the resentment of a sufferer from an injury unless we disapprove of the motives of the causing agent.

> In the same manner we cannot at all sympathize with the resentment of one man against another, merely because this other has been the cause of his misfortune, unless he has been the cause of it from motives which we cannot enter into. Before we can adopt the resentment of the sufferer, we must disapprove of the motives of the agent, and feel that our heart renounces all sympathy with the affections which influenced his conduct. If there appears to have been no impropriety in these, how fatal soever the tendency of the action which proceeds from them to those against whom it is directed, it does not seem to deserve any punishment, or to be the proper object of any resentment. (*TMS*, p. 104)

We cannot adopt the resentment of the suffering from an injurious act unless we disapprove of the motives and affections of the harming agent. If there is no impropriety in an injurious act, there can be no sympathy for the resentment felt by the injured victim of the action.

We heartily sympathize with the resentment of the sufferer when the hurtfulness and propriety of the action join and we abhor all sense of fellow-feeling with the agent.

> [W]hen to the hurtfulness of the action is joined the impropriety of the affection from whence it proceeds, when our heart rejects with abhorrence all fellow-feeling with the motives of the agent, we then heartily and entirely sympathize with the resentment of the sufferer. Such actions seem then to deserve…to call aloud for, a proportionable punishment; and we entirely enter into, and thereby approve of, that resentment which prompts to inflict it. The offender necessarily seems then to be the proper object of punishment, when we thus entirely sympathize with, and thereby approve of, that sentiment which prompts to punish. In this case too, when we approve, and go along with, the affection from which the action proceeds, we must necessarily approve of the action, and regard the person against whom it is directed, as its proper and suitable object. (*TMS*, p. 104)

When the hurtfulness of an action is acknowledged by others, and thus its impropriety established socially, we entirely sympathize with the resentment felt by the harmed person toward the agent who caused the harm.

We must disapprove of the motives of the agent before we can embrace the resentment of the sufferer.

> [W]e cannot at all sympathize with the resentment of one man against another, merely because this other has been the cause of his misfortune, unless he has been the cause of it from motives which we cannot enter into. Before we can adopt the resentment of the sufferer, we must disapprove of the motives of the agent, and feel that our heart renounces all sympathy with the affections which influenced his conduct. If there appears to have been no impropriety in these, how fatal soever the tendency of the action which proceeds from them to those against whom it is directed, it does not seem to deserve any punishment, or to be the proper object of any resentment. (*TMS*, p. 104)

Before we can sympathize with the resentment felt by a person who is injured because of the action of another, we must disapprove of the motives that inspired the injurious action. If there is no disapproval of the motives of an injurious action there can be no sympathy felt for the injured party.

CHAPTER 18

The analysis of the sense of merit and demerit

Our sense of propriety arises from our direct sympathy for the motives of the benefacting agent, whereas our sense of the merit of the reward response is an indirect sympathy for the gratitude of the beneficiary.

> As our sense…of the propriety of conduct arises from…a direct sympathy with the affections and motives of the person who acts, so our sense of its merit arises from…an indirect sympathy with the gratitude of the person who is…acted upon. As we cannot indeed enter thoroughly into the gratitude of the person who receives the benefit, unless we beforehand approve of the motives of the benefactor, so, upon this account, the sense of merit seems to be a compounded sentiment, and to be made up of two distinct emotions; a direct sympathy with the sentiments of the agent, and an indirect sympathy with the gratitude of those who receive the benefit of his actions. (*TMS*, p. 105)

The propriety of an action stems from our direct sympathy with the affections and motives of the benefacting agent. Our sense of the merit of the response action in rewarding that favor originates in the indirect sympathy we feel for the gratitude of that person toward their benefactor. Merit is thus compounded (or a concatenation) of a prior sympathy for the propriety of the benefactor's action and the sympathy for the gratitude felt by the target recipient of the benefit. Propriety is determined by a

Vernon L. Smith, *Adam Smith's Theory of Society*,
https://doi.org/10.1007/978-3-031-68494-4_18

social consensus on the fitness and appropriateness of the agent's motives. But only the gratitude felt by the recipient can properly serve to evaluate its worth.

Notice here the importance of the consumer of a benefit in measuring its value. Also, we see the importance of common knowledge of what a "benefit" is if the primal agent is to not miss their mark.

Sympathetic learning from personal observations of benefactors and beneficiaries of other-regarding action prepares our imagination to admire and honor greatness in historical and iconic figures.

> We may, upon many different occasions, plainly distinguish those two different emotions combining and uniting together in our sense of the good desert of a particular character or action. When we read in history concerning actions of proper and beneficent greatness of mind, how eagerly do we enter into such designs? How much are we animated by that high-spirited generosity which directs them? How keen are we for their success? How grieved at their disappointment? In imagination we become the very person whose actions are represented to us: we transport ourselves in fancy to the scenes of those distant and forgotten adventures…Nor is the indirect sympathy with those who receive the benefit of such actions less sensibly felt. Whenever we place ourselves in the situation of these last, with what warm and affectionate fellow-feeling do we enter into their gratitude towards those who served them so essentially? We embrace…their benefactor along with them. Our heart readily sympathizes with the highest transports of their grateful affection. No honours, no rewards, we think, can be too great for them to bestow upon him. When they make this proper return for his services, we heartily applaud and go along with them; but are shocked…if by their conduct they appear to have little sense of the obligations conferred upon them. Our whole sense, in short, of the merit and good desert of such actions, of the propriety and fitness of recompensing them, and making the person who performed them rejoice in his turn, arises from the sympathetic emotions of gratitude and love, with which, when we bring home to our own breast the situation of those principally concerned, we feel ourselves naturally transported towards the man who could act with such proper and noble beneficence. (*TMS*, pp. 105–106)

Our sympathetic identification with individuals in our communities who intentionally act to benefit others, and whose gratitude toward their benefactors we also sympathize with, well-prepare us to heartily sympathize with the great heroes and heroines of history who perform meritorious acts of greatness for their companions, community, and country. Our experiences with others in our neighborhoods scale up to our ability to bring current and historical cases home to our own situation, in our imagination, though we only read or hear of their good deeds. Hongkonger Jimmy Li I have the honor of calling friend and world freedom patriot.

The demerit of a hurtful action derives from our direct antipathy toward the agent's motives and an indirect sympathy for the resentment of the sufferer.

> In the same manner as our sense of the impropriety of conduct arises from a want of sympathy, or from a direct antipathy to the affections and motives of the agent, so our sense of its demerit arises from…an indirect sympathy with the resentment of the sufferer…As we cannot…enter into the resentment of the sufferer, unless our heart beforehand disapproves the motives of the agent, and renounces all fellow-feeling with them; so upon this account the sense of demerit, as well as that of merit, seems to be a compounded sentiment, and to be made up of two distinct emotions; a direct antipathy to the sentiments of the agent, and an indirect sympathy with the resentment of the sufferer. (*TMS*, pp. 106–107)

The demerit we feel toward they who act to injure another is compounded by our sympathetic disapproval of the motives and affections of the acting agent and of the sympathy we feel for the resentment of the victim toward the perpetrator of harm who chose the injurious action.

We distinguish our antipathy toward the conduct and motives of the agent of cruel harm toward others from the distress of the innocent sufferer, the harm done to them, and our fellow-feeling for the justified resentment they feel.

> We may…upon many different occasions, plainly distinguish…two different emotions combining and uniting together in our sense of the ill-desert of a particular character or action. When we read in history concerning the perfidy and cruelty of a Borgia or a Nero, our heart rises up against the detestable sentiments which influenced their conduct, and renounces with horror and abomination all fellow-feeling with such execrable motives. So far our sentiments are founded upon the direct antipathy to the affections

> of the agent: and the indirect sympathy with the resentment of the sufferers is still more sensibly felt. When we bring home to ourselves the situation of the persons whom those scourges of mankind insulted, murdered, or betrayed, what indignation do we not feel against such insolent and inhuman oppressors of the earth? Our sympathy with the unavoidable distress of the innocent sufferers is not more real nor more lively, than our fellow-feeling with their just and natural resentment. The former sentiment only heightens the latter, and the idea of their distress serves only to inflame and blow up our animosity against those who occasioned it. When we think of the anguish of the sufferers, we take part with them more earnestly against their oppressors; we enter with more eagerness into all their schemes of vengeance, and feel ourselves every moment wreaking, in imagination, upon such violators of the laws of society, that punishment which our sympathetic indignation tells us is due to their crimes. Our sense of the horror and dreadful atrocity of such conduct, the delight which we take in hearing that it was properly punished, the indignation which we feel when it escapes this due retaliation, our whole sense and feeling, in short, of its ill desert, of the propriety and fitness of inflicting evil upon the person who is guilty of it, and of making him grieve in his turn, arises from the sympathetic indignation which naturally boils up in the breast of the spectator, whenever he thoroughly brings home to himself the case of the sufferer. (*TMS*, pp. 107–108)

This distinction between the two sources of demerit identified in *TMS*—our direct antipathy toward the motives and action of the harming agent and our indirect sympathy for the suffering and resentment of the victim—has critical significance for society, because, as we shall see, resentment is what fires justice in punishing and deterring harm in Smith's theory of the bottom-up emergence of jurisprudence as seeking security from injury.

Smith has now completed the formulation of his elementary model of human sociability, with origins in sympathy, contextual experience, and the human ability to change places with another in their imagination. He will proceed next with its applications to the law in society and in nation states, and the role of government in permitting that process to flourish.

PART V

Section II: Of justice and beneficence

CHAPTER 19

Comparison [and contrast] of those two virtues

Beneficence proposition (Bp 1). Circumstances and gratitude-based responses to beneficent action.

> Actions of a beneficent tendency, which proceed from proper motives, seem alone to require a reward; because such alone are the approved objects of gratitude, or excite the sympathetic gratitude of the spectator. (*TMS*, p. 112)

Beneficence concerns all the good things we do for each other in our neighborhoods and communities. Here is a neighborhood narrative of reciprocity that illustrates proposition BP 1.

Parable of the Trash Barrel:

> It is Monday morning, trash pickup day. So, before leaving for the office you wheel your trash barrel from behind your gate to street curbside. That evening, returning from work preoccupied with the day's events, you forget to bring in your trash barrel from the street. This is important because early Tuesday Morning the street sweeper cleans the streets, and you could receive a citation for failing to bring in your trash barrel.

Vernon L. Smith, *Adam Smith's Theory of Society*,
https://doi.org/10.1007/978-3-031-68494-4_19

> Later, however, your neighbor, in the process of bringing in her trash barrel notices that you did not bring in yours. So, she wheels it in for you.
>
> The following Saturday you are harvesting some avocados from your two trees in the back yard. You pick a dozen additional avocados, put them in a separate bag, and take them to your neighbor. She is not at home, so you leave them on her doorstep.
>
> She will know where they came from.

Your neighbor performed an action of a "beneficent tendency" for you. Her action was "properly motivated" in that it was entirely voluntary and intentional. She did not have to do it. Moreover, the action was meritorious as it was costly in time and trouble for her and was valuable to you in assuring that you would not be penalized by the city. Observe that she could have simply informed you, which might have been interpreted as a mild reprimand. She did not; she just brought in your barrel.

Your gratitude for her action was expressed the following Saturday when you incurred the cost of picking a dozen extra avocados and took them to your neighbor. Thus, according to BP 1, you felt an inner obligation—a requirement—to reward her. It was indeed a reward for you knew that she liked avocados—not everyone likes them. She knows that you like avocadoes, and that in picking some for her she knew that you were giving up something of value, just as she had incurred a personal cost in wheeling in your trash barrel.

If any locally informed third party, another neighbor, observed this scenario, they would heartily approve of the action. Hence, the reciprocal actions between you and your neighbor would receive the approbation or implicit consent of the community.

Moreover, in the parable observe that the order of moves is irrelevant as good neighbors eschew and sort of account-keeping: Nothing is changed as an illustration of BP1 if you had harvested some avocados for your neighbor the Saturday before the Monday when she brought in your trash barrel.

The narrative also illustrates the extent of local information embedded in the neighborhood and which underlies the described exchange: Trash pickup schedules, street sweeper schedules, who has avocado trees, and who likes avocados. Change the information and you change the content of the parable, but not the abstract principles described in BP 1.

Surprisingly, BP 1 and other testable propositions in *TMS* predict action in laboratory trust (and ultimatum) games, studied extensively beginning in the 1990s, with replicable results that defied explanation and understanding in terms of extant theory wherein being self-interested meant acting in your self-interest. See Smith, Vernon L. and Bart J. Wilson (2019, Chapters 8 and 10) *Humanomics*, Cambridge: Cambridge University Press.

As an abstract proposition, BP 1 is independent of particular circumstances, which as variables, are subject to wide variation, from neighborhood scenarios to behavior in two-person laboratory ultimatum and trust games. Note the mathematical structure of BP1: Z (reward) = f (X; an action of a beneficent tendency), conditional on Y (X is properly motivated as judged in determining its propriety). The function f (.) can represent an indicator function or a "degree of" function; that is, the degree of reward depending on the degree of benefit. Smith calls them "general rules;" Hayek refers to them as "abstract rules." They are both; they are general, Z = f (X, Y) and abstract, i.e., defined by variable components (Z, X, Y).

Smith is a rigorous theorist of the mainsprings of community order whose thinking and narrative language are precise and can be expressed in mathematical form.

Justice proposition (Jp 1). Circumstances and resentment-based punishment responses to hurtful action.

> Actions of a hurtful tendency, which proceed from improper motives, seem alone to deserve punishment; because such alone are the approved objects of resentment or excite the sympathetic resentment of the spectator. (*TMS*, p. 112)

Justice, in Smith's conception of it, is entirely and exclusively concerned with the limitation, control, and discouragement of intentionally hurtful actions. The origins of justice reside in people's natural resentment and proclivity for lashing out with a punishment response to deliberately or incautiously hurtful actions directed toward them. Though hurtful actions directly cause resentment, the avenging punishment response indirectly discourages hurtful action.

Hence, JP 1 is the obverse of beneficence, BP 1. Beneficence functions socially to increase human happiness through beneficent action, while justice functions to decrease human unhappiness by controlling and limiting hurtful action. Through justice, society seeks security from injury. We tend strongly to sympathize with the victims, with the impropriety, of intentionally hurtful actions, and rejoice when those guilty of such offenses are brought to justice.

Here is an illustrative narrative:

> Your neighbors return from a movie about midnight and as they are pulling into their garage, burglars in their home are leaving via the back door with valuable silver ware and candelabras. Your neighbors find the experience very unsettling and fearful. You completely identify with the terror they feel, easily imagining what it must be like. Someone had burglarized your house before you bought it, so you felt a bit vulnerable living in that upper middle-class neighborhood.
>
> Your neighbors immediately called the police and supplied a complete description of the stolen merchandise. The amateurish burglars had fenced off the goods quickly and locally. Unusual for burglary cases, the police fully recovered the stolen goods offered to a local antique store. They also held two suspects in custody. You sympathetically fellow feel with your neighbors' sense of relief that their goods were returned and the thieves apprehended.

Beneficence proposition (Bp 2). Beneficence is free, cannot be extorted, and the want of it exposes to no punishment.

> Beneficence is always free, it cannot be extorted by force, the mere want of it exposes to no punishment, because the mere want of beneficence tends to do no real positive evil.
>
> It may disappoint of the good which might reasonably have been expected, and upon that account it may justly excite dislike and disapprobation: it cannot, however, provoke any resentment which mankind will go along with. The man who does not recompense his benefactor, when he has it in his power, and when his benefactor needs his assistance, is, no doubt, guilty of the blackest ingratitude. The heart of every impartial spectator rejects all fellow-feeling with the selfishness of his motives, and he is the proper object of the highest disapprobation. But still he does no positive hurt to any body. He only does not do that good which in propriety he ought to have done. He is the object of hatred, a passion which is naturally excited by impropriety of sentiment and behaviour; not of resentment, a passion which is never properly called forth but by actions which tend to do real and positive hurt to some particular persons. His want of gratitude, therefore, cannot be punished. To oblige him by force to perform what in gratitude he ought to perform, and what every impartial spectator would

> approve of him for performing, would, if possible, be still more improper than his neglecting to perform it. His benefactor would dishonour himself if he attempted by violence to constrain him to gratitude, and it would be impertinent for any third person, who was not the superior of either, to intermeddle. But of all the duties of beneficence, those which gratitude recommends to us approach nearest to what is called a perfect and complete obligation. What friendship, what generosity, what charity, would prompt us to do with universal approbation, is still more free, and can still less be extorted by force than the duties of gratitude. We talk of the debt of gratitude, not of charity, or generosity, nor even of friendship, when friendship is mere esteem, and has not been enhanced and complicated with gratitude for good offices. (*TMS*, pp. 112–113)

Inherently, beneficence must always be freely given, and can never be coerced for then it is no longer beneficence. Beneficence loses all meaning if people are not free to choose not to benefit another. If it is zero—no benefit is offered—then no real positive harm has been done, it deserves zero resentment and zero punishment. Among the set of values for beneficent action, this proposition serves formally to fix the zero point, which is contained strictly within the set—nothing changes in substance, only degree, with zero benefit and no punishment is justified.

The circumstances of the proposition arise naturally in 2-person interaction games.

In single-play 2-person trust games, it has been established that when Players 2 are given the opportunity to moderately punish, at moderate cost, their counterpart Players 1 for not offering to cooperate with them, they forego the option at overwhelming rates (Smith and Wilson, *Humanomics*, 2019, pp. 149–150). On the other hand, 24 percent of Players 1 choose a costly option to punish their Player 2 counterparts for defecting after Players 1 have offered to cooperate with them (Smith and Wilson, 2019, pp. 152–154). In effect, the right to not voluntarily offer to benefit another is overwhelmingly respected by people in these games. But deliberately positive hurtful action is punished by nearly one quarter of the victims by people in the same cohort. Hence, the model in *TMS* provides both a set of circumstances when punishment will not be used and a set where punishment will be invoked. No modern theory has been able to offer such action-predictive propositions.

In political discourse many people seem to believe that the rich ought to provide benefits to the poor. Consistent with that belief we have progressive income taxation in which the rich are taxed at higher marginal rates than the poor. This phenomenon is foreign to Smith's proposition BP 2 on beneficence because taxation is not voluntary.

Indeed, majority rule is obviously coercive of minority preferences. Is there a practical alternative? In 2007, Ryan D. Oprea, Abel M. Winn and I published an article called "A compensation election for binary social choice" (*Proceedings National American Academy of Science*, V. 104 (3), pp. 1093–1096) that talks about just this. Some takeaways are provided below.

We study individual decision behavior in a compensation election procedure that is designed to implement a simple binary choice group decision between two options. Think of the group decision problem as a choice between a proposition for a new rule and the status quo. For example, a particular plot of land is to be rezoned to allow a service station to be built. Those living close to the station do not like the increased traffic; those living further from it like the convenience. The rule and the status quo are each common outcomes that apply across all people living in the neighborhood, but the value or cost to each resident differs according to their circumstances and preferences: some gain, some lose, and others are unaffected by a change from old to new.

Rather than casting yes/no coercive votes, each subject in the experiment submits a bid reflecting their willingness to pay to have their preferred option win; also, they enter the amount they wish to be reimbursed if the dis-preferred alternative option is selected by the electorate. We assign each subject a win value and a cost loss, so we know their circumstances, and all payments are made in US dollars cash.

Our Compensation Election selects the option that receives the highest sum of bids. Out of the resulting pool of winning willingness to pay contributions, the losers are each paid the amount they indicated as their loss for the losing option. Although the experiment allows subjects to strategically bid above their value, or below their cost (or even for the option they do not prefer), such behavior is not prominent and declines with repetition. (E.g., you might bid below your value for your best option and above your cost for the worst, hoping thereby to profit from the losing alternative.) We also find that subjects bid more truthfully in revealing their assigned values and costs when we increase the number of individuals participating in the election. Honest bidding increases with experience and electoral numbers.

The constitutional prohibition of alcohol and recreational drug consumption illustrates the contrary case of BP 2 in which the law attempts to prohibit the free exchange of goods whose consumption can be harmful, and is harmful if imbibed in excess.[1] The widespread lack of voluntary compliance in such cases renders unenforceable such top-down control as we experienced with federal alcohol prohibition. An unintended consequence of prohibition was an escalation of violence associated with the illegal domestic production and distribution of alcohol which led to its repeal. Similarly, the lack of voluntary compliance accounts for the failure, and escalation of violence, in the public policy "war on drugs." The same conditions and forces also apply to the policy "war on poverty." Poverty has so far not been eliminated in free economies because of a low-productivity labor sector, and the want of sufficient voluntary bottom-up beneficence, which cannot be coerced. Drug avoidance, like temperance in alcohol consumption, requires voluntary action to not consume, and if lacking, cannot be effectively enforced from the top-down.

In symmetry with Beneficence Proposition 2, we also have your next reading.

Justice proposition (Jp 2): the observance of the rules of justice deserves not to be rewarded.

> Though the breach of justice…exposes to punishment, the observance of the rules of that virtue seems scarce to deserve any reward. There is, no doubt, a propriety in the practice of justice, and it merits, upon that account, all the approbation which is due to propriety. But as it does no real positive good, it is entitled to very little gratitude. Mere justice is, upon most occasions, but a negative virtue, and only hinders us from hurting our neighbour. The man who barely abstains from violating either the person or the estate, or the reputation, of his neighbours, has surely very little positive merit. He fulfils, however, all the rules of what is peculiarly called justice, and does every thing which his equals can with propriety force him to do, or which they can punish him for not doing. We may often fulfil all the rules of justice by sitting still and doing nothing. (*TMS*, p. 117)

Smith insightfully and logically identifies just two categories of outcomes consequent to the intentional action of one person toward another.

[1] Constitutional Prohibition reduced sclerosis by 10–20%: Dills, Angela K. and Jeffrey A. Miron (2003) "Alcohol prohibition and cirrhosis." Working Paper 9681, National Bureau of Economic Research, May.

First, we have a set of positive beneficent outcomes. This set, Smith emphasizes, also contains the null outcome, zero; that is, the lack of beneficial action, or the choice not to act beneficially, does no positive harm, invokes no resentment, and invites no punishment. Benefit, gratitude, and the debt of gratitude reward are zero.

Secondly, we have a set of negative hurtful outcomes. The set contains the null outcome, zero; that is, lack of any hurtful action causes no explicit positive benefit, invokes no gratitude, and invites no reward. Hence, there is no reward for obeying the law—for driving through green lights; rather, you are fined for not stopping at a red light.

Hence, in nature's law, just as failure to act beneficially is not regarded as a punishable offense, symmetrically, the failure to act hurtfully is not regarded as a rewardable benefit.

Implicitly, in Smith's natural law of jurisprudence, we see why it must emerge, or not, as a bottom-up process, if and only if, society is free. If we are not free to act mistakenly and badly, then we are not free to avoid acting so.

I believe that this explains why the American experiment survives populist and recurrent individual excesses—from the extreme conflict of Civil War to a jolting contemporary reminder that Black Lives Matter—relentlessly expanding the scope and inclusiveness of the "self-evident" truth that all people are created equally, and each should be left perfectly free—so long as they do not violate the laws of justice—to "pursue their own interest their own way" (*WN*, Vol. II, p. 184).

None of these populist diversions, as mob demands, provide substance for sustainable change; after running their course, perhaps serving to remind us that there ought to be a better way and that we need to be more sensitive to our unintended transgressions, the rules of beneficence, and the rules of justice supported by our constitution, predominantly return to normal in our routine treatment of each other.

Resentment is the safeguard of justice and the security of innocence.

> Resentment seems to have been given us by nature for defence, and for defence only. It is the safeguard of justice and the security of innocence. It prompts us to beat off the mischief which is attempted to be done to us, and to retaliate that which is already done, that the offender may be made to repent of his injustice, and that others, through fear of the like punishment, may be terrified from being guilty of the like offence. It must be reserved, therefore, for these purposes, nor can the spectator ever go

> along with it when it is exerted for any other. But the mere want of the beneficent virtues, though it may disappoint us of the good which might reasonably be expected, neither does, nor attempts to do, any mischief from which we can have occasion to defend ourselves. (*TMS*, pp. 113–114)

The emotion of resentment is the foundation of justice. Resentment prompts us to vigorously beat off every evil that is attempted to be done to us and to retaliate for any such evil already done. Offenders are thereby made to repent of the evil they have committed, and this tends to deter potential offenders by instilling a fear of the consequences of their actions.

Smith knew that justice is more critical to society than beneficence for no society can subsist when many are ready to hurt others without cause. Consequently, the first responsibility of the civil order is to support the emergent norms of society, the most crucial of which is justice as security from injury.

The retail chain, Target, announced the closing of nine stores that was attributed to rising theft.[2] The failure to enforce laws against theft undermines the principle inherent in all voluntary exchange among free people: you must give in order to receive.

In nature the violation of justice is injury from motives that are disapproved of and invoking the strictest of all obligations to justice as a virtue.

> There is…another virtue, of which the observance is not left to the freedom of our own wills, which may be extorted by force, and of which the violation exposes to resentment, and consequently to punishment. This virtue is justice. the violation of justice is injury: it does real and positive hurt to some particular persons, from motives which are naturally disapproved of. It is, therefore, the proper object of resentment, and of punishment, which is the natural consequence of resentment. As mankind go along with, and approve of, the violence employed to avenge the hurt which is done by injustice, so they much more go along with, and approve of, that which is employed to prevent and beat off the injury, and to restrain the offender from hurting his neighbours. The person himself who meditates an injustice is sensible of this, and feels that force may, with the

[2] Maruf, Ramishah, Parija Kavilanz, and Cheri Mossburg (2023) "Target says it will close nine stores in major cities across four states because of theft and organized crime." *CNN*, September 27, 2023.

> utmost propriety, be made use of, both by the person whom he is about to injure, and by others, either to obstruct the execution of his crime, or to punish him when he has executed it. And upon this is founded that remarkable distinction between justice and all the other social virtues...that we feel ourselves to be under a stricter obligation to act according to justice, than agreeably to friendship, charity, or generosity; that the practice of these last-mentioned virtues seems to be left...to our own choice, but that...we feel ourselves to be in a peculiar manner tied, bound, and obliged, to the observation of justice...and... with the utmost propriety, and with the approbation of all mankind, be made use of to constrain us to observe the rules of the one, but not to follow the precepts of the other. (*TMS*, p. 114)

Nature, abhorring injustice, arms us with resentment to motivate the punishment of offenders. Universal sympathy for the victims of injustice solidifies our sense of strict obligation to do our part in implementing the rules of justice. Without resentment there can be no urge to retaliate against and punish injustice, and hence no property in law-abiding actions. Consequently, weak decentralized governments are put on alert that they should deliver offenders to friends and family of victims for determination of what is to be done. Strong centralized governments, if they are to command broad citizen support must prosecute all crimes against the public—murder, theft, and robbery which violate property in one's body and in the products of mind and body.

That we feel "tied, bound, and obliged, to the observation of justice" is nature's way of acknowledging that it is the most important pillar of society.

Blameworthiness and praiseworthiness arise from extraordinary acts of unkindness or of kindness.

> We must always, however, carefully distinguish what is only blameable, or the proper object of disapprobation, from what force may be employed either to punish or to prevent. That seems blameable which falls short of that ordinary degree of proper beneficence which experience teaches us to expect of every body; and, on the contrary, that seems praiseworthy which goes beyond it. The ordinary degree itself seems neither blameable nor praiseworthy. A father, a son, a brother, who behaves to the correspondent relation neither better nor worse than the greater part of men commonly do, seems properly to deserve neither praise nor blame. He who surprises us by extraordinary and unexpected, though still proper and

> suitable, kindness, or, on the contrary, by extraordinary and unexpected, as well as unsuitable, unkindness, seems praiseworthy in the one case, and blameable in the other. (*TMS*, p. 115)

Small hurts are not subject to blame, and small benefits are not worthy of praise. When either is extraordinary, and serves thereby to surprise us, we feel required to reward a benefactor out of our gratitude for their praiseworthy action and to punish out of our resentment their blamability if any evil doer intentionally harms us.

Prior to civil government every person has a recognized natural right to defend against injury and to punish those who have injured them. Nor can force be justified to extract kindness not offered.

> Among equals each individual is naturally, and antecedent to the institution of civil government, regarded as having a right both to defend himself from injuries, and to exact a certain degree of punishment for those which have been done to him. Every generous spectator not only approves of his conduct when he does this, but enters so far into his sentiments as often to be willing to assist him. When one man attacks, or robs, or attempts to murder, another, all the neighbours take the alarm, and think that they do right when they run, either to revenge the person who has been injured, or to defend him who is in danger of being so. But when a father fails in the ordinary degree of parental affection towards a son; when a son seems to want that filial reverence which might be expected to his father; when brothers are without the usual degree of brotherly affection; when a man shuts his breast against compassion, and refuses to relieve the misery of his fellow-creatures, when he can with the greatest ease; in all these cases, though every body blames the conduct, nobody imagines that those who might have reason, perhaps, to expect more kindness, have any right to extort it by force. The sufferer can only complain, and the spectator can intermeddle no other way than by advice and persuasion. Upon all such occasions, for equals to use force against one another, would be thought the highest degree of insolence and presumption. (*TMS*, pp. 115–116)

In pre-civil government communities, every individual is by nature regarded as having the right to defend themselves from injuries and to punish appropriately those who have committed injuries against them. Nor is there in nature any right to extract beneficial action by employing the threat of punishment. Nature, therefore, prepares us for forming and following orderly rules that promote voluntary acts of beneficence and discourage unjust acts of harm.

Why capital punishment? It prevails in all modern nations but was not the norm in so-called "barbarous" nations that joined punishment with victim compensation.[3]

In Adam Smith's *Lectures on Jurisprudence* (hereafter *LJ*), it is observed that all civilized nations impose capital punishment for the crime of murder. The natural punishment was seen as death, not as compensation, but rather as a reasonable retaliation (*LJ*, p. 476).[4]

Smith, both knowledgeable and sensitive to the history of rule-governed action, notes that in "barbarous" nations the punishment was much less severe than in civilized states, perhaps involving only a pecuniary fine. The cause of this limited involvement was the weakness of early governments in communities where it was a matter of some delicacy to meddle in the affairs of individuals, and their families accustomed to a long-established tradition of rule-following norms; in particular, where it involved the emotions of the family and friends of the contesting parties in the case of murder.

In such early periods of society, governmental authorities intervened only as mediators. The primary motive was peacekeeping in efforts to avoid an escalation of the conflict due to resentment by the family and friends of a slain person toward the person identified as the guilty party (*LJ*, p. 106).

To accomplish its peacekeeping objectives the authorities needed to involve the whole community, particularly the family and friends of the victim as well as those of the murderer. The tradition was for guilty parties to be presented to the family and friends of the victim so that they could decide what was to be done and be compensated for their loss of life. The practice of victim compensation survives today in recovery suits for violation of contract, a civil offense. However, this process was not static in antiquity. Procedures evolved and developed over the course of time and experience into the specification of an atonement rate schedule, wherein the rate charged for murder depended on the person's rank in the society.

[3] This entry is from *Lectures on Jurisprudence* that supplement the previous entry from *TMS*.

[4] Smith, Adam (1978) Lectures on *Jurisprudence* edited by R.L. Meek, D.D. Raphael, and P.G. Stein: Oxford University Press, Liberty Fund Edition.

Observe that victim compensation implies formal recognition that life has a value to the family and friends of the slain and, therefore, to society. Since not all lives are of equal value to a society, elementary economics and common sense combine to account for the emergence of a compensation schedule.[5]

In these early weak-government, victim-compensated, regimes, the officials intervened to specify rates for the atonement of actions causing death. The compensatory payment, known as the wingild, were established for the death of persons of every rank in the state from the king to the slave. The wingild varied according to a person's recognized rank in the hierarchy of the community. Those of higher rank were from family and friend enclaves that were more powerful in wealth, prestige, and subservience and would expect, and could negotiate, a higher satisfying compensation than those of low rank. Consequently, the wingild payment for a king would be much above that of a Thain [one who held land granted by a king or nobleman], above that of an Earl, a Baron, greater than that of a simple free man, which was still more than the value of a slave (*LJ*, p. 107).

The process that evolved was a fine-grained victim compensation scheme. Ranks involved a social consensus on worth, to be negotiated like any other item of exchange. A person of higher rank would constitute a higher loss to the family and society. Thus, the social exchange system, which is an informal market, dutifully determines the value or price of life when the community is in need of it.

The determination of victim compensation was an evolutionary process.[6]

Where a person could not pay compensation for a death they caused, then they were confined originally in a tent reserved for the purpose

[5] To the modern mind this might seem to constitute a shocking extension of mercenary pricing into the sacrosanctity of personal ethical matters. However, markets and cultures implicitly value and, therefore, price life. For example, wages paid workers in high accident-risk occupations include compensation premiums paid to overcome worker reluctance to be exposed to death. There is a substantial literature concerned with measuring the "value of a statistical life" and determining its variation across countries. For example, T. R. Miller (2000) "Variations between countries in values of statistical life," Journal of Transport Economics and Policy, vol. 34, no. 2, May, pp. 169–188 HTTPS://WWW.JSTOR.ORG/STABLE/20053838.

[6] *LJ*, p. 107.

of eliciting payment, called the "wingild room". The guilty person was initially asked to pay for it. If they were unable to pay, then family and friends were asked separately. If there was still not adequate payment, then they were assembled and asked publicly as a group three times. [What I tell you three times must be true!] If all these attempts failed to yield the compensatory payment, then the victim was offered up to the friends of the slain for capital punishment or for whatever fate they wished to declare. Relatives served as both judges and executioners. In the modern state public officials serve as professional executioners (*LJ*, p. 107).

In *LJ*, Smith articulates a historical social evaluation procedure for dealing with murder founded on community consent processes, which, in important ways, was naturally superior to that which has survived into the modern centralized state. It had a deterrence value comparable to that of modern punishment which, in the contest between plaintiff and defendant, blameworthiness determines the death penalty or term of imprisonment. But more importantly, there was a consensual community effort to partially restore the victim's loss relative to their previous state. A family loses a husband and father but receives some compensatory support payments. Such action as an emergent expression of our humanity has been lost in favor of a schedule of "crimes against the public," which focuses only on punishment and deterrence.

Superiors, parents toward children, children toward parents, and civil magistrates toward citizens, are obliged by approbation to prescribe rules that restrain injustice and promote prosperity among their charges.

> A superior may, indeed, sometimes, with universal approbation, oblige those under his jurisdiction to behave, in this respect, with a certain degree of propriety to one another. The laws of all civilized nations oblige parents to maintain their children, and children to maintain their parents, and impose upon men many other duties of beneficence. The civil magistrate is entrusted with the power not only of preserving the public peace by restraining injustice, but of promoting the prosperity of the common-wealth, by establishing good discipline, and by discouraging every sort of vice and impropriety; he may prescribe rules, therefore, which not only prohibit mutual injuries among fellow-citizens, but command mutual good offices to a certain degree (*TMS*, p. 116).

Magistrates and other administrative superiors may, with community consent, sometimes oblige those under their jurisdiction to behave with propriety toward each other. Similarly, the laws of civilized nations require parents to care for their children, children as adults to care for parents, and to impose certain duties of beneficence. This is the historical origin and background of modern progressive or "liberal" programs for benefiting the poor or the disadvantaged, and of classical liberal or "conservative" programs for rewarding people for meritorious actions and achievements and holding individuals accountable for their hurtful actions toward others.

Great sensitivity is required that a sovereign neither neglect proper duty, nor push too far and destroy liberty, security, and justice.

> When the sovereign commands what is merely indifferent, and what, antecedent to his orders, might have been omitted without any blame, it becomes not only blameable but punishable to disobey him. When he commands, therefore, what, antecedent to any such order, could not have been omitted without the greatest blame, it surely becomes much more punishable to be wanting in obedience. Of all the duties of a lawgiver, however, this, perhaps, is that which requires the greatest delicacy and reserve to execute with propriety and judgment. To neglect it altogether exposes the commonwealth to many gross disorders and shocking enormities, and to push it too far is destructive of all liberty, security, and justice. (*TMS*, p. 116)

Smith clearly has in mind that the rules which emerge naturally in community are founded on self-command, a force that is widely distributed "among equals." The rules are importantly evaluated by approbation and admitted to a tradition. Rule traditions must be respected and supported by civil authority if their orderly evolution is to continue as a bottom-up process. Civil authority and its growth, however, tends to reflect increasing concentrations of power, a corollary of its role of defending against foreign encroachments and the management of police in the provision of domestic security from injury. Hence, the requirement placed on the lawgiver is of "the greatest delicacy and reserve to execute with propriety and judgment." Social harm may follow from neglect while a government that pushes too far can destroy "liberty, security, and justice."

The "delicacy and reserve" exercised by civil authority in our history has aligned first with slavery, then civil war, followed by racial discrimination in Southern state law and in Northern state social practice, and finally, unproductive, and enormously destructive intervention into unpopular foreign conflicts such as WWI and the Vietnam War. But true to Smith's classical liberalism, captured in our constitution, we have long had a strong-voiced tradition of dissent, that opposed slavery, racial discrimination, US entry into WWI and the Vietnam War. In WWII we witnessed the internment of over 110,000 Japanese citizens after the Pearl Harbor attack in December 1941, opposed by many of us. In all these cases the dissenters were subsequently vindicated and recognized. Today's dissenters, when aligned with classical liberal principles of freedom, have tended to be tomorrow's victors.

The merit of a reward response is increasing in gratitude felt, which is increasing in the approbation of the propriety of a beneficial action.

> Though the mere want of beneficence seems to merit no punishment from equals, the greater exertions of that virtue appear to deserve the highest reward. By being productive of the greatest good, they are the natural and approved objects of the liveliest gratitude. (*TMS*, p. 117)

In *TMS*, "propriety" means social approval of an action, as when your neighbor brings in your trash barrel which you had forgotten to do. Other neighbors who happened to notice this deed would naturally think it was fitting and appropriate. The same neighbors would approve of your action in rewarding the neighbor's action, and thus returning the favor. The general open-ended rule is to do favors for neighbors, such exertions being applauded but never punishable if not freely offered; another rule is to return favors. All these are qualitative community norms. "The greater exertions" of virtue, however, adds a judgment of the merit of the action. Merit introduces a quantitative "degree of" benefit into norms, thereby enabling people to convey the strength of their approbation or disapprobation of an action.

Nature urges us to retaliate against that evil which has been done to us.

> As every man doth, so it shall be done to him, and retaliation seems to be the great law which is dictated to us by nature. Beneficence and generosity

> we think due to the generous and beneficent. Those whose hearts never open to the feelings of humanity, should, we think, be shut out in the same manner, from the affections of all their fellow-creatures, and be allowed to live in the midst of society, as in a great desert, where there is nobody to care for them, or to enquire after them. The violator of the laws of justice ought to be made to feel himself that evil which he has done to another; and since no regard to the sufferings of his brethren is capable of restraining him, he ought to be overawed by the fear of his own. The man who is barely innocent, who only observes the laws of justice with regard to others, and merely abstains from hurting his neighbours, can merit only that his neighbours in their turn should respect his innocence, and that the same laws should be religiously observed with regard to him. (*TMS*, pp. 117–118)

The Golden Rule, "do unto others what you would have them do unto you" constitutes a propriety-merit-reward-benefit calculus corresponding to Beneficence Proposition 1 (BP 1) in *TMS* (p. 112). But the Rule does not work for justice as security from injury. The beneficence version of The Golden Rule is most prominently associated with the Abrahamic religions of Christianity and Islam. There are versions in Buddhism, Confucianism, and Hinduism of the form, "do not unto others as you would have them not do unto you," that concerns the set of harmful actions, and of reducing harm, as in Justice Proposition 1 (JP 1) in *TMS* (p. 112). Both describe norms that societies must internalize for success. Religion can inspire kind action or the prohibition of unkind action, or both. National and state political constitutions can only specify the prohibition of certain actions harmful to others. These, however, must be enforceable. Otherwise, as in the American experience with alcohol and drug prohibition, the harm done can overwhelm whatever good is accomplished. The fact that the harm exceeded the benefit was publicly recognized in the Constitutional amendment that repealed prohibition. But the damage from drug criminalization, as distinct from declaring it only an illegal civil violation, continues so long as we follow what Senator Biden once championed as the "Lock 'em up and throw away the key" policy.

CHAPTER 20

Of the sense of justice, of remorse, and of the consciousness of merit

There is no justification for harming our neighbor except in retaliation for evil they have done to us.

> There can be no proper motive for hurting our neighbour, there can be no incitement to do evil to another which mankind will go along with, except just indignation for evil which that other has done to us. To disturb his happiness merely because it stands in the way of our own, to take from him what is of real use to him merely because it may be of equal or of more use to us, or to indulge, in this manner, at the expense of other people, the natural preference which every man has for his own happiness above that of other people, is what no impartial spectator can go along with. Every man is, no doubt, by nature, first and principally recommended to his own care; and as he is fitter to take care of himself, than of any other person, it is fit and right that it should be so. Every man, therefore, is much more deeply interested in whatever immediately concerns himself, than in what concerns any other man: and to hear, perhaps, of the death of another person, with whom we have no particular connection, will give us less concern, will spoil our stomach, or break our rest, much less than a very insignificant disaster which has befallen ourselves. (*TMS*, p. 119)

Thus, in leading up to Smith's key ideas on actions governed by one's own versus other's interest, it is here emphasized that there can be no proper motive for hurting out neighbor except in the form of just indignation for an unprovoked evil that our neighbor has done to us. We must

Vernon L. Smith, *Adam Smith's Theory of Society*,
https://doi.org/10.1007/978-3-031-68494-4_20

never take from another anything simply because we think it is of equal of greater benefit to us. This last prohibition has long been violated by progressive income taxation which requires rich citizens to pay disproportionately more in financing government expenditures than those of more modest means.

Our self-love cannot be allowed to let us ruin our neighbor to prevent misfortune to ourselves.

> [T]hough the ruin of our neighbour may affect us much less than a very small misfortune of our own, we must not ruin him to prevent that small misfortune, nor even to prevent our own ruin. We must here, as in all other cases, view ourselves not so much according to that light in which we may naturally appear to ourselves, as according to that in which we naturally appear to others. Though every man may, according to the proverb, be the whole world to himself, to the rest of mankind he is a most insignificant part of it. Though his own happiness may be of more importance to him than that of all the world besides, to every other person it is of no more consequence than that of any other man. Though it may be true, therefore, that every individual, in his own breast, naturally prefers himself to all mankind, yet he dares not look mankind in the face, and avow that he acts according to this principle. He feels that in this preference they can never go along with him, and that how natural soever it may be to him, it must always appear excessive and extravagant to them. When he views himself in the light in which he is conscious that others will view him, he sees that to them he is but one of the multitude, in no respect better than any other in it. (*TMS*, pp. 119–120)

Here, carefully introduced, is Smith's key methodological distinction between being self-interested and acting self-interestedly. We are all strictly self-interested, but as a means to "go along" with humankind we are very careful in our actions to always view ourselves in the light of how others view us. There is no denial that people are rightly and justly self-interested, but we must screen and modify our actions to take into account that to others we are "but one of the multitude, in no respect better than any other in it."

On humbling the arrogance of Our self-love to bring it down to what others can go along with.

> If he would act so as that the impartial spectator may enter into the principles of his conduct, which is what of all things he has the greatest desire to do, he must upon this, as upon all other occasions, humble the arrogance of his self-love, and bring it down to something which other men can go along with. They will indulge it so far as to allow him to be more anxious about, and to pursue with more earnest assiduity, his own happiness than that of any other person. Thus far, whenever they place themselves in his situation, they will readily go along with him. In the race for wealth, and honours, and preferments, he may run as hard as he can, and strain every nerve and every muscle, in order to outstrip all his competitors. But if he should justle, or throw down any of them, the indulgence of the spectators is entirely at an end. It is a violation of fair play, which they cannot admit of. This man is to them, in every respect, as good as he: they do not enter into that self-love, by which he prefers himself so much to this other, and cannot go along with the motive from which he hurt him. They readily, therefore, sympathize with the natural resentment of the injured, and the offender becomes the object of their hatred and indignation. He is sensible that he becomes so, and feels that those sentiments are ready to burst out from all sides against him. (*TMS*, pp. 120–121)

To properly consider and benefit from the interest of others whenever we act, we must humble the arrogance of our self-love reducing it to a level that others can go along with. Actions are neither self-interested nor altruistic (a nineteenth-century English word) but are rule-governed and promote harmony in community and society. We are all part of a social consensus that enables each of us to benefit without taking advantage of others by foul means—a rule-socializing process that began in antiquity. In many societies, however, this natural development has not been a central part of rulemaking and following by the government.

Observe that primitive utility inters this process in the form of a "desire to get along with others" which, it can be argued, arises because others are willing to give you more if you are willing to give them more although Smith does not accept this interpretation in his first beneficence proposition which has a strong good-hearted first-mover motivation not an expectation of a reward. But Smith's proposition in the above passage is about our attitude toward independent action by others. He says that we are entirely willing to see them pursue their own ends as vigorously and effectively as they wish but we cannot tolerate any action designed to disable others in that pursuit. In this sense businesspersons are depicted as fair-play, no foul, rule devotees. I believe this is also a proper modern model of antitrust. Success ought to be championed so long as one business does not "justle and throw down" another. So, Pfizer, Amazon, or Google are not to be reprimanded unless they do this to a competitor or a customer. Since buying a competitor might be a means of avoiding that alternative, antitrust must show some concern for horizontal mergers. Limiting consumer choice among independent producers may constitute a form of justling.

Greater evil done implies greater resentment and greater punishment.

> The greater and more irreparable the evil that is done, the resentment of the sufferer runs naturally the higher: so does likewise the sympathetic indignation of the spectator, as well as the sense of guilt in the agent. Death is the greatest evil which one man can inflict upon another, and excites the highest degree of resentment in those who are immediately connected with the slain. Murder, therefore, is the most atrocious of all crimes which affect individuals only, in the sight both of mankind and of the person who has committed it. To be deprived of that which we are possessed of, is a greater evil than to be disappointed of what we have only the expectation. Breach of property, therefore, theft and robbery, which take from us what we are possessed of, are greater crimes than breach of contract, which only disappoints us of what we expected. The most sacred laws of justice, therefore, those whose violation seems to call loudest for vengeance and punishment, are the laws which guard the life and person of our neighbour; the next are those which guard his property and possessions; and last of all come those which guard what are called his personal rights, or what is due to him from the promises of others. (*TMS*, p. 121)

And thus does Adam Smith articulate the origins of property in the natural feelings of resentment for intentional harm inflicted, and punishment proportional to, or increasing in, the resentment felt, in society and economy:

- Without societal protection against murder, there can be no property in one's body.
- Without protection from theft and robbery, there can be no property in the products of a person's body and mind.
- Without protection from violation of contract, there can be no property, and therefore no trust, in each other's promises.

Justice as Property provides security from injury as the necessary foundation for stable society and economy. Justice combined with Beneficence constitutes necessary and sufficient conditions for stability and prosperity in society and economy.

Smith also notes that "Breach of property…theft and robbery, which take from us what we are possessed of, are greater crimes than breach of contract, which only disappoints us of what we expected." Although he does not say so explicitly this is an application of his important proposition on the asymmetry between joy and sorrow (see entry below) and therefore between gain and loss. Thus does Smith's theory explain why theft and robbery draw greater penalties than violation of contractual promises, nowhere so insightfully explained in modern economics, behavioral economics, and psychology.

Justice as naturally sacred law requires violators to reflect and know shame, horror, and consternation for their actions.

> The violator of the more sacred laws of justice can never reflect on the sentiments which mankind must entertain with regard to him, without feeling all the agonies of shame, and horror, and consternation. When his passion is gratified, and he begins coolly to reflect on his past conduct, he can enter into none of the motives which influenced it. They appear now as detestable to him as they did always to other people. By sympathizing with the hatred and abhorrence which other men must entertain for him, he becomes in some measure the object of his own hatred and abhorrence. The situation of the person, who suffered by his injustice, now calls upon his pity. He is grieved at the thought of it; regrets the unhappy effects of his own conduct, and feels at the same time that they have rendered him the proper object of the resentment and indignation of mankind, and of what is the natural consequence of resentment, vengeance and punishment. The thought of this perpetually haunts him, and fills him with terror and amazement. He dares no longer look society in the face, but imagines himself, as it were, rejected, and thrown out from the affections of all mankind. He cannot hope for the consolation of sympathy in this his greatest and most dreadful distress. The remembrance of his crimes has shut out all fellow-feeling with him from the hearts of his fellow-creatures. The sentiments which they entertain with regard to him, are the very thing which he is most afraid of. Every thing seems hostile, and he would be glad to fly to some inhospitable desert, where he might never more behold the face of a human creature, nor read in the countenance of mankind the condemnation of his crimes. But solitude is still more dreadful than society.

> His own thoughts can present him with nothing but what is black, unfortunate, and disastrous, the melancholy forebodings of incomprehensible misery and ruin. The horror of solitude drives him back into society, and he comes again into the presence of mankind, astonished to appear before them loaded with shame and distracted with fear, in order to supplicate some little protection from the countenance of those very judges, who he knows have already all unanimously condemned him. Such is the nature of that sentiment, which is properly called remorse; of all the sentiments which can enter the human breast the most dreadful. It is made up of shame from the sense of the impropriety of past conduct; of grief for the effects of it; of pity for those who suffer by it; and of the dread and terror of punishment from the consciousness of the justly-provoked resentment of all rational creatures. (*TMS*, pp. 121–122)

The sentiment in this proposition is reflected for Christians in the Lord's Prayer, wherein we ask our father in heaven to "forgive us our trespasses as we forgive those who trespass against us." Smith's graphic description of the role of feelings, and the powerful urge to confront and deter the hurtful actions "of all rational creatures," did not mean that Smith saw deterrence, in the modern state's focus on the punishment of crimes against the public, as the only viable public policy practice. As we have seen in his examination of the history of jurisprudence in *TMS*, p. 145, he observes that in early societies with weak governments, their principal concern for peacekeeping led them to support indigenous community rules requiring victim compensation via a social consensus which serves not only to punish the violator, but also to cool the passions of the family and friends of the victim who feel that their loss is thereby partially recompensed as well as avenged.

Today, we are aware of a small subset of recalcitrant cases, referred to as sociopaths, who are incapable of feeling the remorse Smith saw as properly visited on the perpetrator of crimes against innocents. In fact, Smith's model of human sociability articulates why the vast majority of people are not sociopaths. But a small percentage of all populations of people never enter the Great School of Self-Command.

Linda Mealey's "The sociobiology of sociopathy: An integrated evolutionary model" (*Behavioral and Brain Sciences*, 1995) reports that although sociopaths make up about 3–4 percent of the male population and less than 1 percent of females, they are believed to comprise some 20 percent of the US prison population and 33–80 percent of chronic criminal offenders.[1] Sociopaths are described as irresponsible and unreliable in conduct and behavior. They are considered egocentric, impulsive, and incapable of forming long-term personal relationships. Their actions are always self-interested and others they likewise believe act in their own interest; so, their interest and that of all others are strictly opposed.

This is the abstract world that traditional interactive game theory modeled—a population of interacting self-interested agents in strict opposition to each other; a world without any natural security from injury supported by a community consensus on justice. But agents were permitted to punish, and to risk, defection from offers to cooperate. The only justice is what you can achieve via the threat of loss or reduced payoff (injury). Game theoretic experiments find evidence of both gratitude and resentment in interactive play.

Game theory was said to be about "poker, business, and war." Adam Smith's model explains why this is not an entirely correct conception of business, except for the mercantilist government-business coalition, and thus we have the applicable situations for game theory reduced to poker and war, although we should add political opponents who commonly see themselves as in struct opposition to each other as they seek to align themselves with the largest possible interest among their constituents.

Dan Ellsberg, hired as a Vietnam-era game-theoretic consultant to the federal government, discovered and came to believe, that the image of US war actions as defensive was an illusion that the government maintained by lying to its own people. More recently, Snowden made similar claims that the government was lying to, and spying on, its own people, and leaked classified evidence in support of his claim. I believe that Dan Ellsberg was a patriot, comparable to our many war heroes, who was upholding the constitution which he was sworn to defend and was part of an ennobling history of dissent in the American experiment. Snowden was also in that vein but unlike Ellsberg and our war heroes, Snowden was not willing to face the consequences of his decision. Ellsberg escaped the certainty of imprisonment only because egocentric President Nixon violated Ellsberg's rights as a citizen and blew the government's case

[1] This male and female difference in the incidence of sociopathology accounts for the far greater incarceration rate for men than women. As of June 7, 2025, the Federal Bureau of Prisons (BOP) indicates that men make up 93.5 percent of approximately 155,000 federal inmates ("Inmate Sex," Federal BOP. June 2025. https://www.bop.gov/about/statistics/statistics_inmate_gender.jsp).

against him. Hence the vengeance-satisfying proposition that "in time, all heals are wounded."

In both prospect and retrospect generous persons feel themselves the object of sympathy, esteem, and approbation by humankind and thereby are made conscious of their merit or deserved reward.

> The man who, not from frivolous fancy, but from proper motives, has performed a generous action, when he looks forward to those whom he has served, feels himself to be the natural object of their love and gratitude, and, by sympathy with them, of the esteem and approbation of all mankind. And when he looks backward to the motive from which he acted, and surveys it in the light in which the indifferent spectator will survey it, he still continues to enter into it, and applauds himself by sympathy with the approbation of this supposed impartial judge. In both these points of view, his own conduct appears to him every way agreeable. His mind, at the thought of it, is filled with cheerfulness, serenity, and composure. He is in friendship and harmony with all mankind, and looks upon his fellow-creatures with confidence, and benevolent satisfaction, secure that he has rendered himself worthy of their most favourable regards. In the combination of all these sentiments, consists the consciousness of merit, or of deserved reward. (*TMS*, p. 123)

They who perform properly motivated generous actions toward others can look forward to being the natural object of their love and gratitude. Because of the natural human capacity for sympathy, we are thereby in harmony with the esteem and approbation of humankind generally.

And when they who so act look back to survey their actions in the light of a fair, cool, and impartial spectator, they will continue to see their actions as consistent with that of an impartial judge—agreeable, and therefore in friendship and harmony with all humankind, an enduring source of cheerfulness, serenity, and composure. These sentiments give life to one's consciousness of personal merit or deserved reward. They reflect our deepest desire to love and be loved.

Because society is necessary for people to subsist, nature adapted them to a social role supportive of a stable society.

> It is thus that man, who can subsist only in society, was fitted by nature to that situation for which he was made. All the members of human society stand in need of each other's assistance, and are likewise exposed to mutual injuries. Where the necessary assistance is reciprocally afforded from love, from gratitude, from friendship, and esteem, the society flourishes and is happy. All the different members of it are bound together by the agreeable bands of love and affection, and are, as it were, drawn to one common centre of mutual good offices.
>
> But though the necessary assistance should not be afforded from such generous and disinterested motives, though among the different members of the society there should be no mutual love and affection, the society, though less happy and agreeable, will not necessarily be dissolved. Society may subsist among different men, as among different merchants, from a sense of its utility, without any mutual love or affection; and though no man in it should owe any obligation, or be bound in gratitude to any other, it may still be upheld by a mercenary exchange of good offices according to an agreed valuation. (*TMS*, p. 124)

Although he is skeptical of utilitarian accounts of human social action, Smith's intention seems to be to allow for the possibility of a viable utilitarian alternative to his concept of Beneficence because, as we shall see in the next entry, there is no such viable alternative to his concept of Justice. Much later, in Part VII of *TMS*, he attributes to Thomas Hobbes the idea that we adopt a civil order and give authority to a civil magistrate in order to avoid a state of war:

> It is well known to have been the doctrine of Mr Hobbes, that a state of nature is a state of war; and that antecedent to the institution of civil government, there could be no safe or peaceable society among men. To preserve society…was to support civil government, and to destroy civil government, was the same thing as to put an end to society." Civil government thus depends essentially on "the obedience that is paid to the supreme magistrate." By this doctrine, self-preservation teaches us to follow the authority of the civil magistrate as otherwise "all government is at an end." "The laws of the civil magistrate, therefore, ought to be regarded as the sole ultimate standards of what was just and unjust, of what was right and wrong." (*TMS*, p. 467)

The *TMS* model insightfully establishes the reverse of this Hobbesian scenario. What actions are just or unjust, right or wrong, emerge as a community consensus prior to a civil magistrate. As populations of socialized individuals grew beyond small bands and tribes, continued development required more centralized authority, and thus a civil order of government was fashioned to better provide security from internal and external sources of injury. To be sure there were those with darker intent, explaining why government was sometimes the problem and not the solution. But pre-civil historical communities had routinely invoked natural resentments and corresponding punishments with built-in deterrence incentives that the civil magistrate was later called upon to support, which they have tended to do in Western democracies. Yet these have been marred by populist riots against black migration North during the WWI, and later eruptions in protest of police actions in Watts and recently in Minneapolis.

Justice is essential to society which cannot subsist among those ready always to hurt and injure one another.

> Society, however, cannot subsist among those who are at all times ready to hurt and injure one another. The moment that injury begins, the moment that mutual resentment and animosity take place, all the bands of it are broken asunder, and the different members of which it consisted, are, as it were, dissipated and scattered abroad by the violence and opposition of their discordant affections. If there is any society among robbers and murderers, they must at least, according to the trite observation, abstain from robbing and murdering one another. Beneficence, therefore, is less essential to the existence of society than justice. Society may subsist, though not in the most comfortable state, without beneficence; but the prevalence of injustice must utterly destroy it. (*TMS*, pp. 124–125)

Hence the important conclusion is that justice is more crucial to society than beneficence. But implicitly, justice is manifest as property in our bodies, its products, and in their investment in capital goods, which accounts for wealth creation. So, the flowering of beneficence is facilitated by, and dependent on, justice achieving minimal levels of harm.

While nature encourages humankind to reward acts of beneficence, she has not thought it necessary to use punishment to enforce its practice should it be neglected.

> But Though nature…exhorts mankind to acts of beneficence, by the pleasing consciousness of deserved reward, she has not thought it necessary to guard and enforce the practice of it by the terrors of merited punishment

> in case it should be neglected. It is the ornament which embellishes, not the foundation which supports the building, and which it was, therefore, sufficient to recommend, but by no means necessary to impose. Justice, on the contrary, is the main pillar that upholds the whole edifice. If it is removed, the great, the immense fabric of human society, that fabric which, to raise and support, seems, in this world, if I may say so, to have been the peculiar and darling care of nature, must in a moment crumble into atoms. In order to enforce the observation of justice, therefore, nature has implanted in the human breast that consciousness of ill desert, those terrors of merited punishment, which attend upon its violation, as the great safeguards of the association of mankind, to protect the weak, to curb the violent, and to chastise the guilty. Men, though naturally sympathetic, feel so little for another, with whom they have no particular connection, in comparison of what they feel for themselves; the misery of one, who is merely their fellow-creature, is of so little importance to them in comparison even of a small conveniency of their own; they have it so much in their power to hurt him, and may have so many temptations to do so, that if this principle did not stand up within them in his defence, and overawe them into a respect for his innocence, they would, like wild beasts, be at all times ready to fly upon him; and a man would enter an assembly of men as he enters a den of lions. (*TMS*, pp. 125–126)

Beneficence is the ornament that pleases and embellishes the best things in life. But without justice, as security from intentional or careless injury, the seeds of beneficence fall on barren ground with no pathway to flower. Therefore, let justice reign, keeping uppermost that without it, beneficence is just a hollow promise of unattainable good. The modern illusion that justice is entirely about distributional outcomes, leaves bad things only to find their origin in bad people, the heart and soul of pessimism. It is the modern error that *TMS* sought to guard against because it is neither accurate nor grounds for inspiring optimism in people's natural ability to overcome. It cannot account for the survival and persistence of Western democracies in the face of repeated insults both domestic and foreign. Smith is always about the science of prediction and of confronting it with cases, viz "experiments." But he was also always concerned as to what conduct was moral, right, and to be followed. What was best for society was best for the individual and vice versa.

In the harmonious motion of all matter, we distinguish means from their final ends; yet in accounting for natural order in society we are likely to attribute its harmony to our conscious reason.

> In every part of the universe we observe means adjusted with the nicest artifice to the ends which they are intended to produce; and in the mechanism of a plant, or animal body, admire how every thing is contrived for advancing the two great purposes of nature, the support of the individual, and the propagation of the species. But in these, and in all such objects, we still distinguish the efficient from the final cause of their several motions and organizations. The digestion of the food, the circulation of the blood, and the secretion of the several juices which are drawn from it, are operations all of them necessary for the great purposes of animal life. Yet we never endeavour to account for them from those purposes as from their efficient causes, nor imagine that the blood circulates, or that the food digests of its own accord, and with a view or intention to the purposes of circulation or digestion. The wheels of the watch are all admirably adjusted to the end for which it was made, the pointing of the hour. All their various motions conspire in the nicest manner to produce this effect. If they were endowed with a desire and intention to produce it, they could not do it better. Yet we never ascribe any such desire or intention to them, but to the watch-maker, and we know that they are put into motion by a spring, which intends the effect it produces as little as they do. But though, in accounting for the operations of bodies, we never fail to distinguish in this manner the efficient from the final cause, in accounting for those of the mind, we are very apt to confound these two different things with one another. When by natural principles we are led to advance those ends which a refined and enlightened reason would recommend to us, we are very apt to impute to that reason, as to their efficient cause, the sentiments and actions by which we advance those ends, and to imagine that to be the wisdom of man, which in reality is the wisdom of God. Upon a superficial view, this cause seems sufficient to produce the effects which are ascribed to it; and the system of human nature seems to be more simple and agreeable, when all its different operations are in this manner deduced from a single principle. (*TMS*, pp. 126–127)

In “the two great purposes of nature, the support of the individual, and the propagation of the species” Smith states succinctly his evolutionary theory of nature manifest in culture, which, is completely modern in its essence yet far more sophisticated than a mere selfish gene, itself only a manifestation of utilitarianism in nature.

Smith also articulates his essential distinction between the origins (or “final cause”) of action and the consequences of action. Physical systems, the motions of the planets, solid bodies, and particles such as the electron, all follow systematic laws that boggle our imaginations, but we do not attribute agency, or intentionality, to them. It is another matter for human systems of order in neighborhood, community, society, economy, and nation. Surely, some believe, these were part of human design, the work of some remote genius, or in antiquity of a prophet like Moses who received them from God on the mountain. People everywhere have a need to explain, find meaning in who we are. We are so insatiably curious that we defied God, ate the apple, and found knowledge. Thus, did we find in knowledge of ourselves both the best of the good and the worst of the evil, but above all we found order in the bottom-up voluntary rules that we fashion as we follow them. That process allows us to recover from the consequences of the worst of our sins but that is a narrow path and broad are the wide ways to oblivion.

Humans found and have benefitted from diversity in nature long, long, before our contemporaries, some of whom can't shut up about their current simplistic negative versions of it.

The efficiency of an orderly society is a consequence of the rules of justice we learn to follow, not its cause.

> As society cannot subsist unless the laws of justice are tolerably observed, as no social intercourse can take place among men who do not generally abstain from injuring one another; the consideration of this necessity, it has been thought, was the ground upon which we approved of the enforcement of the laws of justice, by the punishment of those who violated them. Man, it has been said, has a natural love for society, and desires that the union of mankind should be preserved for its own sake, and though he himself was to derive no benefit from it. The orderly and flourishing state of society is agreeable to him, and he takes delight in contemplating it. Its disorder and confusion, on the contrary, is the object of his aversion, and he is chagrined at whatever tends to produce it. He is sensible, too, that his own interest is connected with the prosperity of society, and that the happiness, perhaps the preservation of his existence, depends upon its preservation. Upon every account, therefore, he has an abhorrence at whatever can tend to destroy society, and is willing to make use of every means, which can hinder so hated and so dreadful an event. Injustice necessarily tends to destroy it. Every appearance of injustice, therefore, alarms him, and he runs, if I may say so, to stop the progress of what, if allowed to go on, would quickly put an end to every thing that is dear to him. If he cannot restrain it by gentle and fair means, he must bear it down by force and violence, and at any rate must put a stop to its further progress.

> Hence it is, they say, that he often approves of the enforcement of the laws of justice, even by the capital punishment of those who violate them. The disturber of the public peace is hereby removed out of the world, and others are terrified by his fate from imitating his example. (*TMS*, pp. 127–128)

And thus, is reaffirmed the human pretense and propensity to attribute reason and fine deliberative public intentions and planning to anything that works, however little we understand it and however so autonomically and unthinkingly we act to follow rules of order that have created it.

Nor do we follow moral rules because they are a product of reason.

> Sometimes, too, we have occasion to defend the propriety of observing the general rules of justice, by the consideration of their necessity to the support of society. We frequently hear the young and the licentious ridiculing the most sacred rules of morality, and professing, sometimes from the corruption, but more frequently from the vanity of their hearts, the most abominable maxims of conduct. Our indignation rouses, and we are eager to refute and expose such detestable principles. But though it is their intrinsic hatefulness and detestableness which originally inflames us against them, we are unwilling to assign this as the sole reason why we condemn them, or to pretend that it is merely because we ourselves hate and detest them. The reason, we think, would not appear to be conclusive. Yet, why should it not; if we hate and detest them because they are the natural and proper objects of hatred and detestation? But when we are asked why we should not act in such or such a manner, the very question seems to suppose that, to those who ask it, this manner of acting does not appear to be for its own sake the natural and proper object of those sentiments. We must shew them, therefore, that it ought to be so for the sake of something else. Upon this account we generally cast about for other arguments, and the consideration which first occurs to us, is the disorder and confusion of society which would result from the universal prevalence of such practices. We seldom fail, therefore, to insist upon this topic. (*TMS*, pp. 128–129)

Are we to follow the opinions of those who claim to be self-less seekers of office who desire only to do good in our name and oppose evil by any name? The wise are skeptical of all such self-serving prescriptions that rely only on the proffered, reasoned, social compass of those who ask us to follow them.

Few have reflected on the necessity of justice for the existence of society.

> But though it commonly requires no great discernment to see the destructive tendency of all licentious practices to the welfare of society, it is seldom this consideration which first animates us against them. All men, even the most stupid and unthinking, abhor fraud, perfidy, and injustice, and delight to see them punished. But few men have reflected upon the necessity of justice to the existence of society, how obvious soever that necessity may appear to be. Such is the account commonly given of our approbation of the punishment of injustice. And so far this account is undoubtedly true, that we frequently have occasion to confirm our natural sense of the propriety and fitness of punishment, by reflecting how necessary it is for preserving the order of society. When the guilty is about to suffer that just retaliation, which the natural indignation of mankind tells them is due to his crimes; when the insolence of his injustice is broken and humbled by the terror of his approaching punishment; when he ceases to be an object of fear, with the generous and humane he begins to be an object of pity. The thought of what he is about to suffer extinguishes their resentment for the sufferings of others to which he has given occasion. They are disposed to pardon and forgive him, and to save him from that punishment, which in all their cool hours they had considered as the retribution due to such crimes. Here, therefore, they have occasion to call to their assistance the consideration of the general interest of society. They counterbalance the impulse of this weak and partial humanity, by the dictates of a humanity that is more generous and comprehensive. They reflect that mercy to the guilty is cruelty to the innocent, and oppose to the emotions of compassion which they feel for a particular person, a more enlarged compassion which they feel for mankind. (*TMS*, p. 129)

But how effective and efficient is the criminal justice system in providing security from injury by preventing "licentious practices?" According to one report, bail bond reduction in New York, in 2020, was associated with increased theft.[2]

It is said to be controversial as to how bail bond reform has impacted theft in California, Illinois, and New York. But there is a Brookings study of the enormous economic opportunity cost of pretrial detention that

[2] Lehman, Charles Fain (2022).
"Yes, New York's Bail Reform Has Increased Crime. New data prove it." *City Journal*, September. https://www.city-journal.org/new-yorks-bail-reform-has-increased-crime.

strongly suggests the need for some kind of reform.[3] It mentions the following in its abstract, which I include here to provide you with more context:

> Two thirds of the jail population and one quarter of the total incarcerated population consist of pretrial detainees. These shares have risen over time, fueling questions about the impacts of pretrial detention and the system of monetary bail that largely governs it. New research indicates that pretrial detention has a substantially negative economic impact on individuals, disrupting their labor market activities and causing increased recidivism. In addition to summarizing this research, we characterize key trends in pretrial detention and the bail system: increasing use of money bail, increasing time from arrest to adjudication, and rising median bail requirements, all of which have occurred across major offense categories. We conclude by discussing costs and benefits of money bail and the bail bonds industry.[4]

Incarceration rates have been enormously increased by the policy war on drugs.[5]

Under the principle that murder, theft, and robbery are resented by the victims, and criminal by approbation, Smith observes that "mercy to the guilty is cruelty to the innocent." In the war on drugs, the possessors of drugs were deemed criminal with so many imprisoned under that law that those guilty of only petty theft and robbery are released on bail pending a prison vacancy. Hence, the trend among states of leniency toward mere drug possession, a modern version of prohibition repeal to reduce incarceration. Society cannot declare any criminal form of voluntary exchange without generating insurmountable obstacles to enforcement. Better models of control are those governing alcohol and tobacco which forbid sales to minors and use warning labels. Society,

[3] Liu, Patrick, Ryan Nunn, and Jay Shambaugh (2018) "The economics of bail and pretrial detention." *Brookings*, December 19. https://www.brookings.edu/research/the-economics-of-bail-and-pretrial-detention/.

[4] Liu, Patrick, Ryan Nunn, and Jay Shambaugh (2018) "The economics of bail and pretrial detention." *Brookings*, December 19. https://www.brookings.edu/research/the-economics-of-bail-and-pretrial-detention/.

[5] American Association of Family Practitioners Incarceration and Health (2022) "A Family Medicine Perspective (Position Paper)." AAFP, January.https://www.aafp.org/about/policies/all/incarceration.html.

therefore, registers its consensus view that a substance ought not to be consumed, but to do so is not criminal.

Intellectually, we occasionally defend the rules of justice because of their necessity to the support of society, but the real reason is that we hate and despise acts of injustice.

> Sometimes, too, we have occasion to defend the propriety of observing the general rules of justice, by the consideration of their necessity to the support of society. We frequently hear the young and the licentious ridiculing the most sacred rules of morality, and professing, sometimes from the corruption, but more frequently from the vanity of their hearts, the most abominable maxims of conduct. Our indignation rouses, and we are eager to refute and expose such detestable principles. But though it is their intrinsic hatefulness and detestableness which originally inflames us against them, we are unwilling to assign this as the sole reason why we condemn them, or to pretend that it is merely because we ourselves hate and detest them. The reason, we think, would not appear to be conclusive. Yet, why should it not; if we hate and detest them because they are the natural and proper objects of hatred and detestation? But when we are asked why we should not act in such or such a manner, the very question seems to suppose that, to those who ask it, this manner of acting does not appear to be for its own sake the natural and proper object of those sentiments. We must shew them, therefore, that it ought to be so for the sake of something else. Upon this account we generally cast about for other arguments, and the consideration which first occurs to us, is the disorder and confusion of society which would result from the universal prevalence of such practices. We seldom fail, therefore, to insist upon this topic. (*TMS*, pp. 129–130)

In defending the use of punishment to deter criminal acts, we resort to the argument that in their absence society would face disorder and confusion. However, in our ancestral history, we applied forms of victim compensation as the basis for punishment, through the assistance of the authorities when governments were weak. Because the goal of deterring future crimes helped not at all in dealing with the pain of a current crime, the local resources of family and friends of the offender were marshaled to compensate those of the victim in some way alleviating, while avenging for, the suffering. But the administration of victim compensation by the modern centralized state seems beyond practical consideration, especially given that the resources of the courts and police have been overwhelmed in the failed attempt to enforce the criminality of recreational drug consumption. The current political trend toward state liberalization of marijuana consumption opens the promise of some reversal of this failed costly strategy.

We abhor injustice as destructive, but it is seldom this consideration which first animates us against them.

> [T]hough it commonly requires no great discernment to see the destructive tendency of all licentious practices to the welfare of society, it is seldom this consideration which first animates us against them. All men, even the most stupid and unthinking, abhor fraud, perfidy, and injustice, and delight to see them punished. But few men have reflected upon the necessity of justice to the existence of society, how obvious soever that necessity may appear to be. (*TMS*, p. 129)

Contemporary attitudes reveal a lack of serious reflection on the concept of justice as security from injury. Rather, the emphasis is on justice as a concern for "fair" outcomes, which, in *TMS* is the exclusive concern of beneficence not of justice. In contemporary social and political interpretation, no meaningful distinction is made between justice and beneficence—only justice matters. Thus, it is just and proper that the "rich" give to the "poor." The incoherence of policy is matched with the muddled thinking from which it sprung. A just society is represented as concerned only with policies providing a more equal distribution of gains, a proposition that, in *WN* and contemporary economic analysis, is found to reduce wealth unless public and private poverty programs are directed toward helping the poor help themselves via increasing their value—labor and products—to others, which is the historical practiced means for increasing wealth through markets.

Exchange improves your return only in so far as it improves that of others. An individual's mere existence is insufficient to assure a living. All those of able body and mind must give to receive and to receive benefit at least in proportion to their giving. You observe this in friendly neighborhoods and communities in which favors done for another, are approved via the approbation of others, and generate a return from multiple agents greater than that given.

Similarly, in markets, prices reveal active buyers willing to pay at least the amounts paid and active sellers willing to accept at least the amounts received. The publicity of these prices then empowers people to make decisions that better themselves through their choice of work, goods, and services.

Insofar as innovation increases the productivity of labor by reducing the unit cost of the goods and services labor produces, consumers and producers benefit. If the productivity increases come from artificial intelligence nothing in principle is changed. The increase in product value or decrease in product cost is due to the action of the individual or firm that found or used the artificial intelligence that functioned better than the alternatives available. That individual or firm will collect the profits made possible by the discovery. Thus, algorithms enabling passengers and drivers to be matched in real time and space have greatly benefited passenger services and drivers who better utilize their work and automobile capacity by self-employing both as little or as much as they voluntarily choose.

Our impulse to punish crime arises not from a need to preserve society but from our fellow-feelings of resentment and the impulse to punish the deliberately hurtful actions of others, giving cause for the emergent societal rules governing hurtful actions that are society-preserving.

> That it is not a regard to the preservation of society, which originally interests us in the punishment of crimes committed against individuals, may be demonstrated by many obvious considerations. The concern which we take in the fortune and happiness of individuals, does not, in common cases, arise from that which we take in the fortune and happiness of society. We are no more concerned for the destruction or loss of a single man, because this man is a member or part of society, and because we should be concerned for the destruction of society, than we are concerned for the loss of a single guinea, because this guinea is part of a thousand guineas, and because we should be concerned for the loss of the whole sum. In neither case does our regard for the individuals arise from our regard for the multitude; but in both cases our regard for the multitude is compounded and made up of the particular regards which we feel for the different individuals of which it is composed. As when a small sum is unjustly taken from us, we do not so much prosecute the injury from a regard to the preservation of our whole fortune, as from a regard to that particular sum which we have lost; so when a single man is injured, or destroyed, we demand the punishment of the wrong that has been done to him, not so much from a concern for the general interest of society, as from a concern for that

> very individual who has been injured. It is to be observed, however, that this concern does not necessarily include in it any degree of those exquisite sentiments which are commonly called love, esteem, and affection, and by which we distinguish our particular friends and acquaintances. The concern which is requisite for this, is no more than the general fellow-feeling which we have with every man, merely because he is our fellow-creature. We enter into the resentment even of an odious person, when he is injured by those to whom he has given no provocation. Our disapprobation of his ordinary character and conduct does not in this case altogether prevent our fellow-feeling with his natural indignation; though with those who are not either extremely candid, or who have not been accustomed to correct and regulate their natural sentiments by general rules, it is very apt to damp it. (*TMS*, pp. 129–30)

It is not from a concern for the welfare or general interest of society that we want to punish crimes against individuals, but from our sympathy and particular fellow-feeling toward that individual victim who has been harmed. We naturally enter and relate to the victim's distress and feelings of resentment toward the person who has acted harmfully toward this other. If we have respect and sympathy for a whole community or nation it is because we have respect and sympathy for certain individuals who are part of that whole.

We know someone that we trust, a result growing from our personal experience, who has, nevertheless, broken the law, but we are far from judging them as a lawbreaker. Trust serves to dampen the escalation of resentment and its urge to lash out in punishment for the hurtful action. Trust has its origin in the good-hearted intentional actions of someone and their propensity to reward such actions by others.

In acquiring a sense of what is best for the multitude, our opinion involves the compounding of our sense of sympathy toward the individuals who make up the society. We will think well of the Scotch, the Belgians, and the Chinese if we have had pleasant experiences with individuals from those countries—experiences in which they help others and are attentive in rewarding those who help them.

The same considerations apply to the formation of our attitude toward organizations and companies.

In 1964 I bought a new International Harvester all-wheel drive Scout in Lafayette, Indiana where I was employed at Purdue. I vacationed with it that summer in Southeastern Utah and Southwestern Colorado, negotiating the many "Jeep" trails in that region. But my Scout had an operating problem: On very steep upgrades the vehicle surged intermittently with black smoke emitted from the exhaust, consistent with a too-rich fuel mixture.

Upon returning home I drove to the IHC dealer who had sold me the Scout. Instead of learning from my experience, they doubted that it could be true because the IHC so thoroughly tested their vehicles in their test facility in Arizona—no problem-solving satisfaction there. So, I went to the library, found out who was the President of IHC, and wrote him a letter describing my experience. He answered in a return post, thanking me for alerting him to the problem, and stating that a regional engineering representative of IHC would be in contact with me to deal with the issue.

I soon heard from the regional engineer, and we arranged a meeting at the local IHC dealer. On site, they had a truck with an adjustable flatbed that they raised to a steep incline, according to my instruction, and I drove up the inclined truck bed. The Scout's engine started to surge then cut out, surge again. We had just the right test platform. It was an educational experience for the local dealer who had been simply making up the facts to avoid engagement. And for me, I was learning about the competence of the IHC upper management and their eagerness to engage.

My experience would get better.

I next received a call from the Holley Carburetor representative who was full time with the IHC plant in Ft Wayne, Indiana. He knew precisely what my problem was and suggested we meet at the local IHC retail facility. There, he lifted my Scout's engine hood showing me that the fuel intake line is attached to the rear of the carburetor. Hence, in a steep upgrade the carburetor bowl tilts up, the fuel level tilts down, the float attached to the intake valve opens, excess fuel enters, and the fuel/air vapor ratio increases, causing a too-rich mixture to enter the cylinders with ensuing black exhaust smoke and erratic power delivery to the wheels.

He explained that he had been trying to get IHC to buy a new carburetor with fuel intake from the side. That would work because no idiot is going to drive horizontally on such a steep incline and risk a rollover. But IHC was balking because it would add $50 to the cost of the Carburetor. I immediately realized that he and I had a common interest. My case would help him sell IHC a different carburetor, and he would solve my problem, which he was eager to do. He said he was working on a redesigned carburetor with a spring-loaded needle valve that would resist opening when the carburetor was tilted. There is no proving-ground substitute for customer feedback from the thousands who buy a vehicle. He would prepare such a carburetor for me and install it. He indicated that if it did not work, he could always install an adapter, enabling him to turn my carburetor 180 degrees so that the problem only occurs in backing up a steep incline which I rarely had occasion to do.

A few weeks later he had everything ready, and I drove up to Ft Wayne. He installed his custom-designed carburetor and we drove out to a local sand pit with steeply inclined sides and our test of the redesigned carburetor failed; we still had the intermittent fuel flow problem. So, he now implemented plan two. He installed his adapter and turned the carburetor 180 degrees. In the sand pit, it worked beautifully in forward motion but in reverse we had engine hiccups. I was satisfied because I had the only Scout in the world that could go forward up a steep incline.

In 1972, I bought a new Scout II model after lifting the hood and noting that the fuel intake was at the side of the carburetor. It felt good that I had helped IHC solve a significant problem. But I kept the old scout, likely still the only one in the world that performs smoothly up a steep incline. And I became a fan of IHC whose management was into problem-solving and customer satisfaction. But unfortunately, they encountered financial trouble, sold their farm machinery business and other divisions in 1985, and closed the Scout and light truck divisions, surviving as a leading commercial truck manufacturer renamed Navistar.[6]

[6] Volkswagen has recently acquired Navistar and reported that it is building a new Scout as an EV brand in the US: "VW has previously tried to break out of its niche to become a more significant brand in the U.S. Although it is the world's second-largest auto maker by sales behind Toyota Motor Corp., it commands a market share of less than 5% in the U.S.

Despite this modest footprint, VW's electric vehicles are selling faster than its conventional cars in the U.S. VW said it has around 8% of the U.S. EV market, second behind Tesla Inc….

From the 1960s until it stopped production in 1980, Scout was a fierce rival to Land Rover, Jeep, and the Ford Bronco….

VW acquired the rights to the Scout brand name with its acquisition of Navistar International Corp. in 2020. Navistar was created in 1985 when International Harvester, which owned the Scout brand, went out of business….VW plans to use the Scout brand name, which still inspires fan clubs and devoted collectors on social media…" Boston, William (2022) "Volkswagen Is Bringing Back the Scout, the SUV Pioneer, as an EV." *Wall Street Journal.* May 10. As Yogi would say, it's not over til' it's over.

On cases wherein punishment is based on the general interest of society.

> Upon some occasions, indeed, we both punish and approve of punishment, merely from a view to the general interest of society, which, we imagine, cannot otherwise be secured. Of this kind are all the punishments inflicted for breaches of what is called either civil police, or military discipline. Such crimes do not immediately or directly hurt any particular person; but their remote consequences, it is supposed, do produce, or might produce, either a considerable inconveniency, or a great disorder in the society. A sentinel, for example, who falls asleep upon his watch, suffers death by the laws of war, because such carelessness might endanger the whole army. This severity may, upon many occasions, appear necessary, and, for that reason, just and proper. When the preservation of an individual is inconsistent with the safety of a multitude, nothing can be more just than that the many should be preferred to the one. Yet this punishment…always appears to be excessively severe. The natural atrocity of the crime seems to be so little, and the punishment so great, that it is with great difficulty that our heart can reconcile itself to it. Though such carelessness appears very blameable, yet the thought of this crime does not naturally excite any such resentment, as would prompt us to take such dreadful revenge. A man of humanity must recollect himself, must make an effort, and exert his whole firmness and resolution, before he can bring himself either to inflict it, or to go along with it…It is not, however, in this manner, that he looks upon the just punishment of an ungrateful murderer or parricide. His heart, in this case, applauds with ardour, and even with transport, the just retaliation which seems due to such detestable crimes, and which, if, by any accident, they should happen to escape, he would be highly enraged and disappointed. The very different sentiments with which the spectator views those different punishments, is a proof that his approbation of the one is far from being founded upon the same principles with that of the other. He looks upon the sentinel as an unfortunate victim, who, indeed, must and ought to be devoted to the safety of numbers, but whom still, in his heart, he would be glad to save; and he is only sorry that the interest of the many should oppose it. But if the murderer should escape from punishment, it would excite his highest indignation, and he would call upon God to avenge, in another world, that crime which the injustice of mankind had neglected to chastise upon earth. (*TMS*, pp. 131–132)

There are occasions in which we observe a dereliction of duty with civil police or military service and thereby invoke capital punishment. Such is the case of an army sentinel who faces execution for falling asleep while on duty. By reason, we accept the logic that such action must be deterred. This sentinel, however, was a good person, husband, and father. Yet, he cannot be excused; the execution must go forward; otherwise, the punishment as a rule will be without credibility; and the trustworthiness of sentinels questioned. But there is no victim as in ordinary hurtful action by one person toward another where we naturally sympathize with the victim. This law, concerning the sentinel, has no victim, although potentially many. It commands not the same sympathetic resentment for them who are the victim of a crime, carelessly if unintentionally endangering others, as toward they who intentionally commit a crime against an individual. Indeed, we may see the sentinel as an unfortunate victim of his own failing, and regret that he must be held accountable for that failing and that his wife and children will suffer the loss of a husband and father. Smith's sentinel example insightfully serves to illustrate the dramatic difference between a punishment rule based on reason and one based on widely shared feelings of resentment for the hurtful actions of one person toward another. The example helps us to appreciate the power of ground-level voluntary learnt rules of propriety in accounting for the stability and durability of society.

From whence comes our desire that the punishment of injustice pursue the evil doer even unto the afterlife?

> [I]t well deserves to be taken notice of, that we are so far from imagining that injustice ought to be punished in this life, merely on account of the order of society, which cannot otherwise be maintained, that nature teaches us to hope, and religion, we suppose, authorizes us to expect, that it will be punished even in a life to come. Our sense of its ill desert pursues it…even beyond the grave, although the example of its punishment there cannot serve to deter the rest of mankind, who see it not, who know it not, from being guilty of the like practices here. The justice of God, however, we think, still requires that He should hereafter avenge the injuries of the widow and the fatherless, who are here so often insulted with impunity. In every religion, and in every superstition that the world has ever beheld, accordingly, there has been a Tartarus as well as an Elysium; a place provided for the punishment of the wicked, as well as one for the reward of the just. (*TMS*, pp. 132–133)

Although our concern that crimes be punished does not arise directly out of the principle that it preserves order in society, nature has not entirely abandoned us to a sense of purposelessness for the whole. Accordingly, nature teaches us to hope, while religion teaches us to expect, that wrongdoing will be judged and punished, and thereby avenged in the afterlife. Even the widow and orphans of the sentinel will find peace in that afterlife where every wrong is righted. Human law must be rule based. God's law is human—love and be loved—based. The most primitive of religious superstitions made provision for the punishment of wickedness and the reward of the just beyond our own deaths. Christians are urged to follow the commandments, for wide is the gate, and broad is the way, that leadeth to destruction, and many will find it, while narrow is the way which leadeth unto life, and only a few will find it.

PART VI

Section III: Of the influence of fortune upon the sentiments of mankind, with regard to the merit or demerit of actions

CHAPTER 21

Of the causes of the influence of fortune

A. The cause of irregularity in our sentiment.

The causes of pain and pleasure, whatever they are, or however they operate, seem to be the objects, which, in all animals, immediately excite those two passions of gratitude and resentment. They are excited by inanimated, as well as by animated objects. We are angry, for a moment, even at the stone that hurts us. A child beats it, a dog barks at it, a choleric man is apt to curse it. The least reflection, indeed, corrects this sentiment, and we soon become sensible, that what has no feeling is a very improper object of revenge. When the mischief, however, is very great, the object which caused it becomes disagreeable to us ever after, and we take pleasure to burn or destroy it. We should treat, in this manner, the instrument which had accidentally been the cause of the death of a friend, and we should often think ourselves guilty of a sort of inhumanity, if we neglected to vent this absurd sort of vengeance upon it.

We conceive, in the same manner, a sort of gratitude for those inanimated objects which have been the causes of great or frequent pleasure to us. The sailor, who, as soon as he got ashore, should mend his fire with the plank upon which he had just escaped from a shipwreck, would seem to be guilty of an unnatural action. We should expect that he would rather preserve it with care and affection, as a monument that was, in some measure, dear to him. A man grows fond of a snuff-box, of a pen-knife, of a staff which he has long made use of, and conceives something like a real love and affection for them. If he breaks or loses them, he is vexed out of all proportion to

Vernon L. Smith, *Adam Smith's Theory of Society*,
https://doi.org/10.1007/978-3-031-68494-4_21

the value of the damage. The house which we have long lived in, the tree whose verdure and shade we have long enjoyed, are both looked upon with a sort of respect that seems due to such benefactors. The decay of the one, or the ruin of the other, affects us with a kind of melancholy, though we should sustain no loss by it. The dryads and the lares of the ancients, a sort of genii of trees and houses, were probably first suggested by this sort of affection which the authors of those superstitions felt for such objects, and which seemed unreasonable, if there was nothing animated about them. (*TMS*, pp. 136–137)

So sensitized are we to the principle that the action that hurts us deserves to be punished that we unwittingly strike back at the beam on which we accidentally bumped our head—curse this thing that was in my way. In *TMS* this provides evidence for our rule-following nature, including impromptu but critical fight-or-flight responses where deliberation would be catastrophic. Objects of lasting use and comfort to us—a custom-made wristwatch band that has survived several watches, a treasured walking stick—may become objects of deep affection that we anxiously guard against loss.

B. The object of gratitude or resentment must be capable of feeling pleasure or pain.

[B]efore any thing can be the proper object of gratitude or resentment, it must not only be the cause of pleasure or pain; it must likewise be capable of feeling them. Without this other quality, those passions cannot vent themselves with any sort of satisfaction upon it. As they are excited by the causes of pleasure and pain, so their gratification consists in retaliating those sensations upon what gave occasion to them; which it is to no purpose to attempt upon what has no sensibility. Animals, therefore, are less improper objects of gratitude and resentment than inanimated objects. The dog that bites, the ox that gores, are both of them punished…nor is this merely for the security of the living, but, in some measure, to revenge the injury of the dead. Those animals, on the contrary, that have been remarkably serviceable to their masters, become the objects of a very lively gratitude. But, though animals are not only the causes of pleasure and pain, but are also capable of feeling those sensations they are still far from being complete and perfect objects either of gratitude or resentment; and those passions still feel, that there is something wanting to their entire gratification. (*TMS*, p. 137)

If the emotions of gratitude or resentment are to have their full impact on individuals and their society, in properly and efficiently reinforcing the actions of reward and punishment, the participant observers must be capable of these sentiments and feelings. Humans are paramount relative to other animals in this regard.

C. The greater purpose or design in the rules of beneficence and justice is for every person who is the object of praise or blame to be made to feel that it was their conduct that required reward or deserved punishment.

> What gratitude chiefly desires is not only to make the benefactor feel pleasure in his turn, but to make him conscious that he meets with this reward on account of past conduct, to make him pleased with that conduct, and to satisfy him that the person upon whom he bestowed his good offices was not unworthy of them. What most of all charms us in our benefactor, is the concord between his sentiments and our own…We are delighted to find a person who values us as we value ourselves, and distinguishes us from the rest of mankind, with an attention not unlike that with which we distinguish ourselves...A generous mind often disdains the interested thought of extorting new favours from its benefactor, by what may be called the importunities of its gratitude. But to preserve and to increase his esteem, is an interest which the greatest mind does not think unworthy of its attention…when we cannot enter into the motives of our benefactor, when his conduct and character appear unworthy of our approbation, yet his services have been ever so great, our gratitude is always sensibly diminished… The object, on the contrary, which resentment is chiefly intent upon, is not so much to make our enemy feel pain in his turn, as to make him conscious that he feels it upon account of his past conduct, to make him repent of that conduct, and to make him sensible, that the person whom he injured did not deserve to be treated in that manner. What chiefly enrages us against the man who injures or insults us, is the little account which he seems to make of us…The glaring impropriety of this conduct, the gross insolence and injustice which it seems to involve in it, often shock and exasperate us more than all the mischief which we have suffered. To bring him back to a more just sense of what is due to other people, to make him sensible of what he owes us, and of the wrong that he has done to us, is frequently the principal end proposed in our revenge…When our enemy appears to have done us no injury, when we are sensible that he acted quite properly, that, in his situation, we should have done the same thing, and that we deserved from him all the mischief we met with; in that case, if we

> have the least spark either of candour or justice, we can entertain no sort of resentment. (*TMS*, pp. 138–139)

Gratitude is a natural response by a person who has received a favor from a benefactor who recognizes that the person is worthy of their good offices. What chiefly pleases us all is the natural harmony between the benefactors' sentiments and ours. The social betterment purpose of gratitude is to make all benefactors conscious that they meet with spontaneous socially based rewards, because of their past conduct, to make them pleased with that conduct, and to satisfy them that the person whom they favored was judged worthy of their good action. The urge to reward reinforces the judgment and the worth of the benefactor's action. As we saw in Parable of the Trash Barrel (Chapter 19), the sense of a required reward for acts of good neighborliness encourages and fosters good neighbors.

Likewise, the social function of resentment is not simply to make the wrongdoer feel the pain of punishment but to make them conscious that they feel it because of their past unacceptable conduct, to make them repent of that conduct, and to sensible that the person who was injured did not deserve such treatment. Therefore, does society, through bottom-up individual action, safeguard innocence by deterring injurious acts.

The exception—not available to Smith's careful research, concerns the sociopath. For beneficent actions, sociopaths are less likely to return the favor, and will thereby tend to be self-isolated from the company of social others. For hurtful actions, they are less likely to be deterred or corrected by punishment. Since sociopaths are super-proportionally represented among incarcerated offenders, their societal isolation is not so much justified as correctional, as for the protection of the general law-abiding population.

Being isolated from society, prison inmates generally are also isolated from free entry-exit disciplinary interactions of markets for the sale of labor and the purchase of consumption goods. Hence, food, clothing, utilities, and shelter are imposed in equal available amounts for all. A prison is a truly egalitarian mini society. Suppose, instead, that only the barest minimum of these comforts was equally supplied for all. Those desiring to purchase these amenities in greater than minimal amounts would work at whatever wages their skill levels commanded, using the proceeds to buy better comfort levels or to accumulate savings to take with them when released.

Having withdrawn from private labor markets they would merely be reentering but private business is likely to be hostile to their competitive reentry. Hence, the challenge of all such top-down policies. The achievements of that which enters by approbation from social origins cannot be attained by imposition from above.

In conclusion summary

> Before any thing...can be the complete and proper object, either of gratitude or resentment, it must possess three different qualifications.
> First, it must be the cause of pleasure in the one case and of pain in the other. Secondly, it must be capable of feeling those sensations.
> And, thirdly, it must not only have produced those sensations, but it must have produced them from design, and from a design that is approved of in the one case and disapproved of in the other. It is by the first qualification that any object is capable of exciting those passions: it is by the second, that it is in any respect capable of gratifying them: the third qualification is not only necessary for their complete satisfaction, but, as it gives a pleasure or pain that is both exquisite and peculiar, it is likewise an additional exciting cause of those passions. (*TMS*, pp. 139)

Smith thus states the necessary conditions for the emotions of gratitude and resentment to serve the betterment of a voluntary human society. He then argues that its success may be mixed, because our judgment of intentions is biased in favor of the outcomes that are in fact experienced, which may be a consequence of an intentional action combined with a random event that distorts the incidence of the intended reward or punishment. Noise would thus distort the signal.

If an actor fails to produce the good or the evil intended, then less gratitude or resentment is due to their action.

> As what gives pleasure or pain, therefore, either in one way or another, is the sole exciting cause of gratitude and resentment; though the intentions of any person should be ever so proper and beneficent, on the one hand, or ever so improper and malevolent on the other; yet, if he has failed in producing either the good or the evil which he intended, as one of the exciting causes is wanting in both cases, less gratitude seems due to him in the one, and less resentment in the other. And, on the contrary, though in the intentions of any person, there was either no laudable degree of

> benevolence on the one hand, or no blameable degree of malice on the other; yet, if his actions should produce either great good or great evil, as one of the exciting causes takes place upon both these occasions, some gratitude is apt to arise towards him in the one, and some resentment in the other. A shadow of merit seems to fall upon him in the first, a shadow of demerit in the second. And, as the consequences of actions are altogether under the empire of fortune, hence arises her influence upon the sentiments of mankind with regard to merit and demerit. (*TMS*, pp. 139–140)

Nature teaches that it is the conjunction of intentions and the quality of that which is actually delivered that justifies the full expression of gratitude or resentment. If an action fails to yield either the good or the evil that was intended, then less gratitude seems due to the benefactor, or less resentment is due to the offender, than otherwise. Where the final good or evil that was intended fails, due to the intervening empire of chance, then it diminishes the merit or demerit of humankind's sentiment toward the actor. The chance of failure to deliver the full promise of the design compromises the full expression of gratitude and resentment. However, as *TMS* pushes further into this important topic, the propositions yield less predictive success. Smith's motivation is to fully flesh out his theory which is methodologically highly to be desired for if any of the downstream propositions fail, we learn more about where and what in the theory was on track, or not. It is what every experimentalist wants and rejoices to see in any theory he is attempting to test.

CHAPTER 22

Of the extent of this influence of fortune

Further examination of the circumstances and consequences, due to chance, in which intentions fail to benefit or hurt another.

Experimental Tests Fail to Confirm the Extended Predictions

> [T]hough the intentions of any person should be ever so proper and beneficent on the one hand, or ever so improper or malevolent on the other, yet, if they fail [due to the vagaries of "chance"] in producing their effects, his merit seems imperfect in the one case, and his demerit incomplete in the other. Nor is this irregularity of sentiment felt only by those who are immediately affected by the consequences of any action. It is felt, in some measure, even by the impartial spectator. The man who solicits an office for another, without obtaining it, is regarded as his friend, and seems to deserve his love and affection. But the man who not only solicits, but procures it, is more peculiarly considered as his patron and benefactor, and is entitled to his respect and gratitude. The person obliged…may with some justice, imagine himself on a level with the first: but we cannot enter into his sentiments, if he does not feel himself inferior to the second. It is common indeed to say, that we are equally obliged to the man who has endeavoured to serve us, as to him who actually did so. It is the speech which we constantly make upon every unsuccessful attempt of this kind; but which, like all other fine speeches, must be understood with a grain of allowance...When they lose those advantages…they seem to lose but a

Vernon L. Smith, *Adam Smith's Theory of Society*,
https://doi.org/10.1007/978-3-031-68494-4_22

> trifle, which is scarce worth regarding. They still, however, lose something. Their pleasure, therefore, and consequently their gratitude, is not perfectly complete: and accordingly, if between the friend who fails, and the friend who succeeds, all other circumstances are equal, there will, even in the noblest and best mind, be some little difference of affection in favour of him who succeeds. Nay, so unjust are mankind in this respect, that though the intended benefit should be procured, yet if it is not procured by the means of a particular benefactor, they are apt to think that less gratitude is due to the man, who with the best intentions in the world could do no more than help it a little forward. As their gratitude is in this case divided among the different persons who contributed to their pleasure, a smaller share of it seems due to any one. Such a person, we hear men commonly say, intended no doubt to serve us; and we really believe exerted himself to the utmost of his abilities for that purpose. We are not, however, obliged to him for this benefit; since, had it not been for the concurrence of others, all that he could have done would never have brought it about. This consideration, they imagine, should even in the eyes of the impartial spectator diminish the debt which they owe to him. The person himself who has unsuccessfully endeavoured to confer a benefit, has by no means the same dependency upon the gratitude of the man whom he meant to oblige, nor the same sense of his own merit towards him, which he would have had in the case of success. (*TMS*, pp. 141–143)

Where a friend solicits an office and fails, while another succeeds, may illustrate the potential mixing of pure chance with elements of skill. The successful case may reflect a comparative skill edge. Important laboratory experiments control for any skill effects by examining the effect of reversing the first movers' intended outcome with "pure" probability 0.25. Second movers respond at rates approximately the same as when offers to cooperate are known to be intended, giving first movers the benefit of the doubt concerning intentions known to be unreliable in 25% of the cases. It seems that these responders to cooperative offers may be somewhat concerned not to discourage favorable social behavior if it was intended. The empirical laboratory finding that the actor tends to be favored with the benefit of the doubt, functions to serve as an additional source of social stability overlooked in *TMS*. It appears consistent with a bias toward optimism and against pessimism.[1]

[1] Cox, James C. and Cary A. Deck (2006) "Assigning Intentions When Actions Are Unobservable: The Impact of Trembling in the Trust Game." *Southern Economic Journal* Vol. 73, No. 2 (October), pp. 307–314.

Unintended error in skillful plans, executions, and results, diminish praise or blame.

> Even the merit of talents and abilities which some accident has hindered from producing their effects, seems in some measure imperfect, even to those who are fully convinced of their capacity to produce them. The general who has been hindered by the envy of ministers from gaining some great advantage over the enemies of his country, regrets the loss of the opportunity for ever after....He laments that he was hindered from performing an action which would have added a new lustre to his character in his own eyes, as well as in those of every other person. It satisfies neither himself nor others to reflect that the plan or design was all that depended on him...He still did not execute it; and though he might deserve all the approbation which is due to a magnanimous and great design, he still wanted the actual merit of having performed a great action.... It mortifies an architect when his plans are either not executed at all, or when they are so far altered as to spoil the effect of the building. The plan, however, is all that depends upon the architect. The whole of his genius is, to good judges, as completely discovered in that as in the actual execution. But a plan does not, even to the most intelligent, give the same pleasure as a noble and magnificent building...the amusement derived from the first never approaches to the wonder and admiration which are sometimes excited by the second...The superiority of virtues and talents has not, even upon those who acknowledge that superiority, the same effect with the superiority of achievements. (*TMS*, pp. 143–144)

Achievement is what humankind is most willing to praise or blame, and they do not afford similar recognition of the design only, however well-constructed and planned. The proposition is captured, as well as verified, in the ancient adage that: "The proof of the pudding is in the eating." Adages reveal much about the rules followed by the speakers of a language, as we saw in "debt of gratitude" and with Smith's contemporary, Booby Burns: "O wad some Power the giftie gie us To see oursels as ithers see us! It wad frae mony a blunder free us, An' foolish notion: What airs in dress an' gait wad lea'e us, An' ev'n devotion!"

Smith, in this example, cleanly illustrates his consistent methodology that the propositional implications of a theory must be rich enough to allow the theory's error properties to be spelled out and evaluated. Hence, if the theory fails a test, one can ask and explore which of its conditions were responsible for its failure.

In markets, consumers commonly do not ask what went into a product they like, as they are the judges that count on their willingness to pay for its output. However, since ingredients can be dangerous, consumer protection has focused on truth-in-labeling and non-deceptive advertising. The Food and Drug Administration (1906) was a government move to replace Caveat emptor, the buyer beware rule, with new government-sanctioned rules, as the only needed criteria. But the principal long-term private forces at work to assure quality are still to be found in reputation and branding, while shorter-term forces have emerged via independent testing organizations, e.g., *Consumer Reports*. Nor can the resources of government predict frost in the Florida orange groves as effectively as the Florida Orange Juice Futures. Information on key uncertain events is fundamentally dispersed widely; private markets effectively filter and aggregate that information. Government by its nature, cannot and does not.

Treason excepted, the design to commit crime is never punished so severely as its actual commission.

> The design to commit a crime, how clearly soever it be proved, is scarce ever punished with the same severity as the actual commission of it. The case of treason is perhaps the only exception. That crime immediately affecting the being of the government itself, the government is naturally more jealous of it than of any other. In the punishment of treason, the sovereign resents the injuries which are immediately done to himself: in the punishment of other crimes, he resents those which are done to other men. It is his own resentment which he indulges in the one case: it is that of his subjects which by sympathy he enters into in the other. In the first case, therefore, as he judges in his own cause, he is very apt to be more violent and sanguinary [involving or causing much bloodshed] in his punishments than the impartial spectator can approve of. His resentment too rises here upon smaller occasions, and does not always, as in other cases, wait for the perpetration of the crime, or even for the attempt to commit it. A treasonable concert, though nothing has been done, or even attempted in consequence of it, nay, a treasonable conversation, is in many countries punished in the same manner as the actual commission of treason. With regard to all other crimes, the mere design, upon which no attempt has followed, is seldom punished at all, and is never punished severely. A criminal design, and a criminal action, it be said, indeed, do not necessarily suppose the same degree of depravity, and ought not therefore to be subjected to the same punishment. We are capable, it

> be said, of resolving, and even of taking measures to execute, many things which, when it comes to the point, we feel ourselves altogether incapable of executing. But this reason can have no place when the design has been carried the length of the last attempt. The man, however, who fires a pistol at his enemy but misses him, is punished with death by the laws of scarce any country. By the old law of Scotland, though he should wound him, yet, unless death ensues within a certain time, the assassin is not liable to the last punishment. The resentment of mankind, however, runs so high against this crime, their terror for the man who shews himself capable of committing it, is so great, that the mere attempt to commit it ought in all countries to be capital. The attempt to commit smaller crimes is almost always punished very lightly, and sometimes is not punished at all. The thief, whose hand has been caught in his neighbour's pocket before he had taken any thing out of it, is punished with ignominy only. If he had got time to take away a handkerchief, he would have been put to death. The house-breaker, who has been found setting a ladder to his neighbour's window, but had not got into it, is not exposed to the capital punishment. The attempt to ravish is not punished as a rape. The attempt to seduce a married woman is not punished at all, though seduction is punished severely. Our resentment against the person who only attempted to do a mischief, is seldom so strong as to bear us out in inflicting the same punishment upon him, which we should have thought due if he had actually done it. In the one case, the joy of our deliverance alleviates our sense of the atrocity of his conduct; in the other, the grief of our misfortune increases it. His real demerit, however, is undoubtedly the same in both cases, since his intentions were equally criminal; and there is in this respect, therefore, an irregularity in the sentiments of all men, and a consequent relaxation of discipline, in the laws of, I believe, all nations, of the most civilized, as well as of the most barbarous. The humanity of a civilized people disposes them either to dispense with, or to mitigate punishments wherever their natural indignation is not goaded on by the consequences of the crime. Barbarians, on the other hand, when no actual consequence has happened from any action, are not apt to be very delicate or inquisitive about the motives. (*TMS*, pp. 144–146)

What matters most in crimes is the actual commission, not the design intention for there is room for many a slip between design and execution. What appeals to an imagined design may be unappealing when it becomes real. Also, we more abhor finding the innocent guilty, than failing to apprehend and punish the guilty. So, the consequences of error are not all equal and are highly asymmetric in their perceived cost.

But crimes against the government such as treason are a different matter, as the government is much more jealous even of the intention to do it harm than in the case of harmful intention by one citizen to another.

What is felt by the guilty who by accident are not found out?

> The person himself who, either from passion or from the influence of bad company, has resolved, and perhaps taken measures, to perpetrate some crime, but who has fortunately been prevented by an accident which put it out of his power, is sure, if he has any remains of conscience, to regard this event all his life after as a great and signal deliverance. He can never think of it without returning thanks to Heaven for having been thus graciously pleased to save him from the guilt in which he was just ready to plunge himself, and to hinder him from rendering all the rest of his life a scene of horror, remorse, and repentance. But though his hands are innocent, he is conscious that his heart is equally guilty as if he had actually executed what he was so fully resolved upon. It gives great ease to his conscience, however, to consider that the crime was not executed, though he knows that the failure arose from no virtue in him. He still considers himself as less deserving of punishment and resentment; and this good fortune either diminishes, or takes away altogether, all sense of guilt. To remember how much he was resolved upon it, has no other effect than to make him regard his escape as the greater and more miraculous: for he still fancies that he has escaped, and he looks back upon the danger to which his peace of mind was exposed, with that terror, with which one who is in safety sometimes remember the hazard he was in of falling over a precipice, and shudder with horror at the thought. (*TMS*, pp. 146–147)

TMS is concerned with reasonable propositions among reasonable people who are not unreasonably sociopathic. Hence, they who know they are guilty can be ecstatic and forever grateful that they escaped being found guilty. But they recall in horror the precipice on which they so fortunately rescued.

Our sense of merit or demerit is increased beyond what is justified when chance causes extraordinary pleasure or pain.

> The second effect of this influence of fortune, is to increase our sense of the merit or demerit of actions beyond what is due to the motives or affection from which they proceed, when they happen to give occasion to

extraordinary pleasure or pain. The agreeable or disagreeable effects of the action often throw a shadow of merit or demerit upon the agent, though in his intention there was nothing that deserved either praise or blame, or at least that deserved them in the degree in which we are apt to bestow them. Thus, even the messenger of bad news is disagreeable to us; and, on the contrary, we feel a sort of gratitude for the man who brings us good tidings. For a moment we look upon them both as the authors, the one of our good, the other of our bad fortune, and regard them in some measure as if they had really brought about the events which they only give an account of. The first…is naturally the object of a transitory gratitude: we embrace him with warmth and affection, and should be glad, during the instant of our prosperity, to reward him as for some signal service. By the custom of all courts, the officer who brings the news of a victory is entitled to considerable preferments, and the general always chooses one of his principal favourites to go upon so agreeable an errand. The first author of our sorrow is, on the contrary, just as naturally the object of a transitory resentment. We can scarce avoid looking upon him with chagrin and uneasiness; and the rude and brutal are apt to vent upon him that spleen which his intelligence gives occasion to. Tigranes, King of Armenia, struck off the head of the man who brought him the first account of the approach of a formidable enemy. To punish in this manner the author of bad tidings, seems barbarous and inhuman: yet, to reward the messenger of good news, is not disagreeable to us; we think it suitable to the bounty of kings. But why do we make this difference, since, if there is no fault in the one, neither is there any merit in the other? It is because any sort of reason seems sufficient to authorize the exertion of the social and benevolent affections; but it requires the most solid and substantial to make us enter into that of the unsocial and malevolent. (*TMS*, pp. 147–48)

Ordinarily, we can suppose that gratitude is proportional to the merit of praise-able actions, resentment asymmetrically proportional to the demerit of blame-able actions. *TMS* predicts that when chance produces extraordinary pleasure or harm, then gratitude or resentment, in its proportionality, is increased. Thus, the innocent messenger of bad news is famously beheaded, returned on horseback to his army, and thus is conveyed the clearest of possible nonverbal responses to the original announcement.

Chance and ambivalence toward the punishment of gross negligence.

But though in general we are averse to enter into the unsocial and malevolent affections, though we lay it down for a rule that we ought never to approve of their gratification, unless so far as the malicious and unjust intention of the person against whom they are directed renders him their proper object; yet, upon some occasions, we relax of this severity. When the negligence of one man has occasioned some unintended damage to another, we generally enter so far into the resentment of the sufferer, as to approve of his inflicting a punishment upon the offender much beyond what the offence would have appeared to deserve, had no such unlucky consequence followed from it.

There is a degree of negligence, which would appear to deserve some chastisement though it should occasion no damage to any body. Thus, if a person should throw a large stone over a wall into a public street without giving warning to those who might be passing by, and without regarding where it was likely to fall, he would undoubtedly deserve some chastisement. A very accurate police would punish so absurd an action, even though it had done no mischief. The person who has been guilty of it, shews an insolent contempt of the happiness and safety of others. There is real injustice in his conduct. He wantonly exposes his neighbour to what no man in his senses would choose to expose himself, and evidently wants [lacks] that sense of what is due to his fellow-creatures, which is the basis of justice and of society. Gross negligence, therefore, is, in the law, said to be almost equal to malicious design. When any unlucky consequences happen from such carelessness, the person who has been guilty of it is often punished as if he had really intended those consequences; and his conduct, which was only thoughtless and insolent, and what deserved some chastisement, is considered as atrocious, and as liable to the severest punishment. Thus if, by the imprudent action above mentioned, he should accidentally kill a man, he is, by the laws of many countries, particularly by the old law of Scotland, liable to the last punishment. And though this is no doubt excessively severe, it is not altogether inconsistent with our natural sentiments. Our just indignation against the folly and inhumanity of his conduct is exasperated by our sympathy with the unfortunate sufferer. Nothing, however, would appear more shocking to our natural sense of equity, than to bring a man to the scaffold merely for having thrown a stone carelessly into the street without hurting any body. The folly and inhumanity of his conduct, however, would in this case be the same; but still our sentiments would be very different. The consideration of this difference satisfy us how much the indignation even of the spectator is apt to be animated by the actual consequences of the action. In cases of this kind there will, if I am not mistaken, be found a great degree of severity in the laws of almost all nations; as…in those of an opposite kind there was a very general relaxation of discipline. (*TMS*, pp. 148–151)

I am reminded of a senseless neighborhood murder by a burglar surprised to find the two lady occupants at home. I learned that a policeman who lived nearby, in the tense neighborhood aftermath, had long prepared and equipped his wife for defensive action. He now added to her instruction, that if she had to use the gun, to be sure to kill the intruder to guard against any claim by the intruder that her fear was excessive. Fear, however, justified by the circumstances at the time, is a difficult ex post defense when it produces an extraordinary outcome.

Why might gross negligence be punished to the same extent as if it were intended, which seems excessive? Ask, rather, what might be the consequences if this were not the rule. Then there would be no need for caution, and gross negligence might become very gross, blurring the line between intentions and accident. The law regularly reflects the opportunity cost of a rule—of the avoidable consequences of not having the rule. Indeed, rules emerge in response to events occurring absent the rule thereby making evident the consequences of its absence. To prevent this is to cause error.

The law does not normally determine what is right. It is the other way around: experience determines what actions are right, which then determines what the law must be. Where rule A has long been in force, the history of not-A is lost and with it the rational for A.

Legislative bodies make law in the absence of experience comparable to that which accumulates in common law. Gideon John Tucker (10, 1826–July 1899) was an American lawyer, newspaper editor, and politician. In 1866, as Surrogate of New York County, he wrote in a decision on a legal malpractice claim against a deceased lawyer's estate: "No man's life, liberty or property are safe while the Legislature is in session."

Negligence combined with unintended harm deserves some blame, the guilty are required to compensate.

> There is another degree of negligence which does not involve in it any sort of injustice. The person who is guilty of it treats his neighbour as he treats himself, means no harm to any body, and is far from entertaining any insolent contempt for the safety and happiness of others. He is not, however, so careful and circumspect in his conduct as he ought to be, and deserves upon this account some degree of blame and censure, but no sort of punishment. Yet if, by a negligence of this kind, he should occasion some damage to another person, he is by the laws of, I believe,

> all countries, obliged to compensate it. And though this is no doubt a real punishment, and what no mortal would have thought of inflicting upon him, had it not been for the unlucky accident which his conduct gave occasion to; yet this decision of the law is approved of by the natural sentiments of all mankind. Nothing, we think, can be more just than that one man should not suffer by the carelessness of another; and that the damage occasioned by blameable negligence, should be made up by the person who was guilty of it. (*TMS*, p. 151)

Victim compensation, prominent in early weak-government societies, between families involving murder, survives into the modern period in the form of civil action to recover unintended damage to another person from want of ordinary carefulness. You are painting your house and failing to secure the scaffold against winds that damage your neighbor's property or person. You have committed no crime but are liable in a civil suit for the damage caused by your carelessness.

More dramatically, O. J. Simpson was a famous football star accused of murdering his wife and her lover. Although Simson was acquitted in his criminal trial, he had to pay damages in his subsequent civil trial: "Although Simpson was acquitted in the criminal case, he was also sued by the victims' families for wrongful death, and the civil trial began in October 1996. Less than four months later, that jury found him responsible for the deaths of Nicole Brown Simpson and Ronald Goldman and awarded their families $33.5 million in damages" (History & Society (2024) "O. J. Simpson trial." Britannica, law case. https://www.britannica.com/event/O-J-Simpson-trial).

The ambivalence in guilt with neglect of close attention to causing harm.

> There is another species of negligence, which consists merely in a want of the most anxious timidity and circumspection with regard to all the possible consequences of our actions. The want of this painful attention, when no bad consequences follow from it, is so far from being regarded as blameable, that the contrary quality is rather considered as such. That timid circumspection which is afraid of every thing, is never regarded as a virtue, but as a quality which, more than any other, incapacitates for action and business. Yet when, from a want of this excessive care, a person happens to occasion some damage to another, he is often by the law obliged to compensate it. Thus, by the Aquilian law, the man, who not being able to

> manage a horse that had accidentally taken fright, should happen to ride down his neighbour's slave, is obliged to compensate the damage. When an accident of this kind happens, we are apt to think that he ought not to have rode such a horse, and to regard his attempting it as an unpardonable levity; though without this accident we should not only have made no such reflection, but should have regarded his refusing it as the effect of timid weakness, and of an anxiety about merely possible events, which it is to no purpose to be aware of. The person himself, who by an accident even of this kind has involuntarily hurt another, seems to have some sense of his own ill desert with regard to him. He naturally runs up to the sufferer to express his concern for what has happened, and to make every acknowledgment in his power. If he has any sensibility, he necessarily desires to compensate the damage, and to do every thing he can to appease that animal resentment, which he is sensible will be apt to arise in the breast of the sufferer. To make no apology, to offer no atonement, is regarded as the highest brutality. Yet why should he make an apology more than any other person? Why should he, since he was equally innocent with any other by-stander, be thus singled out from among all mankind, to make up for the bad fortune of another? This task would surely never be imposed upon him, did not even the impartial spectator feel some indulgence for what be regarded as the unjust resentment of that other. (*TMS*, pp. 151–152)

The horse you are riding takes fright when the wind dislodges a previously broken tree branch. The cause was the wind in conjunction with a previous storm that broke the tree branch. Both events are beyond your control—acts of God. What is your liability? For a contemporary response to Smith's proposition, I asked BingChat to get an AI answer: "In most states, an equine activity sponsor or equine professional is not liable for any injury to, or the death of, a participant in equine activities resulting from the inherent risks of equine activities. However, if there was negligence on the part of the rider or if there was a failure to warn of a known danger, then there be liability."

A very general, not very astute answer. That there is no negligence, and no injury to the rider was specified as conditions.

CHAPTER 23

Of the final cause of the irregularity of sentiments

Chance bad or good outcome events influence praise or blame judgments by a world of man made for action.

> Such is the effect of the good or bad consequence of actions upon the sentiments both of the person who performs them, and of others; and thus, fortune, which governs the world, has some influence where we should be least willing to allow her any, and directs in some measure the sentiments of mankind, with regard to the character and conduct both of themselves and others. That the world judges by the event, and not by the design, has been in all ages the complaint, and is the great discouragement of virtue. Every body agrees to the general maxim, that as the event does not depend on the agent, it ought to have no influence upon our sentiments, with regard to the merit or propriety of his conduct. But when we come to particulars, we find that our sentiments are scarce in any one instance exactly conformable to what this equitable maxim would direct. The happy or unprosperous event of any action, is not only apt to give us a good or bad opinion of the prudence with which it was conducted, but almost always too animates our gratitude or resentment, our sense of the merit or demerit of the design. Nature, however, when she implanted the seeds of this irregularity in the human breast, seems, as upon all other occasions, to have intended the happiness and perfection of the species. If the hurtfulness of the design, if the malevolence of the affection, were alone the causes which excited our resentment, we should feel all the furies of that passion against any person in whose breast we suspected or believed such designs

Vernon L. Smith, *Adam Smith's Theory of Society*,
https://doi.org/10.1007/978-3-031-68494-4_23

or affections were harboured, though they had never broken out into any actions. Sentiments, thoughts, intentions, would become the objects of punishment; and if the indignation of mankind run as high against them as against actions; if the baseness of the thought which had given birth to no action, seemed in the eyes of the world as much to call aloud for vengeance as the baseness of the action, every court of judicature would become a real inquisition. There would be no safety for the most innocent and circumspect conduct. Bad wishes, bad views, bad designs, might still be suspected; and while these excited the same indignation with bad conduct, while bad intentions were as much resented as bad actions, they would equally expose the person to punishment and resentment. Actions, therefore, which either produce actual evil, or attempt to produce it, and thereby put us in the immediate fear of it, are by the Author of nature rendered the only proper and approved objects of human punishment and resentment. Sentiments, designs, affections, though it is from these that according to cool reason human actions derive their whole merit or demerit, are placed by the great Judge of hearts beyond the limits of every human jurisdiction, and are reserved for the cognizance of his own unerring tribunal. That necessary rule of justice, therefore, that men in this life are liable to punishment for their actions only, not for their designs and intentions, is founded upon this salutary and useful irregularity in human sentiments concerning merit or demerit, which at first sight appears so absurd and unaccountable. But every part of nature, when attentively surveyed, equally demonstrates the providential care of its Author; and we admire the wisdom and goodness of God even in the weakness and folly of men. Nor is that irregularity of sentiments altogether without its utility, by which the merit of an unsuccessful attempt to serve, and much more that of mere good inclinations and kind wishes, appears to be imperfect. *Man was made for action*, and to promote by the exertion of his faculties such changes in the external circumstances both of himself and others, as seem most favourable to the happiness of all. He must not be satisfied with indolent benevolence, nor fancy himself the friend of mankind, because in his heart he wishes well to the prosperity of the world. That he call forth the whole vigour of his soul, and strain every nerve, in order to produce those ends which it is the purpose of his being to advance, Nature has taught him, that neither himself nor mankind can be fully satisfied with his conduct, nor bestow upon it the full measure of applause, unless he has actually produced them. He is made to know, that the praise of good intentions, without the merit of good offices, will be but of little avail to excite either the loudest acclamations of the world, or even the highest degree of self-applause. The man who has performed no single action of importance, but whose whole conversation and deportment express the justest, the noblest, and most

> generous sentiments, can be entitled to demand no very high reward, even though his inutility should be owing to nothing but the want of an opportunity to serve. We can still refuse it him without blame. We can still ask him, What have you done? What actual service can you produce, to entitle you to so great a recompence? We esteem you and love you; but we owe you nothing. To reward indeed that latent virtue which has been useless only for want of an opportunity to serve, to bestow upon it those honours and preferments, which, though in some measure it may be said to deserve them, it could not with propriety have insisted upon, is the effect of the most divine benevolence. To punish, on the contrary, for the affections of the heart only, where no crime has been committed, is the most insolent and barbarous tyranny. The benevolent affections seem to deserve most praise, when they do not wait till it becomes almost a crime for them not to exert themselves. The malevolent, on the contrary, can scarce he too tardy, too slow, or deliberate. (*TMS*, pp. 152–155; italics added)

Nature teaches us to give weight to realized outcomes rather than intentions only, which appears to discourage virtue. But if all reward and all punishment are to be levied on they who are good or evil in their hearts, by what invasive inquisition and suspension of freedom are such judgments to be made? We cringe in horror at the thought of governments, as in North Korea, Russia, etc., inviting citizens to earn the favor of the government by spying on their neighbors. As publicized in the revelations of Ellsberg and Snowden, the jealousies of our own government drove the leaders to commit these same authoritarian interventions. The important difference is that the revelations were revealed by dissent and that is why we are free and why others are not.

The necessary rule of justice in this world must focus on actions and their consequences, not goodness or badness of heart. They who are free to take good actions must also be free to make mistakes and suffer the consequences howsoever unintended and motivated by high principle. There is no reward in the court of impartial judgment for high-sounding rhetoric disconnected from actions and consequences. These principles follow from the underlying axiom in *TMS*, that humankind was made for action in the service of their own and others' happiness. "Made for action" was Adam Smith's theme with no applause for indolent benevolence, nor good intentions that so often go awry. Moral sentiments are about moral consequences that follow actions. You must not only give but deliver, if you are to receive, which also requires delivery.

Humankind revere happiness, and desire not hurting their brethren even by accident.

> It is even of considerable importance that the evil which is done without design should be regarded as a misfortune to the doer as well as to the sufferer. Man is thereby taught to reverence the happiness of his brethren, to tremble lest he should, even unknowingly, do any thing that can hurt them, and to dread that animal resentment which, he feels, is ready to burst out against him, if he should, without design, be the unhappy instrument of their calamity. As, in the ancient heathen religion, that holy ground which had been consecrated to some god, was not to be trod upon but upon solemn and necessary occasions, and the man who had even ignorantly violated it, became piacular [atoning, reparative] from that moment, and, until proper atonement should be made, incurred the vengeance of that powerful and invisible being to whom it had been set apart; so, by the wisdom of Nature, the happiness of every innocent man is, in the same manner, rendered holy, consecrated, and hedged round against the approach of every other man; not to be wantonly trod upon, not even to be, in any respect, ignorantly and involuntarily violated, without requiring some expiation, some atonement in proportion to the greatness of such undesigned violation. A man of humanity, who accidentally, and without the smallest degree of blameable negligence, has been the cause of the death of another man, feels himself piacular, though not guilty. During his whole life he considers this accident as one of the greatest misfortunes that could have befallen him. If the family of the slain is poor, and he himself in tolerable circumstances, he immediately takes them under his protection, and without any other merit, thinks them entitled to every degree of favour and kindness. If they are in better circumstances, he endeavours by every submission, by every expression of sorrow, by rendering them every good office which he can devise, or they accept of, to atone for what has happened, and to propitiate, as much as possible, their, perhaps natural, though no doubt most unjust resentment for the great, though involuntary, offence which he has given them. (*TMS*, pp. 155–156)

Why does nature teach that even that evil which is done without design is a misfortune both to the doer and the victim? Because thereby we experience the lesson that we are here to revere the happiness of humankind, to fear that, unintentionally, even unknowingly, to unjustly harm another brings retribution for which one must atone in proportion to the harm inflicted. That felt responsibility supports a common sense of duty to society. Just as heathen religion taught that holy ground was not to be violated without punishment, so other people are holy ground not to be violated even when it is done totally without design, and, though judged innocent, the sensitive actor feels they must still atone in proportion to the unhappiness inflicted. Hence, historically, the strong motives of weak government authorities to help enforce appropriate compensation that victims be restored as completely and wholly as it is materially possible. Also, the modern plea bargaining process brings forms of compensation to the table.

Even with primitive religion where ignorant superstition is usually claimed to reign, Smith finds evidence in support of these interpretations; for to him no shared, repeated, human experience, fails to find meaning or function.

Revealed also is Smith's theory, that the social function of resentment that is individually felt and automatically supported by third-party sympathetic observers, inspires the law of property in body, its products, and all assets formed from such products.

Where the vagaries of chance distort perceptions of our reputation, we must seek support from candid observers capable of seeing our truer selves.

> Notwithstanding…all these seeming irregularities of sentiment, if man should unfortunately either give occasion to those evils which he did not intend, or fail in producing that good which he intended, Nature has not left his innocence altogether without consolation, nor his virtue altogether without reward. He then calls to his assistance that just and equitable maxim, that those events which did not depend upon our conduct, ought not to diminish the esteem that is due to us. He summons up his whole magnanimity and firmness of soul, and strives to regard himself, not in the light in which he at present appears, but in that in which he ought to appear, in which he would have appeared had his generous designs been crowned with success, and in which he would still appear, notwithstanding their miscarriage, if the sentiments of mankind were either altogether candid and equitable, or even perfectly consistent with themselves. The more candid and humane part of mankind entirely go along with the efforts which he thus makes to support himself in his own opinion. They exert their whole generosity and greatness of mind, to correct in themselves this irregularity of human nature, and endeavour to regard his unfortunate magnanimity in the same light in which, had it been successful, they

> would, without any such generous exertion, have naturally been disposed to consider it. (*TMS*, pp. 156–157)

Our best defense against the vagaries of guilt from harm we have inflicted, despite well-intended actions, is to have, or work to restore, a reputation for kind action consistent with what we wish to see happen. Such a reputation will instill in others a disbelief in our guilt if intentions go awry or build confidence that we are dedicated to making amends for unintended harm done. Treasure good friends who can bear expert testimony as to any of our virtues that go unheeded.

PART VII

Of the foundation of our judgments concerning our own sentiments and conduct and of the sense of duty

CHAPTER 24

Of the principle of self-approbation and self-disapprobation

The principle by which we judge ourselves should be the same as that by which we judge others.

The principle by which we naturally either approve or disapprove of our own conduct, seems to be altogether the same with that by which we exercise the like judgments concerning the conduct of other people. We either approve or disapprove of the conduct of another man, according as we feel that, when we bring his case home to ourselves, we either can or cannot entirely sympathize with the sentiments and motives which directed it. And, in the same manner, we either approve or disapprove of our own conduct, according as we feel that, when we place ourselves in the situation of another man, and view it, as it were, with his eyes and from his station, we either can or cannot entirely enter into and sympathize with the sentiments and motives which influenced it. We can never survey our own sentiments and motives, we can never form any judgment concerning them, unless we remove ourselves, as it were, from our own natural station, and endeavour to view them as at a certain distance from us. But we can do this in no other way than by endeavouring to view them with the eyes of other people, or as other people are likely to view them. Whatever judgment we can form concerning them, accordingly, must always bear some secret reference, either to what are, or to what, upon a certain condition, would be, or to what, we imagine, ought to be the judgment of others. We endeavour to examine our own conduct as we imagine any other fair [cool] and impartial spectator would examine it. If, upon placing ourselves in his

Vernon L. Smith, *Adam Smith's Theory of Society*,
https://doi.org/10.1007/978-3-031-68494-4_24

> situation, we thoroughly enter into all the passions and motives which influenced it, we approve of it, by sympathy with the approbation of this supposed equitable judge. If otherwise, we enter into his disapprobation, and condemn it. (*TMS*, pp. 161–162)

The principle by which we naturally judge the propriety, or impropriety, of our own conduct is one and the same by which we judge the conduct of another and vice versa. We must always examine our own conduct from the perspective of a fair [meaning fair-play] and [cool] impartial spectator, applying the same standards to any other whose conduct we judge. This rule, when applied generally, enables people without design or intention to be part of a process that can create a stable and cohesive community and society. It is the stuff by which great nations of opportunity are created without planning to do so. Let those who would achieve national good by planning it, begin by planning to better treat their neighbors. Gandhi's insightful modern version of this maxim is to be the change you would want to see in the world.

Smith's gedankenexperiment, which imagines one growing up in the absence of any contact with another person enables us to see why and how our being is social.

> Were it possible that a human creature could grow up to manhood in some solitary place, without any communication with his own species, he could no more think of his own character, of the propriety or demerit of his own sentiments and conduct, of the beauty or deformity of his own mind, than of the beauty or deformity of his own face. All these are objects which he cannot easily see, which naturally he does not look at, and with regard to which he is provided with no mirror which can present them to his view. Bring him into society, and he is immediately provided with the mirror which he wanted before. It is placed in the countenance and behaviour of those he lives with, which always mark when they enter into, and when they disapprove of his sentiments; and it is here that he first views the propriety and impropriety of his own passions, the beauty and deformity of his own mind. To a man who from his birth was a stranger to society, the objects of his passions, the external bodies which either pleased or hurt him, would occupy his whole attention. The passions themselves, the desires or aversions, the joys or sorrows, which those objects excited, though of all things the most immediately present to him, could scarce ever be the objects of his thoughts. The idea of them could never interest him so much as to call upon his attentive consideration. The consideration of his joy could

> in him excite no new joy, nor that of his sorrow any new sorrow, though the consideration of the causes of those passions might often excite both. Bring him into society, and all his own passions will immediately become the causes of new passions. He will observe that mankind approve of some of them, and are disgusted by others. He will be elevated in the one case, and cast down in the other; his desires and aversions, his joys and sorrows, will now often become the causes of new desires and new aversions, new joys and new sorrows: they will now, therefore, interest him deeply, and often call upon his most attentive consideration. (*TMS*, pp. 162–163)

Smith's perceptive mental experiment is an insightful parable establishing why and how we are social and why and how our sociability defines who we are as individuals, each uniquely different and empowered by others to achieve all that we might become. The metaphor of the social mirror powerfully captures the key to Smith's bottom-up theory of society. If there is no social mirror, there can be no society of humankind.

Our social maturation requires us to suppose ourselves the spectators of our own behavior, imagining what effect it would produce upon us and seeing ourselves through a social mirror as others see us.

> In the same manner our first moral criticisms are exercised upon the characters and conduct of other people; and we are all very forward to observe how each of these affects us. But we soon learn, that other people are equally frank with regard to our own. We become anxious to know how far we deserve their censure or applause, and whether to them we must necessarily appear those agreeable or disagreeable creatures which they represent us. We begin, upon this account, to examine our own passions and conduct, and to consider how these must appear to them, by considering how they would appear to us if in their situation. We suppose ourselves the spectators of our own behaviour, and endeavour to imagine what effect it would, in this light, produce upon us. This is the only looking-glass by which we can, in some measure, with the eyes of other people, scrutinize the propriety of our own conduct. If in this view it pleases us, we are tolerably satisfied. We can be more indifferent about the applause, and, in some measure, despise the censure of the world; secure that, however misunderstood or misrepresented, we are the natural and proper objects of approbation. On the contrary, if we are doubtful about it, we are often, upon that very account, more anxious to gain their approbation, and, provided we have not already, as they say, shaken hands with

> infamy, we are altogether distracted at the thoughts of their censure, which then strikes us with double severity. (*TMS*, pp. 163–164)

The three-step process whereby we become social, by socializing with each other, begins with our recognition of the moral actions of others and applies our capacity to imagine changing places with others to form a sense of what they must feel. Next, we become aware that our own actions similarly affect them. Lastly, we learn to screen and modify our own actions in the light of how we appear to others, as would any impartial spectator of the fair-play rules of sociality that we learn to follow in good propriety.

We are concerned about our own appearance of beauty or deformity only because of how it appears to others.

> Our first ideas of personal beauty and deformity are drawn from the shape and appearance of others, not from our own. We soon become sensible, however, that others exercise the same criticism upon us. We are pleased when they approve of our figure, and are disobliged when they seem to be disgusted. We become anxious to know how far our appearance deserves either their blame or approbation. We examine our persons limb by limb, and by placing ourselves before a looking-glass, or by some such expedient, endeavour, as much as possible, to view ourselves at the distance and with the eyes of other people. If, after this examination, we are satisfied with our own appearance, we can more easily support the most disadvantageous judgments of others. If, on the contrary, we are sensible that we are the natural objects of distaste, every appearance of their disapprobation mortifies us beyond all measure. A man who is tolerably handsome, will allow you to laugh at any little irregularity in his person; but all such jokes are commonly unsupportable to one who is really deformed. It is evident, however, that we are anxious about our own beauty and deformity, only upon account of its effect upon others. If we had no connection with society, we should be altogether indifferent about either. (*TMS*, pp. 164)

Our own conceptions of beauty and ugliness are derived from the appearance of others. Since we recognize that others form the same conceptions by viewing us, we become anxious to know whether our appearance deserves their approbation or disapprobation. We examine our limbs, use a looking glass to view them at a distance, and judge our appearance from the perspective of others. If we are satisfied with this assessment, that we compare favorably with others, then we can better fend against any misrepresentations by others. If we see that our appearance is distasteful it is mortifying.

Smith's point is that such things matter only because we are part of society and that if we had no such connections then it would not matter.

Modern methods of treatment, exercise, nutrition, and cosmetic surgery can change appearance. But more important is that there are many dimensions of appearance besides the physical, so that our expertise in business, science, sport, or a profession can easily outweigh and render irrelevant one's physical appearance. The genius and scientific contributions of Albert Einstein or Stephen Hawking have a way of being beautiful that makes physical appearance irrelevant, even disgusting if mentioned.

Also notice the close parallel between Smith's description of how we judge physical appearance and the process whereby our conduct is socialized. Order in appearance is like order in conduct from which an orderly society emerges.

In examining my own conduct, it is as if I were two different characters; the person who is the examiner and judge—the spectator—and the person whose conduct is to be judged of—the acting agent, myself, of whose conduct I am forming an opinion.

> When I endeavour to examine my own conduct, when I endeavour to pass sentence upon it, and either to approve or condemn it, it is evident that, in all such cases, I divide myself, as it were, into two persons; and that I, the examiner and judge, represent a different character from that other I, the person whose conduct is examined into and judged of. The first is the spectator, whose sentiments with regard to my own conduct I endeavour to enter into, by placing myself in his situation, and by considering how it would appear to me, when seen from that particular point of view. The second is the agent, the person whom I properly call myself, and of whose conduct, under the character of a spectator, I was endeavouring to form some opinion. The first is the judge; the second the person judged of. But that the judge should, in every respect, be the same with the person judged of, is as impossible as that the cause should, in every respect, be the same with the effect. (*TMS*, pp. 164–165)

In examining our own conduct, we operate through two mental states. The first is that of the spectator, examiner, and judge of that conduct, conceptually distinct and separate from the second, the agent of action whose conduct is examined into and judged of. The first is the spectator, whose sentiments with regard to my own conduct I strive to enter into, by placing myself in their situation, and considering how it appears to me, from that perspective. The second is the agent of action, my acting self, whose conduct I form an opinion of so that my actions will be consistent with my natural desire to get along with others.

Virtue is not said to be amiable or meritorious because it is the object of its own love but because it excites those sentiments in others.

> To be amiable and to be meritorious; that is, to deserve love and to deserve reward, are the great characters of virtue; and to be odious and punishable, of vice. But all these characters have an immediate reference to the sentiments of others. Virtue is not said to be amiable, or to be meritorious, because it is the object of its own love, or of its own gratitude; but because it excites those sentiments in other men. The consciousness that it is the object of such favourable regards, is the source of that inward tranquillity and self-satisfaction with which it is naturally attended, as the suspicion of the contrary gives occasion to the torments of vice. What so great happiness as to be beloved, and to know that we deserve to be beloved? What so great misery as to be hated, and to know that we deserve to be hated? (*TMS*, p. 165)

Virtue consists of being amiable, meritorious, deserving of love, and deserving of reward recognition by others; not because virtue is the object of its own love or gratitude, but because it excites these sentiments in others. Our consciousness of the favorable attitude of others toward us is a source of inner peace, self-satisfaction, and happiness.

Vice, as the opposite of virtue, is to be odious, to be hated, and to deserve hatred, and is the source of the greatest misery and unhappiness.

Standard contemporary utility theory gets it wrong by supposing Max U (outcome), without a theory of how and why those outcomes got into U(.) and, therefore, is incompetent to explain why and how we are social.

CHAPTER 25

Of the love or praise, and of that of praise-worthiness; and of the dread or blame, and of that of blame-worthiness

Nature inspires in us the desire to be loved, to be lovely; the dread of being hated, being hateful; the desire for praise, to be praiseworthy; the dread of blame, to be blameworthy.

> Man naturally desires, not only to be loved, but to be lovely; or to be that thing which is the natural and proper object of love. He naturally dreads, not only to be hated, but to be hateful; or to be that thing which is the natural and proper object of hatred. He desires not only praise, but praise-worthiness; or to be that thing which, though it should be praised by nobody, is, however, the natural and proper object of praise. He dreads, not only blame, but blame-worthiness; or to be that thing which, though it should be blamed by nobody, is, however, the natural and proper object of blame. (*TMS*, p. 166)

"For 'tis love and love alone the world is seeking" (Victor Herbert, "Ah! Sweet Mystery of Life At Last I've Found You," 1910). Nature created humankind to love, be loved, to be lovely. We desire not only praise but to be praiseworthy, the natural object of praise, even if that object is unknown to others. We dread not only hatred, but to be hateful, not only to be blamed but to be blameworthy, even if such be unknown to others. In either case, our desires are not about superficial image, but

Vernon L. Smith, *Adam Smith's Theory of Society*,
https://doi.org/10.1007/978-3-031-68494-4_25

about the substance of their content. Otherwise, we become frauds unto ourselves.

Praiseworthiness is not derived from praise.

> The love of praise-worthiness is by no means derived altogether from the love of praise. Those two principles, though they resemble one another, though they are connected, and often blended with one another, are yet, in many respects, distinct and independent of one another. (*TMS*, p. 166)

To be praised is to enjoy our finest hour, provided only that we are indeed praiseworthy. So also, in our finest hour, is our desire to avoid being blamed provided only that we are indeed not blameworthy.

The desire to excel is rooted in our admiration of excellence in others; for achievement we must become the impartial spectators of our own conduct.

> The love and admiration which we naturally conceive for those whose character and conduct we approve of, necessarily dispose us to desire to become ourselves the objects of the like agreeable sentiments, and to be as amiable and as admirable as those whom we love and admire the most. Emulation, the anxious desire that we ourselves should excel, is originally founded in our admiration of the excellence of others. Neither can we be satisfied with being merely admired for what other people are admired. We must at least believe ourselves to be admirable for what they are admirable. But, in order to attain this satisfaction, we must become the impartial spectators of our own character and conduct. We must endeavour to view them with the eyes of other people, or as other people are likely to view them. When seen in this light, if they appear to us as we wish, we are happy and contented. But it greatly confirms this happiness and contentment when we find that other people, viewing them with those very eyes with which we, in imagination only, were endeavouring to view them, see them precisely in the same light in which we ourselves had seen them. Their approbation necessarily confirms our own self-approbation. Their praise necessarily strengthens our own sense of our own praise-worthiness. In this case, so far is the love of praise worthiness from being derived altogether from that of praise, that the love of praise seems, at least in a great measure, to be derived from that of praise-worthiness. (*TMS*, pp. 166–167)

Our desire to excel stems from our admiration of others. If indeed we are to excel, we must become the impartial spectators of our own conduct, develop by this means our praiseworthiness, and thus earn the praise of others.

Proof of praiseworthiness must underlie praise if it is to be pleasurable. Soberly correct the mistaken perceptions of others.

> The most sincere praise can give little pleasure when it cannot be considered as some sort of proof of praise worthiness. It is by no means sufficient that, from ignorance or mistake, esteem and admiration should, in some way or other, be bestowed upon us. If we are conscious that we do not deserve to be so favourably thought of, and that if the truth were known, we should be regarded with very different sentiments, our satisfaction is far from being complete. The man who applauds us either for actions which we did not perform, or for motives which had no sort of influence upon our conduct, applauds not us, but another person. We can derive no sort of satisfaction from his praises. To us they should be more mortifying than any censure, and should perpetually call to our minds the most humbling of all reflections, the reflection of what we ought to be, but what we are not. A woman who paints could derive, one should imagine, but little vanity from the compliments that are paid to her complexion…To be pleased with such groundless applause is a proof of the most superficial levity and weakness. It is what is properly called vanity, and is the foundation of the most ridiculous and contemptible vices, the vices of affectation and common lying; follies which, if experience did not teach us how common they are, one should imagine the least spark of common sense would save us from. The foolish liar, who endeavours to excite the admiration of the company by the relation of adventures which never had any existence; the important coxcomb, who gives himself airs of rank and distinction which he well knows he has no just pretensions to; are both of them, no doubt, pleased with the applause which they fancy they meet with. But their vanity arises from so gross an illusion of the imagination, that it is difficult to conceive how any rational creature should be imposed upon by it. When they place themselves in the situation of those whom they fancy they have deceived, they are struck with the highest admiration for their own persons. They look upon themselves, not in that light in which, they know, they ought to appear to their companions, but in that which they believe their companions actually look upon them. Their superficial weakness and trivial folly hinder them from ever turning their eyes inwards, or from seeing themselves in that despicable point of view in which their own consciences must

> tell them that they would appear to every body, if the real truth should ever come to be known. (*TMS*, pp. 167–168)

Praise, if accepted without correction, where there is no praiseworthiness, must surely be one of the most corrupt and corrupting of the many forms of self-deceit. Or, if one is much admired, the correction will be dismissed as due to excessive modesty. Moreover, your correction will be believed. An example is Mae West, whose response to "Goodness, what diamonds" was that "Goodness had nothing to do with it."

Truth is equally corrupted by accepting blame without correction when there is no blameworthiness, but then the correction may not be believed. Recall that President Richard Nixon, blamed for the Watergate break-in, did not gain credibility when he resigned by asserting that "I am not a crook." Most interesting in Nixon's case is that he seems to have thought that he had not been a crook but had been merely pursuing his own interest in his own acceptable way.

Real comfort is to feel that our conduct has been deserving of praise because our actions have been praiseworthy.

> As ignorant and groundless praise can give no solid joy, no satisfaction that will bear any serious examination, so, on the contrary, it often gives real comfort to reflect, that though no praise should actually be bestowed upon us, our conduct, however, has been such as to deserve it, and has been in every respect suitable to those measures and rules by which praise and approbation are naturally and commonly bestowed. We are pleased, not only with praise, but with having done what is praiseworthy. We are pleased to think that we have rendered ourselves the natural objects of approbation, though no approbation should ever actually be bestowed upon us: and we are mortified to reflect that we have justly merited the blame of those we live with, though that sentiment should never actually be exerted against us. The man who is conscious to himself that he has exactly observed those measures of conduct which experience informs him are generally agreeable, reflects with satisfaction on the propriety of his own behaviour. When he views it in the light in which the impartial spectator would view it, he thoroughly enters into all the motives which influenced it. He looks back upon every part of it with pleasure and approbation, and though mankind should never be acquainted with what he has done, he regards himself, not so much according to the light in which they actually regard him, as according to that in which they would regard him if they were better informed...Men have voluntarily thrown away life to acquire after death

> a renown which they could no longer enjoy. Their imagination, in the meantime, anticipated that fame which was in future times to be bestowed upon them. Those applauses which they were never to hear rung in their ears; the thoughts of that admiration, whose effects they were never to feel, played about their hearts, banished from their breasts the strongest of all natural fears, and transported them to perform actions which seem almost beyond the reach of human nature. But in point of reality there is surely no great difference between that approbation which is not to be bestowed till we can no longer enjoy it, and that which, indeed, is never to be bestowed, but which would be bestowed, if the world was ever made to understand properly the real circumstances of our behaviour. If the one often produces such violent effects, we cannot wonder that the other should always be highly regarded. (*TMS*, pp. 168–170)

It is a source of deep, lasting, and genuine comfort to know that our actions are praiseworthy, and to know that they would have drawn much deserved praise if others had been better informed. Smith asks: Is there, in reality, any difference between great approbation to be bestowed only after death, when we can no longer enjoy it, and that which would be bestowed only if the world could be made to understand properly the true circumstances of our behavior? My view is that our true circumstances are likely to become known. Indeed, Smith's own model predicts that others will find out our true circumstances because we will not be able to prevent them from being revealed in our social relationships. Sociopathology is an exception and is truly a most unfortunate disease of the mind that leverages unbounded egocentricity restrained not by the social mirror. But if all that fails, does that change our aspirations? Does it change what we would most want to be though none would ever know? As George Bernard Shaw put it in Major Barbara, "What price salvation now?"

Nature prepares us for society by endowing us with an original desire to please, and an aversion for offending our brethren, but also with a desire to being approved of and for being praiseworthy.

> Nature, when she formed man for society, endowed him with an original desire to please, and an original aversion to offend his brethren. She taught him to feel pleasure in their favourable, and pain in their unfavourable regard. She rendered their approbation most flattering and most agreeable to him for its own sake; and their disapprobation most mortifying and most offensive. But this desire of the approbation, and this aversion to

> the disapprobation of his brethren, would not alone have rendered him fit for that society for which he was made. Nature, accordingly, has endowed him, not only with a desire of being approved of, but with a desire of being what ought to be approved of; or of being what he himself approves of in other men. The first desire could only have made him wish to appear to be fit for society. The second was necessary in order to render him anxious to be really fit. The first could only have prompted him to the affectation of virtue, and to the concealment of vice. The second was necessary in order to inspire him with the real love of virtue, and with the real abhorrence of vice. In every well-informed mind this second desire seems to be the strongest of the two. It is only the weakest and most superficial of mankind who can be much delighted with that praise which they themselves know to be altogether unmerited. A weak man sometimes be pleased with it, but a wise man rejects it upon all occasions. But, though a wise man feels little pleasure from praise where he knows there is no praiseworthiness, he often feels the highest in doing what he knows to be praiseworthy, though he knows equally well that no praise is ever to be bestowed upon it. To obtain the approbation of mankind, where no approbation is due, can never be an object of any importance to him...But to be that thing which deserves approbation, must always be an object of the highest. (*TMS*, pp. 170–171)

Nature prepares us for society by first endowing us with a desire to please and to avoid offending others. Secondly, she made the approbation from others pleasing to us, and their disapprobation mortifying. These reciprocal features, however, were not alone sufficient to make us fit for society. Nature also has endowed us to aspire to be what ought to be approved of, or that which we approve of, in others. The first desire only makes us wish to appear fit by prompting us to the affection of virtue. The second renders us anxious to be really fit by inspiring us with a real love of virtue and an abhorrence of vice. As in Lord Acton: "Liberty is not the power of doing what we like, but the right of being able to do what we ought."

Contemptible vanity is to desire or accept praise where none is due; to desire it where it is really due is to desire no more than is just.

> To desire, or even to accept of praise, where no praise is due, can be the effect only of the most contemptible vanity. To desire it where it is really due, is to desire no more than that a most essential act of justice should be done to us. The love of just fame, of true glory, even for its own sake, and independent of any advantage which he can derive from it, is not unworthy even of a wise man. He sometimes, however, neglects, and even despises

> it; and he is never more apt to do so than when he has the most perfect assurance of the perfect propriety of every part of his own conduct. His self-approbation, in this case, stands in need of no confirmation from the approbation of other men. It is alone sufficient, and he is contented with it. This self-approbation, if not the only, is at least the principal object, about which he can or ought to be anxious. The love of it is the love of virtue. (*TMS*, pp. 171–173)

To love praise where none is due defines the most contemptible vanity.

To desire it when it is due defines just fame.

To aspire to and seek the most perfect propriety of conduct constitutes the love of virtue.

Seek always to love virtue, detest vice, and be these things that God in His love created you for and to overcome the sinfulness he created for the purpose of testing your resolve. Only tested resolve can be meaningful, credible, and creditworthy.

Love and admiration for some characters, hatred and contempt for others, are proper models for our own sentiments.

> As the love and admiration which we naturally conceive for some characters dispose us to wish to become ourselves the proper objects of such agreeable sentiments; so the hatred and contempt which we as naturally conceive for others, dispose us, perhaps still more strongly, to dread the very thought of resembling them in any respect. Neither is it…so much the thought of being hated and despised that we are afraid of, as that of being hateful and despicable.…The man who has broken through all those measures of conduct which can alone render him agreeable to mankind, though he should have the most perfect assurance that what he had done was for ever to be concealed from ever human eye, it is all to no purpose. When he looks back upon it, and views it in the light in which the impartial spectator would view it, he finds that he can enter into none of the motives which influenced it…His imagination…anticipates the contempt and derision from which nothing saves him but the ignorance of those he lives with. He still feels that he is the natural object of these sentiments, and still trembles at the thought of what he would suffer, if they were ever actually exerted against him. But if what he had been guilty of was not merely one of those improprieties which are the objects of simple disapprobation, but one of those enormous crimes which excite detestation and resentment, he could never think of it as long as he had any sensibility left, without feeling all the agony of horror and remorse; and

> though he could be assured that no man was ever to know it, and could even bring himself to believe that there was no God to revenge it, he would still feel enough of both these sentiments to embitter the whole of his life: he would still regard himself as the natural object of the hatred and indignation of all his fellow-creatures...These natural pangs of an affrighted conscience are the demons, the avenging furies, which, in this life, haunt the guilty, which allow them neither quiet nor repose, which often drive them to despair and distraction, from which no assurance of secrecy can protect them, from which no principle of irreligion can entirely deliver them. (*TMS*, pp. 171–173)

The pangs of a guilty conscience, where the ignorance of others protects one from the social consequences of the vilest of conduct, are the demon from which there is no escape, even in the refuge of silent denial, of religion, and God, in the reality of one's hatred and hatefulness.

For do we not praise Jesus because He lived and taught the life of love and loveliness but most especially because He said follow me as I follow God in heaven and these things will follow you all the days of your life.

The horror of crimes that escape detection does not always relieve the guilt of the harm-doer.

> Men of the most detestable characters, who, in the execution of the most dreadful crimes, had taken their measures so coolly as to avoid even the suspicion of guilt, have sometimes been driven, by the horror of their situation, to discover, of their own accord, what no human sagacity could ever have investigated. By acknowledging their guilt, by submitting themselves to the resentment of their offended fellow-citizens, and, by thus satiating that vengeance, of which they were sensible that they had become the proper objects, they hoped by their death to reconcile themselves, at least in their own imagination, to the natural sentiments of mankind; to be able to consider themselves as less worthy of hatred and resentment; to atone, in some measure, for their crimes, and, by thus becoming the objects, rather of compassion than of horror, if possible to die in peace, and with the forgiveness of all their fellow-creatures. Compared to what they felt before the discovery, even the thought of this, it seems, was happiness. In such cases, the horror of blameworthiness seems, even in persons who cannot be suspected of any extraordinary delicacy or sensibility of character, completely to conquer the dread of blame. In order to allay that horror, in order to pacify, in some degree, the remorse of their own consciences, they

> voluntarily submitted themselves both to the reproach and to the punishment which they knew were due to their crimes, but which, at the same time, they might easily have avoided. (*TMS*, pp. 173–174)

Let the greatest praise be reserved for they who are found innocent, but who, knowing their own guilt, confess and reveal all.

Unmerited praise that delights is frivolous; unmerited reproach is capable of mortifying.

> They are the most frivolous and superficial of mankind only who can be much delighted with that praise which they themselves know to be altogether unmerited. Unmerited reproach, however, is frequently capable of mortifying very severely even men of more than ordinary constancy. Men of the most ordinary constancy, indeed, easily learn to despise those foolish tales which are so frequently circulated in society, and which, from their own absurdity and falsehood, never fail to die away in the course of a few weeks, or of a few days. But an innocent man, though of a more than ordinary constancy, is often, not only shocked, but most severely mortified by the serious, though false, imputation of a crime; especially when that imputation happens unfortunately to be supported by some circumstances which give it an air of probability. He is humbled to find that any body should think so meanly of his character as to suppose him capable of being guilty of it. Though perfectly conscious of his own innocence, the very imputation seems often, even in his own imagination, to throw a shadow of disgrace and dishonour upon his character. His just indignation, too, at so very gross an injury, which, however, it frequently be improper, and sometimes even impossible to revenge, is itself a very painful sensation. There is no greater tormentor of the human breast than violent resentment which cannot be gratified. An innocent man, brought to the scaffold by the false imputation of an infamous or odious crime, suffers the most cruel misfortune which it is possible for innocence to suffer. The agony of his mind, in this case, frequently be greater than that of those who suffer for the like crimes, of which they have been actually guilty. Profligate criminals, such as common thieves and highwaymen, have frequently little sense of the baseness of their own conduct, and consequently no remorse. Without troubling themselves about the justice or injustice of the punishment, they have always been accustomed to look upon the gibbet as a lot very likely to fall to them. When it does fall to them, therefore, they consider themselves only as not quite so lucky as some of their companions, and submit to their fortune, without any other uneasiness than what arise from the fear of death; a fear which, even by such worthless wretches,

> we frequently see, can be so easily, and so very completely conquered. The innocent man, on the contrary, over and above the uneasiness which this fear occasion, is tormented by his own indignation at the injustice which has been done to him. He is struck with horror at the thoughts of the infamy which the punishment shed upon his memory, and foresees, with the most exquisite anguish, that he is hereafter to be remembered by his dearest friends and relations, not with regret and affection, but with shame, and even with horror for his supposed disgraceful conduct: and the shades of death appear to close round him with a darker and more melancholy gloom than naturally belongs to them…
> To persons in such unfortunate circumstances, that humble philosophy which confines its views to this life, can afford, perhaps, but little consolation. Every thing that could render either life or death respectable is taken from them. They are condemned to death and to everlasting infamy. Religion can alone afford them any effectual comfort. She alone can tell them, that it is of little importance what man think of their conduct, while the all-seeing Judge of the world approves of it. She alone can present to them the view of another world; a world of more candour, humanity, and justice, than the present; where their innocence is in due time to be declared, and their virtue to be finally rewarded: and the same great principle which can alone strike terror into triumphant vice, affords the only effectual consolation to disgraced and insulted innocence. (*TMS*, pp. 174–176)

There is no personally greater loss, torment, and suffering than that of an innocent person found guilty. Hence, the fundamental asymmetry in the error properties of beneficence and justice. To praise in error is nothing in comparison to blame for error. Hence, the proposition in Smith supports the classical liberal first amendment constitutional commitment to the principle that the accused are to be treated as innocent until proved guilty, and are entitled to due process, and judgment from a jury of peers.

We have, regretfully, deviated in three prominently dangerous ways from those first principles: (1) DOE Title IX guidelines for combatting sexual harassment in which victims do not face their accusers [as of 2023, such university campus cases that have gotten to the courts have ruled that the victim's constitutional rights had been violated[1]]; (2) in "whistle-blower" cases the goal of ferreting out wrongdoing protects accusers from

[1] See https://www.thefire.org/research-learn/sexual-harassment-college-campuses.

being known to, and confronted by, the accused.[2] (3) Civil Forfeiture whereby property connected in some way, even innocently, with a crime, can be seized by local police and sold for their slush fund accounts without recourse for recovery.[3]

Unjust imputation can be more hurtful than actual guilt felt.

> In smaller offences, as well as in greater crimes, it frequently happens that a person of sensibility is much more hurt by the unjust imputation than the real criminal is by the actual guilt. A woman of gallantry laughs even at the well-founded surmises which are circulated concerning her conduct. The worst-founded surmise of the same kind is a mortal stab to an innocent virgin. The person who is deliberately guilty of a disgraceful action, we lay it down, I believe, as a general rule, can seldom have much sense of the disgrace; and the person who is habitually guilty of it, can scarce ever have any. (*TMS*, p. 176)

The real criminal's sense of their own guilt for the violation of justice is small compared with the depth of feeling by those who are unjustly found guilty. The consequences of error must always be sensitive to the asymmetries in their impact on individuals and, therefore, in their implications for society. One of the great technological breakthroughs is the ability to detect traces of DNA that has enabled many old cases of unjustified guilt being re-evaluated and corrected.

Every wise person despises unmerited applause but why is unmerited reproach capable of mortifying?

> When every man, even of middling understanding, so readily despises unmerited applause, how it comes to pass that unmerited reproach should often be capable of mortifying so severely men of the soundest and best judgment, perhaps deserve some consideration.
> Pain, I have already had occasion to observe, is, in almost all cases, a more pungent sensation than the opposite and correspondent pleasure. The one almost always depresses us much more below the ordinary, or what may

[2] But these protections hare been removed by the state in espionage charges. https://www.whistleblowers.org/news/the-case-of-edward-snowden/.

[3] https://www.cato.org/policing-in-america/chapter-4/civil-asset-forfeiture#:~:text=Civil%20asset%20forfeiture%20is%20a,is%20involved%20with%20criminal%20activity.

be called the natural state of our happiness, than the other ever raises us above it. A man of sensibility is apt to be more humiliated by just censure than he is ever elevated by just applause. Unmerited applause a wise man rejects with contempt upon all occasions; but he often feels very severely the injustice of unmerited censure. By suffering himself to be applauded for what he has not performed, by assuming a merit which does not belong to him, he feels that he is guilty of a mean falsehood, and deserves, not the admiration, but the contempt, of those very persons who, by mistake, had been led to admire him. It, perhaps, give him some well-founded pleasure to find that he has been, by many people, thought capable of performing what he did not perform. But, though he may be obliged to his friends for their good opinion, he would think himself guilty of the greatest baseness if he did not immediately undeceive them. It gives him little pleasure to look upon himself in the light in which other people actually look upon him, when he is conscious that, if they knew the truth, they would look upon him in a very different light. A weak man, however, is often much delighted with viewing himself in this false and delusive light. He assumes the merit of every laudable action that is ascribed to him, and pretends to that of many which nobody ever thought of ascribing to him. He pretends to have done what he never did, to have written what another wrote, to have invented what another discovered; and is led into all the miserable vices of plagiarism and common lying. But though no man of middling good sense can derive much pleasure from the imputation of a laudable action which he never performed, yet a wise man suffer great pain from the serious imputation of a crime which he never committed. Nature, in this case, has rendered the pain not only more pungent than the opposite and correspondent pleasure, but she has rendered it so in a much greater than the ordinary degree. A denial rids a man at once of the foolish and ridiculous pleasure; but it will not always rid him of the pain. When he refuses the merit which is ascribed to him, nobody doubts his veracity. It may be doubted when he denies the crime which he is accused of. He is at once enraged at the falsehood of the imputation, and mortified to find that any credit should be given to it. He feels that his character is not sufficient to protect him. He feels that his brethren, far from looking upon him in that light in which he anxiously desires to be viewed by them, think him capable of being guilty of what he is accused of. He knows perfectly that he has not been guilty: he knows perfectly what he has done; but, perhaps, scarce any man can know perfectly what he himself is capable of doing. What the peculiar constitution of his own mind or not admit of, is, perhaps, more or less a matter of doubt to every man. The trust and good opinion of his friends and neighbours tend more than any thing to relieve him from this most disagreeable doubt; their distrust and unfavourable opinion,

> to increase it. He thinks himself very confident that their unfavourable judgment is wrong: but this confidence can seldom be so great as to hinder that judgment from making some impression upon him; and the greater his sensibility, the greater his delicacy, the greater his worth, in short, this impression is likely to be the greater. (*TMS*, pp. 176–178)

Because pain is asymmetrically felt as more pungent than its opposite in joy, we can suffer more from pain than we can ever gain from joy. To this, however, must be appended a greater and more unsettling asymmetry: No one doubts, and all immediately accept, the veracity of they who reject praise as undeserved and not praiseworthy. But no one routinely accepts another's denial of guilt. This follows most logically from Adam Smith's distinction between the origins of action and the consequences of action.

The importance of the agreement or disagreement of our own sentiments and judgments with that of others is identical with the same sentiments toward ourselves.

> The agreement or disagreement both of the sentiments and judgments of other people with our own, is, in all cases, it must be observed, of more or less importance to us, exactly in proportion as we ourselves are more or less uncertain about the propriety of our own sentiments, about the accuracy of our own judgments. A man of sensibility sometimes feel great uneasiness lest he should have yielded too much even to what be called an honourable passion; to his just indignation, perhaps, at the injury which have been done either to himself or to his friend. He is anxiously afraid lest, meaning only to act with spirit, and to do justice, he, from the too great vehemence of his emotion, have done a real injury to some other person; who, though not innocent, not have been altogether so guilty as he at first apprehended. The opinion of other people becomes, in this case, of the utmost importance to him. Their approbation is the most healing balsam; their disapprobation, the bitterest and most tormenting poison that can be poured into his uneasy mind. When he is perfectly satisfied with every part of his own conduct, the judgment of other people is often of less importance to him. (*TMS*, pp. 178–179)

As we judge ourselves, so we expect others to judge us and vice versa.

They who are most comfortable with their self-judgments are less likely to be anxious as to the judgments of others.

For they who are perfectly and justly satisfied with their own conduct the judgments of others may become less important to them.

Anxiety about public opinion affects variously, the uncertainty or certainty of our own tastes in the arts and sciences.

> There are some very noble and beautiful arts, in which the degree of excellence can be determined only by a certain nicety of taste, of which the decisions, however, appear always, in some measure, uncertain. There are others, in which the success admits, either of clear demonstration, or very satisfactory proof. Among the candidates for excellence in those different arts, the anxiety about the public opinion is always much greater in the former than in the latter.
>
> The beauty of poetry is a matter of such nicety, that a young beginner can scarce ever be certain that he has attained it. Nothing delights him so much, therefore, as the favourable judgments of his friends and of the public; and nothing mortifies him so severely as the contrary. The one establishes, the other shakes, the good opinion which he is anxious to entertain concerning his own performances. Experience and success in time give him a little more confidence in his own judgment. He is at all times, however, liable to be most severely mortified by the unfavourable judgments of the public. Racine was so disgusted by the indifferent success of his Phædra, the finest tragedy, perhaps, that is extant in any language, that, though in the vigour of his life, and at the height of his abilities, he resolved to write no more for the stage...The extreme sensibility of Voltaire to the slightest censure of the same kind is well known to every body. The Dunciad of Mr Pope is an everlasting monument of how much the most correct, as well as the most elegant and harmonious of all the English poets, had been hurt by the criticisms of the lowest and most contemptible authors. Gray...is said to have been so much hurt by a foolish and impertinent parody of two of his finest odes, that he never afterwards attempted any considerable work. Those men of letters who value themselves upon what is called fine writing in prose, approach somewhat to the sensibility of poets. Mathematicians, on the contrary, who have the most perfect assurance both of the truth and of the importance of their discoveries, are frequently very indifferent about the reception which they meet with from the public. The two greatest mathematicians that I ever have had the honour to be known to, and, I believe, the two greatest that have lived in my time, Dr Robert Simson of Glasgow, and Dr Matthew Stewart of Edinburgh, never seemed to feel even the slightest uneasiness from the neglect with which the ignorance of the public received some of their most valuable works. The great work of Sir Isaac Newton, his Mathematical Principles of Natural Philosophy, I have been told, was for several years neglected by the public. The tranquillity of that great man, it is probable, never suffered, upon that account, the interruption of a single

> quarter of an hour. Natural philosophers, in their independency upon the public opinion, approach nearly to mathematicians, and, in their judgments concerning the merit of their own discoveries and observations, enjoy some degree of the same security and tranquillity. (*TMS*, pp. 179–181)

Students of calculus today will be interested to learn that Simson (now Simpson), of Simpson's rule for the differentiation of an integral, was a Glasgow colleague of Smith's.

Smith's proclamations that academics and great figures like Newton were immune to the critical opinions of the public must constitute his largest failure of explanation and prediction concerning the future of factions and cabals in academia.

As some wag has claimed, academic infighting is endemic because the stakes are so low, implying that where the economic stakes are low the non-monetary payoffs become bitterly and exaggeratedly contentious without external restraint and order in its formation process.

Because of their independence from public opinion, mathematicians and natural philosophers are not tempted to factions and cabals.

> Mathematicians and natural philosophers, from their independency upon the public opinion, have little temptation to form themselves into factions and cabals, either for the support of their own reputation, or for the depression of that of their rivals. They are almost always men of the most amiable simplicity of manners, who live in good harmony with one another, are the friends of one another's reputation, enter into no intrigue in order to secure the public applause, but are pleased when their works are approved of, without being either much vexed or very angry when they are neglected. It is not always the same case with poets, or with those who value themselves upon what is called fine writing. They are very apt to divide themselves into a sort of literary factions; each cabal being often avowedly, and almost always secretly, the mortal enemy of the reputation of every other, and employing all the mean arts of intrigue and solicitation to pre-occupy the public opinion in favour of the works of its own members, and against those of its enemies and rivals. In France, Despreaux and Racine did not think it below them to set themselves at the head of a literary cabal, in order to depress the reputation, first of Quinault and Perrault, and afterwards of Fontenelle and La Motte, and even to treat the good La Fontaine with a species of most disrespectful kindness. In England, the amiable Mr Addison did not think it unworthy of his gentle and modest character to set himself at the head of a little

> cabal of the same kind, in order to keep down the rising reputation of Mr Pope. Mr Fontenelle, in writing the lives and characters of the members of the academy of sciences, a society of mathematicians and natural philosophers, has frequent opportunities of celebrating the amiable simplicity of their manners; a quality which, he observes, was so universal among them as to be characteristical rather of that whole class of men of letters than of any individual. Mr D'Alembert, in writing the lives and characters of the members of the French Academy, a society of poets and fine writers, or of those who are supposed to be such, seems not to have had such frequent opportunities of making any remark of this kind, and nowhere pretends to represent this amiable quality as characteristical of that class of men of letters whom he celebrates. (*TMS*, pp. 181–182)

Some of the best mathematicians I knew cared so little of their public image that I do not think they knew how to find it and did not know what it was. They were, however, quite interested to know of the opinions of other mathematicians they knew and respected. But I believe that natural philosophers and today's physicists and astronomers are another matter. Although, my colleague at the University of Arizona, Roger Angel, surely is comfortable with his incredible and much deserved scientific reputation. So surely was that of my colleague at Purdue, Seymour Benzer the Purdue physicist who, after distinguishing himself with great success in the early development of transistors, became a great pioneering behavioral geneticist.

Our anxiety to think favorably of ourselves also drives our natural desire to know what opinion others have of us.

> Our uncertainty concerning our own merit, and our anxiety to think favourably of it, should together naturally enough make us desirous to know the opinion of other people concerning it; to be more than ordinarily elevated when that opinion is favourable, and to be more than ordinarily mortified when it is otherwise: but they should not make us desirous either of obtaining the favourable, or of avoiding the unfavourable opinion, by intrigue and cabal. When a man has bribed all the judges, the most unanimous decision of the court, though it gain him his law-suit, cannot give him any assurance that he was in the right: and had he carried on his law-suit merely to satisfy himself that he was in the right, he never would have bribed the judges. But though he wished to find himself in the right, he wished likewise to gain his law-suit; and therefore he bribed the judges. If

> praise were of no consequence to us, but as a proof of our own praiseworthiness, we never should endeavour to obtain it by unfair[-play] means. But though to wise men it is, at least in doubtful cases, of principal consequence upon this account, it is likewise of some consequence upon its own account; and therefore (we cannot, indeed, upon such occasions, call them wise men, but) men very much above the common level have sometimes attempted both to obtain praise and to avoid blame by very unfair means. (*TMS*, pp. 182–183)

We are anxious to learn about ourselves from others because that is the only way we can know ourselves. That learning is most valuable to us and others if we are always very honest with others in all interactions with them. We should avoid intrigue, strategizing, and cabal in seeking the opinion of others about ourselves. For they who bribe judges to win a judgment cannot know if their case is right, whereas those who pursue their lawsuit to see if they are right would never have bribed the judges.

As we have already discussed, classical game theory applied to poker, war, and politics concerned environments in which people mutually identified each other as being in strict opposition (see Chapter 20). Adam Smith saw certain attitudes as bound to poison the attainment of stable and productive communities and societies. Intrigue, strategy, and cabal are what undermine justice, and crowd out beneficence. Indeed, being an effective neighbor, co-worker in a business, or educator requires one to avoid any actions that might brand you as a strategist in your relevant socio-economic group. And if you try to restrict your display of those proclivities to those outside your group it might prejudice how you are viewed within your group!

Praise and blame concern what are, but praiseworthiness and blameworthiness ought to drive our conduct and be what others want to know of us.

> Praise and blame express what actually are; praiseworthiness and blameworthiness what naturally ought to be the sentiments of other people with regard to our character and conduct. The love of praise is the desire of obtaining the favourable sentiments of our brethren. The love of praiseworthiness is the desire of rendering ourselves the proper objects of those sentiments. So far those two principles resemble and are akin to one another. The like affinity and resemblance take place between the dread of blame and that of blameworthiness.

> The man who desires to do, or who actually does, a praiseworthy action, likewise desire the praise which is due to it, and sometimes, perhaps, more than is due to it. The two principles are in this case blended together. How far his conduct have been influenced by the one, and how far by the other, frequently may be unknown even to himself. It must almost always be so to other people. They who are disposed to lessen the merit of his conduct, impute it chiefly or altogether to the mere love of praise, or to what they call mere vanity. They who are disposed to think more favourably of it, impute it chiefly or altogether to the love of praiseworthiness; to the love of what is really honourable and noble in human conduct; to the desire not merely of obtaining, but of deserving, the approbation and applause of his brethren. The imagination of the spectator throws upon it either the one colour or the other, according either to his habits of thinking, or to the favour or dislike which he bear to the person whose conduct he is considering. (*TMS*, pp. 183–184)

They who diminish the merit of another's good conduct attribute it to that other's vain pursuit of the love of praise. They who think favorably of another's impulse to good action, attribute it to the love of praiseworthiness. By such expressions of how they interpret the actions of their companions, we will come to know how to interpret their actions toward others and toward us.

Splenetic and peevish philosophers have confounded praise and praiseworthiness in judging vanity.

> Some splenetic philosophers, in judging of human nature, have done as peevish individuals are apt to do in judging of the conduct of one another, and have imputed to the love of praise, or to what they call vanity, every action which ought to be ascribed to that of praiseworthiness…
>
> Very few men can be satisfied with their own private consciousness that they have attained those qualities, or performed those actions, which they admire and think praiseworthy in other people; unless it is at the same time generally acknowledged that they possess the one, or have performed the other; or, in other words, unless they have actually obtained that praise which they think due both to the one and to the other. In this respect…men differ considerably… Some seem indifferent about the praise, when, in their own minds, they are perfectly satisfied that they have attained the praiseworthiness. Others appear much less anxious about the praiseworthiness than about the praise.

> No man can be completely or even tolerably satisfied with having avoided every thing blameworthy in his conduct; unless he has likewise avoided the blame or the reproach. A wise man frequently neglect praise, even when he has best deserved it; but, in all matters of serious consequence, he will most carefully endeavour so to regulate his conduct as to avoid, not only blameworthiness, but, as much as possible, every probable imputation of blame. He will never, indeed, avoid blame by doing any thing which he judges blameworthy; by omitting any part of his duty, or by neglecting any opportunity of doing any thing which he judges to be really and greatly praiseworthy. But, with these modifications, he will most anxiously and carefully avoid it. To shew much anxiety about praise, even for praiseworthy actions, is seldom a mark of great wisdom, but generally of some degree of weakness. But, in being anxious to avoid the shadow of blame or reproach, there may be no weakness, but frequently the most praiseworthy prudence. (*TMS*, pp. 184–185)

Some, not at all anxious to receive praise, are completely comfortable with their own praiseworthiness. Others, preoccupied by their image in the world, will be much less secure in their own sense of praiseworthiness and may be anxious for the praise they receive.

But no one can be entirely comfortable with having avoided all blameworthiness unless they also avoid all blame. The wise person often neglects praise, even when well deserved, but must carefully nurture their conduct to avoid, not only blameworthiness, but all chances of blame. If you have to say "I am not a crook" you have revealed that surely you must be a crook.

Cicero's Inconsistency Seems Founded on What We Learn from the Principles of an All-Wise Author of Nature.

> "Many people," says Cicero, "despise glory, who are yet most severely mortified by unjust reproach; and that most inconsistently." This inconsistency, however, seems to be founded in the unalterable principles of human nature. The all-wise Author of Nature has, in this manner, taught man to respect the sentiments and judgments of his brethren; to be more or less pleased when they approve of his conduct, and to be more or less hurt when they disapprove of it. He has made man... the immediate judge of mankind; and has in this respect, as in many others, created him after his own image, and appointed him his vicegerent upon earth, to superintend the behaviour of his brethren. They are taught by nature to acknowledge that power and jurisdiction which has thus been conferred upon him, to be

> more or less humbled and mortified when they have incurred his censure, and to be more or less elated when they have obtained his applause. (*TMS*, p. 185)

The Author of Nature has wisely taught us to always respect the approval and disapproval judgments of each other and has thus made humans the judge of humankind and in this has made plain to all that humankind is created in His image as His vicegerent upon earth, to superintend the conduct of our brethren. Thus, will His victory or failure be ours, and ours His? Smith's insightful and guiding theme is that we can only know God and carry out His purpose through each other and thereby find or not, His purpose.

Distinguishing the jurisdiction of the man without from that of the man within.

> But though man has, in this manner, been rendered the immediate judge of mankind, he has been rendered so only in the first instance; and an appeal lies from his sentence to a much higher tribunal, to the tribunal of their own consciences, to that of the supposed impartial and well-informed spectator, to that of the man within the breast, the great judge and arbiter of their conduct. The jurisdictions of those two tribunals are founded upon principles which, though in some respects resembling and akin, are, however, in reality different and distinct. The jurisdiction of the man without is founded altogether in the desire of actual praise, and in the aversion to actual blame. The jurisdiction of the man within is founded altogether in the desire of praiseworthiness, and in the aversion to blame-worthiness; in the desire of possessing those qualities, and performing those actions, which we love and admire in other people; and in the dread of possessing those qualities, and performing those actions, which we hate and despise in other people. If the man without should applaud us, either for actions which we have not performed, or for motives which had no influence upon us; the man within can immediately humble that pride and elevation of mind which such groundless acclamations might otherwise occasion, by telling us, that as we know that we do not deserve them, we render ourselves despicable by accepting them. If, on the contrary, the man without should reproach us, either for actions which we never performed, or for motives which had no influence upon those which we have performed; the man within immediately correct this false judgment, and assure us, that we are by no means the proper objects of that censure which has so unjustly been bestowed upon us. But in this, and in some

> other cases, the man within seems sometimes, as it were, astonished and confounded by the vehemence and clamour of the man without. The violence and loudness with which blame is sometimes poured out upon us, seems to stupify and benumb our natural sense of praiseworthiness and blameworthiness; and the judgments of the man within, though not, perhaps, absolutely altered or perverted, are, however, so much shaken in the steadiness and firmness of their decision, that their natural effect, in securing the tranquillity of the mind, is frequently, in a great measure, destroyed. We scarce dare to absolve ourselves, when all our brethren appear loudly to condemn us. The supposed impartial spectator of our conduct seems to give his opinion in our favour with fear and hesitation; when that of all the real spectators, when that of all those with whose eyes and from whose station he endeavours to consider it, is unanimously and violently against us. In such cases, this demigod within the breast appears, like the demigods of the poets, though partly of immortal, yet partly too of mortal extraction. When his judgments are steadily and firmly directed by the sense of praiseworthiness and blameworthiness, he seems to act suitably to his divine extraction: but when he suffers himself to be astonished and confounded by the judgments of ignorant and weak man, he discovers his connection with mortality, and appears to act suitably rather to the human than to the divine part of his origin. (*TMS*, pp. 185–187)

Smith identifies the human desire for praise and to avoid blame with a person's outward orientation to the source of all observations and evidence of interactive social influence—The Man Without. Separately and distinctly, he identifies the human desire for praiseworthiness and to avoid blameworthiness with a person's inward orientation to matters of the heart—The Man Within. The former is subject to error, but they who admit that the praise was unjustified meet with ready acceptance and respect; the latter are also subject to error but they who claim to be not guilty as charged meet with skepticism. Since in Smith's model, we necessarily must have common knowledge that all are self-interested, the credibility of one's "honest" confession in the first case is accepted because it is contrary to their self-interested incentives, whereas the credibility of their denial in the second case is entirely consistent with their self-interest. We imagine no one dishonestly claiming that praise was unjustified, but easily imagine anyone dishonestly claiming to be not guilty.

The resolution of the conflict between the man without and the man within lies in the appeal to a still higher tribunal.

> In such cases, the only effectual consolation of humbled and afflicted man lies in an appeal to a still higher tribunal, to that of the all-seeing Judge of the world, whose eye can never be deceived, and whose judgments can never be perverted. A firm confidence in the unerring rectitude of this great tribunal, before which his innocence is in due time to be declared, and his virtue to be finally rewarded, can alone support him under the weakness and despondency of his own mind, under the perturbation and astonishment of the man within the breast, whom nature has set up as, in this life, the great guardian, not only of his innocence but of his tranquillity. Our happiness in this life is thus, upon many occasions, dependent upon the humble hope and expectation of a life to come; a hope and expectation deeply rooted in human nature, which can alone support its lofty ideas of its own dignity, can alone illumine the dreary prospect of its continually approaching mortality, and maintain its cheerfulness under all the heaviest calamities to which, from the disorders of this life, it sometimes be exposed. That there is a world to come, where exact justice will be done to every man; where every man will be ranked with those who, in the moral and intellectual qualities, are really his equals; where the owner of those humble talents and virtues which, from being depressed by fortune, had, in this life, no opportunity of displaying themselves; which were unknown, not only to the public, but which he himself could scarce be sure that he possessed, and for which even the man within the breast could scarce venture to afford him any distinct and clear testimony; where that modest, silent, and unknown merit will be placed upon a level, and sometimes above those who, in this world, had enjoyed the highest reputation, and who, from the advantage of their situation, had been enabled to perform the most splendid and dazzling actions; is a doctrine, in every respect so venerable, so comfortable to the weakness, so flattering to the grandeur of human nature, that the virtuous man who has the misfortune to doubt of it, cannot possibly avoid wishing most earnestly and anxiously to believe it. It could never have been exposed to the derision of the scoffer, had not the distribution of rewards and punishments, which some of its most zealous assertors have taught us was to be made in that world to come, been too frequently in direct opposition to all our moral sentiments. (*TMS*, pp. 187–188)

Nature has created in humankind faith in a higher tribunal, "the all-seeing Judge of the world" and in an afterlife in which every person will be ranked and judged in regard to their good deeds and rewarded, with bad deeds judged and punished, even though these have escaped detection, judgment, and their deserved consequences in this life. In this, nature seeks to support our happiness in this world and to believe that we are born into a world founded on justice. Without faith in the existence of such a tribunal, how could we be led to form an image of perfection against which we make judgments of relative attainment? How can we know justice as a means for allowing beneficence into our lives and communities?

The roads to preferment in the adulated courtier versus the faithful and merited. Is preferment to be denied the military officer?

> That the assiduous courtier is often more favoured than the faithful and active servant; that attendance and adulation are often shorter and surer roads to preferment than merit or service; and that a campaign at Versailles or St James's is often worth two either in Germany or Flanders, is a complaint which we have all heard from many a venerable but discontented old officer. But what is considered as the greatest reproach even to the weakness of earthly sovereigns, has been ascribed, as an act of justice, to divine perfection; and the duties of devotion, the public and private worship of the Deity, have been represented, even by men of virtue and abilities, as the sole virtues which can either entitle to reward, or exempt from punishment, in the life to come. They were the virtues, perhaps, most suitable to their station, and in which they themselves chiefly excelled; and we are all naturally disposed to overrate the excellencies of our own characters. In the discourse which the eloquent and philosophical Massillon pronounced, on giving his benediction to the standards of the regiment of Catinat, there is the following address to the officers:—"What is most deplorable in your situation, gentlemen, is, that in a life hard and painful, in which the services and the duties sometimes go beyond the rigour and severity of the most austere cloisters; you suffer always in vain for the life to come, and frequently even for this life. Alas! the solitary monk in his cell, obliged to mortify the flesh and to subject it to the spirit, is supported by the hope of an assured recompence, and by the secret unction of that grace which softens the yoke of the Lord. But you, on the bed of death, can you dare to represent to him your fatigues and the daily hardships of your employment? can you dare to solicit him for any recompence? and in all the exertions that you have made, in all the violences that you have done to yourselves, what is there that he ought to place to his own account? The best days of your life, however, have been sacrificed to your profession, and ten years' service has more worn out your body, than would,

> perhaps, have done a whole life of repentance and mortification. Alas! my brother, one single day of those sufferings, consecrated to the Lord, would, perhaps, have obtained you an eternal happiness. One single action, painful to nature, and offered up to Him, would, perhaps, have secured to you the inheritance of the saints. And you have done all this, and in vain, for this world." (*TMS*, pp. 188–189)

Can it be that a military life devoted to duty and sacrifice, with little time for repentance, fail to find its proper judgment and reward in the afterlife to come? Or will the monk's life or repentance, also doing his duty assure its reward?

For the monks eternal heaven, yet no quarter for the heroes, statesman, lawgiver, poets, and philosophers, nor the protectors, instructors, and benefactors of humankind?

> To compare, in this manner, the futile mortifications of a monastery, to the ennobling hardships and hazards of war; to suppose that one day, or one hour, employed in the former should, in the eye of the great Judge of the world, have more merit than a whole life spent honourably in the latter, is surely contrary to all our moral sentiments; to all the principles by which nature has taught us to regulate our contempt or admiration. It is this spirit, however, which, while it has reserved the celestial regions for monks and friars, or for those whose conduct and conversation resembled those of monks and friars, has condemned to the infernal all the heroes, all the statesmen and lawgivers, all the poets and philosophers of former ages; all those who have invented, improved, or excelled in the arts which contribute to the subsistence, to the conveniency, or to the ornament of human life; all the great protectors, instructors, and benefactors of mankind; all those to whom our natural sense of praiseworthiness forces us to ascribe the highest merit and most exalted virtue. Can we wonder that so strange an application of this most respectable doctrine should sometimes have exposed it to contempt and derision? with those at least who had themselves, perhaps, no great taste or turn for the devout and contemplative virtues? (*TMS*, pp. 189–190)

That the great Judge of the Universe should elevate monks, because of their unusual piety, to a station above the heroes, statesmen, lawgivers, poets, and philosophers, and the protectors, instructors, and benefactors of humankind are entirely contrary to everything that nature teaches us to love about praise and praiseworthiness, and to hate about blame and blameworthiness.

So, says *TMS*, if in doubt: listen to Nature! Perhaps in this is embodied the Holy Spirit!

The influence and approbation of human conscience and the impartial spectator.

> But though the approbation of his own conscience can scarce, upon some extraordinary occasions, content the weakness of man; though the testimony of the supposed impartial spectator of the great inmate of the breast cannot always alone support him; yet the influence and authority of this principle is, upon all occasions, very great; and it is only by consulting this judge within that we can ever see what relates to ourselves in its proper shape and dimensions; or that we can ever make any proper comparison between our own interests and those of other people. (*TMS*, p. 191)

Our conscience is the judge within, disciplined and informed by the fair-play impartial spectator who evaluates what relates to ourselves in its proper shape and dimensions. We often attribute the individual's ability to overcome temptation and take the right action to their conscience; but behind that concept is an emergent evolutionary system modeled in *TMS*. God speaks indirectly to us through learning from the experience of His creations. Forget not that Jesus was first and foremost The Son of Man. And we were asked not to follow him, but His God as did He.

CHAPTER 26

Of the influence and authority of conscience

Views from near and far give perspective to vision.

> As to the eye of the body, objects appear great or small, not so much according to their real dimensions as according to the nearness or distance of their situation; so do they likewise to what be called the natural eye of the mind: and we remedy the defects of both these organs pretty much in the same manner. In my present situation, an immense landscape of lawns and woods, and distant mountains, seems to do no more than cover the little window which I write by, and to be out of all proportion less than the chamber in which I am sitting. I can form a just comparison between those great objects and the little objects around me, in no other way than by transporting myself, at least in fancy, to a different station, from whence I can survey both at nearly equal distances, and thereby form some judgment of their real proportions. Habit and experience have taught me to do this so easily and so readily, that I am scarce sensible that I do it; and a man must be, in some measure, acquainted with the philosophy of vision, before he can be thoroughly convinced how little those distant objects would appear to the eye, if the imagination, from a knowledge of their real magnitudes, did not swell and dilate. (*TMS*, pp. 191–192)

The eye of the mind transports us by fancy from a common reality to different stations, and thus different perspectives, which are not altogether the same because of our manner of viewing them. The consequence is a

Vernon L. Smith, *Adam Smith's Theory of Society*,
https://doi.org/10.1007/978-3-031-68494-4_26

perspective and understanding far greater than any of its parts, the great gift of humankind.

In a similar manner, an impartial perspective comes neither only from own nor only from other but also from that of an imagined impartial third-party observer.

> In the same manner, to the selfish and original passions of human nature, the loss or gain of a very small interest of our own appears to be of vastly more importance, excites a much more passionate joy or sorrow, a much more ardent desire or aversion, than the greatest concern of another with whom we have no particular connection. His interests, as long as they are surveyed from his station, can never be put into the balance with our own, can never restrain us from doing whatever tend to promote our own, how ruinous soever to him. Before we can make any proper comparison of those opposite interests, we must change our position. We must view them, neither from our own place nor yet from his, neither with our own eyes nor yet with his, but from the place and with the eyes of a third person, who has no particular connection with either, and who judges with impartiality between us. Here, too, habit and experience have taught us to do this so easily and so readily, that we are scarce sensible that we do it; and it requires, in this case, too, some degree of reflection, and even of philosophy, to convince us, how little interest we should take in the greatest concerns of our neighbour, how little we should be affected by whatever relates to him, if the sense of propriety and justice did not correct the otherwise natural inequality of our sentiments. (*TMS*, pp. 192–193)

In like manner, to judge our own or another's selfish loss or gain from our, or that of the other's particular perspective, fails to lead to a proper balancing of these distinct experiences. For that balance, we need more than our view and not only that of the other but rather that of a third person with no particular connection with either of us but who can sensibly judge between us. Yet, that is precisely what we do through our "sense of propriety and justice" which forms within us, to correct the natural inequality between our sentiments and those of our neighbor. Smith has referred to this transformational process with the metaphor of the impartial spectator but here he is re-articulating what must be, if we are to understand by what process we escape the painful myopia of separation and isolationism. To envision this, he notes how much reflection and philosophy is needed. But Smith's key methodological tool of inquiry is to ask after the opportunity cost consequences if things were otherwise, or as we say abstractly in theory, by appropriate choice of counterfactuals. And hence, to learn requires experience with the rule and with not the rule, as in the emergent common (peoples') law founded on fair-play versus foul.

Why should we care that myriads of inhabitants of china are swallowed by a great earthquake?

> Let us suppose that the great empire of China, with all its myriads of inhabitants, was suddenly swallowed up by an earthquake, and let us consider how a man of humanity in Europe, who had no sort of connection with that part of the world, would be affected upon receiving intelligence of this dreadful calamity. He would, I imagine, first of all express very strongly his sorrow for the misfortune of that unhappy people, he would make many melancholy reflections upon the precariousness of human life, and the vanity of all the labours of man, which could thus be annihilated in a moment. He would, too, perhaps, if he was a man of speculation, enter into many reasonings concerning the effects which this disaster might produce upon the commerce of Europe, and the trade and business of the world in general. And when all this fine philosophy was over, when all these humane sentiments had been once fairly expressed, he would pursue his business or his pleasure, take his repose or his diversion, with the same ease and tranquillity as if no such accident had happened. The most frivolous disaster which could befall himself would occasion a more real disturbance. If he was to lose his little finger tomorrow, he would not sleep to-night; but, provided he never saw them, he will snore with the most profound security over the ruin of a hundred millions of his brethren, and the destruction of that immense multitude seems plainly an object less interesting to him than this paltry misfortune of his own. To prevent, therefore, this paltry misfortune to himself, would a man of humanity be willing to sacrifice the lives of a hundred millions of his brethren, provided he had never seen them? Human nature startles with horror at the thought, and the world, in its greatest depravity and corruption, never produced such a villain as could be capable of entertaining it. But what makes this difference? When our passive feelings are almost always so sordid and so selfish, how comes it that our active principles should often be so generous and so noble? When we are always so much more deeply affected by whatever concerns ourselves than by whatever concerns other men; what is it which prompts the generous upon all occasions, and the mean upon many,

> to sacrifice their own interests to the greater interests of others? (*TMS*, pp. 192–193)

Why should an eighteenth-century European care that a hundred million people in a distant country such as China, be lost to an unavoidable natural disaster? Such a question startles us as horrific. But why harbor such passive selfish feelings when we so frequently find occasion to be actively generous? What accounts for this difference?

We care about the loss of our brethren because of the inner voice from the breast of reason, principle, and conscience.

> It is not the soft power of humanity, it is not that feeble spark of benevolence which Nature has lighted up in the human heart, that is thus capable of counteracting the strongest impluses of self-love. It is a stronger power, a more forcible motive, which exerts itself upon such occasions. It is reason, principle, conscience, the inhabitant of the breast, the man within, the great judge and arbiter of our conduct. It is he who, whenever we are about to act so as to affect the happiness of others, calls to us, with a voice capable of astonishing the most presumptuous of our passions, that we are but one of the multitude, in no respect better than any other in it; and that when we prefer ourselves so shamefully and so blindly to others, we become the proper objects of resentment, abhorrence, and execration. It is from him only that we learn the real littleness of ourselves, and of whatever relates to ourselves, and the natural misrepresentations of self-love can be corrected only by the eye of this impartial spectator. It is he who shews us the propriety of generosity and the deformity of injustice; the propriety of resigning the greatest interests of our own for the yet greater interests of others; and the deformity of doing the smallest injury to another in order to obtain the greatest benefit to ourselves. It is not the love of our neighbour, it is not the love of mankind, which upon many occasions prompts us to the practice of those divine virtues. It is a stronger love, a more powerful affection, which generally takes place upon such occasions; the love of what is honourable and noble, of the grandeur, and dignity, and superiority of our own characters. (*TMS*, pp. 193–194)

Nature's great judge and arbiter of our conduct also monitors that conduct—our impartial spectator—so that we always see ourselves as only one of a multitude, no better than any other, and who reveals above our own great and important interest, a still greater interest of other's that we cannot tread upon.

What would motivate an honorable person to sacrifice his little finger if it could avoid a great disaster for his brethren is his love for "what is honourable and noble, of the grandeur, and dignity, and superiority of our own characters."

Also, as we shall, see wise Nature does not divert our attention to preoccupations with concerns that we can do nothing about, that lie beyond our power to influence. Her rules that we make and follow focus us on what we can do, influence, and accomplish.

The looming contempt of our brethren reminds the call from within that we must prefer not our self-love to the many.

> When the happiness or misery of others depends in any respect upon our conduct, we dare not, as self-love might suggest to us, prefer the interest of one to that of many. The man within immediately calls to us, that we value ourselves too much and other people too little, and that, by doing so, we render ourselves the proper object of the contempt and indignation of our brethren. Neither is this sentiment confined to men of extraordinary magnanimity and virtue. It is deeply impressed upon every tolerably good soldier, who feels that he would become the scorn of his companions if he could be supposed capable of shrinking from danger, or of hesitating either to expose or to throw away his life when the good of the service required it. (*TMS*, pp. 194–195)

We have here illustrated Smith's important methodological distinction between being self-interested and acting self-interestedly. Our conduct, distinct from our opinions, beliefs, and expectations, is about patterns in our relationships with, and between ourselves and, others. Where the welfare of others depends upon our conduct it cannot admit of a preferment of any one other over that of many. This is as true for one of ordinary standing as for those of great virtue such as the soldier who is exposed to great danger in service to his compatriots in battle.

The call of the man within allows that the poor man must never hurt or injure another to benefit himself even if that other be rich. This is because a beneficent society fails if beneficence is thought to be coercer-able.

> One individual must never prefer himself so much even to any other individual as to hurt or injure that other in order to benefit himself, though the benefit to the one should be much greater than the hurt or injury to the other. The poor man must neither defraud nor steal from the rich, though the acquisition might be much more beneficial to the one than the loss could be hurtful to the other. The man within immediately calls to him in this case, too, that he is no better than his neighbour, and that by his unjust preference, he renders himself the proper object of the contempt and indignation of mankind, as well as of the punishment which that contempt and indignation must naturally dispose them to inflict, for having thus violated one of those sacred rules, upon the tolerable observation of which depend the whole security and peace of human society. There is no commonly honest man who does not more dread the inward disgrace of such an action, the indelible stain which it would for ever stamp upon his own mind, than the greatest external calamity which, without any fault of his own, could possibly befall him; and who does not inwardly feel the truth of that great stoical maxim, that for one man to deprive another unjustly of any thing, or unjustly to promote his own advantage by the loss or disadvantage of another, is more contrary to nature than death, than poverty, than pain, than all the misfortunes which can affect him, either in his body, or in his external circumstances. (*TMS*, p. 195)

Smith provides no moral comfort for the modern populist sentiment that the poor deserve to derive benefit from involuntary transfers from the rich. Later, when he wrote *WN*, though he argues that we have property law because the rich want to prevent the poor from taking their property, all benefit from the wealth created by the division of labor supported, in turn, by markets and property law. In *TMS* it is justice, as morality, all the way up from the inner person; otherwise, there can be no society. There can be no society where the exception to freedom empowers the poor to violate the rights of the rich simply because of their riches. This exception defines the slipperiest slope into all forms of authoritarianism and ultimately, prosperity for no one.

Do I think the rich ought to help the poor? YES, but only voluntarily and not under either threat of, or application of, top-down coercive power—the Trojan Horse that can only destroy the beneficent order of a free society. It is the mortal moral sin of man written large.

When our interests are detached from others, we feel less impelled to regard them, but two schools, one of propriety and one of philosophy, offer different paths to proper conduct. The first is prior but direct, the second is after but confirms.

> When the happiness or misery of others, indeed, in no respect depends upon our conduct, when our interests are altogether separated and detached from theirs, so that there is neither connection nor competition between them, we do not always think it so necessary to restrain, either our natural, and, perhaps, improper anxiety about our own affairs, or our natural, and, perhaps, equally improper indifference about those of other men. The most vulgar education teaches us to act, upon all important occasions, with some sort of impartiality between ourselves and others, and even the ordinary commerce of the world is capable of adjusting our active principles to some degree of propriety. But it is the most artificial and refined education only, it has been said, which can correct the inequalities of our passive feelings; and we must for this purpose, it has been pretended, have recourse to the severest, as well as to the profoundest, philosophy. (*TMS*, pp. 195–196)

Philosophy pretends that its profound lessons are needed in education to overcome the natural inequalities inherent in our passive feelings toward others. Yet the lessons of propriety in life, uninformed by philosophical discussions, teach us to act with some form of impartiality between ourselves and others.

One set of moral philosophers teach that we guide ourselves to increase our sensibility to the interests of others; the other set work to diminish that sensitivity to our own interest. Some reproach us for feeling happy when others are in misery. Nature teaches us to be little concerned about those who are beyond our power to help.

> Two different sets of philosophers have attempted to teach us this hardest of all the lessons of morality. One set have laboured to increase our sensibility to the interests of others; another, to diminish that to our own. The first would have us feel for others as we naturally feel for ourselves. The second would have us feel for ourselves as we naturally feel for others. Both, perhaps, have carried their doctrines a good deal beyond the just standard of nature and propriety. The first are those whining and melancholy moralists who are perpetually reproaching us with our happiness, while so many of our brethren are in misery, who regard as impious the

> natural joy of prosperity, which does not think of the many wretches that are at every instant labouring under all sorts of calamities, in the langour of poverty, in the agony of disease, in the horrors of death, under the insults and oppression of their enemies....ought, they think, to damp the pleasures of the fortunate...But, first of all, this extreme sympathy with misfortunes which we know nothing about seems altogether absurd and unreasonable...This artificial commiseration, besides...seems altogether unattainable; and those who affect this character have commonly nothing but a certain affected and sentimental sadness, which, without reaching the heart, serves only to render the countenance and conversation impertinently dismal and disagreeable. And...this disposition of mind, though it could be attained, would be perfectly useless, and could serve no other purpose than to render miserable the person who possessed it. Whatever interest we take in the fortune of those with whom we have no acquaintance or connection, and who are placed altogether out of the sphere of our activity, can produce only anxiety to ourselves, without any manner of advantage to them. To what purpose should we trouble ourselves about the world in the moon? All men, even those at the greatest distance, are no doubt entitled to our good wishes, and our good wishes we naturally give them. But if, notwithstanding, they should be unfortunate, to give ourselves any anxiety upon that account seems to be no part of our duty. *That we should be little interested, therefore, in the fortune of those whom we can neither serve nor hurt, and who are in every respect so very remote from us, seems wisely ordered by Nature*; and if it were possible to alter in this respect the original constitution of our frame, we could yet gain nothing by the change. (*TMS*, pp. 196–197; italics added)

One school of philosophy teaches us to care for others as we care for ourselves, the other to care for ourselves as we care for others. The school of natural propriety teaches us to care for both in proper balance in all our actions and to bother with neither if the circumstances are beyond our capacity to influence. Hence, eighteenth-century Europeans could do nothing to alleviate the suffering by the people of China if a great earthquake should strike.

On viewing ourselves stoically as would any other citizen of the world.

> It is never objected to us that we have too little fellow feeling with the joy of success. Wherever envy does not prevent it, the favour which we bear to prosperity is rather apt to be too great; and the same moralists who blame

> us for want of sufficient sympathy with the miserable, reproach us for the levity with which we are too apt to admire and almost to worship the fortunate, the powerful, and the rich. Among the moralists who endeavour to correct the natural inequality of our passive feelings by diminishing our sensibility to what peculiarly concerns ourselves, we count all the ancient sects of philosophers; but, particularly, the ancient Stoics. Man, according to the Stoics, ought to regard himself, not as something separated and detached, but as a citizen of the world, a member of the vast commonwealth of nature. To the interest of this great community he ought at all times to be willing that his own little interest should be sacrificed. Whatever concerns himself ought to affect him no more than whatever concerns any other equally important part of this immense system. We should view ourselves, not in the light in which our own selfish passions are apt to place us, but in the light in which any other citizen of the world would view us. What befalls ourselves we should regard as what befalls our neighbour, or, what comes to the same thing, as our neighbour regards what befalls us. "When our neighbour," says Epictetus, "loses his wife, or his son, there is nobody who is not sensible that this is a human calamity, a natural event altogether according to the ordinary course of things; but, when the same thing happens to ourselves, then we cry out, as if we had suffered the most dreadful misfortune. We ought, however, to remember how we were affected when this accident happened to another, and such as we were in his case, such ought we to be in our own." (*TMS*, p. 198)

We imagine the pain and dislocation of a major calamity for another to be even greater if it happens to us. The ancient Stoics taught that all of us ought to consider ourselves citizens of the world. And hence, that we ought each to see ourselves as impacted by calamities in no way different than how we view their impact upon our neighbor.

Accounting for differential emotions toward others suffering from private misfortunes. The decalogue commanded us to honor our fathers and mothers. But the love of our children is not mentioned because nature had long sufficiently prepared us for the performance of this latter duty.

> Those private misfortunes, for which our feelings are apt to go beyond the bounds of propriety, are of two different kinds. They are either such as affect us only indirectly, by affecting, in the first place, some other persons who are particularly dear to us; such as our parents, our children, our brothers and sisters, our intimate friends; or they are such as affect

> ourselves immediately and directly, either in our body, in our fortune, or in our reputation; such as pain, sickness, approaching death, poverty, disgrace, &c. In misfortunes of the first kind, our emotions, no doubt, go very much beyond what exact propriety will admit of; but they likewise fall short of it, and they frequently do so. The man who should feel no more for the death or distress of his own father or son than for those of any other man's father or son, would appear neither a good son nor a good father. Such unnatural indifference, far from exciting our applause, would incur our highest disapprobation. Of those domestic affections, however, some are most apt to offend by their excess, and others by their defect. Nature, for the wisest purposes, has rendered in most men, perhaps in all men, parental tenderness a much stronger affection than filial piety. The continuance and propagation of the species depend altogether upon the former, and not upon the latter. In ordinary cases, the existence and preservation of the child depend altogether upon the care of the parents. Those of the parents seldom depend upon that of the child. Nature, therefore, has rendered the former affection so strong, that it generally requires not to be excited, but to be moderated; and moralists seldom endeavour to teach us how to indulge, but generally how to restrain our fondness, our excessive attachment, the unjust preference which we are disposed to give to our own children above those of other people. They exhort us, on the contrary, to an affectionate attention to our parents, and to make a proper return to them in their old age for the kindness which they had shewn to us in our infancy and youth. In the Decalogue we are commanded to honour our fathers and mothers. No mention is made of the love of our children. Nature had sufficiently prepared us for the performance of this latter duty. Men are seldom accused of affecting to be fonder of their children than they really are. They have sometimes been suspected of displaying their piety to their parents with too much ostentation. The ostentatious sorrow of widows has, for a like reason, been suspected of insincerity. We should respect, could we believe it sincere, even the excess of such kind affections; and though we might not perfectly approve, we should not severely condemn it. That it appears praiseworthy, at least in the eyes of those who affect it, the very affectation is a proof. (*TMS*, pp. 199–200)

TMS maintains that Nature has rendered parental concern for their children as stronger than that of the concern of children for their parents. Why should this be? Because nature is wise to the need to maintain and propagate the species. It is, therefore, much more important to nurture the child to better assure its survival than the parent. Hence, in the Decalogue, we are importuned to honor our father and mother, but no mention is made or needs to be made of our children. Nature builds into our sentiments the need to provide for our children in case it be otherwise neglected.

Nature also creates an aversion for murder, theft, and robbery, then includes them in the Decalogue adding that Thou Shalt Not Bear False Witness Nor Covet The Possessions of Thy Neighbor. These commands rightfully receive double imprinting because without them there can be no orderly society or tradition that children can follow in.

Offensive excesses of beneficence might be blamable; but they never appear odious.

> Even the excess of those kind affections which are most apt to offend by their excess, though it appear blameable, never appears odious. We blame the excessive fondness and anxiety of a parent, as something which, in the end, prove hurtful to the child, and which, in the meantime, is excessively inconvenient to the parent; but we easily pardon it, and never regard it with hatred and detestation. But the defect of this usually excessive affection appears always peculiarly odious. The man who appears to feel nothing for his own children, but who treats them upon all occasions with unmerited severity and harshness, seems of all brutes the most detestable. The sense of propriety, so far from requiring us to eradicate altogether that extraordinary sensibility, which we naturally feel for the misfortunes of our nearest connections, is always much more offended by the defect than it ever is by the excess of that sensibility. The stoical apathy is, in such cases, never agreeable, and all the metaphysical sophisms by which it is supported can seldom serve any other purpose than to blow up the hard insensibility of a coxcomb to ten times its native impertinence. The poets and romance writers, who best paint the refinements and delicacies of love and friendship, and of all other private and domestic affections, Racine and Voltaire, Richardson, Marivaux, and Riccoboni, are, in such cases, much better instructors than Eno, Chrysippus, or Epictetus. (*TMS*, pp. 200–201)

An offensive excess of affection does not imply that the excess is deemed odious. We feel for our children an excess that others do not share, but our excess of affection, even if blamable because it might undermine their normal development of independence, is not seen as odious by others. We leave to the private business of others their balancing of affection and discipline toward their children.

Propriety is more likely offended by excess when misfortune happens to us than when it happens to others.

> That moderated sensibility to the misfortunes of others, which does not disqualify us for the performance of any duty—the melancholy and affectionate remembrance of our departed friends...are by no means undelicious sensations. Though they outwardly wear the features of pain and grief, they are all inwardly stamped with the ennobling characters of virtue and self-approbation. It is otherwise in the misfortunes which affect ourselves immediately and directly, either in our body, in our fortune, or in our reputation. The sense of propriety is much more apt to be offended by the excess than by the defect of our sensibility, and there are but very few cases in which we can approach too near to the stoical apathy and indifference. (*TMS*, p. 201)

Outwardly, our sensibility toward the misfortunes of others exhibits our pain and grief, while inwardly it represents ennobling characteristics of virtue and self-approbation. But it is otherwise in the misfortunes which affect ourselves in our body, fortune, or reputation. With us, the sense of propriety is much more likely to be offended by an excess than by a deficiency of our sensibility. Better to bear our burdens more stoically.

Bodily harm occasions the liveliest sympathy, but they who suffer it with ease, are never offensive.

> That we have very little fellow-feeling with any of the passions which take their origin from the body, has already been observed. That pain which is occasioned by an evident cause, such as the cutting or tearing of the flesh, is, perhaps, the affection of the body with which the spectator feels the most lively sympathy. The approaching death of his neighbour, too, seldom fails to affect him a good deal. In both cases, however, he feels so very little in comparison of what the person principally concerned feels, that the latter can scarce ever offend the former by appearing to suffer with too much ease. (*TMS*, p. 201)

To bear the pain of body or of emotion, as in the death of a dear friend, engenders a full sympathetic understanding from others. But moderating our expressions of sorrow, in Stoic acceptance, will hardly be offensive.

We applaud the ranking of character and conduct over fortune.

> The mere want of fortune, mere poverty, excites little compassion. Its complaints are too apt to be the objects rather of contempt than of fellow-feeling. We despise a beggar; and, though his importunities extort an alms from us, he is scarce ever the object of any serious commiseration. The fall from riches to poverty, as it commonly occasions the most real distress to the sufferer, so it seldom fails to excite the most sincere commiseration in the spectator. Though in the present state of society this misfortune can seldom happen without some misconduct, and some very considerable misconduct, too, in the sufferer, yet he is almost always so much pitied, that he is scarce ever allowed to fall into the lowest state of poverty; but, by the means of his friends, frequently by the indulgence of those very creditors who have much reason to complain of his imprudence, is almost always supported in some degree of decent, though humble, mediocrity. To persons under such misfortunes we could, perhaps, easily pardon some degree of weakness; but, at the same time, they who carry the firmest countenance, who accommodate themselves with the greatest ease to their new situation, who seem to feel no humiliation from the change, but to rest their rank in the society, not upon their fortune, but upon their character and conduct, are always the most approved of, and never fail to command our highest and most affectionate admiration. (*TMS*, pp. 201–202)

Here we have the proposition that though we give alms to a beggar we give them little sympathy or sorrow, and generally the want of fortune only, is not something that excites our compassion. Perhaps we are as likely to feel contempt as fellow-feeling, especially today with drug use, except we must recognize the downward spiral of addiction, helped not a whit by the outrage of criminalization. Why does not poverty alone excite compassion? If we have known poverty and escaped it, why should not others have done so also? Perhaps we had opportunities that they did not, which inspires respect for those who are dedicated to finding systematic ways to help the poor bootstrap themselves into a more abundant life.

The homeless being visible disturbs our tranquility. We call the police, so what are they to do? Some are not homeless—they have cars, trailers, or tents to sleep in; they are merely houseless. One whom I see regularly hangs out with his faithful and much-loved dog near the local supermarket, often in Starbucks having coffee. I bought him a Starbucks gift card. Handing it to him I said, "take care of your dog." He replies, "I do. He is first ahead of me." He merely verified what I suspected, but to be sure I ensured by giving him a Starbucks credit, not cash.

We admire sensibility and indifference in the innocent whose loss of reputation is undeserved, or the aged whose long experience of folly and injustice in this world has armored them with indifference.

> As of all the external misfortunes which can affect an innocent man immediately and directly, the undeserved loss of reputation is certainly the greatest; so a considerable degree of sensibility to whatever can bring on so great a calamity does not always appear ungraceful or disagreeable. We often esteem a young man the more when he resents…any unjust reproach that have been thrown upon his character or his honour. The affliction of an innocent young lady, on account of the groundless surmises which have been circulated concerning her conduct, appears often perfectly amiable. Persons of an advanced age, whom long experience of the folly and injustice of the world has taught to pay little regard either to its censure or to its applause, neglect and despise obloquy, and do not even deign to honour its futile authors with any serious resentment. This indifference, which is founded altogether on a firm confidence in their own well-tried and well-established characters, would be disagreeable in young people, who neither can nor ought to have any such confidence. It might in them be supposed to forebode in their advancing years a most improper insensibility to real honour and infamy. (*TMS*, pp. 202–203)

The elderly see duty as a service to be neither censored nor applauded. We esteem a young man who resents any unjust reproach to their honor. At one time this esteem was so strong that it provided social support for dueling. Indeed, the challenge to duel was a measure of justified resentment and of presumed innocence. He who dueled and won received a unanimous opinion of innocence.

The virtue of self-command is disciplined by the supposed spectator of our conduct and is essential for the emergence of a bottom-up rule-governed free society.

> If we examine the different shades and gradations of weakness and self-command, as we meet with them in common life, we shall very easily satisfy ourselves that this control of our passive feelings must be acquired, not from the abstruse syllogisms of a quibbling dialectic, but from that great discipline which Nature has established for the acquisition of this and of every other virtue; a regard to the sentiments of the real or supposed spectator of our conduct. (*TMS*, p. 145)

The inner voice of the impartial spectator of our own conduct, whether weak, middling, or strong, determines the effectiveness of our self-command. The voice must speak strongly enough in the many to trump the temptations of inappropriate self-loving action if a stable free society is to emerge.

Growing up, we find that our first playmates have not the indulgent partiality of our parents, we moderate our passions to please them, thus entering the great school of self-command, a lifelong rule-learning process supporting the free society.

> A very young child has no self-command; but, whatever are its emotions, whether fear, or grief, or anger, it endeavours always, by the violence of its outcries, to alarm, as much as it can, the attention of its nurse, or of its parents. While it remains under the custody of such partial protectors, its anger is the first, and, perhaps, the only passion which it is taught to moderate. By noise and threatening they are, for their own ease, often obliged to frighten it into good temper; and the passion which incites it to attack, is restrained by that which teaches it to attend to its own safety. When it is old enough to go to school, or to mix with its equals, it soon finds that they have no such indulgent partiality. It naturally wishes to gain their favour, and to avoid their hatred or contempt. Regard even to its own safety teaches it to do so; and it soon finds that it can do so in no other way than by moderating, not only its anger, but all its other passions, to the degree which its play-fellows and companions are likely to be pleased with. It thus enters into the great school of self-command; it studies to be more and more master of itself; and begins to exercise over its own feelings a discipline which the practice of the longest life is very seldom sufficient to bring to complete perfection. (*TMS*, pp. 203–204)

Smith, who never married and had no children, rather brilliantly traces his critically important concept of self-command to the natural environment in which he saw children growing up. In contrast, I lived on a Kansas farm, aged 5–7, had no remembered playmates from recess in a one-room schoolhouse for grades 1–8, and no neighborly children as farmhouses stood far apart. I was largely a loner with only a few close friends, through grade, intermediate, high, and undergrad schools, surely stunting my social development and accounting for my academic career! All mammals acquire essential skills in their early periods of play with brothers, sisters, and/or neighborhood playmates. Mine was with animals, dog, cats, cows, chickens—I made a play-mate pet of a treasured young chicken.

For Smith, the very young child is without self-command. The indulgence and necessary protections of its nurse or parents in attending to the discomforts of its fears, grief, or anger, bring largely and only the partial controls of safety. A sea-change occurs when the child enters school (or pre-school today) by age 4 or 5. The child now mixes with its equals, and soon finds that they have not the indulgent partiality of its parents. Things go better if the child gains their favor and avoids their hatred and disgust. The only way to do this is for the child to moderate its anger and other passions to the extent that their playfellows are pleased by letting us know which of our actions they like or not.

Thus, does the child enter the Great School of Self-command where it studies to increase its mastery of itself and begins to acquire a discipline over its own feelings, the practice of which the longest life is unlikely to bring to complete perfection. This constitutes Smith's elementary bottom-up theory of voluntary, social rule-following, norms that account for the emergence of a stable self-sustaining society.

The three entries to follow concern a hypothetical person suffering from private misfortunes of pain, sickness, or sorrow who receives a visitor, who thereby will focus on your misfortune: "How are you?" Smith's aim is to examine the effect of different degrees of attainment in the social and socializing skills of self-command. Accordingly, the person suffering misfortune is, respectively, weakly, somewhat firmly, or thoroughly, schooled in self-command. The exercise serves to articulate and establish the central importance of Self-command in his theory of society.

When in pain, sickness, or sorrow, our attention to a visitor diverts us from our own view of ourselves to their view of us; the case of the visited who are weak in self-command.

> In all private misfortunes, in pain, in sickness, in sorrow, the weakest man, when his friend, and still more when a stranger visit him, is immediately impressed with the view in which they are likely to look upon his situation. Their view calls off his attention from his own view; and his breast is, in some measure, becalmed the moment they come into his presence. This effect is produced instantaneously, and, as it were, mechanically; but, with a weak man, it is not of long continuance. His own view of his situation immediately recurs upon him. He abandons himself, as before, to sighs,

> and tears, and lamentations; and endeavours, like a child that has not yet gone to school, to produce some sort of harmony between his own grief and the compassion of the spectator, not by moderating the former, but by importunately calling upon the latter. (*TMS*, p. 204)

The visit of a friend, and still more a stranger, has the effect of diverting our attention from our view of ourselves to how the visitor views us. This circumstance has an immediate becalming effect on us. But for one who is weak in self-command, this effect will be short-lived as their sorrow for themselves returns to dominate their mental state.

The case of the person with some firmness in self-command.

> With a man of a little more firmness, the effect is somewhat more permanent. He endeavours, as much as he can, to fix his attention upon the view which the company are likely to take of his situation. He feels, at the same time, the esteem and approbation which they naturally conceive for him when he thus preserves his tranquillity; and, though under the pressure of some recent and great calamity, appears to feel for himself no more than what they really feel for him. He approves and applauds himself by sympathy with their approbation, and the pleasure which he derives from this sentiment supports and enables him more easily to continue this generous effort. In most cases he avoids mentioning his own misfortune; and his company, if they are tolerably well bred, are careful to say nothing which can put him in mind of it. He endeavours to entertain them, in his usual way, upon indifferent subjects, or, if he feels himself strong enough to venture to mention his misfortune, he endeavours to talk of it as he thinks they are capable of talking of it, and even to feel it no further than they are capable of feeling it. If he has not, however, been well inured to the hard discipline of self-command, he soon grows weary of this restraint. A long visit fatigues him; and, towards the end of it, he is constantly in danger of doing, what he never fails to do the moment it is over, of abandoning himself to all the weakness of excessive sorrow. Modern good manners, which are extremely indulgent to human weakness, forbid for some time the visits of strangers to persons under great family distress, and permit those only of the nearest relations and most intimate friends. The presence of the latter, it is thought, will impose less restraint than that of the former; and the sufferers can more easily accommodate themselves to the feelings of those from whom they have reason to expect a more indulgent sympathy. Secret enemies, who fancy that they are not known to be such, are frequently fond of making those charitable visits as early as the most

> intimate friends. The weakest man in the world, in this case, endeavours to support his manly countenance, and, from indignation and contempt of their malice, to behave with as much gaiety and ease as he can. (*TMS*, p. 205)

They who are somewhat firm in their self-command enter into the visitor's sympathy, esteem, and approbation in seeing us thus as preserving our tranquility in their presence, appearing to feel no more for ourselves than they feel for us, for their approval and applause for us in their approbation of our conduct in not dwelling on ourselves. But a long visit fatigues us and endangers our return to our own sorrowful state.

Finally, the case of those thoroughly bred in the great scholl of self-command.

> The man of real constancy and firmness, the wise and just man who has been thoroughly bred in the great school of self-command, in the bustle and business of the world, exposed, perhaps, to the violence and injustice of faction, and to the hardships and hazards of war, maintains this control of his passive feelings upon all occasions; and whether in solitude or in society, wears nearly the same countenance, and is affected very nearly in the same manner. In success and in disappointment, in prosperity and in adversity, before friends and before enemies, he has often been under the necessity of supporting this manhood. He has never dared to forget for one moment the judgment which the impartial spectator would pass upon his sentiments and conduct. He has never dared to suffer the man within the breast to be absent one moment from his attention. With the eyes of this great inmate he has always been accustomed to regard whatever relates to himself. This habit has become perfectly familiar to him: he has been in the constant practice…of modelling, or of endeavouring to model, not only his outward conduct and behaviour, but, as much as he can, even his inward sentiments and feelings, according to those of this awful and respectable judge. He does not merely affect the sentiments of the impartial spectator; he really adopts them. He almost identifies himself with, he almost becomes himself that impartial spectator, and scarce even feels but as that great arbiter of his conduct directs him to feel. (*TMS*, pp. 205–206)

One who is strong in self-command maintains their passive feelings, adopting nearly the same countenance whether in solitude or in society. They encourage the voice within to guide and model the person's outward actions and even somewhat the feelings within. They affect but also adopt the sentiments of the fair-play impartial spectator.

Self-approbation is proportioned to the degree of self-command necessary to obtain that self-approbation. your and societies' moral compass.

> The degree of the self-approbation with which every man upon such occasions [of pain and misfortune] surveys his own conduct, is higher or lower, exactly in proportion to the degree of self-command which is necessary in order to obtain that self-approbation. Where little self-command is necessary, little self-approbation is due. The man who has only scratched his finger cannot much applaud himself, though he should immediately appear to have forgot this paltry misfortune. The man who has lost his leg by a cannon shot, and who, the moment after, speaks and acts with his usual coolness and tranquillity, as he exerts a much higher degree of self-command, so he naturally feels a much higher degree of self-approbation. With most men, upon such an accident, their own natural view of their own misfortune would force itself upon them with such a vivacity and strength of colouring, as would entirely efface all thought of every other view. They would feel nothing, they could attend to nothing, but their own pain and their own fear; and not only siddent the judgment of the ideal man within the breast, but that of the real spectators who might happen to be present, would be entirely overlooked and disregarded. (*TMS*, pp. 206–207)

The extent of one's self-approbation is proportional to the degree of self-command and vice versa. The person who is stoically cool in the face of calamity sees beyond its disruptive intervention to a return to a better state, and this is because of the strength of their self-command; they are the heroes of conflict, war, and unpopular dissent from the ephemeral opinions and deceptions of the mob.

This is Smith's key proposition on how society is built by people who, through people, discover and find themselves, and thereby create a free society. It is Your and Societies' Moral Compass.

I am reminded of an influential popular book of my teen years *On Being a Real Person*, by Harry Emerson Fosdick (1943). Fosdick's Real person sought their Moral Compass.

The disruptions of Covid-19 tri-forked into proposals first to limit socialization to only the most essential socio-economic interactions, close all schools and public/private gatherings; second, impose limits only on vulnerable populations; third, let all self-limit and restrain in response to public disclosure of ongoing information. These accord well with Smith's weak, firm, and thorough education in self-command. The first option is for the wards of the authoritarian state, the second for the timid and cautious leader, and the third is for a nation with a Moral Compass.

Nature rewards good behavior under misfortune in direct proportion to the degree of that good behavior.

> The reward which Nature bestows upon good behaviour under misfortune is thus exactly proportioned to the degree of that good behaviour. The only compensation she could possibly make for the bitterness of pain and distress is thus, too, in equal degrees of good behaviour, exactly proportioned to the degree of that pain and distress. In proportion to the degree of the self-command which is necessary in order to conquer our natural sensibility, the pleasure and pride of the conquest are so much the greater; and this pleasure and pride are so great that no man can be altogether unhappy who completely enjoys them. Misery and wretchedness can never enter the breast in which dwells complete self-satisfaction; and though it may be too much, perhaps, to say with the Stoics, that, under such an accident as that above mentioned, the happiness of a wise man is in every respect equal to what it could have been under any other circumstances; yet it must be acknowledged, at least, that this complete enjoyment of his own self-applause, though it not altogether extinguish, must certainly very much alleviate his sense of his own sufferings. (*TMS*, pp. 207–208)

Nature rewards good behavior in the face of pain and distress in proportion to that good behavior, which is the only fit compensation for pain and distress overcome, and in proportion to the self-command that conquers the natural feelings of sorrow. Misery and distress cannot penetrate the breasts of they who are well-schooled in self-command.

Nature's reward for self-command under duress leaves some reward for the internal satisfaction of having overcome.

> In such paroxysms of distress…the wisest and firmest man, in order to preserve his equanimity, is obliged, I imagine, to make a considerable, and even a painful exertion. His own natural feeling of his own distress, his own natural view of his own situation, presses hard upon him, and he cannot, without a very great effort, fix his attention upon that of the impartial spectator. Both views present themselves to him at the same time. His

> sense of honour, his regard to his own dignity, directs him to fix his whole attention upon the one view. His natural, his untaught and undisciplined feelings, are continually calling it off to the other. He does not, in this case, perfectly identify himself with the ideal man within the breast, he does not become himself the impartial spectator of his own conduct. The different views of both characters exist in his mind separate and distinct from one another, and each directing him to a behaviour different from that to which the other directs him. When he follows that view which honour and dignity point out to him, Nature does not, indeed, leave him without a recompense. He enjoys his own complete self-approbation, and the applause of every candid and impartial spectator. By her unalterable laws, however, he still suffers; and the recompense which she bestows, though very considerable, is not sufficient completely to compensate the sufferings which those laws inflict. Neither is it fit that it should. If it did completely compensate them, he could, from self-interest, have no motive for avoiding an accident which must necessarily diminish his utility both to himself and to society; and Nature, from her parental care of both, meant that he should anxiously avoid all such accidents. He suffers, therefore, and though, in the agony of the paroxysm, he maintains not only the manhood of his countenance but the sedateness and sobriety of his judgment, it requires his utmost and most fatiguing exertions to do so. (*TMS*, p. 208)

In the paroxysms of distress, a wise person focuses on both the protestations of the impartial spectator to take account of others and the temptations of self-love to defect from service to others. Nature's reward for complete self-command in the face of sorrow and distress allows for some built-in compensation from the self-approbation of a task well performed. Your Moral Compass bears dividends.

Why nature assures that agony can never be permanent.

> By the constitution of human nature, however, agony can never be permanent; and if he survives the paroxysm, he soon comes, without any effort, to enjoy his ordinary tranquillity. A man with a wooden leg suffers, no doubt, and foresees that he must continue to suffer during the remainder of his life, a very considerable inconveniency. He soon comes to view it, however, exactly as every impartial spectator views it, as an inconveniency under which he can enjoy all the ordinary pleasures both of solitude and of society. He soon identifies himself with the ideal man within the breast; he soon becomes himself the impartial spectator of his own situation. He no longer weeps, he no longer laments, he no longer grieves over it, as

> a weak man sometimes do in the beginning. The view of the impartial spectator becomes so perfectly habitual to him, that, without any effort, without any exertion, he never thinks of surveying his misfortune in any other view. (*TMS*, p. 209)

Nature ever adapts her guidance in the measured process-balancing of our necessary self-interested actions against our heartfelt desire to humble our self-love to bring it down to actions that others will go along with. This is accomplished through the norm-forming other-regarding rules we follow in which nature trusts us to know when and where to substitute the urgent demands of our self-interest without abandoning your Moral Compass. Your neighbor might well not bring in your trash barrel when you neglected to do so, if her husband needed to be taken to the emergency room or to urgent care. Her freedom to choose is integral to your trust in each other.

We accommodate that which becomes our permanent situation.

> The never-failing certainty with which all men, sooner or later, accommodate themselves to whatever becomes their permanent situation, perhaps, induce us to think that the Stoics were, at least, thus far very nearly in the right; that, between one permanent situation and another, there was, with regard to real happiness, no essential difference: or that, if there were any difference, it was no more than just sufficient to render some of them the objects of simple choice or preference, but not of any earnest or anxious desire; and others, of simple rejection, as being fit to be set aside or avoided, but not of any earnest or anxious aversion. Happiness consists in tranquillity and enjoyment. Without tranquillity there can be no enjoyment; and where there is perfect tranquillity there is scarce anything which is not capable of amusing. But in every permanent situation, where there is no expectation of change, the mind of every man, in a longer or shorter time, returns to its natural and usual state of tranquillity. In prosperity, after a certain time, it falls back to that state; in adversity, after a certain time, it rises up to it... (*TMS*, pp. 209–210)

Nature ever seeks psychologically to return us to those states of tranquility in which we accept our lot, our duty to a higher purpose, whether we lost a leg in war, or must give up our treasured independence to care for an orphaned younger sibling, an older paralyzed sibling, or nurse our mother back to an uncertain better health. The Moral Compass is a permanent guide. Thus in 2 Corinthians 4 17–18 "this too shall pass" (New Testament, KJV).

Make the best of whatever is now and the next will follow.

> The great source of both the misery and disorders of human life seems to arise from overrating the difference between one permanent situation and another. Avarice overrates the difference between poverty and riches: ambition, that between a private and a public station: vainglory, that between obscurity and extensive reputation. The person under the influence of any of those extravagant passions is not only miserable in his actual situation, but is often disposed to disturb the peace of society in order to arrive at that which he so foolishly admires…in all the ordinary situations of human life, a well-disposed mind be equally calm, equally cheerful, and equally contented. Some of those situations, no doubt, deserve to be preferred to others; but none of them can deserve to be pursued with that passionate ardour which drives us to violate the rules either of prudence or of justice; or to corrupt the future tranquillity of our minds, either by shame from the remembrance of our own folly, or by remorse from the horror of our own injustice. Wherever prudence does not direct, wherever justice does not permit, the attempt to change our situation, the man who does attempt it, plays at the most unequal of all games of hazard, and stakes every thing against scarce any thing. What the favourite of the King of Epirus said to his master, be applied to men in all the ordinary situations of human life. When the king had recounted to him, in their proper order, all the conquests which he proposed to make, and had come to the last of them—"And what does your Majesty propose to do then?" said the favourite.—"I propose then," said the King, "to enjoy myself with my friends, and endeavour to be good company over a bottle."—"And what hinders your Majesty from doing so now?" replied the favourite. In the most glittering and exalted situation that our idle fancy can hold out to us, the pleasures from which we propose to derive our real happiness are almost always the same with those which, in our actual though humble station, we have at all times at hand and in our power. Except the frivolous pleasures of vanity and superiority, we find, in the most humble station, where there is only personal liberty, every other which the most exalted can afford; and the pleasures of vanity and superiority are seldom consistent with perfect tranquillity, the principle and foundation of all real and satisfactory enjoyment. Neither is it always certain that, in the splendid situation which we aim at, those real and satisfactory pleasures can be enjoyed with the same security as in the humble one which we are so very eager to abandon. Examine the records of history, recollect what has happened

> within the circle of your own experience, consider with attention what has been the conduct of almost all the greatly unfortunate, either in private or public life, whom you have either read of, or heard of, or remember, and you will find that the misfortunes of by far the greater part of them have arisen from their not knowing when they were well, when it was proper for them to sit still and to be contented. The inscription upon the tombstone of the man who had endeavoured to mend a tolerable constitution by taking physic [a cathartic]—"I was well, I wished to be better; here I am," generally may be applied with great justness to the distress of disappointed avarice and ambition. (*TMS*, pp. 210–211)

Smith brilliantly summarizes three of the great obsessions of humankind:

> Avarice overrates the difference between poverty and riches; ambition, that between a private and a public station; vainglory, that between obscurity and extensive reputation.

These obsessions were identified by the great naysayers of humanity in the eighteenth century.

But have they changed in the twenty-first century? Those constantly berating progress because of persistent differences between the rich and the "poor," who are less rich, are today as voluble as ever.

Private reputational achievement is today widely respected and acknowledged, while politics still attracts the most ego centrical who we know and identify because they seek and find public attention in politics and acting.

Be not the king who seeks a series of conquests to overcome, then to retire in ease and repose, when, if that be his most preferred state, he might simply do that today.

Seek not the epitaph: "Here lies the happy man, who took an untested potion that his happiness might be increased, only to die poisoned."

Be not among they who sacrifice some treasured freedom for more security, and in so doing, to sacrifice both.

Some for the sinful glorious pleasures of this world, while others pursue the prophets' paradise to come; be not the one who takes the cash and lets the credit go, but he who gives in gratitude, receives in abundance, and makes kindness the parent of kindness. Pursue security from injury but make the punishment fit the crime and require a measure of victim compensation from they who are found guilty of hurtful action.

From misery, time ever recomposes and redirects our effort.

> It may be thought a singular, but I believe it to be a just observation, that, in the misfortunes which admit of some remedy, the greater part of men do not either so readily or so universally recover their natural and usual tranquillity, as in those which plainly admit of none. In misfortunes of the latter kind, it is chiefly in what may be called the paroxysm, or in the first attack, that we can discover any sensible difference between the sentiments and behaviour of the wise and those of the weak man. In the end, time, the great and universal comforter, gradually composes the weak man to the same degree of tranquillity which a regard to his own dignity and manhood teaches the wise man to assume in the beginning. The case of the man with the wooden leg is an obvious example of this. In the irreparable misfortunes occasioned by the death of children, or of friends and relations, even a wise man for some time indulge himself in some degree of moderated sorrow. An affectionate, but weak woman, is often upon such occasions almost perfectly distracted. Time, however, in a longer or shorter period, never fails to compose the weakest woman to the same degree of tranquility as the strongest man. In all the irreparable calamities which affect himself immediately and directly, a wise man endeavours, from the beginning, to anticipate and to enjoy beforehand, that tranquillity which he foresees the course of a few months or a few years will certainly restore to him in the end. (*TMS*, pp. 211–212)

Time heals all wounds, for the healthy and wise know that all wounds eventually heal, that all heals get their due, and this helps them to find their Moral Compass.

Misfortunes that seem to admit of remedy, but that are out of reach, disrupt the return of natural tranquility.

> In the misfortunes for which the nature of things admits, or seems to admit, of a remedy, but in which the means of applying that remedy are not within the reach of the sufferer, his vain and fruitless attempts to restore himself to his former situation, his continual anxiety for their success, his repeated disappointments upon their miscarriage, are what chiefly hinder him from resuming his natural tranquillity, and frequently render miserable, during the whole of his life, a man to whom a greater misfortune, but which plainly admitted of no remedy, would not have given a fortnight's disturbance. In the fall from royal favour to disgrace, from power to insignificancy, from riches to poverty, from liberty to confinement, from strong health to some lingering, chronical, and, perhaps, incurable disease;

> the man who struggles the least, who most easily and readily acquiesces in the fortune which has fallen to him, very soon recovers his usual and natural tranquillity, and surveys the most disagreeable circumstances of his actual situation in the same light, or, perhaps, in a much less unfavourable light, than that in which the most indifferent spectator is disposed to survey them. Faction, intrigue, and cabal, disturb the quiet of the unfortunate statesman. Extravagant projects, visions of gold mines, interrupt the repose of the ruined bankrupt. The prisoner, who is continually plotting to escape from his confinement, cannot enjoy that careless security which even a prison can afford him. The medicines of the physician are often the greatest torment of the incurable patient... (*TMS*, pp. 212–213)

The person of vanity, who falls from royalty, power, riches, or health, where nature admits no remedy, fruitlessly pursues the restoration of their tranquility with an anxiety itself hindering success. In such misfortunes, they who struggle least, accept their fortune, and soon recover that tranquility by knowing and accepting that which they cannot change. If your affliction is incurable view your medical treatment as a means only of reducing your immediate discomfort.

Self-command and our sensibility to others are teammates in celebrating their joy, being compassionate in their sorrow, while moderating both in ourselves.

> Our sensibility to the feelings of others, so far from being inconsistent with the manhood of self-command, is the very principle upon which that manhood is founded. The very same principle or instinct which, in the misfortune of our neighbour, prompts us to compassionate his sorrow, in our own misfortune, prompts us to restrain the abject and miserable lamentations of our own sorrow. The same principle or instinct which, in his prosperity and success, prompts us to congratulate his joy, in our own prosperity and success, prompts us to restrain the levity and intemperance of our own joy. In both cases, the propriety of our own sentiments and feelings seems to be exactly in proportion to the vivacity and force with which we enter into and conceive his sentiments and feelings. (*TMS*, pp. 213–214)

Self-command is founded on the same principles that enliven a natural compassion for our neighbor. As their life goes, so goes ours, and out of our compassion is born the self-restraint that social effectiveness demands, and this is also what constitutes the moral life.

Perfect virtue and perfect self-command join in creating our highest love and admiration.

> The man of the most perfect virtue, the man whom we naturally love and revere the most, is he who joins, to the most perfect command of his own original and selfish feelings, the most exquisite sensibility both to the original and sympathetic feelings of others. The man who, to all the soft, the amiable, and the gentle virtues, joins all the great, the awful [awe-filled], and the respectable, must surely be the natural and proper object of our highest love and admiration. (*TMS*, p. 214)

They who are blessed with the most perfect virtue combine their self-command with their original sympathetic feelings toward others and are in company with the most loved, admired, and revered.

They who are most fit for self-command also feel the most for the joys and sorrows of others but such virtues fail if not well practiced.

> The person best fitted by nature for acquiring … [the soft, amiable, and gentile] virtues is likewise necessarily best fitted for acquiring [self-command]…. The man who feels the most for the joys and sorrows of others, is best fitted for acquiring the most complete control of his own joys and sorrows. The man of the most exquisite humanity is naturally the most capable of acquiring the highest degree of self-command. He may not, however, always have acquired it; and it very frequently happens that he has not. He may have lived too much in ease and tranquillity. He may have never been exposed to the violence of faction, or to the hardships and hazards of war. He may have never experienced the insolence of his superiors, the jealous and malignant envy of his equals, or the pilfering injustice of his inferiors. When in an advanced age some accidental change of fortune exposes him to all these, they all make too great an impression upon him. He has the disposition which fits him for acquiring the most perfect self-command, but he has never had the opportunity of acquiring it. Exercise and practice have been wanting; and without these no habit can ever be tolerably established. Hardships, dangers, injuries, misfortunes, are the only masters under whom we can learn the exercise of this virtue. But these are all masters to whom nobody willingly puts himself to school. (*TMS*, pp. 214–215)

Those who nature disposes of as most fit for acquiring the soft, amiable, and gentle virtues are likewise those who are best fitted for the most perfect self-command. But only practice makes perfect. Hardships, dangers, injuries, and misfortunes are the effective masters from whom we learn the exercise of this virtue.

They who are themselves at ease, and they who are most exposed to hardship, best attend distress in others.

> The situations in which the gentle virtue of humanity can be most happily cultivated, are by no means the same with those which are best fitted for forming the austere virtue of self-command. The man who is himself at ease can best attend to the distress of others. The man who is himself exposed to hardships is most immediately called upon to attend to, and to control his own feelings. In the mild sunshine of undisturbed tranquillity, in the calm retirement of undissipated and philosophical leisure, the soft virtue of humanity flourishes the most, and is capable of the highest improvement. But, in such situations, the greatest and noblest exertions of self-command have little exercise. Under the boisterous and stormy sky of war and faction, of public tumult and confusion, the sturdy severity of self-command prospers the most, and can be the most successfully cultivated. But, in such situations, the strongest suggestions of humanity must frequently be stifled or neglected; and every such neglect necessarily tends to weaken the principle of humanity. As it frequently be the duty of a soldier not to take, so it sometimes may be his duty not to give quarter [pity, mercy]; and the humanity of the man who has been several times under the necessity of submitting to this disagreeable duty, can scarce fail to suffer a considerable diminution. For his own ease, he is too apt to learn to make light of the misfortunes which he is so often under the necessity of occasioning; and the situations which call forth the noblest exertions of self-command, by imposing the necessity of violating sometimes the property, and sometimes the life of our neighbour, always tend to diminish, and too often to extinguish altogether, that sacred regard to both, which is the foundation of justice and humanity. It is upon this account that we so frequently find in the world men of great humanity who have little self-command, but who are indolent and irresolute, and easily disheartened, either by difficulty or danger, from the most honourable pursuits; and, on the contrary, men of the most perfect self-command, whom no difficulty can discourage, no danger appal, and who are at all times ready for the most daring and desperate enterprizes, but who, at the same time, seem to be hardened against all sense either of justice or humanity. (*TMS*, pp. 215–216)

Self-command does not find the most favorable soil in those who most easily pursue the gentle virtues of humanity. Rather, self-command grows in the tumult of adversity wherein people find ways to overcome.

Low birthright combines with defeat-able adversity to nurture self-command.

I am reminded of my friend, John Fei (1923–1996), at MIT when I was at Harvard. We met while both were employed on the Leontief project. John had fought in the army of Generalissimo Chiang Kai-shek against the Chinese communist revolutionaries, retreated with him to Formosa, then emigrated to the United States and to the University of Washington, Seattle. Somehow, he found his way into Doug North's economic history class, where he excelled as a student, and Doug got him into MIT. John became a leading development economist. For several decades he actively advised the Taiwanese government on economic policy issues.

John's brother, Charles Fei, also fought for the Generalissimo, but at one point simply defected to the other side, taking his entire regiment with him. Following John, he also showed up at the University of Washington, Seattle, still wearing his Red Army jacket but with the red star torn off its upper left front leaving its faded symbol, a clear mark of the fame he and the communists sought.

There is an inspiring documentary book directly on Smiths theme in *The Railway Man: A POW's Searing Account of War, Remembrance, and Forgiveness* (Vintage Books, 1996). His publisher says this about the book: "Eric Lomax, sent to Malaya in World War II, was taken prisoner by the Japanese and put to punishing work on the notorious Burma-Siam railway. After the radio he illicitly helped to build in order to follow war news was discovered, he was subjected to two years of starvation and torture. He would never forget the interpreter at these brutal sessions. Fifty years after returning home from the war, marrying, and gaining the strength from his wife Patti to fight his demons, he learned the interpreter was alive. Through letters and meeting with his former torturer, Lomax bravely moved beyond bitterness drawing on an extraordinary will to extend forgiveness." In his need, his captor movingly sought his forgiveness.

The exaggerations of solitude are relieved by conversation.

> In solitude, we are apt to feel too strongly whatever relates to ourselves: we are apt to overrate the good offices we have done, and the injuries we have suffered: we are apt to be too much elated by our own good, and too much dejected by our own bad fortune. The conversation of a friend brings us to a better, that of a stranger to a still better temper. The man within the breast, the abstract and ideal spectator of our sentiments and conduct, requires often to be awakened and put in mind of his duty, by the presence of the real spectator: and it is always from that spectator, from whom we can expect the least sympathy and indulgence, that we are likely to learn the most complete lesson of self-command. (*TMS*, p. 216)

If in solitude one is vainly preoccupied with their own good works and the avoidance of evil and its doing, both tending to be overrated by the individual, let in the conversation of others who bring the beacon of a different perspective, including that of failed good intentions and succeeding bad intentions from which spring new learning. Let the spectator awaken the beast within to broker a better way in the company of others.

Are you in adversity? In the darkness of deep sorrow return to society. Seek not the too indulgent friend but strangers and show them you are above the calamity.

> Do not mourn in the darkness of solitude, do not regulate your sorrow according to the indulgent sympathy of your intimate friends; return, as soon as possible, to the daylight of the world and of society. Live with strangers, with those who know nothing, or care nothing about your misfortune; do not even shun the company of enemies; but give yourself the pleasure of mortifying their malignant joy, by making them feel how little you are affected by your calamity, and how much you are above it. (*TMS*, pp. 216–217)

Mourn not in darkness, solitude, and the indulgence of close friends only. Return to the bright light of society, nation, and world. Rejoice in strangers, even enemies whose hopes for your fate were roundly defeated. Let them burn in the envies of their own creation.

In prosperity share your joy with independents, past superiors in your unsuccess, and all who modesty in you they might value.

> Are you in prosperity? Do not confine the enjoyment of your good fortune to your own house, to the company of your own friends, perhaps of your flatterers, of those who build upon your fortune the hopes of mending their own; frequent those who are independent of you, who can value you only for your character and conduct, and not for your fortune. Neither seek nor shun, neither intrude yourself into, nor run away from, the society of those who were once your superiors, and who be hurt at finding you their equal, or, perhaps, even their superior. The impertinence of their pride, perhaps, render their company too disagreeable: but if it should not, be assured that it is the best company you can possibly keep; and if by the simplicity of your unassuming demeanour you can gain their favour and kindness, you rest satisfied that you are modest enough, and that your head has been in no respect turned by your good fortune. (*TMS*, p. 217)

If you are in prosperity wallow not in the house of your good fortune and in company only with those trying to emulate your triumph. Let an unassuming demeanor of curiosity be your beacon of discovery with a mix of new and old associates.

Befriend those younger than you, for you are less likely to outlive them. Let the sleeping dogs of envy lie undisturbed.

Moral propriety is corrupted by the indulgent spectator when the indifferent one is distant.

> The propriety of our moral sentiments is never so apt to be corrupted as when the indulgent and partial spectator is at hand, while the indifferent and impartial one is at a great distance. (*TMS*, p. 217)

Reject the partial, indulgent, corrupted, and corrupting spectator, too close at hand, in favor of the distant, indifferent, and impartial spectator of our actions.

Among nations the neutral are the impartial, but also at greatest distance; in unjust wars the sovereigns are commonly guilty.

> Of the conduct of one independent nation towards another, neutral nations are the only indifferent and impartial spectators. But they are placed at so great a distance that they are almost quite out of sight. When two nations are at variance, the citizen of each pays little regard to the sentiments which foreign nations entertain concerning his conduct. His whole ambition is

> to obtain the approbation of his own fellow-citizens; and as they are all animated by the same hostile passions which animate himself, he can never please them so much as by enraging and offending their enemies. The partial spectator is at hand: the impartial one at a great distance. In war and negotiation, therefore, the laws of justice are very seldom observed. Truth and fair dealing are almost totally disregarded. Treaties are violated; and the violation, if some advantage is gained by it, sheds scarce any dishonour upon the violator. The ambassador who dupes the minister of a foreign nation is admired and applauded. The just man who disdains either to take or to give any advantage, but who would think it less dishonourable to give than to take one—the man who in all private transactions would be the most beloved and the most esteemed, in those public transactions is regarded as a fool and an idiot, who does not understand his business, and he incurs always the contempt, and sometimes even the detestation, of his fellow-citizens. In war, not only what are called the laws of nations are frequently violated, without bringing (among his own fellow-citizens, whose judgments he only regards) any considerable dishonour upon the violator; but those laws themselves are, the greater part of them, laid down with very little regard to the plainest and most obvious rules of justice. That the innocent, though they have some connection or dependency upon the guilty (which, perhaps, they themselves cannot help), should not upon that account suffer or be punished for the guilty, is one of the plainest and most obvious rules of justice. In the most unjust war, however, it is commonly the sovereign or the rulers only who are guilty. The subjects are almost always perfectly innocent. Whenever it suits the conveniency of a public enemy, however, the goods of the peaceable citizens are seized both at land and at sea; their lands are laid waste, their houses are burnt, and they themselves, if they presume to make any resistance, are murdered or led into captivity; and all this in the most perfect conformity to what are called the laws of nations. (*TMS*, pp. 217–218)

As I recall, echoing Adam Smith, when the United Nations (UN) was formed after WWII, some wag described how it would work: If two small nations fight, the UN will intervene and that will be the end of the two nations. If a large nation and a small nation fight, the UN will intervene and that will be the end of the small nation. If two large nations fight that will be the end of the UN.

Among strong nations, constructed from strong communities of endogenously rule-governed citizens are likely to be found the neutral sober peacekeepers. These, however, are also likely to reside on political pathways at the greatest distance from the centers of influence. If contrarywise, they do enter the political fray, they are likely to be castigated fools and idiots, led astray by their own impractical and lofty seeking after unachievable ideals. Would the return of Jesus be otherwise construed with the many now washing their hands in populist conformity with they who fear and resent dissent.

In Dan Ellsberg's unauthorized release of the *Pentagon Papers*, the injustice of the Vietnam War was matched only by the guilt of the sovereign who lied to all of us and declared that Ellsberg was the most dangerous man in America. Dan became a loyal patriot, as truth and fair dealing were served with loyalty because Dan's pledge was to the constitution not to the sovereign representative.

In due time the heals all got their wounds, signaling their erstwhile need to explore their Moral Compass.

Factions, civil or ecclesiastical, within nations can be more furious toward each other than among hostile nations.

> The animosity of hostile factions, whether civil or ecclesiastical, is often still more furious than that of hostile nations, and their conduct towards one another is often still more atrocious. What may be called the laws of faction have often been laid down by grave authors with still less regard to the rules of justice than what are called the laws of nations. The most ferocious patriot never stated it as a serious question, Whether faith ought to be kept with public enemies? Whether faith ought to be kept with rebels? Whether faith ought to be kept with heretics? are questions which have been often furiously agitated by celebrated doctors, both civil and ecclesiastical. It is needless to observe, I presume, that both rebels and heretics are those unlucky persons, who, when things have come to a certain degree of violence, have the misfortune to be of the weaker party. In a nation distracted by faction, there are, no doubt, always a few, though commonly but a very few, who preserve their judgment untainted by the general contagion. They seldom amount to more than here and there a solitary individual, without any influence, excluded by his own candour from the confidence of either party, and who, though he may be one of the wisest, is necessarily upon that very account one of the most insignificant men in the society. All such people are held in contempt and derision, frequently in detestation, by the furious zealots of both parties. A true party-man hates and despises candour; and, in reality, there is no vice which could so effectually disqualify him for the trade of a party-man as that single virtue. The real, revered, and impartial spectator, therefore, is upon no occasion at a greater distance than amidst the violence and rage of contending parties.

> To them it may be said, that such a spectator scarce exists anywhere in the universe. Even to the great Judge of the universe they impute all their own prejudices, and often view that divine Being as animated by all their own vindictive and implacable passions. Of all the corrupters of moral sentiments, therefore, faction and fanaticism have always been by far the greatest. (*TMS*, pp. 219–220)

Observe, that we are emersed in entries in which Smith is articulating, in the context of his model of society, an incredible variety of social-psychological personalities operating in the context of independent, national, and institutional affiliations. In effect, the approbation of conduct between and among equals is situation-specific and changes abruptly in domestic politics, ecclesiastical groups, and among friend versus foe nations.

In his day, factions were perhaps more factitious domestically than internationally. In effect nations made war, not vile rhetoric, on each other. An American contemporary, James Madison, saw domestic factions as in the nature of humankind. Differences in wealth, property, and ranking created like-minded clusters that were destabilizing although Madison hoped to limit the effects of factions in politics and the role of political parties in the American constitutional focus on individual rights—a constitution consistent with and much shaped by Smith's theory of society emerging from bottom-up rules of order.

The sensibility of some people is so overwhelming that self-command fails to emerge or prevail.

> Concerning the subject of self-command, I shall only observe further, that our admiration for the man who, under the heaviest and most unexpected misfortunes, continues to behave with fortitude and firmness, always supposes that his sensibility to those misfortunes is very great, and such as it requires a very great effort to conquer or command. The man who was altogether insensible to bodily pain, could deserve no applause from enduring the torture with the most perfect patience and equanimity. The man who had been created without the natural fear of death, could claim no merit from preserving his coolness and presence of mind in the midst of the most dreadful dangers...The sensibility of some men, however, to some of the objects which immediately affect themselves, is sometimes so strong as to render all self-command impossible. No sense of honour can control

> the fears of the man who is weak enough to faint, or to fall into convulsions, upon the approach of danger. Whether such weakness of nerves, as it has been called, not by gradual exercise and proper discipline admit of some cure, perhaps be doubtful. It seems certain that it ought never to be trusted or employed. (*TMS*, p. 220)

Self-command is a virtue predicated on the idea that those who are capable of ordinary sensibilities regulate their expression through this virtue and acquire a sense of honor out of effective self-government. They who are overwhelmed by fear, or who are sociopathic-ally oblivious to others, are outside the reach of self-command.

Smith next considers that "There are two different occasions upon which we examine our own conduct, and endeavour to view it in the light in which the impartial spectator would view it: first, when we are about to act; and, secondly, after we have acted. Our views are apt to be very partial in both cases; but they are apt to be most partial when it is of most importance that they should be otherwise" (*TMS*, p. 221).

As is his style, he considers the error properties of each branch in the action tree. These are each presented, in order, in the next two entries.

CHAPTER 27

Of the nature of self-deceit, and of the origin and nature of general rules

When we are about to act, the passions of the exciting situation overwhelm all indifferent examination.

> When we are about to act, the eagerness of passion will seldom allow us to consider what we are doing with the candour of an indifferent person. The violent emotions which at that time agitate us, discolour our views of things, even when we are endeavouring to place ourselves in the situation of another, and to regard the objects that interest us in the light in which they will naturally appear to him. The fury of our own passions constantly calls us back to our own place, where every thing appears magnified and misrepresented by self-love. Of the manner in which those objects would appear to another, of the view which he would take of them, we can obtain…but instantaneous glimpses, which vanish in a moment, and which, even while they last, are not altogether just. We cannot even for that moment divest ourselves entirely of the heat and keenness with which our peculiar situation inspires us, nor consider what we are about to do with the complete impartiality of an equitable judge. The passions, upon this account…all justify themselves, and seem reasonable and proportioned to their objects as long as we continue to feel them. (*TMS*, pp. 221–222)

As creatures of reason, in principle before we act, we first contemplate, then decide. But in the reality of the moment excited by the circumstances, a contemplative stance is overwhelmed by the feelings that drive

Vernon L. Smith, *Adam Smith's Theory of Society*,
https://doi.org/10.1007/978-3-031-68494-4_27

the rules we have unaware-ally learned to follow on autopilot and that serve us well.

In any situation that excites the propriety of our action, whether fueled by gratitude or resentment, we go into autopilot mode carrying forth from a host of past experiences. The automaticity of our action leaves little space for contemplating this case and the appropriateness of our action in the case. Pre-action error surely may sometimes occur where there is little scope for contemplation, as the rules of morality derive from propriety, not reason. More commonly, reason merely affirms what nature teaches from experience reinforced by the social mirror of approbation or disapprobation. This is because there is so much practical wisdom packed into that process.

When the action is over our capacity for cool reappraisal is lost with the diminution of remote feelings.

> When the action is over…we can enter more coolly into the sentiments of the indifferent spectator. What before interested us is now become almost as indifferent to us as it always was to him, and we can now examine our own conduct with his candour and impartiality. The man of to-day is no longer agitated by the same passions which distracted the man of yesterday: and when the paroxysm of emotion, in the same manner as when the paroxysm of distress, is fairly over, we can identify ourselves, as it were, with the ideal man within the breast, and, in our own character, view, as in the one case our own situation, so in the other our own conduct, with the severe eyes of the most impartial spectator. But our judgments now are often of little importance in comparison of what they were before, and can frequently produce nothing but vain regret and unavailing repentance, without always securing us from the like errors in time to come. It is seldom, however, that they are quite candid even in this case. The opinion which we entertain of our own character depends entirely on our judgment concerning our past conduct. It is so disagreeable to think ill of ourselves, that we often purposely turn away our view from those circumstances which might render that judgment unfavourable. He is a bold surgeon, they say, whose hand does not tremble when he performs an operation upon his own person; and he is often equally bold who does not hesitate to pull off the mysterious veil of self-delusion which covers from his view the deformities of his own conduct. Rather than see our own behaviour under so disagreeable an aspect, we too often, foolishly and weakly, endeavour to exasperate anew those unjust passions which had formerly misled us; we endeavour by artifice to awaken our old hatreds, and

> irritate afresh our almost forgotten resentments: we even exert ourselves for this miserable purpose, and thus persevere in injustice, merely because we once were unjust, and because we are ashamed and afraid to see that we were so. (*TMS*, pp. 221–223)

When an action is over, we can revisit its precipitating circumstances, and enter more coolly into the sentiments of the impartial spectator, but the pungency of the situation that excited it may be diluted by distance and a weakening of the circumstantial spirit that moved us. Since our opinion of ourselves depends upon our judgments of our past conduct, these ex-post evaluations are critical to this alignment reevaluation but may be lost in self-deception.

If humankind but had the power of the indifferent spectator, they could more accurately judge based on their own than on other conduct.

> So partial are the views of mankind with regard to the propriety of their own conduct, both at the time of action and after it; and so difficult is it for them to view it in the light in which any indifferent spectator would consider it. But if it was by a peculiar faculty, such as the moral sense is supposed to be, that they judged of their own conduct, if they were endued with a particular power of perception, which distinguished the beauty or deformity of passions and affections; as their own passions would be more immediately exposed to the view of this faculty, it would judge with more accuracy concerning them than concerning those of other men, of which it had only a more distant prospect. (*TMS*, p. 223)

If we had the power of an indifferent spectator arising say from a supposed special moral sense, then the beauty or deformity of our own passions would be judged more precisely than those of other people because of their direct proximity to our observation as compared with others. This is evidence that such a specialized moral sense we do not have, thus opening us to the hazards of self-deceit, which impinges on the quality of self-command. We see in this passage why we cannot be guided by inborn instinct. Such a source could not be sensitive to experience and adaptation based on the experience of others.

Self-deceit is what prevents our seeing ourselves as would others if they knew all that we know.

> This self-deceit, this fatal weakness of mankind, is the source of half the disorders of human life. If we saw ourselves in the light in which others see us, or in which they would see us if they knew all, a reformation would generally be unavoidable. We could not otherwise endure the sight. (*TMS*, p. 223)

Self-deceit, a key concept in *TMS*, is what blurs, distorts, and corrupts our self-image and our self-command.

We are not by nature entirely abandoned to the delusions of self-love because we learn from each other what is properly fit to be done or avoided.

> Nature, however, has not left this weakness, which is of so much importance, altogether without a remedy; nor has she abandoned us entirely to the delusions of self-love. Our continual observations upon the conduct of others insensibly lead us to form to ourselves certain general rules concerning what is fit and proper either to be done or to be avoided. Some of their actions shock all our natural sentiments. We hear every body about us express the like detestation against them. This still further confirms, and even exasperates, our natural sense of their deformity. It satisfies us that we view them in the proper light, when we see other people view them in the same light. We resolve never to be guilty of the like, nor ever, upon any account, to render ourselves in this manner the objects of universal disapprobation. We thus naturally lay down to ourselves a general rule, that all such actions are to be avoided, as tending to render us odious, contemptible, or punishable,—the objects of all those sentiments for which we have the greatest dread and aversion. Other actions, on the contrary, call forth our approbation, and we hear every body around us express the same favourable opinion concerning them. Every body is eager to honour and reward them. They excite all those sentiments for which we have by nature the strongest desire; the love, the gratitude, the admiration, of mankind. We become ambitions of performing the like; and thus naturally lay down to ourselves a rule of another kind, that every opportunity of acting in this manner is carefully to be sought after. (*TMS*, pp. 223–224)

The delusions of self-deceit are corrected by nature in that, through our observations of others, we learn which of our actions meet with their approbation or their disapprobation, and therefore, what is to be embraced and what is avoided. We seek their love and admiration, and in return to love, honor, and reward them. This interactive process shapes the rules we follow that enable us to live harmoniously, or not, with others.

It is through the experience of each other, that we form and learn general riles of morality, independent of, but conditional on, particular circumstances.

> It is thus that the general rules of morality are formed. They are ultimately founded upon experience of what, in particular instances, our moral faculties, our natural sense of merit and propriety, approve or disapprove of. We do not originally approve or condemn particular actions, because, upon examination, they appear to be agreeable or inconsistent with a certain general rule. The general rule, on the contrary, is formed by finding from experience that all actions of a certain kind, or circumstanced in a certain manner, are approved or disapproved of. To the man who first saw an inhuman murder committed from avarice, envy, or unjust resentment, and upon one, too, that loved and trusted the murderer; who beheld the last agonies of the dying person; who heard him with his expiring breath complain more of the perfidy and ingratitude of his false friend than of the violence which had been done to him; there could be no occasion, in order to conceive how horrible such an action was, that he should reflect, that one of the most sacred rules of conduct was what prohibited the taking away the life of an innocent person, that this was a plain violation of that rule, and, consequently, a very blameable action. His detestation of this crime, it is evident, would arise instantaneously and antecedent to his having formed to himself any such general rule. The general rule, on the contrary, which he might afterwards form, would be founded upon the detestation which he felt necessarily arise in his own breast, at the thought of this and every other particular action of the same kind. (*TMS*, pp. 224–225)

The general rules we follow are formed, not by comparison with a prior standard, but by inference from the trials, evaluations, and adjustments we experience in response to our feelings of gratitude or resentment to the actions of others.

Historical and romantic artistic accounts of generosity and baseness reinforce our personal experience.

> When we read in history or romance the account of actions either of generosity or of baseness, the admiration which we conceive for the one,

> and the contempt which we feel for the other, neither of them arise from reflecting that there are certain general rules which declare all actions of the one kind admirable, and all actions of the other contemptible. Those general rules, on the contrary, are all formed from the experience we have had of the effects which actions of all different kinds naturally produce upon us. (*TMS*, p. 225)

Historical or romantic accounts of human actions are part of the total experience that shapes the rules we learn to follow. We are part of that history, part of its creation, and it is integral to our learning.

General rules can only form out of our observation of the amiable, respectable, or horrid as objects of action.

> An amiable action, a respectable action, an horrid action, are all of them actions which naturally excite for the person who performs them, the love, the respect, or the horror of the spectator. The general rules which determine what actions are, and what are not, the objects of each of those sentiments, can be formed no other way than by observing what actions actually and in fact excite them. (*TMS*, pp. 225–226)

Actions that are amiable, respectable, or horrid excite corresponding feelings in observers, and help to determine which actions that conform to those sentiments result in community approbation or disapprobation and are thereby nurtured or discouraged.

When general rules have formed, we appeal to them as defining standards of judgment unavailable without their emergence from the foundry of experience contrary to the claims of some philosophers.

> When these general rules, indeed, have been formed, when they are universally acknowledged and established, by the concurring sentiments of mankind, we frequently appeal to them as to the standards of judgment, in debating concerning the degree of praise or blame that is due to certain actions of a complicated and dubious nature. They are upon these occasions commonly cited as the ultimate foundations of what is just and unjust in human conduct; and this circumstance seems to have misled several very eminent authors, to draw up their systems in such a manner as if they had supposed that the original judgments of mankind with regard to right and wrong were formed like the decisions of a court of judicatory, by considering first the general rule, and then, secondly, whether the particular

action under consideration fell properly within its comprehension. (*TMS*, p. 226)

Smith again and again takes great pains to make it clear that in *TMS* general rules concerning right and wrong actions do not represent a highly sophisticated application of self-love—that was the modernists and neoclassical economics error—nor do they arise out of any general denial of self-love in favor of "altruism," a nineteenth-century word. Indeed, there is rule-governed universal social disapprobation for those who do not properly attend to their own needs, thus falsifying that explanation. Nor again do they arise from the decisions of some past court of judiciary. These are gross distortions and diversions from the principles developed in *TMS*.

Rather, the *TMS* model is one in which the rules we learn to follow we learn without conscious awareness, are founded on common knowledge that all are self-interested, but that not all our actions are made in our self-loving interest. *Hence, Smith's careful implicit methodological distinction between being self-interested and acting self-interestedly*, which constitutes a way of thinking and modeling foreign to the modern mind. Because the rules are conditional on circumstances including who might be made better off, and who worse off, people can implement the rules only with common knowledge that all are self-interested. Otherwise, the rules cannot have a transparent common meaning. Modern scholars incoherently infer ex post a preference from the observed action and can predict nothing. They imagine that action can only stem from what must have been preference because they cannot imagine action that is not based on outcome utility. They assume altruistic or "social" preferences wherever and in whatever form they arise empirically in any other-regarding action. If that were true, we could not follow rules without knowledge of peoples' preferences—who is altruistic and who is selfish—an infeasible requirement that can guide no one's action. In *TMS*, all such finely structured knowledge of preferences is redundant because action is rule-contingent on common knowledge that all are strictly self-interested. We all depend on knowledge we do not possess, or even need, because we depend on each other and the community of summed knowledge and experience.

In *TMS*, the modern word "altruistic" can only be interpreted as an aspect of Benevolence, that is, one who consistently acts in accordance with the two general rules of Beneficence—reward actions of a good-hearted tendency, and do not attempt to coerce them as they cannot be coerced. Benevolence is not a consequence of "social preference" but a revealed pattern of rule-following enabling the individual to get along with their self-interested neighbors all of whom agree that properly motivated beneficent actions call for reward by the person favored by the action—an observation supported by the universal community tendencies toward reciprocity.

Those general rules serve to correct misrepresentations, ancient and modern, concerning the role of self-love.

> Those general rules of conduct, when they have been fixed in our mind by habitual reflection, are of great use in correcting the misrepresentations of self-love concerning what is fit and proper to be done in our particular situation. The man of furious resentment, if he was to listen to the dictates of that passion, would, perhaps, regard the death of his enemy as but a small compensation for the wrong he imagines he has received, which, however, may be no more than a very slight provocation. But his observations upon the conduct of others have taught him how horrible all such sanguinary revenges appear. Unless his education has been very singular, he has laid it down to himself as an inviolable rule, to abstain from them upon all occasions. This rule preserves its authority with him, and renders him incapable of being guilty of such a violence. Yet the fury of his own temper may be such, that had this been the first time in which he considered such an action, he would undoubtedly have determined it to be quite just and proper, and what every impartial spectator would approve of. But that reverence for the rule which past experience has impressed upon him, checks the impetuosity of his passion, and helps him to abstain from them upon all occasions. This rule preserves its authority with him, and renders him incapable of being guilty of such a violence. Yet the fury of his own temper may be such, that had this been the first time in which he considered such an action, he would undoubtedly have determined it to be quite just and proper, and what every impartial spectator would correct the too partial views which self-love might otherwise suggest of what was proper to be done in his situation. If he should allow himself to be so far transported by passion as to violate this rule, yet, even in this case, he cannot throw off altogether the awe and respect with which he has been accustomed to regard it. At the very time of acting, at the moment in which passion mounts the highest, he hesitates and trembles at the thought of what he is about to do: he is secretly conscious to himself that he is breaking through

> those measures of conduct which, in all his cool hours, he had resolved never to infringe, which he had never seen infringed by others without the highest disapprobation, and the infringement of which, his own mind forebodes, must soon render him the object of the same disagreeable sentiments. Before he can take the last fatal resolution, he is tormented with all the agonies of doubt and uncertainty; he is terrified at the thought of violating so sacred a rule, and at the same time is urged and goaded on by the fury of his desires to violate it. He changes his purpose every moment; sometimes he resolves to adhere to his principle, and not indulge a passion which corrupt the remaining part of his life with the horrors of shame and repentance; and a momentary calm takes possession of his breast, from the prospect of that security and tranquillity which he will enjoy when he thus determines not to expose himself to the hazard of a contrary conduct. But immediately the passion rouses anew, and with fresh fury drives him on to commit what he had the instant before resolved to abstain from. Wearied and distracted with those continual irresolutions, he at length, from a sort of despair, makes the last fatal and irrecoverable step; but with that terror and amazement with which one flying from an enemy throws himself over a precipice, where he is sure of meeting with more certain destruction than from any thing that pursues him from behind. Such are his sentiments even at the time of acting; though he is then, no doubt, less sensible of the impropriety of his own conduct than afterwards, when his passion being gratified and palled, he begins to view what he has done in the light in which others are apt to view it; and actually feels, what he had only foreseen very imperfectly before, the stings of remorse and repentance begin to agitate and torment him. (*TMS*, pp. 226–229)

Smith shows how powerful is our commitment to following general rules of conduct in correcting the immediate misrepresentations of self-love that might otherwise tempt us to act precipitately and inappropriately. General rules encapsulate the experience of many and embody much more information than we can glean from out own more limited experience. *TMS* dwells on the emotional turmoil a person of propriety goes through when they are particularly outraged by the passions of resentment, know that they must contain their excesses of response, but feel particularly challenged in maintaining their composure. I am reminded again of another of those great acerbic comments of Leroy "Satchel" Paige, arguably the greatest pitcher who ever lived, called finally at age 42 to the majors: "Don't look back; something might be gaining on you." Satchel's abiding purpose as a pitcher was to keep his eye on the ball which he fashioned into a beautiful guide to life. No one illustrates more powerfully the principle that society is created out of the whole cloth of simple ordinary people in ordinary circumstances learning from their ordinary experiences that were there from antiquity.

CHAPTER 28

Of the influence and authority of the general rules of morality, and that they are justly regarded as the laws of the deity

The sense of duty derives from the sanctity of general rules.

> The regard to those general rules of conduct is what is properly called a sense of duty, a principle of the greatest consequence in human life, and the only principle by which the bulk of mankind are capable of directing their actions.
>
> Many men behave very decently, and through the whole of their lives avoid any considerable degree of blame, who yet, perhaps, never felt the sentiment upon the propriety of which we found our approbation of their conduct, but acted merely from a regard to what they saw were the established rules of behaviour. The man who has received great benefits from another person, by the natural coldness of his temper, feel but a very small degree of the sentiment of gratitude. If he has been virtuously educated, however, he will often have been made to observe how odious those actions appear which denote a want of this sentiment, and how amiable the contrary. Though his heart, therefore, is not warmed with any grateful affection, he will strive to act as if it was, and will endeavour to pay all those regards and attentions to his patron which the liveliest gratitude could suggest. He will visit him regularly; he will behave to him respectfully; he will never talk of him but with expressions of the highest esteem, and of the many obligations which he owes to him. And, what is more, he will carefully embrace every opportunity of making a proper return for past services. He may do all this, too, without any hypocrisy or blameable dissimulation, without any selfish intention of obtaining new favours, and without any

Vernon L. Smith, *Adam Smith's Theory of Society*,
https://doi.org/10.1007/978-3-031-68494-4_28

> design of imposing either upon his benefactor or the public. The motive of his actions may be no other than a reverence for the established rule of duty, a serious and earnest desire of acting, in every respect, according to the law of gratitude. A wife, in the same manner, sometimes not feel that tender regard for her husband which is suitable to the relation that subsists between them. If she has been virtuously educated, however, she will endeavour to act as if she felt it, to be careful, officious, faithful, and sincere, and to be deficient in none of those attentions which the sentiment of conjugal affection could have prompted her to perform. Such a friend, and such a wife, are neither of them, undoubtedly, the very best of their kinds; and though both of them have the most serious and earnest desire to fulfil every part of their duty, yet they will fail in many nice and delicate regards, they will miss many opportunities of obliging, which they could never have overlooked if they had possessed the sentiment that is proper to their situation. Though not the very first of their kinds, however, they are perhaps the second; and if the regard to the general rules of conduct has been very strongly impressed upon them, neither of them will fail in any very essential part of their duty. None but those of the happiest mould are capable of suiting, with exact justness, their sentiments and behaviour to the smallest difference of situation, and of acting upon all occasions with the most delicate and accurate propriety. The coarse clay of which the bulk of mankind are formed, cannot be wrought up to such perfection. There is scarce any man, however, who by discipline, education, and example, may not be so impressed with a regard to general rules, as to act upon almost every occasion with tolerable decency, and through the whole of his life to avoid any considerable degree of blame. (*TMS*, pp. 229–231)

There are surely those who are naturally insensitive to a feeling of gratitude toward those who have happily benefitted them, but, aware of the duties normally attending to the reward of such action, proceed to follow those rules out of a regard for doing one's duty. Hence, more people may obey the rules than do it out of any gratitude personally felt. As is his wont, Smith is concerned to examine all those exceptions to his model of beneficent action based on gratitude in which beneficent action is normally rewarded out of a "debt of gratitude." Actions are in rule space, contain information that we access through others, and thus obviate the need to download all its particulars.

Without this sacred regard for general rules, including those of good manners, there is no man whose conduct can be much relied upon.

> It is this which constitutes the most essential difference between a man of principle and honour and a worthless fellow. The one adheres, on all occasions, steadily and resolutely to his maxims, and preserves, through the whole of his life, one even tenor of conduct. The other acts variously and accidentally, as humour, inclination, or interest, chance to be uppermost. Nay, such are the inequalities of humour to which all men are subject, that without this principle, the man who, in all his cool hours, had the most delicate sensibility to the propriety of conduct, might often be led to act absurdly upon the most frivolous occasions, and when it was scarce possible to assign any serious motive for his behaving in this manner. Your friend makes you a visit when you happen to be in a humour which makes it disagreeable to receive him; in your present mood his civility is very apt to appear an impertinent intrusion; and if you were to give way to the views of things which at this time occur, though civil in your temper, you would behave to him with coldness and contempt. *What renders you incapable of such a rudeness is nothing but a regard to the general rules of civility and hospitality, which prohibit it.* That habitual reverence which your former experience has taught you for these, enables you to act, upon all such occasions, with nearly equal propriety, and hinders those inequalities of temper, to which all men are subject, from influencing your conduct in any very sensible degree. But if without regard to these general rules, even the duties of politeness, which are so easily observed, and which one can scarce have any serious motive to violate, would yet be so frequently violated, what would become of the duties of justice, of truth, of chastity, of fidelity, which it is often so difficult to observe, and which there be so many strong motives to violate? But upon the tolerable observance of these duties depends the very existence of human society, which would crumble into nothing if mankind were not generally impressed with a reverence for those important rules of conduct. (*TMS*, pp. 231–233; italics added)

Think of your own circumstances in which a friend drops in when you are not in the mood to receive her in good spirits. Never-the-less, rather than receive her in the coldness you moodily feel, you receive her in polite regard for her long friendship and mutual esteem. If it were otherwise, and our current situation always and only reflected our current states of cheer or gloom, what would happen to the great societal duties of justice, truth, chastity, of fidelity, so difficult to maintain in competition with the delusions of our self-love? The existence of a stable society would be in endanger of crumbling to nothing were humankind not able to rise above the moment and maintain a reverence for proper rules of conduct. Similarly, we do not change our outlook on every unfortunate event in world history.

As related by Smith's younger contemporary, Edmund Burke notes: "Manners are of more importance than laws. Upon them, in a great measure, the laws depend." ("Letters on A Regicide Peace," *Select Works of Edmund Burke*. Vol. 3, Liberty Fund, 1796).

Nature armed humankind early with religious beliefs that defined ideals of good and evil that provided models for the rules we learned to follow in our families and neighborhoods.

> This reverence is still further enhanced by an opinion which is first impressed by nature, and afterwards confirmed by reasoning and philosophy, that those important rules of morality are the commands and laws of the Deity, who will finally reward the obedient, and punish the transgressors of their duty.
> This opinion or apprehension…seems first to be impressed by nature. Men are naturally led to ascribe to those mysterious beings, whatever they are, which happen in any country to be the objects of religious fear, all their own sentiments and passions. They have no other, they can conceive no other, to ascribe to them. Those unknown intelligences which they imagine but see not, must necessarily be formed with some sort of resemblance to those intelligences of which they have experience. During the ignorance and darkness of pagan superstition, mankind seem to have formed the ideas of their divinities with so little delicacy, that they ascribed to them, indiscriminately, all the passions of human nature, those not excepted which do the least honour to our species, such as lust, hunger, avarice, envy, revenge. They could not fail, therefore, to ascribe to those beings, for the excellence of whose nature they still conceived the highest admiration, those sentiments and qualities which are the great ornaments of humanity, and which seem to raise it to a resemblance of divine perfection, the love of virtue and beneficence, and the abhorrence of vice and injustice. The man who was injured called upon Jupiter to be witness of the wrong that was done to him, and could not doubt but that divine being would behold it with the same indignation which would animate the meanest of mankind, who looked on when injustice was committed. The man who did the injury felt himself to be the proper object of the detestation and resentment of mankind; and his natural fears led him to impute the same sentiments to those awful beings, whose presence he could not avoid, and whose power he could not resist. These natural hopes, and fears, and suspicions, were propagated by sympathy, and confirmed by education; and the gods were

> universally represented and believed to be the rewarders of humanity and mercy, and the avengers of perfidy and injustice. *And thus religion, even in its rudest form, gave a sanction to the rules of morality, long before the age of artificial reasoning and philosophy.* That the terrors of religion should thus enforce the natural sense of duty, was of too much importance to the happiness of mankind for nature to leave it dependent upon the slowness and uncertainty of philosophical researches. (*TMS*, p. 233; italics added)

Nature, very early in humankind's history, created in the most primitive and superstitious of religious beliefs, models of gods of evil and of good emerging in the rules that defined standards of morality to be followed, or of immorality to be avoided, and that accordingly would be rewarded or punished. These iconic representations captured ideals of perfection in the process of being encased in the rules people followed. Thus, nature supported in practice these ideal representations of perfection in conduct. For Smith, religion was part of experience and, therefore, part of the evidence to be examined for its enduring messages. Religion gave sanction to the rules of moral human action, a condition that was much too important for human happiness and welfare to wait for the slow and uncertainty of philosophical reasoning. Indeed, I would argue that it was that which made the latter possible. Hence, in Smith the importance of God as He appears in the form of the Great Author on Nature to teach His people at ground level what are the rules we are to make and follow. He is here manifest as a Holy Spirit of just conduct.

When philosophical research finally came into being it confirmed by reason that for which nature had long prepared humankind in the rules we learned to follow; to judge, to bestow censure or applause upon all principles in our nature.

> These researches, however, when they came to take place, confirmed those original anticipations of nature. Upon whatever we suppose that our moral faculties are founded, whether upon a certain modification of reason, upon an original instinct, called a moral sense, or upon some other principle of our nature, it cannot be doubted that they were given us for the direction of our conduct in this life. They carry along with them the most evident badges of this authority, which denote that they were set up within us to be the supreme arbiters of all our actions, to superintend all our senses, passions, and appetites, and to judge how far each of them was either to be indulged or restrained. Our moral faculties are by no means, as some have pretended, upon a level in this respect with the other faculties and

> appetites of our nature, endowed with no more right to restrain these last, than these last are to restrain them. No other faculty or principle of action judges of any other. Love does not judge of resentment, nor resentment of love. Those two passions may be opposite to one another, but cannot, with any propriety, be said to approve or disapprove of one another. But it is the peculiar office of those faculties now under our consideration to judge, to bestow censure or applause upon all the other principles of our nature. They may be considered as a sort of senses, of which those principles are the objects. Every sense is supreme over its own objects. There is no appeal from the eye with regard to the beauty of colours, nor from the ear with regard to the harmony of sounds, nor from the taste with regard to the agreeableness of flavours. Each of those senses judges in the last resort of its own objects. Whatever gratifies the taste is sweet, whatever pleases the eye is beautiful, whatever soothes the ear is harmonious. The very essence of each of those qualities consists in its being fitted to please the sense to which it is addressed. It belongs to our moral faculties, in the same manner, to determine when the ear ought to be soothed, when the eye ought to be indulged, when the taste ought to be gratified, when and how far every other principle of our nature ought either to be indulged or restrained. What is agreeable to our moral faculties, is fit, and right, and proper to be done; the contrary, wrong, unfit, and improper. The sentiments which they approve of are graceful and becoming; the contrary, ungraceful and unbecoming. The very words, right, wrong, fit, improper, graceful, unbecoming, mean only what pleases or displeases those faculties. (*TMS*, pp. 233–234)

Nature brought rules allowing humankind to judge, bestow, censer, and encourage our maturation long before the age of reason in which philosophical examination confirmed the efficacy of nature's way. Our moral faculties judge what is fit, right, and proper action, and what is unfit, wrong, and improper action. They approve sentiments that are graceful and becoming; disapprove those that are ungraceful and unbecoming. As this morality develops, and flowers into society, the words, right, wrong, fit, improper, graceful, unbecoming, are formed to express the meaning in that morality.

The moral rules intended to govern human nature are the vicegerents of god within us and are more properly "laws" than those principles that govern motion because they enable us to see order.

> Since these, therefore, were plainly intended to be the governing principles of human nature, the rules which they prescribe are to be regarded as the commands and laws of the Deity, promulgated by those vicegerents which he has thus set up within us. All general rules are commonly denominated laws: thus the general rules which bodies observe in the communication of motion, are called the laws of motion. But those general rules which our moral faculties observe in approving or condemning whatever sentiment or action is subjected to their examination, may much more justly be denominated such. They have a much greater resemblance to what are properly called laws, those general rules which the sovereign lays down to direct the conduct of his subjects. Like them they are rules to direct the free actions of men: they are prescribed most surely by a lawful superior, and are attended too with the sanction of rewards and punishments. Those vicegerents of God within us never fail to punish the violation of them by the torments of inward shame and self-condemnation; and, on the contrary, always reward obedience with tranquillity of mind, with contentment, and self-satisfaction. (*TMS*, pp. 234–235)

Nature's rules are designed to direct the free-will actions of humankind and are surely described by a superior Author causing the sanction of rewards and punishments. Free to choose includes the right to ere and suffer the consequences. Adults are not well served by every program intended to rescue them from their own error in the absence of learning-testing-overcoming experiences. We are born to be remade by others and to help make others.

To gain happiness for humankind and all rational creatures is why the creator brought them into being and to cooperate with nature is to learn moral rules designed to promote that end.

> There are innumerable other considerations which serve to confirm the same conclusion. The happiness of mankind, as well as of all other rational creatures, seems to have been the original purpose intended by the Author of Nature when he brought them into existence. No other end seems worthy of that supreme wisdom and divine benignity which we necessarily ascribe to him; and this opinion, which we are led to by the abstract consideration of his infinite perfections, is still more confirmed by the examination of the works of Nature, which seem all intended to promote happiness, and to guard against misery. But, by acting according to the dictates of our moral faculties, we necessarily pursue the most effectual means for promoting the happiness of mankind, and therefore be said, in some sense, to co-operate with the Deity, and to advance, as far as in

> our power, the plan of providence. By acting otherwise, on the contrary, we seem to obstruct, in some measure, the scheme which the Author of Nature has established for the happiness and perfection of the world, and to declare ourselves…in some measure the enemies of God. Hence we are naturally encouraged to hope for his extraordinary favour and reward in the one case, and to dread his vengeance and punishment in the other. (*TMS*, p. 235)

Nature leads us by an invisible hand to act in accordance with our moral faculties, thereby to promote the happiness of humankind, to cooperate with the Deity, and His plan of providence. To act otherwise would serve to obstruct the grand design of the Author of Nature and thus to become the enemies of God.

Evolutionists please note that Smith's Author of Nature seeks the happiness of "all rational creatures" which includes humankind as we now know and love it. Thus, are we prepared to treat with sober attention even those who bear witness to having seen, or pursued Unidentified Flying Objects!

Humanity does not desire to be great, but to be beloved. It is not in being rich that truth and justice would rejoice.

> There are besides many other reasons, and many other natural principles, which all tend to confirm and inculcate the same salutary doctrine. If we consider the general rules by which external prosperity and adversity are commonly distributed in this life, we shall find, that notwithstanding the disorder in which all things appear to be in this world, yet even here every virtue naturally meets with its proper reward, with the recompence which is most fit to encourage and promote it; and this too so surely, that it requires a very extraordinary concurrence of circumstances entirely to disappoint it. What is the reward most proper for encouraging industry, prudence, and circumspection?—Success in every sort of business. And is it possible that in the whole of life these virtues should fail of attaining it?—Wealth and external honours are their proper recompence, and the recompence which they can seldom fail of acquiring. What reward is most proper for promoting the practice of truth, justice, and humanity?—The confidence, the esteem, and love of those we live with. Humanity does not desire to be great, but to be beloved. It is not in being rich that truth and justice would rejoice, but in being trusted and believed, recompences which those virtues must almost always acquire. By some very extraordinary and unlucky circumstance, a good man may come to be suspected of

> a crime of which he was altogether incapable, and upon that account be most unjustly exposed for the remaining part of his life to the horror and aversion of mankind. By an accident of this kind he may be said to lose his all, notwithstanding his integrity and justice; in the same manner as a cautious man, notwithstanding his utmost circumspection, may be ruined by an earthquake or an inundation. Accidents of the first kind, however, are perhaps still more rare, and still more contrary to the common course of things, than those of the second; and it still remains true, that the practice of truth, justice, and humanity, is a certain and almost infallible method of acquiring what those virtues chiefly aim at, the confidence and love of those we live with. A person may be very easily misrepresented with regard to a particular action; but it is scarce possible that he should be so with regard to the general tenor of his conduct. An innocent man be believed to have done wrong—this, however, will rarely happen. On the contrary, the established opinion of the innocence of his manners will often lead us to absolve him where he has really been in the fault, notwithstanding very strong presumptions. A knave, in the same manner, may escape censure, or even meet with applause, for a particular knavery, in which his conduct is not understood. But no man was ever habitually such, without being almost universally known to be so, and without being even frequently suspected of guilt, when he was in reality perfectly innocent. And so far as vice and virtue can be either punished or rewarded by the sentiments and opinions of mankind, they both, according to the common course of things, meet even here with something more than exact and impartial justice. (*TMS*, pp. 236–237)

What reward does nature consider most proper for promoting the practice of truth, justice, and humanity? None other than the treasured confidence, esteem, and love of those we live with. Humankind desires not to be great, but to be beloved, trusted, and believed, recompenses appropriate for high virtue. Smith argues that good reputations are not easily lost to the watchful cognizance of associates, friends, and enemies. Justice tends to prevail as it has many observant followers.

The industrious knave cultivates the soil; the indolent good man leaves it uncultivated. Who ought to reap the harvest? Who starve and who live in plenty?

> But though the general rules by which prosperity and adversity are commonly distributed, when considered in this cool and philosophical light, appear to be perfectly suited to the situation of mankind in this life,

yet they are by no means suited to some of our natural sentiments. Our natural love and admiration for some virtues is such, that we should wish to bestow on them all sorts of honours and rewards, even those which we must acknowledge to be the proper recompences of other qualities, with which those virtues are not always accompanied. Our detestation, on the contrary, for some vices is such, that we should desire to heap upon them every sort of disgrace and disaster, those not excepted which are the natural consequences of very different qualities. Magnanimity, generosity, and justice, command so high a degree of admiration, that we desire to see them crowned with wealth, and power, and honours of every kind, the natural consequences of prudence, industry, and application; qualities with which those virtues are not inseparably connected. Fraud, falsehood, brutality, and violence, on the other hand, excite in every human breast such scorn and abhorrence, that our indignation rouses to see them possess those advantages which they in some sense may be said to have merited, by the diligence and industry with which they are sometimes attended. The industrious knave cultivates the soil; the indolent good man leaves it uncultivated. Who ought to reap the harvest? Who starve, and who live in plenty? The natural course of things decides it in favour of the knave: the natural sentiments of mankind in favour of the man of virtue. Man judges that the good qualities of the one are greatly over-recompensed by those advantages which they tend to procure him, and that the omissions of the other are by far too severely punished by the distress which they naturally bring upon him; and human laws, the consequences of human sentiments, forfeit the life and the estate of the industrious and cautious traitor, and reward, by extraordinary recompences, the fidelity and public spirit of the improvident and careless good citizen. Thus man is by nature directed to correct, in some measure, that distribution of things which she herself would otherwise have made. The rules which for this purpose she prompts him to follow, are different from those which she herself observes. She bestows upon every virtue, and upon every vice, that precise reward or punishment which is best fitted to encourage the one, or to restrain the other. She is directed by this sole consideration, and pays little regard to the different degrees of merit and demerit which they seem to possess in the sentiments and passions of man. Man, on the contrary, pays regard to this only, and would endeavour to render the state of every virtue precisely proportioned to that degree of love and esteem, and of every vice to that degree of contempt and abhorrence, which he himself conceives for it. The rules which she follows are fit for her, those which he follows for him: but both are calculated to promote the same great end, the order of the world, and the perfection and happiness of human nature. (*TMS*, pp. 237–239)

Nature rewards all those who follow her rules, punishing or not rewarding those who violate them. If the knave cultivates the soil better than the person of virtue, nature will reward the knave. It is the same in the economy, which rewards those who best serve the wants of their customers whether knave or a person of virtue. And again, in neighborhood social exchange, where people help others and are, in turn, rewarded for it. The economy and neighborhood communities are thereby extensions of nature into the institutions of humankind. Cultivate your customers, your neighbors, and your soil.

The best efforts of humankind to interpose in favor of virtue and in opposition to vice sometimes fail. Unavoidably, violence and artifice prevail over sincerity and justice, inciting indignation in the breast of every spectator.

> But though man is thus employed to alter that distribution of things which natural events would make, if left to themselves; though like the gods of the poets he is perpetually interposing, by extraordinary means, in favour of virtue and in opposition to vice, and, like them, endeavours to turn away the arrow that is aimed at the head of the righteous, but to accelerate the sword of destruction that is lifted up against the wicked; yet he is by no means able to render the fortune of either quite suitable to his own sentiments and wishes. The natural course of things cannot be entirely controlled by the impotent endeavours of man: the current is too rapid and too strong for him to stop it; and though the rules which direct it appear to have been established for the wisest and best purposes, they sometimes produce effects which shock all his natural sentiments. That a great combination of men should prevail over a small one; that those who engage in an enterprize with forethought and all necessary preparation, should prevail over such as oppose them without any; and that every end should be acquired by those means only which nature has established for acquiring it, seems to be a rule not only necessary and unavoidable in itself, but even useful and proper for rousing the industry and attention of mankind. Yet when, in consequence of this rule, violence and artifice prevail over sincerity and justice, what indignation does it not excite in the breast of every human spectator? What sorrow and compassion for the sufferings of the innocent, and what furious resentment against the success of the oppressor? We are equally grieved and enraged at the wrong that is done, but often find it altogether out of our power to redress it. When we thus despair of finding any force upon earth which can check the triumph of injustice, we naturally appeal to heaven, and hope that the great Author

> of our nature will himself execute hereafter, what all the principles which he has given us for the direction of our conduct prompt us to attempt even here; that he will complete the plan which he himself has thus taught us to begin; and will, in a life to come, render to every one according to the works which he has performed in this world. And thus we are led to the belief of a future state, not only by the weaknesses, by the hopes and fears of human nature, but by the noblest and best principles which belong to it, by the love of virtue, and by the abhorrence of vice and injustice. (*TMS*, pp. 239–240)

When normally good rules fail, we are grieved and enraged at the unintended wrong that is done, but events are often beyond our poor power to redress. In despair of our failure to check the victory of injustice, humankind has long appealed to the higher power of heaven for assurance that the Great Author of Nature will intervene to complete the plan He has taught us for the direction of our conduct, and will, in a life to come, render to every person according to the works which he has performed in this world through the love of virtue, and the abhorrence of vice and injustice.

When the rules we learn for determining the merit and demerit of our actions our regarded as the laws of an all-powerful being, and be applied in after life, they take on a sacredness requiring the will of the deity to be the supreme governor of our conduct.

> When the general rules which determine the merit and demerit of actions come thus to be regarded as the laws of an all-powerful being, who watches over our conduct, and who, in a life to come, will reward the observance and punish the breach of them—they necessarily acquire a new sacredness from this consideration. That our regard to the will of the Deity ought to be the supreme rule of our conduct, can be doubted of by nobody who believes his existence. The very thought of disobedience appears to involve in it the most shocking impropriety. How vain, how absurd would it be for man, either to oppose or to neglect the commands that were laid upon him by infinite wisdom and infinite power! How unnatural, how impiously ungrateful not to reverence the precepts that were prescribed to him by the infinite goodness of his Creator, even though no punishment was to follow their violation! The sense of propriety, too, is here well supported by the strongest motives of self-interest. The idea that, however we escape the observation of man or be placed above the reach of human punishment, yet we are always acting under the eye and exposed to the punishment of

> God, the great avenger of injustice, is a motive capable of restraining the most headstrong passions, with those at least who, by constant reflection, have rendered it familiar to them. (*TMS*, p. 241)

The important societal function served by belief in an all-powerful Deity, even if in His infinite goodness we are to escape punishment, is to be exposed to His eye as the supreme avenger of injustice and serving to restrain our headstrong passions. Consequently, the general rules of propriety we follow take on a new sacredness.

Religion enforces nature's sense of duty inspiring great confidence in the truly pious believers.

> It is in this manner that religion enforces the natural sense of duty: and hence it is that mankind are generally disposed to place great confidence in the probity of those who seem deeply impressed with religious sentiments. Such persons, they imagine, act under an additional tie, besides those which regulate the conduct of other men. The regard to the propriety of action, as well as to reputation; the regard to the applause of his own breast, as well as to that of others; are motives which, they suppose, have the same influence over the religious man as over the man of the world. But the former lies under another restraint, and never acts deliberately but as in the presence of that great Superior who is finally to recompense him according to his deeds. A greater trust is reposed, upon this account, in the regularity and exactness of his conduct. And wherever the natural principles of religion are not corrupted by the factious and party zeal of some worthless cabal; wherever the first duty which it requires is to fulfil all the obligations of morality; wherever men are not taught to regard frivolous observances as more immediate duties of religion than acts of justice and beneficence; and to imagine, that by sacrifices, and ceremonies, and vain supplications, they can bargain with the Deity for fraud, and perfidy, and violence, the world undoubtedly judges right in this respect, and justly places a double confidence in the rectitude of the religious man's behaviour. (*TMS*, pp. 241–242)

The truly religious person, and Smith was well qualified as a Christian, lies under a restraint, that never acts deliberately except in the presence of that great Superior who is finally to recompense him according to his deeds. A greater trust is reposed, upon this account, in the regularity and exactness of his conduct. And wherever these natural principles of religion are not corrupted by factitious earthly zeal and frivolous observances, we can imagine that by sacrifice, ceremony, and vain supplications that the religious person can bargain with the Deity on matters of fraud, perfidy, and violence, thereby inspiring double confidence in the rectitude of their behavior.

CHAPTER 29

In what cases the sense of duty ought to be the sole principle of our conduct; and in what cases it ought to concur with other motives

Religion has been such a powerful supporter of virtue and restraint of the temptations of vice that many have supposed that such principles are alone sufficient to guide our actions, without need of reward out of gratitude or punishment out of resentment.

> Religion affords such strong motives to the practice of virtue, and guards us by such powerful restraints from the temptations of vice, that many have been led to suppose that religious principles were the sole laudable motives of action. "We ought neither," they say, "to reward from gratitude, nor punish from resentment; we ought neither to protect the helplessness of our children, nor afford support to the infirmities of our parents, from natural affection. All affections for particular objects ought to be extinguished in our breast, and one great affection take the place of all others, the love of the Deity, the desire of rendering ourselves agreeable to him, and of directing our conduct in every respect according to his will. We ought not to be grateful from gratitude, we ought not to be charitable from humanity, we ought not to be public-spirited from the love of our country, nor generous and just from the love of mankind. The sole principle and motive of our conduct in the performance of all those different duties, ought to be a sense that God has commanded us to perform them." I shall not at present take time to examine this opinion particularly; I shall

Vernon L. Smith, *Adam Smith's Theory of Society*,
https://doi.org/10.1007/978-3-031-68494-4_29

> only observe, that we should not have expected to have found it entertained by any sect, who professed themselves of a religion in which, as it is the first precept to love the Lord our God with all our heart, with all our soul, and with all our strength, so it is the second to love our neighbour as we love ourselves; and we love ourselves surely for our own sakes, and not merely because we are commanded to do so. That the sense of duty should be the sole principle of our conduct, is nowhere the precept of Christianity; but that it should be the ruling and the governing one, as philosophy, and as, indeed, common sense, directs. It may be a question, however, in what cases our actions ought to arise chiefly or entirely from a sense of duty, or from a regard to general rules; and in what cases some other sentiment or affection ought to concur, and have a principal influence. (*TMS*, pp. 243–244)

According to Smith, the claim that Christianity's first precept is to love God, the second to love our neighbor as ourselves, fails to make plain that we need to love ourselves for our own sakes and not because we are commanded to do so. The sense of duty is nowhere a precept of Christianity but is a governing precondition in the universe, philosophy, and common sense. Can we really suppose that we need only follow one precept—the Love of God? Smith program is erected on the idea that we need experienced-based guidance to meet new and unfamiliar applications of morality, and God has given us a measure of free will to get it right, or to ere, and to enjoy the gains, or suffer the sorrows that result. Religious belief promises a sense of purpose and zest for life, but to fulfill that promise the Author of Nature creates a practical learning-teaching process of rule formation that underlies community, society, and nation. That is how we find God and His Love. He made us curiosity-driven command-violators and in need of a new covenant emerging from everywhere not just from the top. This message is in the narrative of the apple in Genesis, and everything follows from that. Human curiosity led to sin and demise and will continue to do so but also to prosperity and happiness. We must chart our way through this maze following the rules we fashion.

The two conditions determining whether we act from a sense of duty or in accordance with the applicable general rules.

> The decision of this question [sense of duty versus general rules], which cannot, perhaps, be given with any very great accuracy, will depend upon two different circumstance.

> I. First, I say, it will depend upon the natural agreeableness or deformity of the affection itself, how far our actions ought to arise from it, or entirely proceed from a regard to the general rule.
> All those graceful and admired actions to which the benevolent affections would prompt us, ought to proceed as much from the passions themselves as from any regard to the general rules of conduct. A benefactor thinks himself but ill requited if the person upon whom he has bestowed his good offices repays them merely from a cold sense of duty, and without any affection to his person. A husband is dissatisfied with the most obedient wife, when he imagines her conduct is animated by no other principle besides her regard to what the relation she stands in requires. Though a son should fail in none of the offices of filial duty, yet if he wants that affectionate reverence which it so well becomes him to feel, the parent may justly complain of his indifference. Nor could a son be quite satisfied with a parent who, though he performed all the duties of his situation, had nothing of that fatherly fondness which might have been expected from him. With regard to all such benevolent and social affections, it is agreeable to see the sense of duty employed rather to restrain than to enliven them, rather to hinder us from doing too much, than to prompt us to do what we ought. It gives us pleasure to see a father obliged to check his own fondness, a friend obliged to set bounds to his natural generosity, a person who has received a benefit, obliged to restrain the too sanguine gratitude of his own temper. (*TMS*, pp. 244–245)

Thus, when someone favors us with a beneficial action out of their respect for us, the general rule is to reward that action. But what reward is appropriate? The answer is in our judgment of the merit of each particular case, which is situation-specific, and involves fellow-feeling. To act with coldness, out of a sense that this is what others expect from me, is to fail to enter into the mutual fellow-feeling that is a central part of human sociability. In Parable of the Trash Barrel (Chapter 19), your neighbor might have merely reminded you of what you had neglected to do, which might convey an implicit criticism. Instead, without comment, she wheels the barrel in herself revealing her intimate non-verbale local knowledge of social responsibilities and willingness to fill in for your oversight.

Though we reward from the spontaneous gratitude and generosity That we feel without reluctance, we ought always to punish harmful acts with reluctance in awareness of its design to deter and that the punishment should fit the infraction.

> The contrary maxim takes place with regard to the malevolent and unsocial passions. We ought to reward from the gratitude and generosity of our own hearts, without any reluctance, and without being obliged to reflect how great the propriety of rewarding; but we ought always to punish with reluctance, and more from a sense of the propriety of punishing than from any savage disposition to revenge. Nothing is more graceful than the behaviour of the man who appears to resent the greatest injuries, more from a sense that they deserve, and are the proper objects of resentment, than from feeling himself the furies of that disagreeable passion; who, like a judge, considers only the general rule, which determines what vengeance is due for each particular offence; who, in executing that rule, feels less for what himself has suffered, than for what the offender is about to suffer; who, though in wrath, remembers mercy, and is disposed to interpret the rule in the most gentle and favourable manner, and to allow all the alleviations which the most candid humanity could, consistently with good sense, admit of. (*TMS*, p. 245)

Implicit in the asymmetries between rewarding from gratitude and punishing from resentment are the "alleviations" to be considered in levying punishment. To reward in error is to praise and consider praiseworthy that which is neither, but it is rarely harmful or odious. To blame and consider blameworthy anyone who is innocent is unjust and a calamity for major infractions. Hence, in free countries the constitutional protections for first amendment rights, trial by jury, and attention to due process. Defamation, or wrongful accusations, are subject to recovery, but rarely are gifts retracted in error.

The miser is anxious to restrain trivial expenditures for its own sake, the same concerns by a person of economy and assiduity is their scheme of life.

> As the selfish passions, according to what has formerly been observed, hold in other respects a sort of middle place between the social and unsocial affections, so do they likewise in this. The pursuit of the objects of private interest, in all common, little, and ordinary cases, ought to flow rather from a regard to the general rules which prescribe such conduct, than from any passion for the objects themselves; but upon more important and extraordinary occasions, we should be awkward, insipid, and ungraceful, if the objects themselves did not appear to animate us with a considerable degree of passion. To be anxious, or to be laying a plot either to gain or to save a single shilling, would degrade the most vulgar tradesman in the

> opinion of all his neighbours. Let his circumstances be ever so mean, no attention to any such small matters, for the sake of the things themselves, must appear in his conduct. His situation may require the most severe economy and the most exact assiduity: but each particular exertion of that economy and assiduity must proceed, not so much from a regard for that particular saving or gain, as for the general rule which to him prescribes, with the utmost rigour, such a tenor of conduct. His parsimony to-day must not arise from a desire of the particular threepence which he will save by it, nor his attendance in his shop from a passion for the particular tenpence which he will acquire by it: both the one and the other ought to proceed solely from a regard to the general rule, which prescribes, with the most unrelenting severity, this plan of conduct to all persons in his way of life. In this consists the difference between the character of a miser and that of a person of exact economy and assiduity. The one is anxious about small matters for their own sake; the other attends to them only in consequence of the scheme of life which he has laid down to himself. (*TMS*, pp. 245–246)

The miser is a person universally detested because he symbolizes grasping greed which is odious. To be thrifty in pursuit of a life or business purpose is admired. Yet both are laudable in leaving more goods and services for others to consume through their engagement in trade—giving that they may receive. Good people are glad to accept beneficial things because the flow of goods to them is a consequence of their regard to the general rules which prescribe proper social conduct, rather than from any passion for the objects themselves. That passion is already contained in Smith's postulate that all are strictly self-interested, but that being self-loving is distinct from acting self-interestedly because actions are governed by general rules not only immediate private gain.

I. What is greatness and ambition, and how do these relate to the pursuit of self-interest?

> It is quite otherwise with regard to the more extraordinary and important objects of self-interest. A person appears mean-spirited, who does not pursue these with some degree of earnestness for their own sake. We should despise a prince who was not anxious about conquering or defending a province. We should have little respect for a private gentleman who did not exert himself to gain an estate, or even a considerable office, when he could acquire them without either meanness or injustice. A member

> of Parliament who shews no keenness about his own election, is abandoned by his friends as altogether unworthy of their attachment. Even a tradesman is thought a poor-spirited fellow among his neighbours, who does not bestir himself to get what they call an extraordinary job, or some uncommon advantage. This spirit and keenness constitutes the difference between the man of enterprise and the man of dull regularity. Those great objects of self-interest, of which the loss or acquisition quite changes the rank of the person, are the objects of the passion properly called ambition; a passion which, when it keeps within the bounds of prudence and justice, is always admired in the world, and has even sometimes a certain irregular greatness, which dazzles the imagination when it passes the limits of both these virtues, and is not only unjust but extravagant. Hence the general admiration for heroes and conquerors, and even for statesmen, whose projects have been very daring and extensive, though altogether devoid of justice…The objects of avarice and ambition differ only in their greatness. A miser is as furious about a halfpenny as a man of ambition about the conquest of a kingdom. (*TMS*, pp. 246–247)

The self-interested pursuit of objects whose acquisition quite changes the rank of the person constitutes the passion of ambition which, when it keeps within the bounds of prudence and justice, is always admired. Hence the universal admiration for heroes, conquerors, and statesmen, whose projects have been very daring and extensive. But Smith wants us to understand that in keeping with his theory of society: “A miser is as furious about a halfpenny as a man of ambition about the conquest of a kingdom.”

II. Whether we act from a sense of duty or general rules will depend partly on the latter’s precision or looseness.

> Secondly, I say it will depend partly upon the precision and exactness, or the looseness and inaccuracy of the general rules themselves, how far our conduct ought to proceed entirely from a regard to them.
>
> The general rules of almost all the virtues, the general rules which determine what are the offices of prudence, of charity, of generosity, of gratitude, of friendship, are in many respects loose and inaccurate, admit of many exceptions, and require so many modifications, that it is scarce possible to regulate our conduct entirely by a regard to them. The common proverbial maxims of prudence, being founded in universal experience, are perhaps the best general rules which can be given about it. To affect, however, a very strict and literal adherence to them, would evidently be the most absurd and ridiculous pedantry. Of all the virtues I have just

> now mentioned, gratitude is that, perhaps, of which the rules are the most precise, and admit of the fewest exceptions. That as soon as we can we should make a return of equal, and, if possible, of superior value to the services we have received, would seem to be a pretty plain rule, and one which admitted of scarce any exceptions. Upon the most superficial examination, however, this rule will appear to be in the highest degree loose and inaccurate, and to admit of ten thousand exceptions. If your benefactor attended you in your sickness, ought you to attend him in his? or can you fulfil the obligation of gratitude by making a return of a different kind? If you ought to attend him, how long ought you to attend him? The same time which he attended you, or longer, and how much longer? If your friend lent you money in your distress, ought you to lend him money in his? How much ought you to lend him? When ought you to lend him? Now, or to-morrow, or next month? And for how long a time? It is evident, that no general rule can be laid down by which a precise answer can, in all cases, be given to any of these questions. The difference between his character and yours, between his circumstances and yours, may be such, that you may be perfectly grateful, and justly refuse to lend him a halfpenny: and, on the contrary, you may be willing to lend, or even to give him ten times the sum which he lent you, and yet justly be accused of the blackest ingratitude, and of not having fulfilled the hundredth part of the obligation you lie under. As the duties of gratitude, however, are perhaps the most sacred of all those which the beneficent virtues prescribe to us, so the general rules which determine them are, as I said before, the most accurate. Those which ascertain the actions required by friendship, humanity, hospitality, generosity, are still more vague and indeterminate. (*TMS*, pp. 247–249)

The general rules of almost all the virtues—prudence, charity, generosity, gratitude, and friendship—tend to be loose and inaccurate, admit many exceptions, and require many modifications depending on circumstances. The common proverbial maxims of prudence, being founded in universal experience, are perhaps the most comprehensive of these, while gratitude accounts for the most precise rules. Gratitude requires that as soon as feasible, we should make a return no smaller and preferably of greater value to the services we have received.

The rules of justice are accurate to the highest degree.

> There is, however, one virtue, of which the general rules determine, with the greatest exactness, every external action which it requires. This virtue is Justice. The rules of justice are accurate in the highest degree, and admit

> of no exceptions or modifications but such as be ascertained as accurately as the rules themselves, and which generally, indeed, flow from the very same principles with them. If I owe a man ten pounds, justice requires that I should precisely pay him ten pounds, either at the time agreed upon, or when he demands it. What I ought to perform, how much I ought to perform, when and where I ought to perform it, the whole nature and circumstances of the action prescribed, are all of them precisely fixed and determined. Though it may be awkward and pedantic, therefore, to affect too strict an adherence to the common rules of prudence or generosity, there is no pedantry in sticking fast by the rules of justice. On the contrary, the most sacred regard is due to them; and the actions which this virtue requires are never so properly performed as when the chief motive for performing them is a reverential and religious regard to those general rules which require them. In the practice of the other virtues, our conduct should rather be directed by a certain idea of propriety, by a certain taste for a particular tenor of conduct, than by any regard to a precise maxim or rule; and we should consider the end and foundation of the rule more than the rule itself. But it is otherwise with regard to justice: the man who in that refines the least, and adheres with the most obstinate stead-fastness to the general rules themselves, is the most commendable, and the most to be depended upon. Though the end of the rules of justice be to hinder us from hurting our neighbour, it frequently may be a crime to violate them, though we could pretend, with some pretext of reason, that this particular violation could do no hurt. A man often becomes a villain the moment he begins, even in his own heart, to chicane in this manner. The moment he thinks of departing from the most staunch and positive adherence to what those inviolable precepts prescribe to him, he is no longer to be trusted, and no man can say what degree of guilt he may not arrive at. The thief imagines he does no evil when he steals from the rich, what he supposes they easily want, and what possibly they never even know has been stolen from them. The adulterer imagines he does no evil when he corrupts the wife of his friend, provided he covers his intrigue from the suspicion of the husband, and does not disturb the peace of the family. When once we begin to give way to such refinements, there is no enormity so gross of which we may not be capable. (*TMS*, pp. 249–250)

The rules of justice demand our most sacred and accurate compliance. If you owe someone 10 pounds, you pay them 10 pounds; murder is more serious and commands a higher punishment than theft or robbery. The poor cannot justify robbery simply because the victim is rich. Self-command is always subject to the temptations of self-serving exceptions, recognized in the commandment that you shall not covet the possessions of your neighbor. The slippery slope of corruption begins at home and stays at home with self-deceit.

The rules of justice are analogous to the rules of grammar in their accuracy.

> The rules of justice may be compared to the rules of grammar; the rules of the other virtues to the rules which critics lay down for the attainment of what is sublime and elegant in composition. The one are precise, accurate, and indispensable. The other are loose, vague, and indeterminate, and present us rather with a general idea of the perfection we ought to aim at, than afford us any certain and infallible directions for acquiring it. A man may learn to write grammatically by rule, with the most absolute infallibility; and so, perhaps, he may be taught to act justly. But there are no rules whose observance will infallibly lead us to the attainment of elegance or sublimity in writing: though there are some which help us, in some measure, to correct and ascertain the vague ideas which we might otherwise have entertained of those perfections. And there are no rules by the knowledge of which we can infallibly be taught to act upon all occasions with prudence, with just magnanimity, or proper beneficence: though there are some which enable us to correct and ascertain, in several respects, the imperfect ideas which we might otherwise have entertained of those virtues. (*TMS*, pp. 250–151)

Just as humankind has shaped the rules of grammar to support effective communication based on experience, human social interaction has formed the rules of justice to promote the tranquility of society. But as the rules of grammar cannot alone guarantee fine writing, the rules of justice cannot alone assure just behavior. Each requires dedication and commitment to learning the skills of effective performance for which there are no precise and determinant rules that infallibly assure success.

Though it be our most earnest desire to deserve approbation if we inadvertently ere, it is vain to expect that humankind should never-the-less approve of our behavior.

> It may sometimes happen, that with the most serious and earnest desire of acting so as to deserve approbation, we mistake the proper rules of conduct, and thus maybe misled by that very principle which ought to direct us. It is in vain to expect that in this case mankind should entirely approve of our behaviour. They cannot enter into that absurd idea of duty which influenced us, nor go along with any of the actions which follow

> from it. There is still, however, something respectable in the character and behaviour of one who is thus betrayed into vice, by a wrong sense of duty, or by what is called an erroneous conscience. How fatally soever he may be misled by it, he is still, with the generous and humane, more the object of commiseration than of hatred or resentment. They lament the weakness of human nature, which exposes us to such unhappy delusions, even while we are most sincerely labouring after perfection, and endeavouring to act according to the best principle which can possibly direct us. False notions of religion are almost the only causes which can occasion any very gross perversion of our natural sentiments in this way; and that principle which gives the greatest authority to the rules of duty, is alone capable of distorting our ideas of them in any considerable degree. In all other cases common sense is sufficient to direct us, if not to the most exquisite propriety of conduct, yet to something which is not very far from it; and provided we are desirous in earnest to do well, our behaviour will always, upon the whole, be praiseworthy. That to obey the will of the Deity is the first rule of duty, all men are agreed. But concerning the particular commandments which that will impose upon us, they differ widely from one another. In this, therefore, the greatest mutual forbearance and toleration is due; and though the defence of society requires that crimes should be punished, from whatever motives they proceed, yet a good man will always punish them with reluctance, when they evidently proceed from false notions of religious duty. He will never feel against those who commit them that indignation which he feels against other criminals, but will rather regret, and sometimes even admire, their unfortunate firmness and magnanimity, at the very time that he punishes their crime... (*TMS*, pp. 251–253)

If society is to be defended by its members from destructive internal actions, all crimes must be punished whatever the motives. Good people will regret that a person may be led to the wrong actions by false beliefs or a false sense of religious duty; these cannot be allowed to deflect from the steady hand of justice.

When conduct is not determined by principle, but by human weakness, or by duty, we must withhold the approbation that otherwise would be applied.

> As a person may act wrong by following a wrong sense of duty, so nature may sometimes prevail, and lead him to act right in opposition to it. We cannot in this case be displeased to see that motive prevail, which we think ought to prevail, though the person himself is so weak as to

> think otherwise.[1] As his conduct, however, is the effect of weakness, not principle, we are far from bestowing upon it any thing that approaches to complete approbation. A bigotted Roman Catholic, who, during the massacre of St Bartholomew, had been so overcome by compassion, as to save some unhappy Protestants whom he thought it his duty to destroy, would not seem to be entitled to that high applause which we should have bestowed upon him, had he exerted the same generosity with complete self-approbation. We might be pleased with the humanity of his temper, but we should still regard him with a sort of pity, which is altogether inconsistent with the admiration that is due to perfect virtue. It is the same case with all the other passions. We do not dislike to see them exert themselves properly, even when a false notion of duty would direct the person to restrain them. A very devout quaker, who upon being struck upon one cheek, instead of turning up the other, should so far forget his literal interpretation of our Saviour's[2] precept, as to bestow some good discipline upon the brute that insulted him, would not be disagreeable to us. We should laugh, and be diverted with his spirit, and rather like him the better for it. But we should by no means regard him with that respect and esteem which would seem due to one who, upon a like occasion, had acted properly from a just sense of what was proper to be done. No action can properly be called virtuous, which is not accompanied with the sentiment of self-approbation. (*TMS*, pp. 253–254)

If in a moment of weakness, a person fails to act in the performance of their duty, but we approve of their right action, it does not merit our approbation. In like manner, the approbation for a particular action which is connected to a person's regular line of duty would seem out of place. Thus, the guard who prevents a prisoner from escaping, the fireman who puts out a fire, the soldier who goes to battle, and the lifeguard who rescues a swimmer, are all simply performing the duties that society expects and that they expect of themselves. Only if they act well above the call of ordinary duty do they earn our approbation with special honor. If

[1] Independently of this passage in Smith, recent experiments have tested for the effect of choice action modified by a a random outcome with known probabilities. "We provide experimental evidence that subjects blame others on the basis of events they are not responsible for" (Mehmet Y. Gurdal, Joshua B. Miller, and Aldo Rustichini (2013) "Why Blame?" *Journal of Political Economy*, 121 (6), p. 1205).

[2] It is often claimed that Smith was a Deist as when he writes of God as the Author of Nature, but here he refers explicitly to "our Saviour's precept," adopting the central Christian idea of Christ as humankinds' personal Savior.

it were otherwise in such examples the bottom-up order-creating function of general rules would lose their spontaneity and incisiveness.

PART VIII

Of the effect of utility upon the sentiment of approbation consistenting of one section

CHAPTER 30

Of the beauty which the appearance of utility bestows all the production of art, and of the extensive influence of the species of beauty

The proper role of utility in human pleasure.

> That utility is one of the principal sources of beauty, has been observed by every body who has considered with any attention what constitutes the nature of beauty. The conveniency of a house gives pleasure to the spectator as well as its regularity; and he is as much hurt when he observes the contrary defect, as when he sees the correspondent windows of different forms, or the door not placed exactly in the middle of the building. That the fitness of any system or machine to produce the end for which it was intended, bestows a certain propriety and beauty upon the whole, and renders the very thought and contemplation of it agreeable, is so very obvious, that nobody has overlooked it. (*TMS*, p. 257)

It is right and appropriate that utility has been recognized as a source of universal pleasure in the fitness of a vast number of items in our surroundings to the convenience of our daily existence. Utilitarian services, however, are to be understood as deriving from a system, itself not embodied or embodiable in a utility function! This is the key to understanding and modeling society and to understanding Smith's lasting legacy and relevance to the contemporary continuing evolution of society.

Vernon L. Smith, *Adam Smith's Theory of Society*,
https://doi.org/10.1007/978-3-031-68494-4_30

Why utility causes pleasure; hume versus smith accounts.

> The cause, too, why utility pleases, has of late been assigned by an ingenious and agreeable philosopher, who joins the greatest depth of thought to the greatest elegance of expression, and possesses the singular and happy talent of treating the abstrusest subjects not only with the most perfect perspicuity but with the most lively eloquence.[1] The utility of any object, according to him, pleases the master by perpetually suggesting to him the pleasure or conveniency which it is fitted to promote. Every time he looks at it, he is put in mind of this pleasure; and the object in this manner becomes a source of perpetual satisfaction and enjoyment. The spectator enters by sympathy into the sentiments of the master, and necessarily views the object under the same agreeable aspect. When we visit the palaces of the great, we cannot help conceiving the satisfaction we should enjoy if we ourselves were the masters, and were possessed of so much artful and ingenuously contrived accommodation. A similar account is given why the appearance of inconveniency should render any object disagreeable both to the owner and to the spectator.
> But that this fitness, this happy contrivance of any production of art, should often be more valued than the very end for which it was intended; and that the exact adjustment of the means for attaining any conveniency or pleasure should frequently be more regarded than that very conveniency or pleasure, in the attainment of which their whole merit would seem to consist, has not, so far as I know, been yet taken notice of by any body. (*TMS*, pp. 257–258)

Smith finds a broader conveniency, or utility, not merely in the items, but in the imaginative fitness order within which people arrange them. Smith's theory of society is a system, or process, whose value as a whole is distinct from the utilitarian services that it gives rise to.

Accounting more fully as to why utility pleases.

> That this, however, is very frequently the case, may be observed in a thousand instances, both in the most frivolous and in the most important concerns of human life. When a person comes into his chamber and finds the chairs all standing in the middle of the room, he is angry with

[1] Smith obviously refers to his close friend, David Hume, on whom, faithful to English intellectual style, he first heaps general praise, then rejects decisively Hume's specific utility-based argument.

> his servant, and rather than see them continue in that disorder, perhaps takes the trouble himself to set them all in their places with their backs to the wall. The whole propriety of this new situation arises from its superior conveniency…What he wanted…was not so much this conveniency, as that arrangement of things which promotes it. Yet it is this conveniency which ultimately recommends that arrangement, and bestows upon it the whole of its propriety and beauty. (*TMS*, p. 258)

The arrangement, its propriety, its fitness, yields an outcome that promotes a convenience much superior to anything the items could represent separate from that whole. You go to a superstore to look for couch pillows, lamps, perhaps other things. You find what seems to be just-right pillows, and then search for two lamps. You stumble upon more pillows and realize that you temporarily have chosen some just-wrong pillows. You now have a new vision of your living room born of a more orderly arrangement of form and color.

Some items of consumptive use serve greater purposes in society by assisting our contribution to social order.

> A watch, in the same manner, that falls behind above two minutes in a day, is despised by one curious in watches. He sells it perhaps for a couple of guineas, and purchases another at fifty, which will not lose above a minute in a fortnight. The sole use of watches, however, is to tell us what o'clock it is, and to hinder us from breaking any engagement, or suffering any other inconveniency by our ignorance in that particular point. But the person so nice with regard to this machine will not always be found either more scrupulously punctual than other men, or more anxiously concerned upon any other account to know precisely what time of day it is. What interests him is not so much the attainment of this piece of knowledge, as the perfection of the machine which serves to attain it. (*TMS*, pp. 258–259)

Thus, for Smith, the order that yields society is a well-ordered "machine" or system in which we each have acquired knowledge how to act in an uncountable number of distinct experienced, or to be experienced, situations marked by fellow-feeling with others. That every such instance has utility value to the participants is not the way to comprehend society, whose mainsprings far exceed in depth the sum of the utility services delivered. The gadgets that fascinate us sometimes inadvertently fit that purpose.

Our fascination for items of consumptive use sometimes become ends in themselves, as we lose sight of their purpose.

> How many people ruin themselves by laying out money on trinkets of frivolous utility? What pleases these lovers of toys, is not so much the utility as the aptness of the machines which are fitted to promote it. All their pockets are stuffed with little conveniencies. They contrive new pockets, unknown in the clothes of other people, in order to carry a greater number. They walk about loaded with a multitude of baubles, in weight, and sometimes in value, not inferior to an ordinary Jew's-box, some of which sometimes may be of some little use, but all of which might at all times be very well spared, and of which the whole utility is certainly not worth the fatigue of bearing the burden. (*TMS*, p. 259)

Smith, being Scotch, is here fulfilling their populist image of avoiding frivolous and showy forms of consumption, and again debunking any significant role for utility in accounting for the order in Human Society. I directly learned some continuing aspects of this cultural tradition from my grandmother Smith, who was a McCurdy. Adam Smith's larger vision is to demonstrate that these narrow pursuits deflect from finding satisficing meaning in life.

The displays of the rich inspire youthful imagined utilitarian comforts that, if uncorrected, will fail to produce tranquility of purpose or lasting satisfaction.

> Nor is it only with regard to such frivolous objects that our conduct is influenced by this [utilitarian] principle; it is often the secret motive of the most serious and important pursuits of both private and public life.
> The poor man's son, whom heaven in its anger has visited with ambition, when he begins to look around him, admires the condition of the rich. He finds the cottage of his father too small for his accommodation, and fancies he should be lodged more at his ease in a palace. He is displeased with being obliged to walk afoot, or to endure the fatigue of riding on horseback. He sees his superiors carried about in machines, and imagines that in one of these he could travel with less inconveniency. He feels himself naturally indolent, and willing to serve himself with his own hands as little as possible; and judges that a numerous retinue of servants would save him from a great deal of trouble. He thinks if he had attained all these, he would sit still contentedly, and be quiet, enjoying himself in the thought of the happiness and tranquillity of his situation. He is enchanted with

the distant idea of this felicity. It appears in his fancy like the life of some superior rank of beings, and, in order to arrive at it, he devotes himself for ever to the pursuit of wealth and greatness. To obtain the conveniencies which these afford, he submits in the first year, nay, in the first month of his application, to more fatigue of body and more uneasiness of mind, than he could have suffered through the whole of his life from the want of them. He studies to distinguish himself in some laborious profession. With the most unrelenting industry he labors night and day to acquire talents superior to all his competitors. He endeavors next to bring those talents into public view, and with equal assiduity solicits every opportunity of employment. For this purpose he makes his court to all mankind; he serves those whom he hates, and is obsequious to those whom he despises. Through the whole of his life he pursues the idea of a certain artificial and elegant repose which he never arrives at, for which he sacrifices a real tranquility that is at all times in his power, and which, if in the extremity of old age he should at last attain to it, he will find to be in no respect preferable to that humble security and contentment which he had abandoned for it. It is then, in the last dregs of life, his body wasted with toil and diseases, his mind galled and ruffled by the memory of a thousand injuries and disappointments which he imagines he has met with from the injustice of his enemies, or from the perfidy and ingratitude of his friends, that he begins at last to find that wealth and greatness are mere trinkets of frivolous utility, no more adapted for procuring ease of body or tranquility of mind, than the tweezer-cases of the lover of toys; and like them, too, more troublesome to the person who carries them about with him than all the advantages they can afford him are commodious. There is no other real difference between them, except that the conveniencies of the one are somewhat more observable than those of the other. The palaces, the gardens, the equipage, the retinue of the great, are objects of which the obvious conveniency strikes everybody. They do not require that their masters should point out to us wherein consists their utility. Of our own accord we readily enter into it, and by sympathy enjoy, and thereby applaud the satisfaction which they are fitted to afford him. But the curiosity of a toothpick, of an earpicker, of a machine for cutting the nails, or of any other trinket of the same kind, is not so obvious. Their conveniency perhaps may be equally great, but it is not so striking, and we do not so readily enter into the satisfaction of the man who possesses them. They are therefore less reasonable subjects of vanity than the magnificence of wealth and greatness; and in this consists the sole advantage of these last. They more effectually gratify that love of distinction so natural to man. To one who was to live alone in a desolate island, it might be a matter of doubt perhaps, whether a palace, or a collection of such small conveniencies as are commonly contained in a tweezer-case, would contribute most to his happiness and enjoyment. If he is to live in society, indeed, there can be no comparison, because in this, as in all other cases, we constantly pay more regard to the sentiments of the spectator than to those of the person principally concerned, and consider rather how his situation will appear to other people than how it will appear to himself. If we examine, however, why the spectator distinguishes with such admiration the condition of the rich and the great, we shall find that it is not so much upon account of the superior ease or pleasure which they are supposed to enjoy, as of the numberless artificial and elegant contrivances for promoting this ease or pleasure. He does not even imagine that they are really happier than other people; but he imagines that they possess more means of happiness. And it is the ingenious and artful adjustment of those means to the end for which they were intended that is the principal source of his admiration. But in the langour of disease and the weariness of old age, the pleasures of the vain and empty distinctions of greatness disappear. To one in this situation they are no longer capable of recommending those toilsome pursuits in which they had formerly engaged him. In his heart he curses ambition, and vainly regrets the ease and the indolence of youth, pleasures which are fled forever, and which he has foolishly sacrificed for what, when he has got it, can afford him no real satisfaction. In this miserable aspect does greatness appear to every man when reduced, either by spleen or disease, to observe with attention his own situation, and to consider what it is that is really wanting to his happiness. Power and riches appear then to be, what they are, enormous and operose[2] machines contrived to produce a few trifling conveniencies to the body, consisting of springs the most nice and delicate, which must be kept in order with the most anxious attention, and which, in spite of all our care, are ready every moment to burst into pieces, and to crush in their ruins their unfortunate possessor. They are immense fabrics which it requires the labor of a life to raise, which threaten every moment to overwhelm the person that dwells in them, and which, while they stand, though they save him from some smaller inconveniencies, can protect him from none of the severer inclemencies of the season. They keep off the summer shower, not the winter storm, but leave him always as much, and sometimes more, exposed than before to anxiety, to fear, and to sorrow; to diseases, to danger, and to death. (*TMS*, pp. 259–263)

[2] Rarely used today, "operose" referred to the display of much industry or effort.

The poor man's son is visited with youthful ambition to acquire the trinkets of the rich. He makes his court to all humankind that will listen; he serves those whom he hates and is obsequious to all whom he despises. In the end, having fulfilled his ambition, he learns that wealth and greatness are mere trinkets of frivolous utility. Where is the happiness from all these labors and strivings after? Go for the satisfying and intellectual pursuits that serve you well as you age, make lots of younger such friends, learn, and keep pace with their curiosity.

Philosophy teaches that real satisfaction is not to be found in these contemptible trifling pursuits that we rarely view in abstract light.

> But though this splenetic philosophy, which in time of sickness or low spirits is familiar to every man, thus entirely depreciates those great objects of human desire, when in better health and in better humour, we never fail to regard them under a more agreeable aspect. Our imagination, which in pain and sorrow seems to be confined and cooped up within our own persons, in times of ease and prosperity expands itself to every thing around us. We are then charmed with the beauty of that accommodation which reigns in the palaces and economy of the great; and admire how every thing is adapted to promote their ease, to prevent their wants, to gratify their wishes, and to amuse and entertain their most frivolous desires. If we consider the real satisfaction which all these things are capable of affording, by itself and separated from the beauty of that arrangement which is fitted to promote it, it will always appear in the highest degree contemptible and trifling. But we rarely view it in this abstract and philosophical light. We naturally confound it in our imagination with the order, the regular and harmonious movement of the system, the machine or economy by means of which it is produced. The pleasures of wealth and greatness, when considered in this complex view, strike the imagination as something grand, and beautiful, and noble, of which the attainment is well worth all the toil and anxiety which we are so apt to bestow upon it. (*TMS*, p. 263)

Samuel Johnson defines splenetic as follows: "Sple'netick. adj. [*splenetique*, French.] Troubled with the spleen; fretful; peevish. Thus, 'Horace purged himself from these splentick reflections in odes and epodes, before he undertook his satyrs.' Dryden."

That we are visited by such fretful thoughts "in time of sickness or low spirits is familiar to every man, thus entirely depreciates those great objects of human desire, when in better health and in better humor, we never fail to regard them under a more agreeable aspect." The thoughts are unsettling precisely because they depreciate all that we so deliberately seek after. Yet they quietly and abstractly convey fundamental truth! Do we brush up against truth only in episodes of sickness and low spirits? Yes, because our thoughts are not preoccupied by the hustle and bustle of daily living, and in such circumstances, we are "fretful."

Nature imposes on us to assure that humankind support an economy of abundance to satisfy our material requirements without which we cannot subsist.

> And it is well that nature imposes upon us in this manner. It is this deception which rouses and keeps in continual motion the industry of mankind. It is this which first prompted them to cultivate the ground, to build houses, to found cities and commonwealths, and to invent and improve all the sciences and arts, which ennoble and embellish human life; which have entirely changed the whole face of the globe, have turned the rude forests of nature into agreeable and fertile plains, and made the trackless and barren ocean a new fund of subsistence, and the great high road of communication to the different nations of the earth. The earth, by these labours of mankind, has been obliged to redouble her natural fertility, and to maintain a greater multitude of inhabitants. It is to no purpose that the proud and unfeeling landlord views his extensive fields, and without a thought for the wants of his brethren, in imagination consumes himself the whole harvest that grows upon them. The homely and vulgar proverb, that the eye is larger than the belly, never was more fully verified than with regard to him. The capacity of his stomach bears no proportion to the immensity of his desires, and will receive no more than that of the meanest peasant. The rest he is obliged to distribute among those who prepare, in the nicest manner, that little which he himself makes use of, among those who fit up the palace in which this little is to be consumed, among those who provide and keep in order all the different baubles and trinkets which are employed in the economy of greatness; all of whom thus derive from his luxury and caprice that share of the necessaries of life which they would in vain have expected from his humanity or his justice. The produce of the soil maintains at all times nearly that number of inhabitants which it is capable of maintaining. The rich only select from the heap what is most precious and agreeable. They consume little more than the poor; and in spite of their natural selfishness and rapacity, though they mean only their own conveniency, though the sole end which they propose from the labours of all the thousands whom they employ may be the gratification of their own vain and insatiable desires, they divide with the poor the produce

of all their improvements. *They are led by an invisible hand to make nearly the same distribution of the necessaries of life which would have been made had the earth been divided into equal portions among all its inhabitants; and thus, without intending it, without knowing it, advance the interest of the society, and afford means to the multiplication of the species.* When providence divided the earth among a few lordly masters, it neither forgot nor abandoned those who seemed to have been left out in the partition. These last, too, enjoy their share of all that it produces. In what constitutes the real happiness of human life, they are in no respect inferior to those who would seem so much above them. In ease of body and peace of mind, all the different ranks of life are nearly upon a level, and the beggar, who suns himself by the side of the highway, possesses that security which kings are fighting for. (*TMS*, pp. 263–265; italics added)

Smith's final 6th edition appeared in 1790 over 230 years ago. Economically and functionally the rich did and still importantly "divide with the poor the produce of all their improvements. They are led by an invisible hand to make nearly the same distribution of the necessaries of life which would have been made had the earth been divided into equal portions among all its inhabitants; and thus, without intending it, without knowing it, advance the interest of the society, and afford means to the multiplication of the species."

With the accelerating rate at which 230 plus years later, we today benefit from the application of artificial intelligence to automation in the satisfaction of our material welfare, we can seriously entertain the idea of a universal basic income, UBI, for all. Thanks to the economic principles summarized above by Smith, today we not only can, but must, confront the "splenetic philosopher's" truth that our riches enable us to devote ourselves to finding purpose and meaning in life. It has always been the increase I leisure (non-working) time that has been the enabling source of support for "finding purpose and meaning life," but if that leisure is not generated from the bottom but "given" from the top will it still motivate that "finding." For those self-motivated and eager to employ that leisure such surely will be the predominant outcome, but will it lead to such motivation generally. Look for evidence in any change in the suicide rate.

If all citizens receive a UBI (Universal Basic Income), regardless of sexual identity, skin pigmentation, national origin, or ethnic identity, what is there left to say about inclusion?

Freed from the need for wage work, will humankind find fulfillment in community—the original creative facilitator of the rules that made us rich?

That we most directly experience the processes that produce the ends that are pleasurable and not whether they work or fail to work effectively, serves to recommend institutions that claim to promote public welfare.

> The … love of system, … regard to the beauty of order, of art and contrivance, frequently serves to recommend those institutions which tend to promote the public welfare. When a patriot exerts himself for the improvement of any part of the public police, his conduct does not always arise from pure sympathy with the happiness of those who are to reap the benefit of it. It is not commonly from a fellow-feeling with carriers and waggoners that a public-spirited man encourages the mending of high roads. When the Legislature establishes premiums and other encouragements to advance the linen or woollen manufactures, its conduct seldom proceeds from pure sympathy with the wearer of cheap or fine cloth, and much less from that with the manufacturer or merchant. The perfection of police, the extension of trade and manufactures are noble and magnificent objects. The contemplation of them pleases us, and we are interested in whatever can tend to advance them. They make part of the great system of government, and the wheels of the political machine seem to move with more harmony and ease by means of them. We take pleasure in beholding the perfection of so beautiful and so grand a system, and we are uneasy till we remove any obstruction that can in the least disturb or encumber the regularity of its motions. All constitutions of government, however, are valued only in proportion as they tend to promote the happiness of those who live under them. This is their sole use and end. From a certain spirit of system, however, from a certain love of art and contrivance, we sometimes seem to value the means more than the end, and to be eager to promote the happiness of our fellow-creatures, rather from a view to perfect and improve a certain beautiful and orderly system than from any immediate sense or feeling of what they either suffer or enjoy. There have been men of the greatest public spirit, who have shewn themselves in other respects not very sensible to the feelings of humanity. And, on the contrary, there have been men of the greatest humanity, who seem to have been entirely devoid of public spirit. Every man may find in the circle of his acquaintance instances both of the one kind and the other. Who had ever less humanity or more public spirit than the celebrated legislator of Muscovy? The social

and well-natured James the First of Great Britain seems, on the contrary, to have had scarce any passion, either for the glory or the interest of his country. Would you awaken the industry of the man who seems almost dead to ambition, it will often be to no purpose to describe to him the happiness of the rich and the great; to tell him that they are generally sheltered from the sun and the rain, that they are seldom hungry, that they are seldom cold, and that they are rarely exposed to weariness, or to want of any kind. The most eloquent exhortation of this kind will have little effect upon him. If you would hope to succeed, you must describe to him the conveniency and arrangement of the different apartments in their palaces; you must explain to him the propriety of their equipages, and point out to him the number, the order, and the different offices of all their attendants. If anything is capable of making impression upon him, this will. Yet all these things tend only to keep off the sun and the rain, to save them from hunger and cold, from want and weariness. In the same manner, if you would implant public virtue in the breast of him who seems heedless of the interest of his country, it will often be to no purpose to tell him what superior advantages the subjects of a well-governed state enjoy; that they are better lodged, that they are better clothed, that they are better fed. These considerations will commonly make no great impression. You will be more likely to persuade, if you describe the great system of public police which procures these advantages,—if you explain the connections and dependencies of its several parts, their mutual subordination to one another, and their general subserviency to the happiness of the society; if you shew how this system might be introduced into his own country, what it is that hinders it from taking place there at present, how those obstructions might be removed, and all the several wheels of the machine of government be made to move with more harmony and smoothness, without grating upon one another, or mutually retarding one another's motions. It is scarcely possible that a man should listen to a discourse of this kind, and not feel himself animated to some degree of public spirit…Nothing tends so much to promote public spirit as the study of politics—of the several systems of civil government, their advantages and disadvantages—of the constitution of our own country, its situation, and interest with regard to foreign nations, its commerce, its defence, the disadvantages it labours under, the dangers to which it be exposed, how to remove the one, and how to guard against the other. Upon this account political disquisitions, if just, and reasonable, and practicable, are of all the works of speculation the most useful. Even the weakest and the worst of them are not altogether without their utility. They serve at least to animate the public passions of men, and rouse them to seek out the means of promoting the happiness of the society. (*TMS*, pp. 265–268)

People love politics because they see in it the attempt to improve by methods that seem reasonable, just beneficent [sic], and well-intended. But they are imposed from above, not from inside and below, and can neither serve nor be served but only instruct and issue orders.

CHAPTER 31

Of the beauty which the appearance of utility bestows upon the characters and actions of men; and how far the perception of this beauty may be regarded as one of the original principles of approbation

The government is but an imperfect remedy for deficiencies in the character, wisdom, and virtue of its people. it will fail if it does not also guard against the mischiefs which human wickedness may bring.

The characters of men, as well as the contrivances of art, or the institutions of civil government, may be fitted either to promote or to disturb the happiness both of the individual and of the society. The prudent, the equitable, the active, resolute, and sober character promises prosperity and satisfaction, both to the person himself and to every one connected with him. The rash, the insolent, the slothful, effeminate, and voluptuous, on the contrary, forebodes ruin to the individual, and misfortune to all who have any thing to do with him. The first turn of mind has at least all the beauty which can belong to the most perfect machine that was ever invented for promoting the most agreeable purpose: and the second, all the deformity of the most awkward and clumsy contrivance. What institution of government could tend so much to promote the happiness of mankind as the general prevalence of wisdom and virtue? All government is but an imperfect remedy for the deficiency of these. Whatever beauty, therefore, can belong to civil government upon account of its utility, must in a far superior degree belong to these. On the contrary, what civil policy

Vernon L. Smith, *Adam Smith's Theory of Society*,
https://doi.org/10.1007/978-3-031-68494-4_31

> can be so ruinous and destructive as the vices of men? The fatal effects of bad government arise from nothing, but that it does not sufficiently guard against the mischiefs which human wickedness gives occasion to. (*TMS*, p. 269)

We have been having an in-depth development of Smith's concept of a good society as one whose citizens create and follow rules that build character, wisdom, and virtue while controlling the mischiefs done by human wickedness.

To this he now adds that:

- A good government is but an imperfect remedy for deficiencies in the character, wisdom, and virtue of its people.
- A bad government does not sufficiently guard against the mischiefs which human wickedness gives occasion to.
- Government cannot substitute for the Great School of Self-Command by which its citizens are constantly being educated.

Abstract concepts of virtue and vice are poorly captured in philosophy; it is only in particular instances where the propriety, or impropriety, the merit or demerit, of actions is obvious and discernible.

> This beauty and deformity which characters appear to derive from their usefulness or inconveniency, are apt to strike in a peculiar manner those who consider, in an abstract and philosophical light, the actions and conduct of mankind. When a philosopher goes to examine why humanity is approved of or cruelty condemned, he does not always form to himself, in a very clear and distinct manner, the conception of any one particular action either of cruelty or of humanity, but is commonly contented with the vague and indeterminate idea which the general names of those qualities suggest to him. But it is in particular instances only that the propriety or impropriety, the merit or demerit, of actions is very obvious and discernible. It is only when particular examples are given that we perceive distinctly either the concord or disagreement between our own affections and those of the agent, or feel a social gratitude arise towards him in the one case, or a sympathetic resentment in the other. When we consider virtue and vice in an abstract and general manner, the qualities by which they excite these

> several sentiments seem in a great measure to disappear, and the sentiments themselves become less obvious and discernible. On the contrary, the happy effects of the one, and the fatal consequences of the other, seem then to rise up to the view, and, as it were, to stand out and distinguish themselves from all the other qualities of either. (*TMS*, pp. 269–270)

It is because people learn rules in the context of their various experiences that their meaning becomes obvious and discernible only in particular cases. Smith refers to these not as "Abstract," but as "General Rules," of the form, "given X in condition Y, Z is a consequence. X = actions of a beneficent tendency; Y = that are properly motivated; Z = alone require reward because of the gratitude felt by the observer (including recipient and all third-party observers)."

Hume argued that the rules we follow promote utilitarian conveniency, a fact not to be doubted but this is not why we follow them.

> The same ingenious and agreeable author who first explained why utility pleases, has been so struck with this view of things, as to resolve our whole approbation of virtue into a perception of this species of beauty which results from the appearance of utility. No qualities of the mind, he observes, are approved of as virtuous, but such as are useful or agreeable either to the person himself or to others; and no qualities are disapproved of as vicious, but such as have a contrary tendency. And Nature, indeed, seems to have so happily adjusted our sentiments of approbation and disapprobation, to the conveniency both of the individual and of the society, that after the strictest examination it will be found, I believe, that this is universally the case. But still I affirm, that it is not the view of this utility or hurtfulness which is either the first or principal source of our approbation and disapprobation. These sentiments are, no doubt, enhanced and enlivened by the perception of the beauty or deformity which results from this utility or hurtfulness. But still, I say, they are originally and essentially different from this perception. (*TMS*, pp. 270–271)

Smith's friend David Hume, arguably the greatest English philosopher, is here failing to invoke Smith's important distinction between the origins and the consequences of human action. Hume is much closer to modern utilitarian scholars than was Smith, and shares this error, which is one important reason why Smith's work is still so relevant today in widening our analytical thinking. Rule-following behavior, in *TMS*, provides the version of the invisible hand metaphor that applies to his theory of society in *TMS* and that complements his theory of economy in *WN*.

That utility pleasure, or hurtfulness, should be the principal source of our approbation and disapprobation of actions is doubtful.

> For first of all, it seems impossible that the approbation of virtue should be a sentiment of the same kind with that by which we approve of a convenient and well-contrived building; or, that we should have no other reason for praising a man than that for which we commend a chest of drawers.
> And, secondly, it will be found upon examination, that the usefulness of any disposition of mind is seldom the first ground of our approbation; and that the sentiment of approbation always involves in it a sense of propriety quite distinct from the perception of utility. We observe this with regard to all the qualities which are approved of as virtuous, both those which, according to this system, are originally valued as useful to ourselves, as well as those which are esteemed on account of their usefulness to others. The qualities most useful to ourselves are, first of all, superior reason and understanding, by which we are capable of discerning the remote consequences of all our actions, and of foreseeing the advantage or detriment which is likely to result from them; and, secondly, self-command, by which we are enabled to abstain from present pleasure or to endure present pain, in order to obtain a greater pleasure or to avoid a greater pain in some future time1 In the union of those two qualities consists the virtue of prudence, of all the virtues that which is most useful to the individual. (*TMS*, pp. 271–272)

As I have noted, utility comes into the formation of rules governed by their propriety or impropriety only in the need for common knowledge that all are strictly self-interested and therefore that all have a strong sense of what benefit and hurt mean because this is what human actions convey that meet with a community consensus on approbation or disapprobation.

I do not think Smith had an explicit understanding that his process model of human action based on rules motivated by a desire to "get along with" others was fundamentally and extensively concerned with human relationships and at odds with utilitarianism though it is implicit in his rule defined propositions and examples.

The more abstruse sciences like mathematics are not pursued for their usefulness although they can be so justified only by arguments not easily comprehended.

> [S]uperior reason and understanding are originally approved of as just, and right, and accurate, and not merely as useful or advantageous. It is in the abstruser sciences, particularly in the higher parts of mathematics, that the greatest and most admired exertions of human reason have been displayed. But the utility of those sciences, either to the individual or to the public, is not very obvious, and to prove it, requires a discussion which is not always very easily comprehended. It was not, therefore, their utility which first recommended them to the public admiration. This quality was but little insisted upon, till it became necessary to make some reply to the reproaches of those, who, having themselves no taste for such sublime discoveries, endeavour to depreciate them as useless. (*TMS*, p. 272)

The pursuit of science meets with widespread propriety and approbation but not because of its utilitarian usefulness however true that may be. For example, it is not transparent that the study of prime numbers contributes to human material welfare although the search for algorithms for generating or verifying prime numbers may well enable more economically valuable collateral applications of artificial intelligence.

Self-command restrains our current appetites favoring gifts to others from whom we benefit in vast exchange and thus we are not discounters of future benefit as supposed in economic theory.

> That self-command...by which we restrain our present appetites, in order to gratify them more fully upon another occasion, is approved of as much under the aspect of propriety as under that of utility. When we act in this manner, the sentiments which influence our conduct seem exactly to coincide with those of the spectator. The spectator does not feel the solicitations of our present appetites. To him the pleasure which we are to enjoy a week hence, or a year hence, is just as interesting as that which we are to enjoy this moment. When for the sake of the present, therefore, we sacrifice the future, our conduct appears to him absurd and extravagant in

> the highest degree, and he cannot enter into the principles which influence it. On the contrary, when we abstain from present pleasure, in order to secure greater pleasure to come; when we act as if the remote object interested us as much as that which immediately presses upon the senses, as our affections exactly correspond with his own, he cannot fail to approve of our behaviour; and as he knows from experience how few are capable of this self-command, he looks upon our conduct with a considerable degree of wonder and admiration. Hence arises that eminent esteem with which all men naturally regard a steady perseverance in the practice of frugality, industry, and application, though directed to no other purpose than the acquisition of fortune. The resolute firmness of the person who acts in this manner, and in order to obtain a great though remote advantage, not only gives up all present pleasures, but endures the greatest labour both of mind and body, necessarily commands our approbation. That view of his interest and happiness which appears to regulate his conduct, exactly tallies with the idea which we naturally form of it. There is the most perfect correspondence between his sentiments and our own, and at the same time, from our experience of the common weakness of human nature, it is a correspondence which we could not reasonably have expected. We not only approve, therefore, but in some measure admire his conduct, and think it worthy of a considerable degree of applause. It is the consciousness of this merited approbation and esteem which is alone capable of supporting the agent in this tenor of conduct. The pleasure which we are to enjoy ten years hence interests us so little in comparison with that which we enjoy to-day; the passion which the first excites is naturally so weak in comparison with that violent emotion which the second is apt to give occasion to, that the one could never be any balance to the other, unless it was supported by the sense of propriety, by the consciousness that we merited the esteem and approbation of every body by acting in the one way, and that we became the proper objects of their contempt and derision by behaving in the other. (*TMS*, pp. 272–273)

Irving Fisher extended modern utility theory to the comparison of future value with the current value where the future value is assumed to be always smaller than the current value, implying that people tend to discount the value of future benefits. Behavioral economic psychologists have challenged this with decision research showing that people attribute the same subjective choice value to future goods that they do to current goods. It is called hyperbolic discounting and is considered to violate standard economic theory inherited from Fisher.

In *TMS*, Smith's theory, in which future and current good things are valued at the same rate, is considered as the mark of a mature sense of self-command—something we overcome in growing up. Smith's theory is consistent with modern empirical finding that people are hyperbolic discounters. More significant is that his way of thinking predicted it as a property of the mature and esteemed person who overcomes a weakness in preferring present over future goods.

TMS is also contrary to the modern theory that savings and investment are motivated by positive interest earnings that disincentivizes spending all income on consumption. But if an important motivation for savings is to assure consumption contingent on the event that income is lost, then there is adequate incentive to save even if interest is zero. The adverse event of Covid-19, and the social policy emphasizing lock downs, motivated the increase in home inventories of perishable food stocks and paper products, whatever the interest rate.

Society, as understood in Smith's work, is created out of the aspirations of ordinary people who live in the present, not the future, and whose living creates the future. They know how to live, how to decide, or not, and how to love. Meaning is found in that living and living is found in that meaning.

Humanity and justice are founded on the approbation of the agent and of third-party observers; generosity depends on placing the interest of another above your own.

> Humanity, justice, generosity, and public spirit are qualities most useful to others … the propriety of humanity and justice has been explained [by] … how much our esteem and approbation of those qualities depended upon the concord between the affections of the agent and those of the spectators. The propriety of generosity and public spirit is founded upon the same principle with that of justice. Generosity is different from humanity. Those two qualities, which at first sight seem so nearly allied, do not always belong to the same person. Humanity is the virtue of a woman, generosity of a man. The fair sex, who have commonly much more tenderness than ours, have seldom so much generosity. That women rarely make considerable donations is an observation of the civil law. Humanity consists merely in the exquisite fellow-feeling which the spectator entertains with the sentiments of the persons principally concerned, so as to grieve for their sufferings, to resent their injuries, and to rejoice at their good fortune. The

> most humane actions require no self-denial, no self-command, no great exertion of the sense of propriety. They consist only in doing what this exquisite sympathy would of its own accord prompt us to do. But it is otherwise with generosity. We never are generous except when in some respect we prefer some other person to ourselves, and sacrifice some great and important interest of our own to an equal interest of a friend or of a superior. The man who gives up his pretensions to an office that was the great object of his ambition, because he imagines that the services of another are better entitled to it; the man who exposes his life to defend that of his friend, which he judges to be of more importance, neither of them act from humanity, or because they feel more exquisitely what concerns that other person than what concerns themselves. They both consider those opposite interests, not in the light in which they naturally appear to themselves, but in that in which they appear to others. To every bystander, the success or preservation of this other person justly may be more interesting than their own; but it cannot be so to themselves. When to the interest of this other person, therefore, they sacrifice their own, they accommodate themselves to the sentiments of the spectator, and by an effort of magnanimity act according to those views of things which they feel must naturally occur to any third person. The soldier who throws away his life in order to defend that of his officer, would perhaps be but little affected by the death of that officer if it should happen without any fault of his own; and a very small disaster which had befallen himself might excite a much more lively sorrow. But when he endeavours to act so as to deserve applause, and to make the impartial spectator enter into the principles of his conduct, he feels that to every body but himself his own life is a trifle compared with that of his officer, and that when he sacrifices the one to the other, he acts quite properly and agreeably to what would be the natural apprehensions of every impartial bystander. (*TMS*, pp. 274–275)

Generosity involves placing another's interest above your own. This is manifest in a small way when one gives $5 to a homeless person; in large ways when a soldier sacrifices himself to save a companion. Humans easily engage in interpersonal comparisons, a long-time challenge to utilitarian advances in economic theory. The modern idea of generosity is "altruism," an English word first used in 1852 almost a century after *TMS* appeared. In a review of Thomas Dixon's book, *The Invention of Altruism*:

> Dixon demonstrates that words (and not simply the concepts to which they correspond) do matter. In the case of altruism, the concepts it articulated

> might have been expressed in an older language of 'charity' or 'benevolence', or alternatively in the language of utilitarianism or of co-operation. But if they had been so expressed, their resonance would have been very different. It mattered that it was Comte's neologism that triumphed: the word 'altruism' was explicitly anti-Christian in its origins, and aroused resistance on that account, as well as simply because it was a neologism; and it blurred the distinction between the three main concepts to which it could refer.[1]

In *TMS*, an action taken by one person that benefits another is considered appropriate because it is considered right by the actor and other observers—it commands their approbation. A practice emerges out of community approval just as a word emerges out of community understanding and is used to convey meaning. A benevolent person might take such actions often, and thus be described as "altruistic" today. Modern altruistic preferences have been described as "warm glow" giving, analogous to "fellow-feeling" in *TMS*. Preference theory finds a utility function such that Max U could have produced the observed actions.

When an officer sacrifices his life so that his country can acquire new territory, he views the acquisition from the perspective of the country he fights for, and views it as of the highest importance.

> When a young officer exposes his life to acquire some inconsiderable addition to the dominions of his sovereign, it is not because the acquisition of the new territory is to himself an object more desirable than the preservation of his own life. To him his own life is of infinitely more value than the conquest of a whole kingdom for the state which he serves. But when he compares those two objects with one another, he does not view them in the light in which they naturally appear to himself, but in that in which they appear to the nation he fights for. To them the success of the war is of the highest importance—the life of a private person of scarce any consequence. When he puts himself in their situation, he immediately feels that he cannot be too prodigal of his blood, if by shedding it he can promote so valuable a purpose. In thus thwarting, from a sense of duty and propriety, the strongest of all natural propensities, consists the heroism of his conduct. There is many an honest Englishman, who in his private station would be

[1] Stuart Jones' review of Thomas Dixon's, *The Invention of Altruism* (Making Moral Meanings in Victorian Britain). Oxford, 2008. https://reviews.history.ac.uk/review/757.

> more seriously disturbed by the loss of a guinea than by the national loss of Minorca, who yet, had it been in his power to defend that fortress, would have sacrificed his life a thousand times rather than, through his fault, have let it fall into the hands of the enemy...our admiration is not so much founded upon the utility as upon the unexpected, and on that account the great, the noble, and exalted propriety of such actions. This utility, when we come to view it, bestows upon them undoubtedly a new beauty, and upon that account still further recommends them to our approbation. This beauty, however, is chiefly perceived by men of reflection and speculation, and is by no means the quality which first recommends such actions to the natural sentiments of the bulk of mankind. (*TMS*, pp. 275–276)

Thus did the American Colonists revolt against British rule to take the territory in which they lived away from the control of the occupying British troops. And so also the Ukrainians who are resisting the attempt by Russian troops to retake an independent Ukraine. The Ukrainians see their relationship with Russia in much the same light as the Colonists saw their relationship with the British. That inspires many to a willingness to sacrifice one's own life to reserve a greater value to society—a moral edge hard to defeat.

Insofar as approbation arises from considerations of this "beauty of utility," or usefulness, it is a matter of private taste unrelated to the sentiments of others, such as actions requiring reward or deserving punishment.

> It is to be observed, that so far as the sentiment of approbation arises from the perception of this beauty of utility, it has no reference of any kind to the sentiments of others. If it was possible, therefore, that a person should grow up to manhood without any communication with society, his own actions might, notwithstanding, be agreeable or disagreeable to him on account of their tendency to his happiness or disadvantage. He might perceive a beauty of this kind in prudence, temperance, and good conduct, and a deformity in the opposite behaviour; he might view his own temper and character with that sort of satisfaction with which we consider a well-contrived machine in the one case; or with that sort of distaste and dissatisfaction with which we regard a very awkward and clumsy contrivance in the other. As these perceptions, however, are merely a matter of taste, and have all the feebleness and delicacy of that species of perceptions upon the justness of which what is properly called taste is

> founded, they probably would not be much attended to by one in his solitary and miserable condition. Even though they should occur to him, they would by no means have the same effect upon him, antecedent to his connection with society, which they would have in consequence of that connection. He would not be cast down with inward shame at the thought of this deformity; nor would he be elevated with secret triumph of mind from the consciousness of the contrary beauty. He would not exult from the notion of deserving reward in the one case, nor tremble from the suspicion of meriting punishment in the other. All such sentiments suppose the idea of some other being, who is the natural judge of the person that feels them; and it is only by sympathy with the decisions of this arbiter of his conduct, that he can conceive either the triumph of self-applause or the shame of self-condemnation. (*TMS*, pp. 276–277)

It is only because of our meaningful connections with others that our actions leave us with some sense of personal triumph, or of shame. These feelings are not associated with actions that merely express our private tastes for this or that object. They are born of our desire to get along with others because we value relationships in which we experience a profound source of satisfaction in our sense of fellow-feeling with others.

PART IX

Of the influence of custom and fashion upon the sentiments of moral approbation and disapprobation: Consisting of one section

CHAPTER 32

Of the influence of custom and fashion upon our notions of beauty and deformity

Accounting for cultural variations in the propriety or impropriety of human actions.

There are other principles besides those already enumerated, which have a considerable influence upon the moral sentiments of mankind, and are the chief causes of the many irregular and discordant opinions which prevail in different ages and nations concerning what is blameable or praiseworthy. These principles are custom and fashion, principles which extend their dominion over our judgments concerning beauty of every kind.

When two objects have frequently been seen together, the imagination acquires a habit of passing easily from the one to the other. If the first appear, we lay our account that the second is to follow. Of their own accord they put us in mind of one another, and the attention glides easily along them. Though, independent of custom, there should be no real beauty in their union, yet when custom has thus connected them together, we feel an impropriety in their separation. The one we think is awkward when it appears without its usual companion. We miss something which we expected to find, and the habitual arrangement of our ideas is disturbed by the disappointment. A suit of clothes, for example, seems to want something if they are without the most insignificant ornament which usually accompanies them, and we find a meanness or awkwardness in the absence

Vernon L. Smith, *Adam Smith's Theory of Society*,
https://doi.org/10.1007/978-3-031-68494-4_32

> even of a haunch[1] button. When there is any natural propriety in the union, custom increases our sense of it, and makes a different arrangement appear still more disagreeable than it would otherwise seem to be. Those who have been accustomed to see things in a good taste, are more disgusted by whatever is clumsy or awkward. Where the conjunction is improper, custom either diminishes, or takes away altogether, our sense of the impropriety. Those who have been accustomed to slovenly disorder lose all sense of neatness or elegance. The modes of furniture or dress which seem ridiculous to strangers, give no offence to the people who are used to them. (*TMS*, pp. 281–282)

In several paragraphs here and below, Smith articulates a deep theory of culture emerging out of fashion and tradition. In certain dimensions, like architecture, the change is too slow for people to sense its evolution, while poetry is forever. Few, therefore, may be aware of their taste in music, poetry, and architecture as evolutionary social constructs. In other dimensions like dress and furniture, which Smith relates to the durability of the materials used, people are quite aware of the evolving standard. The foundation for it all is rooted in Smith's model of human sociability although it is expressed differently in different ages.

The modes of dress and furniture are easily recognized by everyone, through their experience, as emerging out of the customs and fashions of different periods.

> Dress and furniture are allowed by all the world to be entirely under the dominion of custom and fashion. The influence of those principles…extends itself to whatever is in any respect the object of taste,—to music, to poetry, to architecture. The modes of dress and furniture are continually changing; and that fashion appearing ridiculous to-day which was admired five years ago, we are experimentally convinced that it owed its vogue chiefly or entirely to custom and fashion. Clothes and furniture are not made of very durable materials. A well-fancied coat is done in a twelvemonth, and cannot continue longer to propagate…that form according to which it was made. The modes of furniture change less rapidly than those of dress; because furniture is commonly more durable. In five or six years, however, it generally undergoes an entire revolution, and every

[1] The "haunch" is located at the hip-thigh conjunction.

man in his own time sees the fashion in this respect change many different ways. The productions of the other arts are much more lasting, and, when happily imagined, continue to propagate the fashion of their make for a much longer time. A well-contrived building may endure many centuries; a beautiful air[2] be delivered down, by a sort of tradition, through many successive generations; a well-written poem last as long as the world; and all of them continue for ages together to give the vogue to that particular style, to that particular taste or manner, according to which each of them was composed. Few men have an opportunity of seeing in their own times the fashion in any of these arts change very considerably. Few men have so much experience and acquaintance with the different modes which have obtained in remote ages and nations, as to be thoroughly reconciled to them, or to judge with impartiality between them and what takes place in their own age and country. Few men, therefore, are willing to allow, that custom or fashion have much influence upon their judgments concerning what is beautiful, or otherwise, in the productions of any of those arts; but imagine that all the rules which they think ought to be observed in each of them are founded upon reason and nature, not upon habit or prejudice. A very little attention, however, convince them of the contrary, and satisfy them that the influence of custom and fashion over dress and furniture is not more absolute than over architecture, poetry, and music.

Can any reason, for example, be assigned why the Doric capital should be appropriated to a pillar, whose height is equal to eight diameters; the Ionic volute to one of nine; and the Corinthian foliage to one of ten? The propriety of each of those appropriations can be founded upon nothing but habit and custom. The eye having been used to see a particular proportion connected with a particular ornament, would be offended if they were not joined together. Each of the five orders has its peculiar ornaments, which cannot be changed for any other, without giving offence to all those who know anything of the rules of architecture. According to some architects, indeed, such is the exquisite judgment with which the ancients have assigned to each order its proper ornaments, that no others can be found which are equally suitable. It seems, however, a little difficult to be conceived that these forms, though no doubt extremely agreeable, should be the only forms which can suit those proportions, or that there should not be five hundred others, which, antecedent to established custom, would have fitted them equally well. When custom, however, has established particular rules of building, provided they are not absolutely unreasonable, it is absurd to think of altering them for others which are only equally good, or even for others which, in point of elegance

2 "An air" as a distinctive manner may be passed down in a cultural community.

> and beauty, have naturally some little advantage over them. A man would be ridiculous who should appear in public with a suit of clothes quite different from those which are commonly worn, though the new dress should in itself be ever so graceful or convenient. And there seems to be an absurdity of the same kind in ornamenting a house after a quite different manner from that which custom and fashion have prescribed; though the new ornaments should in themselves be somewhat superior to the common ones. (*TMS*, pp. 282–284)

Clothes change fashion annually in keeping with a natural rhythm in the durability of their color and texture or appearance. In furniture, which is more durable, the turnover extends to five to six years. Even here, new purchases are more likely motivated by people moving, or by new household formation, than by replacement. Architectural standards and proportions are more durable and lasting, but even then, comes along a Frank Lloyd Wright that upsets existing practices with designs in wood, glass, and stone that reflect, complement, and enhance the exterior environment in which they are placed.

Changing cultural perspectives driven by custom and fashion extend naturally to prominently expressed styles of poetry.

> According to the ancient rhetoricians, a certain measure or verse was by nature appropriated to each particular species of writing, as being naturally expressive of that character, sentiment, or passion which ought to predominate in it. One verse, they said, was fit for grave, and another for gay works, which could not, they thought, be interchanged without the greatest impropriety. The experience of modern times, however, seems to contradict this principle, though in itself it would appear to be extremely probable. What is the burlesque verse in English is the heroic verse in French. The tragedies of Racine and the Henriad of Voltaire are nearly in the same verse with, "Let me have your advice in a weighty affair."
> The burlesque verse in French, on the contrary, is pretty much the same with the heroic verse of ten syllables in English. Custom has made the one nation associate the ideas of gravity, sublimity, and seriousness, to that measure which the other has connected with whatever is gay, flippant, and ludicrous. Nothing would appear more absurd in English than a tragedy written in the Alexandrine verses of the French; or in French, than a work of the same kind in verses of ten syllables.

> An eminent artist will bring about a considerable change in the established modes of each of those arts, and introduce a new fashion of writing, music, or architecture. As the dress of an agreeable man of high rank recommends itself, and how peculiar and fantastical soever, comes soon to be admired and imitated; so the excellencies of an eminent master recommend his peculiarities, and his manner becomes the Fashionable Style In The Art Which He practises. The taste of the Italians in music and architecture has, within these fifty years, undergone a considerable change, from imitating the peculiarities of some eminent masters in each of those arts. Seneca is accused by Quintilian of having corrupted the taste of the Romans, and of having introduced a frivolous prettiness in the room of majestic reason and masculine eloquence. Sallust and Tacitus have by others been charged with the same accusation, though in a different manner. They gave reputation, it is pretended, to a style which, though in the highest degree concise, elegant, expressive, and even poetical, wanted, however, ease, simplicity, and nature, and was evidently the production of the most laboured and studied affectation. How many great qualities must that writer possess who can thus render his very faults agreeable? After the praise of refining the taste of a nation, the highest eulogy, perhaps, which can be bestowed upon any author, is to say that he corrupted it. In our own language, Mr Pope and Dr Swift have each of them introduced a manner different from what was practised before into all works that are written in rhyme, the one in long verses, the other in short. The quaintness of Butler has given place to the plainness of Swift. The rambling freedom of Dryden, and the correct, but often tedious and prosaic languor of Addison, are no longer the objects of imitation, but all long verses are now written after the manner of the nervous precision of Mr Pope. (*TMS*, pp. 284–285)

Smith's, drawing on his knowledge of poetry art, begins with the ancients who thought nature provided distinct categories for each of several forms of verse. Modern verse is viewed as departing from this mold, but this is doubtful: The burlesque verse in French is similar to the heroic verse of ten syllables in English. Custom causes one nation to associate gravity, sublimity, and seriousness, the other with the ensemble of gay, flippant, and ludicrous. A tragedy written in the Alexandrine verses of the French would be an absurdity in English; or in French, a work of the same kind in verses of ten syllables.

A prominent new artist, once recognized, is often associated with changing standards of poetry. I leave further consideration of poetic style and durability to those much more knowledgeable and in Smith's category of expertise if that is indeed a correct evaluation. Nothing is without some influence from the marks of social style, even standards of mathematical proof.

Custom and fashion also change our sense of the beauty of natural objects.

> Neither is it only over the...arts that custom and fashion exert their dominion. They influence our judgments in the same manner with regard to the beauty of natural objects. What various and opposite forms are deemed beautiful in different species of things! The proportions which are admired in one animal are altogether different from those which are esteemed in another. Every class of things has its own peculiar...beauty...distinct from that of every other species. It is upon this account that a learned Jesuit, Father Buffier, has determined that the beauty of every object consists in that form and color, which is most usual among things of that particular sort to which it belongs. Thus in the human form the beauty of each feature lies in a certain middle, equally removed from a variety of other forms that are ugly. A beautiful nose, for example, is one that is neither very long nor very short, neither very straight nor very crooked, but a sort of middle among all those extremes, and less different from any one of them than all of them are from one another.[3] It is the form which Nature seems to have aimed at in them all, which, however, she deviates from in a great variety of ways, and very seldom hits exactly; but to which all those deviations still bear a very strong resemblance. When a number of drawings are made after one pattern, though they all miss it in some respects, yet they will all resemble it more than they resemble one another; the general character of the pattern will run through them all; the most singular and odd will be those which are most wide of it; and though very few will copy it exactly, yet the most accurate delineations will bear a greater resemblance to the most careless, than the careless ones will bear to one another. In the same manner, in each species of creatures, what is most beautiful bears the strongest characters of the general fabric of the species, and has the strongest resemblance to the greater part of the individuals with which it is classed. Monsters, on the contrary, or what is perfectly deformed, are always most singular and odd, and have the least resemblance to the generality of that species to which they belong.

[3] Smith here precisely defines the concept of the median of a set.

> And thus the beauty of each species, though in one sense the rarest of all things, because few individuals hit this middle form exactly, yet in another is the most common, because all the deviations from it resemble it more than they resemble one another. The most customary form therefore is, in each species of things, according to him, the most beautiful. And hence it is that a certain practice and experience in contemplating each species of objects is requisite, before we can judge of its beauty, or know wherein the middle and most usual form consists. The nicest judgment concerning the beauty of the human species will not help us to judge of that of flowers or horses, or any other species of things. It is for the same reason that in different climates, and where different customs and ways of living take place, as the generality of any species receives a different conformation from those circumstances, so different ideas of its beauty prevail. The beauty of a Moorish is not exactly the same with that of an English horse. (*TMS*, pp. 286–288)

The form judged beautiful tends to be a median representation of the distribution of cases. The median nose is the beautiful nose, less different from any one of them than all of them are from one another. While the median is nature's aim, in matters of beauty in the human form, she departs from it in an immense variety of ways. Monsters, contrastingly, tend to be perfectly and singularly deformed, not representable as a median. We choose the ugliest of the outliers. But specialists who abound in the judgment of human beauty provide not a whit of help in judging flowers or horses.

The great variety in standards of natural beauty inspire breadth of meaning and experience across global cultures.

> What different ideas are formed in different nations concerning the beauty of the human shape and countenance! A fair complexion is a shocking deformity upon the coast of Guinea. Thick lips and a flat nose are a beauty. In some nations long ears that hang down upon the shoulders are the objects of universal admiration. In China, if a lady's foot is so large as to be fit to walk upon, she is regarded as a monster of ugliness. Some of the savage nations in North America tie four boards round the heads of their children, and thus squeeze them, while the bones are tender and gristly, into a form that is almost perfectly square. Europeans are astonished at the absurd barbarity of this practice, to which some missionaries have imputed the singular stupidity of those nations among whom it prevails. But when

> they condemn those savages, they do not reflect that the ladies in Europe had, till within these very few years, been endeavouring for near a century past to squeeze the beautiful roundness of their natural shape into a square form of the same kind. And that, notwithstanding the many distortions and diseases which this practice was known to occasion, custom had rendered it agreeable among some of the most civilized nations which perhaps the world ever beheld. (*TMS*, p. 288)

In different regions, climates, and nations the beauty of skin, fair or black, of the nose, flat or erect, the normal foot bound to deform it into a mark of beauty to be admired. In other respects, some of these nations were among the most civilized known. And we have the hypocrisy of Europeans, aghast over native people's using flat boards to recast baby's heads from round to square, expecting their ladies to use corsets to contort their bodies into flatter shapes.

Is our sense of external beauty founded entirely on custom?

> Such is the system of this learned and ingenious father, [the learned Jesuit, Father Buftier] concerning the nature of beauty; of which the whole charm, according to him, would thus seem to arise from its falling in with the habits which custom had impressed upon the imagination, with regard to things of each particular kind. I cannot, however, be induced to believe that our sense even of external beauty is founded altogether on custom. The utility of any form, its fitness for the useful purposes for which it was intended, evidently recommends it, and renders it agreeable to us, independent of custom. Certain colours are more agreeable than others, and give more delight to the eye the first time it ever beholds them. A smooth surface is more agreeable than a rough one. Variety is more pleasing than a tedious undiversified uniformity. Connected variety, in which each new appearance seems to be introduced by what went before it, and in which all the adjoining parts seem to have some natural relation to one another, is more agreeable than a disjointed and disorderly assemblage of unconnected objects. But though I cannot admit that custom is the sole principle of beauty, yet I can so far allow the truth of this ingenious system, as to grant that there is scarce any one external form so beautiful as to please, if quite contrary to custom, and unlike whatever we have been used to in that particular species of things; or so deformed as not to be agreeable, if custom uniformly supports it, and habituates us to see it in every single individual of the kind.(*TMS*, pp. 284–289)

Smith rejects the idea that the Author of Nature uses local custom and tradition as the instrument that shapes even our sense of external beauty. For example, colors vary naturally in their agreeableness; indeed, languages vary in the variety and choice of colors to name. Smooth surfaces are more pleasing than rough ones. Variety can be relieving for its own sake. Complexity of connectedness invokes wonder and admiration. Thus, do some human universals of beauty arising from external stimuli seem to emerge across all cultures regardless of custom and tradition. However, Smith acknowledges that it is unlikely that an external source of beauty can survive where it collides and is discordant with custom and tradition.

CHAPTER 33

The influence of custom and fashion upon moral sentiments

It follows that, if beauty of every kind is influenced by custom and tradition, so must be the beauty of human conduct; but moral principles have an enduring purpose not to be displaced by changing customs and traditions.

> Since our sentiments concerning beauty of every kind are so much influenced by custom and fashion, it cannot be expected that those concerning the beauty of conduct should be entirely exempted from the dominion of those principles. Their influence here, however, seems to be much less than it is everywhere else. There is, perhaps, no form of external objects, how absurd and fantastical soever, to which custom will not reconcile us, or which fashion will not render even agreeable. But the characters and conduct of a Nero, or a Claudius, are what no custom will ever reconcile us to, what no fashion will ever render agreeable; but the one will always be the object of dread and hatred—the other of scorn and derision. The principles of the imagination, upon which our sense of beauty depends, are of a very nice and delicate nature, and easily may be altered by habit and education; but the sentiments of moral approbation and disapprobation are founded on the strongest and most vigorous passions of human nature; and though they may be somewhat warpt, cannot be entirely perverted. (*TMS*, p. 290)

Vernon L. Smith, *Adam Smith's Theory of Society*,
https://doi.org/10.1007/978-3-031-68494-4_33

Although moral principles are affected by custom and fashion, they are founded on the strongest and most vigorous passions of human nature which imparts to them a robustness more enduring than the changing customs and fashions of the times.

Where custom and fashion coincide with natural emergent principles of right and wrong, they leverage virtue and increase our abhorrence of evil.

> But though the influence of custom and fashion upon moral sentiments is not altogether so great, it is, however, perfectly similar to what it is everywhere else. When custom and fashion coincide with the natural principles of right and wrong, they heighten the delicacy of our sentiments, and increase our abhorrence for everything which approaches to evil. Those who have been educated in what is really good company, not in what is commonly called such, who have been accustomed to see nothing in the persons whom they esteemed and lived with, but justice, modesty, humanity, and good order, are more shocked with whatever seems to be inconsistent with the rules which those virtues prescribe. Those, on the contrary, who have had the misfortune to be brought up amidst violence, licentiousness, falsehood, and injustice, lose though not all sense of the impropriety of such conduct, yet all sense of its dreadful enormity, or of the vengeance and punishment due to it. They have been familiarized with it from their infancy, custom has rendered it habitual to them, and they are very apt to regard it as what is called the way of the world, something which either, or must be practised, to hinder us from being the dupes of our own integrity. (*TMS*, p. 291)

Those brought up in communities well-practiced in the rules of justice, modesty, humanity, and good order find shocking any conduct not in keeping with these virtuous rules. The misfortunate brought up amidst violence, licentiousness, falsehood, and injustice, lose not all sense of impropriety, for there must be enough honor among thieves to avoid extinction, and justify their lifestyle as "the way of the world" that if not practiced they become dupes of their own integrity.

On the virtues, vices, and attitudes of the rich and the poor.

> Fashion, too, will sometimes give reputation to a certain degree of disorder, and, on the contrary, discountenance qualities which deserve esteem. In

> the reign of Charles II. a degree of licentiousness was deemed the characteristic of a liberal education. It was connected, according to the notions of those times, with generosity, sincerity, magnanimity, loyalty, and proved that the person who acted in this manner was a gentleman and not a puritan. Severity of manners and regularity of conduct, on the other hand, were altogether unfashionable, and were connected, in the imagination of that age, with cant, cunning, hypocrisy, and low manners. To superficial minds the vices of the great seem at all times agreeable. They connect them, not only with the splendour of fortune, but with many superior virtues which they ascribe to their superiors; with the spirit of freedom and independency, with frankness, generosity, humanity, and politeness. The virtues of the inferior ranks of people, on the contrary, their parsimonious frugality, their painful industry, and rigid adherence to rules, seem to them mean and disagreeable. They connect them both with the meanness of the station to which those qualities commonly belong, and with many great vices which, they suppose, usually accompany them—such as an abject, cowardly, ill-natured, lying, pilfering disposition. (*TMS*, pp. 291–292)

Licentiousness during the reign of Charles II was associated with a liberal education and was an acceptable, approved tradition firmly associated with generosity, sincerity, magnanimity, and loyalty, proving that the follower was a gentleman, not puritanical. For people of superficial mind, those superior in rank view the virtues of the inferior—frugality, industry, and strict rule-following—as marks of a cowardly, ill-natured, pilfering disposition. He was a colonial expansionist and government/business mercantilist sure to inspire the American Revolution.

Different professions are associated with different habitual passions.

> The objects with which men in the different professions and states of life are conversant being very different, and habituating them to very different passions, naturally form in them very different characters and manners. We expect in each rank and profession a degree of those manners which, experience has taught us, belonged to it. But as in each species of things we are particularly pleased with the middle confirmation, which, in every part and feature, agrees most exactly with the general standard which nature seems to have established for things of that kind; so in each rank, or…in each species of men, we are particularly pleased, if they have neither too much nor too little of the character which usually accompanies their particular condition and situation. A man, we say, should look like his trade and profession; yet the pedantry of every profession is disagreeable.

> The different periods of life have, for the same reason, different manners assigned to them. We expect in old age that gravity and sedateness which its infirmities, its long experience, and its worn-out sensibility seem to render both natural and respectable; and we lay our account to find in youth that sensibility, that gaiety and sprightly vivacity, which experience teaches us to expect from the lively impressions that all interesting objects are apt to make upon the tender and unpractised senses of that early period of life. Each of those two ages, however, easily have too much of these peculiarities which belong to it. The flirting levity of youth, and the immoveable insensibility of old age, are equally disagreeable. The young, according to the common saying, are most agreeable when in their behaviour there is something of the manners of the old; and the old, when they retain something of the gaiety of the young. Either of them, however, easily have too much of the manners of the other. The extreme coldness and dull formality which are pardoned in old age, make youth ridiculous. The levity, the carelessness, and the vanity, which are indulged in youth, render old age contemptible. (*TMS*, pp. 292–293)

Each profession has its own distinctive or similar characteristics. So how do we compare individuals across these variations? A man should "look like" his profession, so Smith's "middle confirmation" which corresponds with and defines the median, as a measure of central tendency, has as many elements that are greater as that are less than it. Smith says that we apply the median representation because we want to be able to say that someone has neither too much, nor too little, of that which most characterizes individual members of a profession. Thus, a particular artist has a manner not too ostentatious, a particular mathematician not too reserved; and therefore, we can say that someone is typical of what is expected.

Customary special features, as well as natural variations in their state of life, determine the social characteristics of each rank and profession.

> The peculiar character and manners which we are led by custom to appropriate to each rank and profession, have sometimes, perhaps, a propriety independent of custom, and are what we should approve of for their own sakes, if we took into consideration all the different circumstances which naturally affect those in each different state of life. The propriety of a person's behaviour depends not upon its suitableness to any one circumstance of his situation, but to all the circumstances which, when we bring

his case home to ourselves, we feel should naturally call upon his attention. If he appears to be so much occupied by any one of them as entirely to neglect the rest, we disapprove of his conduct as something which we cannot entirely go along with, because not properly adjusted to all the circumstances of his situation: yet, perhaps, the emotion he expresses for the object which principally interests him does not exceed what we should entirely sympathize with and approve of in one whose attention was not required by any other thing. A parent in private life might, upon the loss of an only son, express without blame a degree of grief and tenderness which would be unpardonable in a general at the head of an army, when glory and the public safety demanded so great a part of his attention. As different objects ought, upon common occasions, to occupy the attention of men of different professions, so different passions ought naturally to become habitual to them; and when we bring home to ourselves their situation in this particular respect, we must be sensible that every occurrence should naturally affect them more or less, according as the emotion which it excites coincides or disagrees with the fixed habit and temper of their minds. We cannot expect the same sensibility to the gay pleasures and amusements of life in a clergyman which we lay our account within an officer. The man whose peculiar occupation is to keep the world in mind of that awful futurity which awaits them, who is to announce what may be the fatal consequences of every deviation from the rules of duty, and who is himself to set the example of the most exact conformity, seems to be the messenger of tidings which cannot, in propriety, be delivered either with levity or indifference. His mind is supposed to be continually occupied with what is too grand and solemn to leave any room for the impressions of those frivolous objects which fill up the attention of the dissipated and the gay. We readily feel, therefore, that independent of custom, there is a propriety in the manners which custom has allotted to this profession, and that nothing can be more suitable to the character of a clergyman than that grave, that austere and abstracted severity which we are habituated to expect in his behaviour… (*TMS*, p. 294)

Off-duty military officers are afforded greater deviation in conduct from their role as commander than off-duty clergymen who are not in church or providing benedictions at social or celebration events. This illustrates the general character of how our expectations concerning the conduct of those in particular social ranks and professions are shaped by their professional specialty. Physicians, housewives, and linemen are expected to be always on call to serve in their role, while many others are expected to be unavailable.

Custom and habit determine our approbation of the demeanor expected of various professions.

> The foundation of the customary character of some other professions is not so obvious, and our approbation of it is founded entirely in habit, without being either confirmed or enlivened by any reflections of this kind. We are led by custom, for example, to annex the character of gaiety, levity, and sprightly freedom, as well as of some degree of dissipation, to the military profession. Yet if we were to consider what mood or tone of temper would be most suitable to this situation, we should be apt to determine, perhaps, that the most serious and thoughtful turn of mind would best become those whose lives are continually exposed to uncommon danger, and who should, therefore, be more constantly occupied with the thoughts of death and its consequences than other men. It is this very circumstance, however, which is not improbably the occasion why the contrary turn of mind prevails so much among men of this profession. It requires so great an effort to conquer the fear of death, when we survey it with steadiness and attention, that those who are constantly exposed to it find it easier to turn away their thoughts from it altogether, to wrap themselves up in careless security and indifference, and to plunge themselves, for this purpose, into every sort of amusement and dissipation. A camp is not the element of a thoughtful or a melancholy man: persons of that cast, indeed, are often abundantly determined, and are capable, by a great effort, of going on with inflexible resolution to the most unavoidable death. But to be exposed to continual, though less imminent danger, to be obliged to exert, for a long time, a degree of this effort, exhausts and depresses the mind, and renders it incapable of all happiness and enjoyment. The gay and careless, who have occasion to make no effort at all, who fairly resolve never to look before them, but to lose, in continual pleasures and amusements, all anxiety about their situation, more easily support such circumstances. Whenever, by any peculiar circumstances, an officer has no reason to lay his account with being exposed to any uncommon danger, he is very apt to lose the gaiety and dissipated thoughtlessness of his character. The captain of a city-guard is commonly as sober, careful, and penurious an animal as the rest of his fellow-citizens. A long peace is, for the same reason, very apt to diminish the difference between the civil and the military character. The ordinary situation, however, of men of this profession, renders gaiety and a degree of dissipation so much their usual character, and custom has, in our imagination, so strongly connected this character with this state of life, that we are very apt to despise any man whose peculiar humour or situation renders him incapable of acquiring it. We laugh at the grave and careful faces of

> a city-guard, which so little resemble those of their profession: they themselves seem often to be ashamed of the regularity of their own manners, and, not to be out of the fashion of their trade, are fond of affecting that levity which is by no means natural to them. Whatever is the deportment which we have been accustomed to see in a respectable order of men, it comes to be so associated in our imagination with that order, that whenever we see the one we lay our account that we are to meet with the other, and when disappointed, miss something which we expected to find. We are embarrassed, and put to a stand, and know not how to address ourselves to a character which plainly affects to be of a different species from those with which we should have been disposed to class it. (*TMS*, pp. 294–296)

We expect off-duty military personnel to adapt to their normal state of living with danger and death, to its opposite, one of escaping it in pleasure-seeking. Interestingly, however, our expectations of off-duty policeman stand in sharp contrast with those of off-duty military personnel. Policemen are expected to be alert to sudden emergency service, be on call, and always alert to exhibit a serious and sober deportment. But the military is expected to unwind and get refreshed before returning to their exposure to accustomed danger.

I think the difference is simple and straight forward to understand. The military man, on duty, is surrounded by other military men in an encampment removed from the enemy, who is also quartered closely in a separate encampment. They are each exposed to danger removed from their immediate environs. Not so for the policeman (or woman) whose call to duty may occur anywhere in his community, near or far from the police station, the local coffee shop, or ACE hardware. And many walk a beat, patrolling between the streetlights. People identify with them as neighbors.

I am reminded of Officer Callahan who was a traffic cop on the Boston side of the Charles River as you come over the Cottage Farm Bridge from Cambridge to Boston. It's the 1952–55 episode in my life when I lived in Cambridge, as a grad student a Harvard. A period in which I was constantly regaled by local events that were a standard part of daily living in the Boston scene. In the Boston area drivers are notoriously aggressive. I would often observe two drivers with windows rolled down shouting obscenities at each other. Drivers do not stop for stop signs and feign not seeing you in an intersection by looking away, thereby bluffing you into slowing for them. Well, coming over the Cottage farm the signs are transparently clear: Right Lane Right turn only. Normally that would mean that you do not hesitate to go straight from the right lane as you bloody well pleased. But not at Callahan's intersection. If you were in the right lane and were about to go straight, Callahan stepped from his traffic box in front of your car to block you, signaling you right. So, one rainy day a city official is blocked from going straight and the official pulls strings to get Calahan busted to a beat.

So, here is Boston's most respected and beloved officer precisely because he enforces the street law and traffic always moves smoothly through his intersection. And the city has seen fit to bust him. No way Boston citizens are going to tolerate that. Angry letters and articles reflecting the same sentiment flood into the Boston Traveler as the community erupts in support of that Irish Officer. Soon, Calahan is returned to his box and Boston cools off.

Different historical periods and countries shape the characters of those who live in them.

> The different situations of different ages and countries are apt, in the same manner, to give different characters to the generality of those who live in them, and their sentiments concerning the particular degree of each quality that is either blameable or praiseworthy, vary according to that degree which is usual in their own country and in their own times. That degree of politeness which would be highly esteemed, perhaps would be thought effeminate adulation, in Russia, would be regarded as rudeness and barbarism at the court of France. That degree of order and frugality which, in a Polish nobleman, would be considered as excessive parsimony, would be regarded as extravagance in a citizen of Amsterdam. Every age and country look upon that degree of each quality which is commonly to be met with in those who are esteemed, among themselves, as the golden mean of that particular talent or virtue; and as this varies according as their different circumstances render excessive different qualities more or less habitual to them, their sentiments, concerning the exact propriety of character and behaviour, vary accordingly. (*TMS*, pp. 296–297)

That which is the ordinarily esteemed expression of politeness might in Russia be thought effeminate adulation, but rude in the Court of France. A common extent of order and frugality would be thought excessively parsimonious to a Polish nobleman, and as extravagance in a citizen of Amsterdam. Every period and national culture creates a golden mean for each virtue to inspire those who are most esteemed.

In this context, Smith discusses the presumptively common European attitude toward the alleged distinctive character of "new world savages" although Scotch social theory at this time was cultivating the more liberal, tolerant, humanitarian attitude toward all individuals generally that we associate with classical liberalism. Hume expressed similar prejudices in a famous footnote, while Smith carries on about the characteristics of savages.[1] I will shorten it without failing to convey the attitude of the times.[2]

Civilized nations are humanitarian while barbarous nations are otherwise.

> Among civilized nations, the virtues which are founded upon humanity are more cultivated than those which are founded upon self-denial and the command of the passions. Among rude and barbarous nations it is quite otherwise—the virtues of self-denial are more cultivated than those of humanity. The general security and happiness which prevail in ages of civility and politeness, afford little exercise to the contempt of danger, to patience in enduring labour, hunger, and pain. Poverty easily may be avoided, and the contempt of it, therefore, almost ceases to be a virtue.[3] The abstinence from pleasure becomes less necessary, and the mind is more

[1] My view is that Hume and Smith deserve neither a cover-up nor castigation, any more than does Mark Twain for his use of the N-word and other expressions, without which his famous novels would have been without credibility. The current "wok" culture demands public castigation—in the spirit of the colonial New England stock for drunkenness—for those who feel and express no guilt for our ancestors' racist attitudes. It is not sufficient to be a dedicated anti-racist. You must also feel shame, guilt, and personal blame for their racist attitudes. Rather than feel pride that one of my Lomax ancestors bought the freedom of two slaves, I ought to feel shame that one of his brothers crossed over to fight for the Confederate South. Progressives seem to be going through a self-imposed purge of our collective sins and no one must be allowed to escape blame. The optimistic view that we have made progress is countered by the claimed more important view that progress has been grossly inadequate. This is not an argument about direction but about speed. Bottom-up processes of change are declared too slow, and change must be imposed from above.

[2] But was Smith a racist, and in what sense, for his time? See: https://www.adamsmith.org/blog/in-support-of-adam-smiths-legacy-against-slavery.

[3] By modern standards poverty was immense, but we have learned from economic historians that by Smith's time the great increase in growth and human economic betterment had started and would continue down to the present.

> at liberty to unbend itself, and to indulge its natural inclinations in all those particular respects.[4] (*TMS*, pp. 293–297)

The rude, savage, barbarous nations are here seen in the interpretation of Europeans as cultures based on the "virtues of self-denial and the command of the passions" with little self-command over selfish needs because of the paucity of surplus over bare subsistence. Yet elsewhere Smith saw moral authority as emanating from religion which, even in primitive superstitious forms, offered symbolic models of good or evil conduct.

In the professions and life states, custom teaches us to adopt manners that concern things not of the greatest importance.

> The different manners which custom teaches us to approve of in the different professions and states of life, do not concern things of the greatest importance. We expect truth and justice from an old man as well as from a young, from a clergyman as well as from an officer; and it is in matters of small moment only that we look for the distinguishing marks of their respective characters. With regard to these, too, there is often some unobserved circumstance, which, if it was attended to, would shew us, that, independent of custom, there was a propriety in the character which custom had taught us to allot to each profession. We cannot complain, therefore, in this case, that the perversion of natural sentiment is very great. Though the manners of different nations require different degrees of the same quality in the character which they think worthy of esteem, yet the worst that can be said to happen even here is, that the duties of one virtue are sometimes extended so as to encroach a little upon the precincts of some other. The rustic hospitality that is in fashion among the Poles encroaches, perhaps, a little upon economy and good order; and the frugality that is esteemed in Holland, upon generosity and good-fellowship. The hardiness demanded of savages diminishes their humanity; and, perhaps, the delicate sensibility required in civilized nations sometimes destroys the masculine firmness of the character. In general the style of manners which takes place in any nation commonly, upon the whole, may be said to be that which is most suitable to its situation. Hardiness is the character most suitable to the circumstances of a savage; sensibility

[4] Smith's model has the implication that our species' escape from bare subsistence was facilitated by sociability, reciprocity, and community rather than the escape being a precondition for our socialization.

to those of one who lives in a very civilized society. Even here, therefore, we cannot complain that the moral sentiments of men are very grossly perverted. (*TMS*, pp. 303–304)

The general principle at work in all nations and cultures is that the style of manners which are observed to prevail are those which are most suitable to its situation. If hardiness is the character that most fits the savage, we cannot complain that our moral sentiments are so grossly perverted. But surely, I would ask, is not the effect of hardiness about matters of small import? I think we have learned in modern ethnologies that the ancients, though primitive in technology, were quite sensitive on matters of truth and justice.

In usage, not general style, customs authorize wide departures from civilized conduct, such as the abuse of children

It is not, therefore, in the general style of conduct or behaviour that custom authorizes the widest departure from what is the natural propriety of action. With regard to particular usages, its influence is often much more destructive of good morals, and it is capable of establishing, as lawful and blameless, particular actions, which shock the plainest principles of right and wrong.

Can there be greater barbarity, for example, than to hurt an infant?—its helplessness, its innocence, its amiableness, call forth the compassion even of an enemy, and not to spare that tender age is regarded as the most furious effort of an enraged and cruel conqueror. What then should we imagine must be the heart of a parent who could injure that weakness which even a furious enemy is afraid to violate? Yet the exposition, that is, the murder of new-born infants, was a practice allowed of in almost all the states of Greece, even among the polite and civilized Athenians; and whenever the circumstances of the parent rendered it inconvenient to bring up the child, to abandon it to hunger, or to wild beasts, was regarded without blame or censure. This practice had, probably, begun in times of the most savage barbarity. The imaginations of men had been first made familiar with it in that earliest period of society, and the uniform continuance of the custom had hindered them afterwards from perceiving its enormity. We find at this day that this practice prevails among all savage nations; and in that rudest and lowest state of society it is undoubtedly more pardonable than in any other. The extreme indigence of a savage is often such that he himself is frequently exposed to the greatest extremity of hunger; he often dies of pure want; and it is frequently impossible for him

> to support both himself and his child. We cannot wonder, therefore, that in this case he should abandon it...That in this state of society, therefore, a parent should be allowed to judge whether he can bring up his child ought not to surprise us so greatly. In the latter ages of Greece, however, the same thing was permitted from views of remote interest or conveniency, which could by no means excuse it. Uninterrupted custom had by this time so thoroughly authorized the practice, that not only the loose maxims of the world tolerated this barbarous prerogative, but even the doctrine of philosophers, which ought to have been more just and accurate, was led away by the established custom; and upon this, as upon many other occasions, instead of censuring, supported the horrible abuse by farfetched considerations of public utility. Aristotle talks of it as of what the magistrate ought, upon many occasions, to encourage. The humane Plato is of the same opinion, and, with all that love of mankind which seems to animate all his writings, nowhere marks this practice with disapprobation. When custom can give sanction to so dreadful a violation of humanity, we well imagine that there is scarce any particular practice so gross which it cannot authorize. Such a thing, we hear men every day saying, is commonly done, and they seem to think this a sufficient apology for what, in itself, is the most unjust and unreasonable conduct.
>
> There is an obvious reason why custom should never pervert our sentiments with regard to the general style and character of conduct and behaviour, in the same degree as with regard to the propriety or unlawfulness of particular usages. There never can be any such custom. No society could subsist a moment, in which the usual strain of men's conduct and behaviour was of a piece with the horrible practice I have just now mentioned. (*TMS*, pp. 304–306)

I believe Smith is here recounting practices that are affected not only by culture, but lower versus higher levels of wealth creation among different cultures. Ceteris paribus, wealthier societies place greater economic value on a human life and will expend more resources to save a life, than poorer societies. Thus abortion, the long-standing means by which married couples have maintained their standard of living, has become highly controversial in modern Western Nations with high standards of living. The narrower interest of equal rights for women which emphasizes the right of women to choose how their body is to be used—child barring or not—collides with the broader interest of society in maintaining the species.

PART X

Of the character of virtue: Consisting of three chapters

CHAPTER 34

Of the character of the individual, so far as it affects his own happiness; or of prudence

Character, as it affects our own or others' happiness, and the virtue of prudence.

> [W]e consider the character of any individual, we naturally view it under two different aspects; first, as it affect his own happiness; and, secondly, as it affect that of other people.
>
> The preservation and healthful state of the body seem to be the objects which nature first recommends to the care of every individual. The appetites of hunger and thirst, the agreeable or disagreeable sensations of pleasure and pain, of heat and cold, be considered as lessons delivered by the voice of Nature herself, directing him what he ought to choose, and what he ought to avoid, for this purpose. The first lessons which he is taught by those to whom his childhood is entrusted, tend, the greater part of them, to the same purpose. Their principal object is to teach him how to keep out of harm's way.
>
> As he grows up, he soon learns that some care and foresight are necessary for providing the means of gratifying those natural appetites, of procuring pleasure and avoiding pain, of procuring the agreeable and avoiding the disagreeable temperature of heat and cold. In the proper direction of this care and foresight consists the art of preserving and increasing what is called his external fortune. Though it is in order to supply the necessities and conveniences of the body that the advantages of external fortune are originally recommended to us, yet we cannot live long in the world without perceiving that the respect of our equals, our credit and rank

Vernon L. Smith, *Adam Smith's Theory of Society*,
https://doi.org/10.1007/978-3-031-68494-4_34

> in the society we live in, depend very much upon the degree in which we possess, or are supposed to possess, those advantages. The desire of becoming the proper objects of this respect, of deserving and obtaining this credit and rank among our equals, is perhaps the strongest of all our desires; and our anxiety to obtain the advantages of fortune is, accordingly, much more excited and irritated by this desire than by that of supplying all the necessities and conveniences of the body, which are always very easily supplied.
> Our rank and credit among our equals, too, depend very much upon what, perhaps, a virtuous man would wish them to depend entirely,—our character and conduct, or upon the confidence, esteem, and good-will, which these naturally excite in the people we live with.
> The care of the health, of the fortune, of the rank and reputation of the individual, the objects upon which his comfort and happiness in this life are supposed principally to depend, is considered as the proper business of that virtue which is commonly called prudence. (*TMS*, pp. 309–311)

The first and most foundational of Nature's virtues is prudence because its proper business is for each individual to govern themselves, their health, fortune, rank, and reputation, the objects on which a person's comfort and happiness in life principally depend. That business connects each to the community of others and each best helps themselves by helping others.

Revisiting the fundamental asymmetry between joy and sorrow.

> We suffer more, it has already been observed (late in Chapter 25), we fall from a better to a worse situation, than we ever enjoy when we rise from a worse to a better. Security, therefore, is the first and the principal object of prudence. It is averse to expose our health, our fortune, our rank, or reputation, to any sort of hazard. It is rather cautious than enterprising, and more anxious to preserve the advantages which we already possess than forward to prompt us to the acquisition of still greater advantages. The methods of improving our fortune, which it principally recommends to us, are those which expose to no loss or hazard; real knowledge and skill in our trade or profession, assiduity and industry in the exercise of it, frugality, and even some degree of parsimony, in all our expenses. (*TMS*, p. 311)

In the earlier entry cited Adam Smith first offers his theory that people's experience of joy and sorrow is fundamentally asymmetric. This feature, as

I have indicated in my discussion, was rediscovered empirically by modern psychologists in the context of choice among probabilistic prospects involving gain or loss measured relative to a reference state.

An implication of this asymmetry, as emphasized and developed in today's entry, is that security is the principal object of prudence. It is averse to expose ourselves to any sort of hazard. It is more in the vein of caution than of enterprise, and seeks real that is established, knowledge in our trade or profession, and in adherence to accepted work skills and standards. Innovative enterprise departs from prudent action and is pursued by those with supreme confidence or vision in departing from this strong norm. Of course, society greatly benefits from successful innovation although few among the innovators succeed. Smith's concept of prudence tells us why, for it says that the innovator throws caution to the winds in pursuit of a vision that is more likely to fail than succeed.

Prudence seeks to understand whatever it professes.

> The prudent man always studies seriously and earnestly to understand whatever he professes to understand, and not merely to persuade other people that he understands it; and though his talents may not always be very brilliant, they are always perfectly genuine. He neither endeavours to impose upon you by the cunning devices of an artful impostor, nor by the arrogant airs of an assuming pedant, nor by the confident assertions of a superficial and impudent pretender: he is not ostentatious even of the abilities which he really possesses. His conversation is simple and modest, and he is averse to all the quackish arts by which other people so frequently thrust themselves into public notice and reputation. For reputation in his profession he is naturally disposed to rely a good deal upon the solidity of his knowledge and abilities; and he does not always think of cultivating the favour of those little clubs and cabals, who, in the superior arts and sciences, so often erect themselves into the supreme judges of merit; and who make it their business to celebrate the talents and virtues of one another, and to decry whatever can come into competition with them. If he ever connects himself with any society of this kind, it is merely in self-defence, not with a view to impose upon the public, but to hinder the public from being imposed upon, to his disadvantage, by the clamours, the whispers, or the intrigues, either of that particular society or of some other of the same kind. (*TMS*, pp. 311–312)

You want your children to know prudent people to help steer them through the vicissitudes of their teen years to young adulthood, yet somehow to depart enough from prudent conduct to succeed and make you proud.

Providence is sincere, truthful, reserved in opinion, though not always frank and open.

> The prudent man is always sincere, and feels horror at the very thought of exposing himself to the disgrace which attends upon the detection of falsehood. But though always sincere, he is not always frank and open; and though he never tells any thing but the truth, he does not always think himself bound, when not properly called upon, to tell the whole truth. As he is cautious in his actions, so he is reserved in his speech, and never rashly or unnecessarily obtrudes his opinion concerning either things or persons. (*TMS*, p. 312)

A prudent person is a rock of integrity. You want them to be many among your fellow-citizens because they will give society its stability in justice allowing the free reign of reciprocal natural beneficence.

Prudence, if not highly sensitive, is capable of friendship.

> The prudent man though not always distinguished by the most exquisite sensibility, is always very capable of friendship. But his friendship is not that ardent and passionate but too often transitory affection, which appears so delicious to the generosity of youth and inexperience. It is a sedate, but steady and faithful attachment to a few well-tried and well-chosen companions; in the choice of whom he is not guided by the giddy admiration of shining accomplishments, but by the sober esteem of modesty, discretion, and good conduct. But though capable of friendship, he is not always much disposed to general sociality. He rarely frequents, and more rarely figures in, those convivial societies which are distinguished for the jollity and gaiety of their conversation. Their way of life might too often interfere with the regularity of his temperance, might interrupt the steadiness of his industry, or break in upon the strictness of his frugality. (*TMS*, p. 313)

The prudent person will be a good if not intimate friend; temperate, dependable, never an embarrassment, always at the center among the middling, neither too far right or too far left. They cheerfully adapt to change but are not wont to make it.

The conversation of the prudent, if not sprightly or diverting, is inoffensive.

> Though his conversation may not always be very sprightly or diverting, it is always perfectly inoffensive. He hates the thought of being guilty of any petulance or rudeness: he never assumes impertinently over any body, and, upon all common occasions, is willing to place himself rather below than above his equals. Both in his conduct and conversation he is an exact observer of decency, and respects, with an almost religious scrupulosity, all the established decorums and ceremonials of society. And in this respect he sets a much better example than has frequently been done by men of much more splendid talents and virtues—who in all ages, from that of Socrates and Aristippus down to that of Dr Swift and Voltaire, and from that of Philip and Alexander the Great down to that of the great Czar Peter of Moscovy, have too often distinguished themselves by the most improper and even insolent contempt of all the ordinary decorums of life and conversation, and who have thereby set the most pernicious example to those who wish to resemble them, and who too often content themselves with imitating their follies without even attempting to attain their perfections. (*TMS*, pp. 313–314)

You should want at least one prudent person on your PhD dissertation committee and at least one innovator. The innovator will help you to push the boundaries of the known/unknown and the prudent person will help you make palatable any new knowledge you discover.

For the prudent, the present, and likely future situations are seen as much the same.

> In the steadiness of his industry and frugality, in his steadily sacrificing the ease and enjoyment of the present moment for the probable expectation of the still greater ease and enjoyment of a more distant but more lasting period of time, the prudent man is always both supported and rewarded by the entire approbation of the impartial spectator, and of the representative of the impartial spectator, the man within the breast. The impartial spectator does not feel himself worn out by the present labour of those whose conduct he surveys; nor does he feel himself solicited by the importunate calls of their present appetites. To him their present, and what is likely to be their future situation, are very nearly the same: he sees them nearly at the same distance, and is affected by them very nearly in the same manner: he knows, however, that to the persons principally concerned they are very

> far from being the same, and that they naturally affect them in a very different manner. He cannot, therefore, but approve, and even applaud, that proper exertion of self-command which enables them to act as if their present and their future situation affected them nearly in the same manner in which they affect him. (*TMS*, p. 314)

As in Part 6, Section 1, entry 7, the prudent person is not a discounter of future versus current circumstances and therefore of the pleasures to be gotten later for the pleasures foregone now, the appetites to be satisfied later in exchange for saying no today. They live as if tomorrow will be at least as heart-warming as today. Mathematically, a "rational" economic investor uses an exponential decay function of time for discounting future outcomes. But in empirical studies people tend to follow an equal value hyperbola decay function of time for discounting future outcomes.

The prudent person is contented with their current income and situation.

> The prudent man lives within his income is naturally contented with his situation, which, by continual, though small accumulations, is growing better and better every day. He is enabled gradually to relax, both in the rigour of his parsimony and in the severity of his application; and he feels with double satisfaction this gradual increase of ease and enjoyment, from having felt before the hardship which attended the want of them. He has no anxiety to change so comfortable a situation, and does not go in quest of new enterprises and adventures, which might endanger, but could not well increase, the secure tranquillity which he actually enjoys. If he enters into any new projects or enterprises, they are likely to be well concerted and well prepared. He can never be hurried or driven into them by any necessity, but has always time and leisure to deliberate soberly and coolly concerning what are likely to be their consequences. (*TMS*, pp. 314–315)

Further, the prudent person is industrious, saves a portion of their income, and feels securely comfortable in their current situation and current earnings. They are deliberative, not prone to be enterprising, but if they do so engage, they will be coordinated, dependable, and well-prepared.

The prudent do not take on responsibilities in excess of those required by their duty.

> [The prudent person] Is not willing to subject himself to any responsibility which his duty does not impose upon him. He is not a bustler in business where he has no concern; is not a meddler in other people's affairs; is not a professed counsellor or adviser, who obtrudes his advice where nobody is asking it: he confines himself, as much as his duty will permit, to his own affairs, and has no taste for that foolish importance which many people wish to derive from appearing to have some influence in the management of those of other people: he is averse to enter into any party disputes, hates faction, and is not always very forward to listen to the voice even of noble and great ambition. When distinctly called upon, he will not decline the service of his country; but he will not cabal in order to force himself into it, and would be much better pleased that the public business were well managed by some other person, than that he himself should have the trouble, and incur the responsibility, of managing it. In the bottom of his heart he would prefer the undisturbed enjoyment of secure tranquillity, not only to all the vain splendour of successful ambition, but to the real and solid glory of performing the greatest and most magnanimous actions. (*TMS*, p. 315)

The prudent do not mind other people's business, keep their own council, and seek not vain splendor or the success of ambition. Others are allowed to rush in to aid an accident victim or to volunteer for tasks beyond their accustomed duties. They do not offer advice where no one is asking for it.

Prudence in personal care is respectable not endearing.

> Prudence…when directed merely to the care of the health, of the fortune, and of the rank and reputation of the individual, though it is regarded as a most respectable, and even, in some degree, as an amiable and agreeable quality, yet it never is considered as one either of the most endearing or of the most ennobling of the virtues. It commands a certain cold esteem, but seems not entitled to any very ardent love or admiration.
> Wise and judicious conduct, when directed to greater and nobler purposes than the care of the health, the fortune, the rank, and reputation, of the individual, is frequently and very properly called Prudence. We talk of the prudence of the great general, of the great statesman, of the great legislator. Prudence is, in all these cases, combined with many greater and more splendid virtues; with valour, with extensive and strong benevolence, with a sacred regard to the rules of justice, and all these supported by a proper degree of self-command. This superior prudence, when carried to

> the highest degree of perfection, necessarily supposes the art, the talent, and the habit or disposition of acting with the most perfect propriety in every possible circumstance and situation. It necessarily supposes the utmost perfection of all the intellectual and of all the moral virtues. It is the best head joined to the best heart. It is the most perfect wisdom combined with the most perfect virtue. It constitutes very nearly the character of the Academical or Peripatetic sage, as the inferior prudence does that of the Epicurean. (*TMS*, pp. 315–316)

Prudence directed only to personal health, fortune, rank, and reputation, is not considered ennobling, but is rather associated with valor, an extensive and strong benevolence, a sacred regard to the rules of justice, and all these are fueled by a proper degree of self-command.

CHAPTER 35

Of the character of the individual, so far as it can affect the happiness of other people

Introduction

Only proper resentment for acts of injustice can justify hurting a neighbor

> The character of every individual, so far as it can affect the happiness of other people, must do so by its disposition either to hurt or to benefit them. Proper resentment for injustice attempted, or actually committed, is the only motive which, in the eyes of the impartial spectator, can justify our hurting or disturbing, in any respect, the happiness of our neighbour. To do so from any other motive is itself a violation of the laws of justice, which force ought to be employed either to restrain or to punish. The wisdom of every state or commonwealth endeavours…to employ the force of the society to restrain those who are subject to its authority from hurting or disturbing the happiness of one another. The rules which it establishes for this purpose constitute the civil and criminal law of each particular state or country. The principles upon which those rules either are or ought to be founded, are the subject of a particular science, of all sciences by far the most important, but hitherto, perhaps, the least cultivated—that of natural jurisprudence; concerning which it belongs not to our present subject to enter into any detail. (*TMS*, p. 319)

Vernon L. Smith, *Adam Smith's Theory of Society*,
https://doi.org/10.1007/978-3-031-68494-4_35

In the eyes of the impartial spectator the only motive that can justify our hurting or disturbing our neighbor in any way is proper resentment and punishment for their unjust actions attempted or committed toward others. To so direct the force of a society as to restrain its citizens from hurting each other is the subject of the science of natural jurisprudence, perhaps the most important of all the sciences for it articulates the rules of proper conduct under which all science may flourish.

Even then, act with caution and sensitivity to the detailed situation. Don't ignite a firestorm.

The innocent and just person has a sacred duty not to disturb the happiness of their neighbor.

> A sacred and religious regard not to hurt or disturb, in any respect, the happiness of our neighbour, even in those cases where no law can properly protect him, constitutes the character of the perfectly innocent and just man; a character which, when carried to a certain delicacy of attention, is always highly respectable and even venerable for its own sake, and can scarce ever fail to be accompanied with many other virtues—with great feeling for other people, with great humanity and great benevolence. It is a character sufficiently understood, and requires no further explanation...(*TMS*, pp. 319–320; italics added)

As we have emphasized, Smith introduces and develops propositions on the two distinct pillars of society—Beneficence and Justice, with the latter being ranked more essential than the former. In the italicized sentence above, Smith expresses his opinion that an individual who is strongly committed to the principles of justice is almost certain also to be committed to great benevolence. Hence, they who are likely to act justly also are likely to act beneficently. Beneficence and justice are not independent as the just are likely also to be beneficent.

> ... I shall only endeavour to explain the foundation of that order which Nature seems to have traced out for the distribution of our good offices, or for the direction and employment of our very limited powers of beneficence; first, towards individuals; and, secondly, towards societies. (*TMS*, pp. 320)

The same unerring wisdom, it will be found, which regulates every other part of her [nature's] conduct, directs, in this respect too, the order of her recommendations; which are always stronger or weaker in proportion as our beneficence is more or less necessary, or can be more or less useful.

of the order in which individual are recommended by nature to our care and attention

The order in which our beneficence is to be bestowed on others

> Every man, as the Stoics used to say, is first and principally recommended to his own care; and every man is certainly, in every respect, fitter and abler to take care of himself than of any other person. Every man feels his own pleasures and his own pains more sensibly than those of other people. The former are the original sensations—the latter the reflected or sympathetic images of those sensations. The former may be said to be the substance—the latter the shadow. After himself, the members of his own family, those who usually live in the same house with him, his parents, his children, his brothers and sisters, are naturally the objects of his warmest affections. They are naturally and usually the persons upon whose happiness or misery his conduct must have the greatest influence. He is more habituated to sympathize with them: he knows better how every thing is likely to affect them, and his sympathy with them is more precise and determinate than it can be with the greater part of other people. It approaches nearer, in short, to what he feels for himself.
>
> This sympathy, too, and the affections which are founded on it, are by nature more strongly directed towards his children than towards his parents, and his tenderness for the former seems generally a more active principle than his reverence and gratitude towards the latter. In the natural state of things...the existence of the child for some time after it comes into the world, depends altogether upon the care of the parent; that of the parent does not naturally depend upon the care of the child. In the eye of nature, it would seem, a child is a more important object than an old man, and excites a much more lively, as well as a much more universal sympathy. It ought to do so. Every thing may be expected, or at least hoped, from the child. In ordinary cases, very little can be either expected or hoped from the old man. The weakness of childhood interests the affections of the most brutal and hard-hearted. It is only to the virtuous and humane that the infirmities of old age are not the objects of contempt and aversion. In ordinary cases an old man dies without being much regretted

> by any body. Scarce a child can die without rending asunder the heart of somebody. (*TMS*, pp. 321–322)

We feel our own sensations of pleasure and pain directly and these constitute the substance and source of the reflection of those images in others, when we change places with them in our imagination. That shadow is the source of our fellow-feeling with others. The first of these associations is with close family such as parents and siblings, then aunts, uncles, and cousins. Nature directs our sympathy more strongly to our children than our parents for they constitute the human future to be protected and nurtured. The death of a person of advanced age is deemed less consequential than a child's death. The former have nearly completed their lifetime contributions to society, the latter are just at the beginning. The former have been there, done that, made that mistake, and learned from it; time to get out of the way of others doing the same.

Continuing the order of recommendations.

> The earliest friendships, the friendships which are naturally contracted when the heart is most susceptible of that feeling, are those among brothers and sisters. Their good agreement, while they remain in the same family, is necessary for its tranquillity and happiness. They are capable of giving more pleasure or pain to one another than to the greater part of other people. Their situation renders their mutual sympathy of the utmost importance to their common happiness; and, by the wisdom of nature, the same situation, by obliging them to accommodate to one another, renders that sympathy more habitual, and thereby more lively, more distinct, and more determinate.
>
> The children of brothers and sisters are naturally connected by the friendship which, after separating into different families, continues to take place between their parents. Their good agreement improves the enjoyment of that friendship—their discord would disturb it. As they seldom live in the same family, however, though of more importance to one another than to the greater part of other people, they are of much less than brothers and sisters. As their mutual current sympathy is less necessary, so it is less habitual, and, therefore, proportionably weaker.
>
> The children of cousins, being still less connected, are of still less importance to one another; and the affection gradually diminishes as the relation grows more and more remote. (*TMS*, pp. 321–323)

Our earliest friendships, formed from heartfelt sympathies, are with siblings whose pleasures and pains are most intimately shared. These sympathies extend naturally, if somewhat weakened, to the children of aunts and uncles. With the decline of large families and migration to cities these connections surely would have been replaced by neighbors who, now next-door at an early age, were more distant and less important in farm communities.

The reality of affection is but habitual sympathy, most prominent in families and in parental tenderness

> What is called affection is in reality nothing but habitual sympathy. Our concern in the happiness or misery of those who are the objects of what we call our affections; our desire to promote the one and to prevent the other, are either the actual feeling of that habitual sympathy, or the necessary consequences of that feeling. Relations being usually placed in situations which naturally create this habitual sympathy, it is expected that a suitable degree of affection should take place among them. We generally find that it actually does take place;—we therefore naturally expect that it should; and we are, upon that account, more shocked when upon any occasion we find that it does not. The general rule is established, that persons related to one another in a certain degree ought always to be affected towards one another in a certain manner, and that there is always the highest impropriety, and sometimes even a sort of impiety, in their being affected in a different manner. A parent without parental tenderness, a child devoid of all filial reverence, appear monsters, the objects, not of hatred only, but of horror. (*TMS*, p. 323)

The horror expressed in *TMS* toward parents without parental tenderness and children who revere not their parents is manifest today in public shootings. This horror is particularly pronounced when the victims are children, or when the crime is committed by a teenager directed to immediate family, friends, or school mates. I wonder if these cases might be exacerbated by fellow-feeling that magnifies disagreement, conflict, and hate where parental tenderness has been absent. Fortunate indeed were my two half sisters in having a stepfather who believed that the best thing that ever happened to him was to find and marry a beautiful widow with two children. And because of this, that widow was convinced that she should have one child by him.

This affection, when diminished by events that separate normal family, is to some extent replaced by respect for the general social rules that emerge from family relations.

> Though in a particular instance the circumstances which usually produce those natural affections [among relatives] by some accident not have taken place, yet respect for the general rule will frequently, in some measure, supply their place, and produce something which, though not altogether the same, bear, however, a very considerable resemblance to those affections. A father is apt to be less attached to a child who, by some accident, has been separated from him in its infancy, and who does not return to him till it is grown up to manhood. The father is apt to feel less paternal tenderness for the child; the child less filial reverence for the father. Brothers and sisters, when they have been educated in distant countries, are apt to feel a similar diminution of affection. With the dutiful and the virtuous, however, respect for the general rule will frequently produce something which, though by no means the same, yet very much resemble those natural affections. Even during the separation, the father and the child, the brothers or the sisters, are by no means indifferent to one another. They all consider one another as persons to and from whom certain affections are due, and they live in the hopes of being some time or another in a situation to enjoy that friendship which ought naturally to have taken place among persons so nearly connected. Till they meet, the absent son, the absent brother, are frequently the favourite son, the favourite brother. They have never offended, or, if they have, it is so long ago that the offence is forgotten as some childish trick not worth the remembering. Every account they have heard of one another, if conveyed by people of any tolerable good nature, has been in the highest degree flattering and favourable. The absent son, the absent brother, is not like other ordinary sons and brothers, but an all-perfect son, an all-perfect brother; and the most romantic hopes are entertained of the happiness to be enjoyed in the friendship and conversation of such persons. When they meet, it is often with so strong a disposition to conceive that habitual sympathy which constitutes the family affection, that they are very apt to fancy they have actually conceived it, and to behave to one another as if they had. Time and experience, however, I am afraid, too frequently undeceive them. Upon a more familiar acquaintance, they frequently discover in one another habits, humours, and inclinations, different from what they expected, to which, from want of habitual sympathy, from want of the real principle and foundation of what is properly called family affection, they cannot now easily accommodate themselves. They have never lived in the situation which almost necessarily forces that easy accommodation, and, though they now

> may be sincerely desirous to assume it, they have really become incapable of doing so. Their familiar conversation and intercourse soon become less pleasing to them, and, upon that account, less frequent. They continue to live with one another in the mutual exchange of all essential good offices, and with every other external appearance of decent regard. But that cordial satisfaction, that delicious sympathy, that confidential openness and ease, which naturally take place in the conversation of those who have lived long and familiarly with one another, it seldom happens that they can completely enjoy. (*TMS*, p. 323–325)

Reader, I am reminded of attending middle school, 1938–1940, with two orphans, a boy and girl both of whom were good students, accepted, and well-liked by their classmates. They grew up in the local Masonic Orphan's Home near Allison Intermediate. This attests to the power of general rules, in a stable society, substituting effectively where separation prevents family values from shaping normal child development. The home was eventually converted to Senior Care, and after 126 years ended in bankruptcy and closed in 2022.

People vastly underestimate the contribution of these private institutions that served the aged, women, and children where families were separated and not able to function.

The survival power of general rules depends on the existence of the dutiful and virtuous.

> It is only, however, with the dutiful and the virtuous that the general rule has even this slender authority. With the dissipated, the profligate, and the vain, it is entirely disregarded. They are so far from respecting it, that they seldom talk of it but with the most indecent derision; and an early and long separation of this kind never fails to estrange them most completely from one another. With such persons respect for the general rule can at best produce only a cold and affected civility (a very slender semblance of real regard); and even this, the slightest offence, the smallest opposition of interest, commonly puts an end to altogether. (*TMS*, p. 325)

The dissipated, profligate, and vain do not naturally respect and propagate the general rules of propriety. They are weak in self-command but their influence, fortunately, has been dominated by the followers of Smith's rules of beneficence and justice in free societies founded on liberal constitutions.

Education in schools distant from family seem to hurt the morals and happiness of a society.

> The education of boys at distant great schools, of young men at distant colleges, of young ladies in distant nunneries and boarding-schools, seems in the higher ranks of life to have hurt most essentially the domestic morals, and consequently the domestic happiness, both of France and England. Do you wish to educate your children to be dutiful to their parents, to be kind and affectionate to their brothers and sisters? Put them under the necessity of being dutiful children, of being kind affectionate brothers and sisters: educate them in your own house. From their parents' house they, with propriety and advantage, go out every day to attend public schools; but let their dwelling be always at home. Respect for you must always impose a very useful restraint upon their conduct; and respect for them frequently impose no useless restraint upon your own. Surely no acquirement which can possibly be derived from what is called a public education can make any sort of compensation for what is almost certainly and necessarily lost by it. Domestic education is the institution of nature—public education the contrivance of man. It is surely unnecessary to say which is likely to be the wisest. (*TMS*, pp. 325–326)

Smith's strongly held view that the morals of young people educated in boarding schools away from home were corrupted was reiterated in the *Wealth of Nations*. It was perhaps shaped by his six years at Oxford from age 17–23, where his elite contemporaries would have attended such preparatory schools. His own characterization of Oxford was that the students would not endanger their health by excessive study as they were required only to attend lecture twice a week and prayer twice a day. Smith's education was secured at Balliol College, Oxford, by an excellent library of classical Greek and Roman literature, where he seems to have spent most of his time.

The alleged wonderful affection of royal blood lines is imaginary.

> In some tragedies and romances we meet with many beautiful and interesting scenes, founded upon what is called the force of blood, or upon the wonderful affection which near relations are supposed to conceive for one another, even before they know that they have any such connection. This force of blood, however, I am afraid, exists nowhere but in tragedies and romances. Even in tragedies and romances it is never supposed to take place between any relations but those who are naturally bred up in the same

> house; between parents and children, between brothers and sisters. To imagine any such mysterious affection between cousins—or even between aunts or uncles, and nephews or nieces—would be too ridiculous. (*TMS*, p. 326)

There is no force of blood, only the force of experience shared in forming the rules that bind in creating community. It is ordinary people, not elites, or royalty, or bloodlines that create neighborly relationships for community, society, and nation. This is because experience, and the desire to get along with others, are what constitute and motivate learning in the great school of self-command.

Pastoralism promotes especially strong cross-family bonds probably necessitated for common defense.

> In pastoral countries, and in all countries where the authority of law is not alone sufficient to give perfect security to every member of the state, all the different branches of the same family commonly choose to live in the neighbourhood of one another.[1] Their association is frequently necessary for their common defence. They are all, from the highest to the lowest, of more or less importance to one another. Their concord strengthens their necessary association—their discord always weakens, and might destroy it. They have more intercourse with one another than with the members of any other tribe. The remotest members of the same tribe claim some connexion with one another; and, where all other circumstances are equal, expect to be treated with more distinguished attention than is due to those who have no such pretensions. It is not many years ago that, in the Highlands of Scotland, the chieftain used to consider the poorest man of his clan as his cousin and relation. The same extensive regard to kindred is said to take place among the Tartars, the Arabs, the Turkomans, and, I believe, among all other nations who are nearly in the same state of society in which the Scots Highlanders were about the beginning of the present century. (*TMS*, pp. 326–327)

Smith saw pastoralism as an intermediate and natural stage standing between hunting and foraging and agriculture. It was also associated

[1] Close-knit Spanish Basque sheepherder communities are prominent in the United States, especially in California and Idaho (even in Telluride, Colorado) with prominent peasant cuisines in Bakersfield, California and Boise, Idaho: https://basquemuseum.eus/see/current-exhibits/basques-in-california/, https://www.basquecenter.com/.

with weak decentralized governments, an intermediate and natural stage prior to the development of centralized government and the emergence of commercial society. Smith was among the stage-builder development historians criticized as insufficiently analytical by Alexander Gerschenkron, my graduate economic history teacher at Harvard, 1952–1953, and one of the then-rising new generations of "Clio-metric" economic historians.

Families as part of the political power structure of society recede in importance in commercial society as the rule of law, not men, became the principal source of order.

> In commercial countries, where the authority of law is always perfectly sufficient to protect the meanest man in the state, the descendants of the same family, having no such motive for keeping together, naturally separate and disperse, as interest or inclination direct. They soon cease to be of importance to one another; and, in a few generations, not only lose all care about one another, but all remembrance of their common origin, and of the connection which took place among their ancestors. Regard for remote relations becomes in every country less and less, according as this state of civilization has been longer and more completely established. It has been longer and more completely established in England than in Scotland; and remote relations are, accordingly, more considered in the latter country than in the former, though in this respect the difference between the two countries is growing less and less every day. Great lords, indeed, are in every country proud of remembering and acknowledging their connection with one another, however remote. The remembrance of such illustrious relations flatters not a little the family pride of them all; and it is neither from affection, nor from any thing which resembles affection, but from the most frivolous and childish of all vanities, that this remembrance is so carefully kept up. Should some more humble, though, perhaps, much nearer, kinsman presume to put such great men in mind of his relation to their family, they seldom fail to tell him that they are bad genealogists, and miserably ill-informed concerning their own family history. It is not in that order, I am afraid, that we are to expect any extraordinary extension of what is called natural affection. (*TMS*, pp. 327–328)

Law trumped the family Lords as the decentralized means whereby order was achieved and persisted in commercial societies. The commercial classes became the sources of wealth creation far in excess of what prevailed in earlier social economies. Being less dependent on a privileged elitist ancestry they were more dispersed and diverse and associated with a middle class between the extremes of poverty and riches.

Natural affection is the effect of the moral connection more than the physical connection between parent and child.

> I consider what is called natural affection as more the effect of the moral than of the supposed physical connection between the parent and the child. A jealous husband, indeed, notwithstanding the moral connection, notwithstanding the child's having been educated in his own house, often regards with hatred and aversion that unhappy child which he supposes to be the offspring of his wife's infidelity. It is the lasting monument of a most disagreeable adventure—of his own dishonour, and of the disgrace of his family. (*TMS*, pp. 328)

Thus, the jealous husband, far from being influenced by this strong physical connection,

often regards with aversion the unhappy child he supposes is the product of his wife's infidelity.

The convenience of mutual accommodation frequently produces a friendship like that within families.

> Among well-disposed people the necessity or conveniency of mutual accommodation very frequently produces a friendship not unlike that which takes place among those who are born to live in the same family. Colleagues in office, partners in trade, call one another brothers, and frequently feel towards one another as if they really were so. Their good agreement is an advantage to all; and, if they are tolerably reasonable people, they are naturally disposed to agree. We expect that they should do so; and their disagreement is a sort of a small scandal. The Romans expressed this sort of attachment by the word necessitudo, which, from the etymology, seems to denote that it was imposed by the necessity of the situation.
>
> Even the trifling circumstance of living in the same neighbourhood has some effect of the same kind. We respect the face of a man whom we see every day, provided he has never offended us. Neighbours can be very convenient, and they can be very troublesome, to one another. If they are good sort of people, they are naturally disposed to agree. We expect their good agreement; and to be a bad neighbour is a very bad character. There

> are certain small good offices, accordingly, which are universally allowed to be due to a neighbour in preference to any other person who has no such connection.
> This natural disposition to accommodate and to assimilate, as much as we can, our own sentiments, principles, and feelings, to those which we see fixed and rooted in the persons whom we are obliged to live and converse a great deal with, is the cause of the contagious effects of both good and bad company. The man who associates chiefly with the wise and the virtuous, though he not himself become either wise or virtuous, cannot help conceiving a certain respect, at least, for wisdom and virtue; and the man who associates chiefly with the profligate and the dissolute, though he not himself become profligate and dissolute, must soon lose at least all his original abhorrence of profligacy and dissolution of manners. The similarity of family characters, which we so frequently see transmitted through several successive generations, may perhaps, be partly owing to this disposition, to assimilate ourselves to those whom we are obliged to live and converse a great deal with. The family character, however, like the family countenance, seems to be owing not altogether to the moral but partly too to the physical connection. The family countenance is certainly altogether owing to the latter. (*TMS*, pp. 328–329)

Colleagues sharing the same office and profession, attending the same meetings and social events, share opportunities for fellow-feeling comparable to that of close-knit families that result in deep friendships. Even the weaker forces at work in neighborhoods have effects of the same kind.

Those attachments founded upon esteem and approbation of good conduct are by far the most respectable. Such friendships, arising from unconstrained natural sympathy and long association, can exist only among persons of virtue.

> But of all attachments to an individual, that which is founded altogether upon esteem and approbation of his good conduct and behaviour, confirmed by much experience and long acquaintance, is by far the most respectable. Such friendships, arising not from a constrained sympathy, not from a sympathy which has been assumed and rendered habitual for the sake of convenience and accommodation, but from a natural sympathy, from an involuntary feeling that the persons to whom we attach ourselves are the natural and proper objects of esteem and approbation, can exist

> only among men of virtue. Men of virtue only can feel that entire confidence in the conduct and behaviour of one another, which can at all times assure them that they can never either offend or be offended by one another. Vice is always capricious—virtue only is regular and orderly. The attachment which is founded upon the love of virtue, as it is certainly of all attachments the most virtuous, so it is likewise the happiest, as well as the most permanent and secure. Such friendships need not be confined to a single person, but safely embrace all the wise and virtuous with whom we have been long and intimately acquainted, and upon whose wisdom and virtue we can upon that account entirely depend. They who would confine friendship to two persons, seem to confound the wise security of friendship with the jealousy and folly of love. The hasty, fond, and foolish intimacies of young people, founded commonly upon some slight similarity of character altogether unconnected with good conduct, upon a taste, perhaps, for the same studies, the same amusements, the same diversions, or upon their agreement in some singular principle or opinion not commonly adopted; those intimacies which a freak begins, and which a freak puts an end to, how agreeable soever they appear while they last, can by no means deserve the sacred and venerable name of friendship. (*TMS*, pp. 330)

Of all our attachments, those most founded on esteem and good conduct—confirmed by experience and long acquaintance—are the are the most virtuous.

Vice is always capricious.

Virtue only is regular and orderly.

Those intimacies which a freak begins, and which a freak puts an end to, how agreeable soever they appear while they last, can by no means deserve the sacred and venerable name of friendship.

Reciprocity: Nature formed humankind to be kind to those who have been kind to them.

> Of all the persons, however, whom nature points out for our peculiar beneficence, there are none to whom it seems more properly directed than to those whose beneficence we have ourselves already experienced. Nature, which formed men for that mutual kindness so necessary for their happiness, renders every man the peculiar object of kindness to the persons to whom he himself has been kind. Though their gratitude should not always correspond to his beneficence, yet the sense of his merit, the sympathetic gratitude of the impartial spectator, will always correspond to it. The

> general indignation of other people against the baseness of their ingratitude will even sometimes increase the general sense of his merit. *No benevolent man ever lost altogether the fruits of his benevolence. If he does not always gather them from the persons from whom he ought to have gathered them, he seldom fails to gather them, and with a tenfold increase, from other people.* Kindness is the parent of kindness; and if to be beloved by our brethren be the great object of our ambition, the surest way of obtaining it is by our conduct to shew that we really love them. (*TMS*, pp. 331; italics added)

Beneficence Proposition 1, in TMS, p 112 as I call it, 1 emphasizes that the origin of the rewardable action was in the heartfelt goodness of the benefactor, not a response to good action from another. It is the good-hearted, uninvited, unilateral action that requires reward out of the debt of gratitude felt!

My interpretation of the above proposition on reciprocity is that once the initiating action is made from such an inner-expressed goodness of heart, it jump-starts the dynamics of reciprocity. Moreover, this also explains and justifies the propensity to truck, barter, and exchange one thing for another in markets as it is developed in *WN*, but whose origins are described there as an unsolved puzzle. Thus, does Smith himself contribute to a compartmentalization of *TMS* and *WN*, a characteristic that led to the "Adam Smith problem" according to which, allegedly, Smith had written two irreconcilable books, an interpretation later judged false, but the more understandable when Smith eschewed all pretense of effecting a reconciliation and in my view contributed to that distraction.

Finally, our beneficence is to be recommended for the extraordinary: the greatly fortunate on whose respect we depend for peace and order, and the greatly unfortunate whose relief from human misery depend upon our compassion.

> After the persons who are recommended to our beneficence, either by their connection with ourselves, by their personal qualities, or by their past services, come those who are pointed out, not indeed to what is called our friendship, but to our benevolent attention and good offices; those who are distinguished by their extraordinary situation—the greatly fortunate and the greatly unfortunate, the rich and the powerful, the poor and the wretched. The distinction of ranks, the peace and order of society, are in a great measure founded upon the respect which we naturally conceive for the former. The relief and consolation of human misery depend altogether

> upon our compassion for the latter. The peace and order of society is of more importance than even the relief of the miserable. Our respect for the great, accordingly, is most apt to offend by its excess—our fellow-feeling for the miserable, by its defect. Moralists exhort us to charity and compassion. They warn us against the fascination of greatness. This fascination, indeed, is so powerful, that the rich and the great are too often preferred to the wise and the virtuous. Nature has wisely judged that the distinction of ranks, the peace and order of society, would rest more securely upon the plain and palpable difference of birth and fortune, than upon the invisible and often uncertain difference of wisdom and virtue. The undistinguishing eyes of the great mob of mankind can well enough perceive the former: it is with difficulty that the nice discernment of the wise and the virtuous can sometimes distinguish the latter. In the order of all those recommendations, the benevolent wisdom of nature is equally evident. (*TMS*, pp. 331–332)

Smith's biographers report that because of his personal generosity the estate he left was modest. In his model, Smith recognizes the value of our compassion for the poor and destitute, yet he believes that our respect and support for the great and powerful is essential to the peace and order of society and consequently must be ranked of more importance than even the relief of the miserable. Thus, our respect for the great is most likely to be offensive in its excess, while our fellow-feeling for the miserable, to be deficient. Nature is thus wise in resting our fascination with birth and fortune in the distinction of ranks, even if imperfectly related to peace and order, because the truly wise and virtuous are so invisible to our judgment. The undistinguishing eyes of the great mob of humankind can well enough perceive who are the poor and miserable (recall "the deplorables" in our political times) and remind us of our charitable duty to them.

When there is no envy in the case, our admiration for the great and our natural tendency toward reciprocity combine to increase our tendency to express kindness toward the great.

> It, perhaps, may be unnecessary to observe, that the combination of two, or more, of those exciting causes of kindness, increases the kindness. The favour and partiality which, when there is no envy in the case, we naturally bear to greatness, are much increased when it is joined with wisdom and virtue. If, notwithstanding that wisdom and virtue, the great man should fall into those misfortunes, those dangers and distresses, to which the most

exalted stations are often the most exposed, we are much more deeply interested in his fortune than we should be in that of a person equally virtuous, but in a more humble situation. The most interesting subjects of tragedies and romances are the misfortunes of virtuous and magnanimous kings and princes. If by the wisdom and manhood of their exertions they should extricate themselves from those misfortunes, and recover completely their former superiority and security, we cannot help viewing them with the most enthusiastic and even extravagant admiration. The grief which we felt for their distress, the joy which we feel for their prosperity, seem to combine together in enhancing that partial admiration which we naturally conceive both for the station and the character. (*TMS*, pp. 323–333)

Here, Smith is again giving us an example of the principle that where two otherwise independent effects of the rules we follow are combined, the result is to magnify the effect of each. We can speak only of a non-additive increase in benefit over that which occurs for each separately. Each leverages the other to an indeterminant extent.

When one beneficent action is in part offset by another action that is costly then what is to be done is resolved in the arbiter of each person's breast.

When those different beneficent affections happen to draw different ways, to determine by any precise rules in what cases we ought to comply with the one, and in what with the other, is perhaps altogether impossible. In what cases friendship ought to yield to gratitude, or gratitude to friendship—in what cases the strongest of all natural affections ought to yield to a regard for the safety of those superiors upon whose safety often depends that of the whole society—and in what cases natural affection, without impropriety, prevail over that regard—must be left altogether to the decision of the man within the breast, the supposed impartial spectator, the great judge and arbiter of our conduct. If we place ourselves completely in his situation, if we really view ourselves with his eyes and as he views us, and listen with diligent and reverential attention to what he suggests to us, his voice will never deceive us. We shall stand in need of no casuistic rules to direct our conduct. These it is often impossible to accommodate to all the different shades and gradations of circumstance, character, and situation, to differences and distinctions which, though not imperceptible, are, by their nicety and delicacy, often altogether undefinable....(*TMS*, p. 333)

When one beneficial action is combined with an action that reduces benefit there may be no net benefit in their joint occurrence that a collective of people can agree upon. Smith's example—"In what cases friendship ought to yield to gratitude, or gratitude to friendship"—suggests that friendship is supported by fellow-feeling that does not require gratitude, the latter being the fellow-feeling that attends beneficial actions directed by one person toward any other—a neighbor or stranger who is not a friend, for friendship defines a relationship that endures in the absence of gratitude. Recall that Smith says: "The earliest friendships, the friendships which are naturally contracted when the heart is most susceptible of that feeling, are those among brothers and sisters." (*TMS*, p. 322).

Also: "Such friendships, arising not from a constrained sympathy, not from a sympathy which has been assumed and rendered habitual for the sake of convenience and accommodation, but from a natural sympathy, from an involuntary feeling that the persons to whom we attach ourselves are the natural and proper objects of esteem and approbation, can exist only among men of virtue. Men of virtue only can feel that entire confidence in the conduct and behaviour of one another, which can at all times assure them that they can never either offend or be offended by one another." (*TMS*, p. 330)[2]

Those Principles That Direct the Order in Which Individuals Are Recommended to Our Beneficence Also Apply to the Order in Which Societies Are Recommended to Our Beneficence

> The same principles that direct the order in which individuals are recommended to our beneficence, direct that likewise in which societies are recommended to it. Those to which it is, or may be of most importance, are first and principally recommended to it. The state or sovereignty in which we have been born and educated, and under the protection of which

[2] Interesting definition because I believe that John Hughes and I had such a friendship. I certainly had a sense of it being "naturally involuntary" and I believe John would have agreed. Indeed, I have even described him as the brother I never had. But neither of us would have thought of these conditions as sufficient for being men of virtue, although I never doubted that John was of incredible virtue grounded in integrity. Moreover, it was not bilateral for it included Stan Reiter, although Stan and I were altogether in agreement that John was the kingpin or pivot of the three-way friendship. (See Smith, Vernon L., A LIFE OF EXPERIMENTAL ECONIMCS, VOLS I AND II; Palgrave Macmillan, 2018).

> we continue to live, is, in ordinary cases, the greatest society upon whose happiness or misery our good or bad conduct can have much influence. It is accordingly by nature most strongly recommended to us. Not only we ourselves, but all the objects of our kindest affections, our children, our parents, our relations, our friends, our benefactors, all those whom we naturally love and revere the most, are commonly comprehended within it; and their prosperity and safety depend, in some measure, upon its prosperity and safety. It is by nature, therefore, endeared to us, not only by all our selfish, but by all our private benevolent affections. Upon account of our own connection with it, its prosperity and glory seem to reflect some sort of honour upon ourselves. When we compare it with other societies of the same kind, we are proud of its superiority, and mortified, in some degree, if it appears in any respect below them. All the illustrious characters which it has produced in former times (for against those of our own times envy sometimes prejudice us a little), its warriors, its statesmen, its poets, its philosophers, and men of letters of all kinds, we are disposed to view with the most partial admiration, and to rank them (sometimes most unjustly) above those of all other nations. The patriot who lays down his life for the safety, or even for the vainglory of this society, appears to act with the most exact propriety. He appears to view himself in the light in which the impartial spectator naturally and necessarily views him, as but one of the multitude, in the eye of that equitable judge, of no more consequence than any other in it, but bound at all times to sacrifice and devote himself to the safety, to the service, and even to the glory, of the greater number. But though this sacrifice appears to be perfectly just and proper, we know how difficult it is to make it, and how few people are capable of making it. His conduct, therefore, excites not only our entire approbation, but our highest wonder and admiration, and seems to merit all the applause which can be due to the most heroic virtue. The traitor, on the contrary, who, in some peculiar situation, fancies he can promote his own little interest by betraying to the public enemy that of his native country; who, regardless of the judgment of the man within the breast, prefers himself, in this respect, so shamefully and so basely, to all those with whom he has any connection, appears to be of all villains the most detestable. (*TMS*, pp. 334–335)

The country in which we were born and educated, that protects us, and in which we continue to live, is in ordinary cases, the greatest society upon whose happiness or misery, our good or bad conduct can have much influence. It is accordingly by nature most strongly recommended to us.

Smith could not have foreseen the immense migration to America and the West from England, Ireland, and his own Scotland in the nineteenth Century, nor its continuance from other regions into the twenty-first century, driven largely by forms of persecution that were not tolerable. Indeed, Smith helped enormously to define the Liberal States to which these migrants would move but neither could he have seen that. These later migrations have maintained the US population in the face of a declining birth rate. The impetus is in people seeing themselves disadvantaged in staying where they were born, often in totalitarian or conflict-torn countries that their citizens come to see as inferior places to raise their children. Or, as with the Ukraine, the migrants remain intensely loyal to their mother country and work to support its independence, thus indicating the truth expressed in *TMS* concerning the order in which societies are to be recommended to their beneficence. Indeed, they honor their heroes, the memory of the loss of citizens they did not know personally, and the places and institutions that reflect their culture. Smith inspired hope and searching for these values for all peoples.

Love of country disposes us to view neighboring countries with jealousy and envy.

> The love of our own nation often disposes us to view, with the most malignant jealousy and envy, the prosperity and aggrandisement of any other neighbouring nation. Independent and neighbouring nations, having no common superior to decide their disputes, all live in continual dread and suspicion of one another. Each sovereign, expecting little justice from his neighbours, is disposed to treat them with as little as he expects from them. The regard for the laws of nations, or for those rules which independent states profess or pretend to think themselves bound to observe in their dealings with one another, is often very little more than mere pretence and profession. From the smallest interest, upon the slightest provocation, we see those rules every day either evaded or directly violated without shame or remorse. Each nation foresees, or imagines it foresees, its own subjugation in the increasing power and aggrandisement of any of its neighbours; and the mean principle of national prejudice is often founded upon the noble one of the love of our own country.…France and England each of them have some reason to dread the increase of the naval and military power of the other; but for either of them to envy the internal happiness and prosperity of the other, the cultivation of its lands, the advancement of its manufactures, the increase of its commerce, the security and number of its ports and harbours, its proficiency in all the liberal arts and sciences, is surely beneath the dignity of two such great nations. These are the real improvements of the world we live in. Mankind are benefited, human nature is ennobled by them. In such improvements each nation ought

> not only to endeavour itself to excel, but, from the love of mankind, to promote, instead of obstructing, the excellence of its neighbours. These are all proper objects of national emulation, not of national prejudice or envy. (*TMS*, pp. 335–336)

The inter-nation jealousy and envy Smith has in mind seem to refer to that among Britain, France, and to a lesser extent Spain, Portugal, and Belgium. Those jealousies made it easier for France to provide naval support for the fledgling new nation in America that had declared its independence from Great Britain. That the French only meant trouble for the British did not make us less beholden to them. In the end we defined a distinct American Liberalism that became the fabric of the American experiment and fueled its emergence elsewhere. Smith supported that experiment which was widely replicated in the West.

The French also came. I had two half sisters that had a French father, thoroughly American, whose brother died in action against WWI Germany.

Love of country does not seem to derive from a larger love of humankind but from our love of country for its own sake.

> The love of our own country seems not to be derived from the love of Humankind. The former sentiment is altogether independent of the latter, and seems sometimes even to dispose us to act inconsistently with it. France may contain, perhaps, near three times the number of inhabitants which Great Britain contains. In the great society of mankind, therefore, the prosperity of France should appear to be an object of much greater importance than that of Great Britain. The British subject, however, who upon that account should prefer upon all occasions the prosperity of the former to that of the latter country, would not be thought a good citizen of Great Britain. We do not love our country merely as a part of the great society of mankind—we love it for its own sake, and independently of any such consideration. That wisdom which contrived the system of human affections, as well as that of every other part of nature, seems to have judged that the interest of the great society of mankind would be best promoted by directing the principal attention of each individual to that particular portion of it which was most within the sphere both of his abilities and of his understanding.
>
> National prejudices and hatreds seldom extend beyond neighbouring nations. We very weakly and foolishly, perhaps, call the French our natural

> enemies; and they, perhaps, as weakly and foolishly consider us in the same manner. Neither they nor we bear any sort of envy to the prosperity of China or Japan. It very rarely happens, however, that our good-will towards such distant countries can be exerted with much effect. (*TMS*, pp. 336–337)

I believe that the model in TMS implies that the origins of our love of country are in our communities, our love for which, arises from our love for our neighbors that grows out of our relationships with each other. Love of country springs from the bottom and ascends to the top. Only this theory explains the robust ability of classical liberal American constitutionalism to overcome adversity and populist excesses on race, gender, and political opinion as we expand ever so naturally our good will toward others. Minority views on race, gender, and sexual orientation have gradually been expanded as enough people agreed to the principle that all people are born free.

Moreover, freedom of choice and its supporting intuitions from Consumer Reports to easy access online investment accounts is the underlying cause of prosperity and poverty reduction.

International peace and tranquility stems from statespersons with sufficient public benevolence to assure the balance of power because that is in accordance with the interest of their respective countries.

> The most extensive public benevolence which can commonly be exerted with any considerable effect is that of the statesmen, who project and form alliances among neighbouring or not very distant nations, for the preservation either of what is called the balance of power, or of the general peace and tranquillity of the states within the circle of their negotiations. The statesmen, however, who plan and execute such treaties, have seldom any thing in view but the interest of their respective countries. Sometimes...their views are more extensive [as with] The Count d'Avaux, the plenipotentiary of France, at the treaty of Munster, would have been willing to sacrifice his life...in order to have restored, by that treaty, the general tranquillity of Europe. King William seems to have had a real zeal for the liberty and independency of the greater part of the sovereign states of Europe; which, perhaps, might be a good deal stimulated by his particular aversion to France, the state from which, during his time, that liberty and independency were principally in danger [and] ... the same

> spirit seems to have descended to the first ministry of Queen Anne. (*TMS*, pp. 337–338)

Smith sees early eighteenth-Century stability in Europe as influenced by the British Monarchs who supported the liberty and independence of the various European states. This was of course the key century for the emergence of Scottish liberal political and economic thought.

The challenge to the stability of a society of greatly diverse orders and powers is to enable each to maintain its privileges against the encroachments of the others.

> Every independent state is divided into many different orders and societies, each of which has its own particular powers, privileges, and immunities. Every individual is naturally more attached to his own particular order or society than to any other. His own interest, his own vanity, the interest and vanity of many of his friends and companions, are commonly a good deal connected with it: he is ambitious to extend its privileges and immunities—he is zealous to defend them against the encroachments of every other order or society.
>
> Upon the manner in which any state is divided into the different orders and societies which compose it, and upon the particular distribution which has been made of their respective powers, privileges, and immunities, depends what is called the constitution of that particular state.
>
> Upon the ability of each particular order or society to maintain its own powers, privileges, and immunities, against the encroachments of every other, depends the stability of that particular constitution. That particular constitution is necessarily more or less altered, whenever any of its subordinate parts is either raised above or depressed below whatever had been its former rank and condition.
>
> All those different orders and societies are dependent upon the state to which they owe their security and protection. That they are all subordinate to that state, and established only in subserviency to its prosperity and preservation, is a truth acknowledged by the most partial member of every one of them. It may often, however, be hard to convince him that the prosperity and preservation of the state require any diminution of the powers, privileges, and immunities of his own particular order or society. This partiality, though it sometimes may be unjust, may not upon that account be useless. It checks the spirit of innovation. It tends to preserve whatever is the established balance among the different orders and societies

> into which the state is divided; and while it sometimes appears to obstruct some alterations of government which may be fashionable and popular at the time, it contributes in reality to the stability and permanency of the whole system. (*TMS*, pp. 338–339)

The security and protection of the different orders of society that compose the state, and to which they are subservient, is acknowledged by their most partial members. Sometimes it is hard to convince them that their powers need to be diminished in the interest of the prosperity and preservation of the state. Their partiality tends to preserve the balance of power among the members and though it appears to obstruct some modifications of government due to popular fashions, it actually contributes to the stability and permanency of the whole system.

I think that what Smith is saying here may have application to current populist movements—black lives matter, WOC (women of color)-rights, critical race theory (CRT; claims that Western society is fundamentally and irreversibly white racist).

These populist waves of fashion which appear, and commonly are intended to be obstructionist, are expressed openly, invite rebuttal, and counteracting arguments that disarm and preserve the permanency of the whole societal system. Each expresses a "truth," if exaggerated and overblown, that bursts on the scene, invokes counterarguments and claims, then fades as new expressions of outrage surface, then fade again. Rapid transmission through social media, the press, and talk shows precipitates rapid responses that peak in clusters, then often suffer correspondingly rapid decay. Dismissively, we used to say: Well, it sells newspapers. It is just ordinary free speech in action. No one has ever claimed that speech must have substance; only the fact of its free expression has substance. And the most prominent institutions are political parties, each of whose presidential and congressional power must be restrained by the other and the courts.

Norman Thomas, the American socialist, six times candidate for president of the United States, for decades the second most popular speaker in America—usually close behind whoever was president—was the most prominent defender of first amendment rights in the American inter-war years. Yet American socialism never achieved a status comparable to that in Europe. American exceptionalism was never socialist and was always based on the right of dissent; even our socialists were committed to and helped to further that principle.

Love of country is manifest in a desire to render the condition of our fellow-citizens as safe, respectable, and happy as we can. It seeks to protect these values in the western liberal tradition based on respect and reverence for the constitutional form of government it helped to establish.

> The love of our country seems, in ordinary cases, to involve in it two different principles; first, a certain respect and reverence for that constitution or form of government which is actually established; and, secondly, an earnest desire to render the condition of our fellow-citizens as safe, respectable, and happy as we can. He is not a citizen who is not disposed to respect the laws and to obey the civil magistrate; and he is certainly not a good citizen who does not wish to promote, by every means in his power, the welfare of the whole society of his fellow-citizens.
> In peaceable and quiet times those two principles generally coincide and lead to the same conduct. The support of the established government seems evidently the best expedient for maintaining the safe, respectable, and happy situation of our fellow-citizens—when we see that this government actually maintains them in that situation. But in times of public discontent, faction, and disorder, those two different principles draw different ways, and even a wise man may be disposed to think some alteration necessary in that constitution or form of government which, in its actual condition, appears plainly unable to maintain the public tranquillity. In such cases, however, it often requires, perhaps, the highest effort of political wisdom to determine when a real patriot ought to support and endeavour to re-establish the authority of the old system, and when he ought to give way to the more daring, but often dangerous, spirit of innovation. (*TMS*, pp. 339–340)

No passages in *TMS* make so plain and transparent Adam Smith's influence on and approval of American and other Western national constitutions. Part VI of *TMS* was entirely new, written and added in the sixth and final edition of *TMS* in 1790 shortly before his death in that year. The Declaration of Independence, the victorious American Revolution, and the American Constitution had all been executed, surely to the quiet, private, elation of Smith who was not prone to ruffle the feathers of the British Administration. He had already pushed the boundaries of that feather-ruffling in the closing pages of *WN* in 1776.

The public spirit is prominently afforded its most splendid opportunity for display in foreign war and civil faction.

> Foreign war and civil faction are the two situations which afford the most splendid opportunities for the display of public spirit. The hero who serves his country successfully in foreign war gratifies the wishes of the whole nation, and is upon that account the object of universal gratitude and admiration. In times of civil discord the leaders of the contending parties, though they may be admired by one-half of their fellow-citizens, are commonly execrated by the other. Their characters, and the merit of their respective services, appear commonly more doubtful. The glory which is acquired by foreign war is, upon this account, almost always more pure and more splendid than that which can be acquired in civil faction.
> The leader of the successful party, however, if he has authority enough to prevail upon his own friends to act with proper temper and moderation (which he frequently has not), sometimes render to his country a service much more essential and important than the greatest victories and the most extensive conquests. He may re-establish and improve the constitution, and from the very doubtful and ambiguous character of the leader of a party, he assume the greatest and noblest of all characters, that of the reformer and legislator of a great state; and, by the wisdom of his institutions, secure the internal tranquillity and happiness of his fellow-citizens for many succeeding generations. (*TMS*, pp. 340–341)

In modern times foreign war has sparked public spirit in their support, as in World War II, but also in opposition, as in World War I and the Vietnam War. Had it not been for the German Submarine attacks on American ships President Wilson might have made good on his promise and desire to keep America out of WWI.

American presidents have routinely failed "to act with proper temper and moderation" although that distinction was associated with Eisenhower, Kennedy, and, I think, Carter who courageously supported the transportation deregulation movement, a great victory for consumers.

Faction mixes with a real spirit of system leading to proposals to achieve imaginary ideals or to re-model the constitution.

> Amidst the turbulence and disorder of faction, a certain spirit of system is apt to mix itself with that public spirit which is founded upon the love of humanity, upon a real fellow-feeling with the inconveniencies and

> distresses to which some of our fellow-citizens may be exposed. This spirit of system commonly takes the direction of that more gentle public spirit, always animates it, and often inflames it, even to the madness of fanaticism. The leaders of the discontented party seldom fail to hold out some plausible plan of reformation, which, they pretend, will not only remove the inconveniencies and relieve the distresses immediately complained of, but will prevent in all time coming any return of the like inconveniencies and distresses. They often propose, upon this account, to new-model the constitution, and to alter in some of its most essential parts that system of government under which the subjects of a great empire have enjoyed, perhaps, peace, security, and even glory, during the course of several centuries together. The great body of the party are commonly intoxicated with the imaginary beauty of this ideal system, of which they have no experience, but which has been represented to them in all the most dazzling colours in which the eloquence of their leaders could paint it. Those leaders themselves, though they originally have meant nothing but their own aggrandizement, become, many of them, in time the dupes of their own sophistry, and are as eager for this great reformation as the weakest and foolishest of their followers. Even though the leaders should have preserved their own heads, as, indeed, they commonly do, free from this fanaticism, yet they dare not always disappoint the expectation of their followers, but are often obliged, though contrary to their principle and their conscience, to act as if they were under the common delusion. The violence of the party refusing all palliatives, all temperaments, all reasonable accommodations, by requiring too much, frequently obtains nothing; and those inconveniencies and distresses which, with a little moderation, might, in a great measure, have been removed and relieved, are left altogether without the hope of a remedy. (*TMS*, pp. 340–342)

Smith's rhetoric reminds me of our sudden withdrawal in 2021 from Afghanistan in a fit of moral outrage over American interventionism. Whatever the merits of better minding our own business in the long view, under American occupancy there had been important advances in women's rights and education that were lost when we suddenly announced our withdrawal without bothering to contact our allies in advance. An impertinent knee-jerk response of great harm.

Picture the political argument that it must be done fast to keep the opposition from gaining steam. The left threw what surely must be its largest constituency, women's rights, under the bus.

Where public spirit is motivated by humanity and benevolence the individual and instiutional orders that constitute the state will command great respect and follow cicero to never do violence to country any more than to parents

> The man whose public spirit is prompted altogether by humanity and benevolence, will respect the established powers and privileges even of individuals, and still more those of the great orders and societies into which the state is divided. Though he should consider some of them as in some measure abusive, he will content himself with moderating, what he often cannot annihilate without great violence. When he cannot conquer the rooted prejudices of the people by reason and persuasion, he will not attempt to subdue them by force, but will religiously observe what by Cicero is justly called the divine maxim of Plato, never to use violence to his country, no more than to his parents. He will accommodate, as well as he can, his public arrangements to the confirmed habits and prejudices of the people, and will remedy, as well as he can, the inconveniencies which flow from the want of those regulations which the people are averse to submit to. When he cannot establish the right, he will not disdain to ameliorate the wrong; but, like Solon, when he cannot establish the best system of laws, he will endeavour to establish the best that the people can bear. (*TMS*, p. 342)

The Cicero principle requires the political leadership and its constituencies to hold very strong characteristics of uncorrupted self-command. I think that is possible but unlikely. The Greeks seem to have executed it tolerably well, but citizenship was restricted and supported economically by a slave class.

Contrarily, the man of system is apt to be wise in his own conceit and ideal plans, imagining that he can arrange the different members of a great society as easily as the hand arranges pieces upon a chess-board with no principles of motion of their own.

> The man of system, on the contrary, is apt to be very wise in his own conceit, and is often so enamoured with the supposed beauty of his own ideal plan of government, that he cannot suffer the smallest deviation from any part of it. He goes on to establish it completely and in all its parts, without any regard either to the great interests or to the strong prejudices which oppose it: he seems to imagine that he can arrange the different members of a great society with as much ease as the hand arranges the different pieces upon a chess-board; he does not consider that the pieces

> upon the chess-board have no other principle of motion besides that which the hand impresses upon them; but that, in the great chess-board of human society, every single piece has a principle of motion of its own, altogether different from that which the legislature might choose to impress upon it. If those two principles coincide and act in the same direction, the game of human society will go on easily and harmoniously, and is very likely to be happy and successful. If they are opposite or different, the game will go on miserably, and the society must be at all times in the highest degree of disorder. (*TMS*, pp. 342–343)

People generally in free societies tend to have their own principles of action and grand private plans for betterment that will succeed or fail to the extent that they are founded or not on bottom-up principles of self- command, justice, and beneficence. People of system in politics hustle votes by supporting fairness in bettering the poorest citizens at the expense of the richest. But markets tend to reward people in accordance with the market value of their contribution, which often seems grossly unfair. [After Harvard's President Claudine Gay was fired amidst charges of plagiarism, she is reported to have continued as a professor at $900,000/year. But her salary pales relative top sport and entertainment figures who earn tens or hundreds of millions based on their market value.] When the reformers cannot establish what is right, let them not disdain to ameliorate what is wrong. A good start is to begin with themselves by being the good they would see in society.

That the state is made for the people and not the other way around is the first principle of statecraft often ignored by the arrogant urge to advance policies despite opposition.

> Some general, and even systematical, idea of the perfection of policy and law, no doubt may be necessary for directing the views of the statesman. But to insist upon establishing, and upon establishing all at once, and in spite of all opposition, every thing which that idea seem to require, must often be the highest degree of arrogance. It is to erect his own judgment into the supreme standard of right and wrong. It is to fancy himself the only wise and worthy man in the commonwealth, and that his fellow-citizens should accommodate themselves to him, and not he to them. It is upon this account that of all political speculators sovereign princes are by far the most dangerous. This arrogance is perfectly familiar to them.

> They entertain no doubt of the immense superiority of their own judgment. When such imperial and royal reformers, therefore, condescend to contemplate the constitution of the country which is committed to their government, they seldom see any thing so wrong in it as the obstructions which it sometimes oppose to the execution of their own will. They hold in contempt the divine maxim of Plato, and consider the state as made for themselves, not themselves for the state. The great object of their reformation, therefore, is to remove those obstructions—to reduce the authority of the nobility—to take away the privileges of cities and provinces, and to render both the greatest individuals and the greatest orders of the state as incapable of opposing their commands as the weakest and most insignificant. (*TMS*, pp. 342–344)

Smith's principle that the state is made for the people rather than that the people are made for the state underlies the Western ideal of government by law rather than government by men. The ideal is perhaps better established in the constitutional, than the political, process and preserves the efforts whereby the bottom-up rules of fair-play justice continue to have power despite all the misguided attempts to reformulate "justice" as top-down rules for the fair distribution of beneficial outcomes. All institutions, including government, serve as tools in the support of, not substitution for, the fair-play rules of neighborly beneficence and of justice that provide security from injury by one citizen acting hurtfully toward another, and in defense from foreign invasion.

Of universal benevolence

Universal beneficence concerns the extent of our good will.

> Though our effectual good offices can very seldom be extended to any wider society than that of our own country, our good will is circumscribed by no boundary, but may embrace the immensity of the universe. We cannot form the idea of any innocent and sensible being whose happiness we should not desire, or to whose misery, when distinctly brought home to the imngination, we should not have some degree of aversion. The idea of a mischievous, though sensible being, indeed naturally provokes our hatred but the ill-will which in this case we bear to it is really the effect of our universal benevolence. It is the effect of the sympathy which we

> feel with the misery and resentment of those other innocent and sensible beings whose happiness is disturbed by its malice." (*TMS*, p. 345)

Good will in substance and extension requires sensibility which unites to surpass all boundaries. Smith asserts, I think insightfully, that we are naturally provoked by the idea of malice by a mischievous though sensible being because of our universal beneficence. Our natural hatred for such a source of ill will is evidence for our universal benevolence.

However noble and generous is the principle of universal benevolence for achieving solid human happiness, without all humans being convinced that it derives from an all-wise being (and not simply a secular form of goodness), the ideal cannot serve the happiness of humankind.

> This universal benevolence, how noble and generous soever, can be the source of no solid happiness to any man who is not thoroughly convinced that all the inhabitants of the universe, the meanest as well as the greatest, are under the immediate care and protection of that great, benevolent, and all-wise Being, who directs all the movements of nature, and who is determined, by his own unalterable perfections, to maintain in it at all times the greatest possible quantity of happiness. To this universal benevolence, on the contrary, the very suspicion of a fatherless world must be the most melancholy of all reflections; from the thought that all the unknown regions of infinite and incomprehensible space be filled with nothing but endless misery and wretchedness. All the splendour of the highest prosperity can never enlighten the gloom with which so dreadful an idea must necessarily overshadow the imagination; nor, in a wise and virtuous man, can all the sorrow of the most afflicting adversity ever dry up the joy which necessarily springs from the habitual and thorough conviction of the truth of the contrary system.
>
> The wise and virtuous man is at all times willing that his own private interest should be sacrificed to the public interest of his own particular order or society. He is at all times willing, too, that the interest of this order or society should be sacrificed to the greater interest of the state or sovereignty of which it is only a subordinate part: he should, therefore, be equally willing that all those inferior interests should be sacrificed to the greater interest of the universe, to the interest of that great society of all sensible and intelligent beings, of which God himself is the immediate administrator and director. If he is deeply impressed with the habitual and

> thorough conviction that this benevolent and all-wise Being can admit into the system of his government no partial evil which is not necessary for the universal good, he must consider all the misfortunes which befall himself, his friends, his society, or his country, as necessary for the prosperity of the universe, and, therefore, as what he ought not only to submit to with resignation, but as what he himself, if he had known all the connections and dependencies of things, ought sincerely and devoutly to have wished for. (*TMS*, pp. 345–346)

I find this assertion by Smith not very Smithian. Elsewhere, in this book, I have been reasonably interpreting Smith's model of society, founded on the discovery of experienced-based rules, as the means whereby humans learn through the Great Author of Nature how to implement God's aspirations for His people. But in this passage Smith appears to want to make plain his belief that there can be no universal benevolence, however generous, that can be a source of solid human happiness for any person who does not personally believe that all rational creatures from meanest to greatest are under the care and protection of an all-wise Being determined to maintain the greatest amount of happiness. A statement in which Smith allows no quarter for free-will learning through experience, an open system not tightly closed by a God who manages every detail. Perhaps this is because for Smith there can be no design without a designer. But then, Adam Ferguson's claim that society is created out "the products of human action but not human design" is not at the foundation of a spontaneous order but a made order by an all-wise God. There is no right path found by experiential free will, subject to error, when all must believe the contrary and know by unquestioning faith that He is in charge. Is it significant that Smith saw no reason to modify this in his 1790 sixth and final edition? Considering all his other passages it may simply be an overlooked anomaly. Otherwise, how can we find deep meaning in the text: "Enter ye in at the strait gate: for wide is the gate, and broad is the way, that leadeth to destruction, and many there be which go in thereat: because strait is the gate, and narrow is the way, which leadeth unto life, and few there be that find it" (Matthew 7:13–14; KJV).

As with good soldiers who follow their trusted general, the magnanimous desire to follow the will of the great director of our universe is not beyond the reach of nature.

> Nor does this magnanimous resignation to the will of the great Director of the universe seem in any respect beyond the reach of human nature. Good soldiers, who both love and trust their general, frequently march with more gaiety and alacrity to the forlorn station, from which they never expect to return, than they would to one where there was neither difficulty nor danger. In marching to the latter, they could feel no other sentiment than that of the dulness of ordinary duty—in marching to the former, they feel that they are making the noblest exertion which it is possible for man to make. They know that their general would not have ordered them upon this station had it not been necessary for the safety of the army, for the success of the war: they cheerfully sacrifice their own little systems to the prosperity of a greater system: they take an affectionate leave of their comrades, to whom they wish all happiness and success, and march out, not only with submissive obedience, but often with shouts of the most joyful exultation, to that fatal but splendid and honourable station to which they are appointed. No conductor of any army can deserve more unlimited trust, more ardent and zealous affection, than the great Conductor of the universe. In the greatest public as well as private disasters, a wise man ought to consider that he himself, his friends and countrymen, have only been ordered upon the forlorn station of the universe; that had it not been necessary for the good of the whole, they would not have been so ordered; and that it is their duty, not only with humble resignation to submit to this allotment, but to endeavour to embrace it with alacrity and joy. A wise man should surely be capable of doing what a good soldier holds himself at all times in readiness to do. (*TMS*, pp. 346–347)

Smith sees our magnanimous desire to follow the will of God as manifest in nature as within our power because we are nature's product. In this we are like the good soldiers who follow their good general, knowing that he has our interest at heart. Nature is simply the means whereby we know and follow God.

But in the previous passage it seems essential that every follower believe that all others believe the same, which is that God's-will not their will is in control.

The care of the happiness of humankind is in the divine, the business of god. to humans are allotted their own happiness.

> The idea of that divine Being, whose benevolence and wisdom have from all eternity contrived and conducted the immense machine of the universe so as at all times to produce the greatest possible quantity of happiness, is certainly, of all the objects of human contemplation, by far the most sublime. Every other thought necessarily appears mean in the comparison. The man whom we believe to be principally occupied in this sublime contemplation, seldom fails to be the object of our highest veneration; and though his life should be altogether contemplative, we often regard him with a sort of religious respect, much superior to that with which we look upon the most active and useful servant of the commonwealth. The meditations of Marcus Antoninus, which turn principally upon this subject, have contributed more, perhaps, to the general admiration of his character than all the different transactions of his just, merciful, and beneficent reign.
> The administration of the great system of the universe, however, the care of the universal happiness of all rational and sensible beings, is the business of God, and not of man. To man is allotted a much humbler department, but one much more suitable to the weakness of his powers, and to the narrowness of his comprehension—the care of his own happiness, of that of his family, his friends, his country: that he is occupied in contemplating the more sublime, can never be an excuse for his neglecting the more humble department; and he must not expose himself to the charge which Avidius Cassius is said to have brought, perhaps unjustly, against Marcus Antoninus, that while he employed himself in philosophical speculations, and contemplated the prosperity of the universe, he neglected that of the Roman empire. The most sublime speculation of the contemplative philosopher can scarce compensate the neglect of the smallest active duty. (*TMS*, pp. 347–348)

And thus can we say that Adam Smith—a profoundly religious man—declared that we ought to render to humans duties appropriate to their limited capability—"the care of his own happiness, of that of his family, his friends, his country"—and to God the management of the great universe and "the care of the universal happiness of all rational and sensible beings."

After Smith's discourse on the respective duties and division of responsibility between the Great Author of the Universe and humankind, he enters the articulation of his most important practicing virtue of humankind: self-command; our authority and dominion over ourselves. If self-command fails, we, and all our noblest hopes of avoiding subjugation, fail, whatever our other professed or claimed virtues. Self-command is the fount of bottom-up, inside out, classical liberal society and economy. They who seek security through involuntary transfers from the acquisitions of others, thus violating their freedom, will discover that freedom and security are complements, not substitutes.

Smith has prominently called our attention to the two pillars of society, beneficence, and justice, of which justice is the more important. But self-command deserves to be considered the third pillar of society because it is essential to the internal regulation and effectiveness of the first two.

CHAPTER 36

Of self-command

They who act in accordance with the rules of perfect justice, prudence, and of proper benevolence are said to be virtuous.

The man who acts according to the rules of perfect prudence, of strict justice, and of proper benevolence, may be said to be perfectly virtuous. But the most perfect knowledge of those rules will not alone enable him to act in this manner; his own passions are very apt to mislead him—sometimes to drive him, and sometimes to seduce him, to violate all the rules which he himself, in all his sober and cool hours, approves of. The most perfect knowledge, if it is not supported by the most perfect self-command, will not always enable him to do his duty.

Some of the best of the ancient moralists seem to have considered those passions as divided into two different classes; first, into those which it requires a considerable exertion of self-command to restrain even for a single moment; and, secondly, into those which it is easy to restrain for a single moment, or even for a short period of time; but which, by their continual and almost incessant solicitations, are, in the course of a life, very apt to mislead into great deviations.

Fear and anger, together with some other passions which are mixed or connected with them, constitute the first class. The love of ease, of pleasure, of applause, and of many other selfish gratifications, constitute the second. Extravagant fear and furious anger [are] … often difficult to restrain even for a single moment. The love of ease, of pleasure, of applause, and other selfish gratifications, it is always easy to restrain for a

Vernon L. Smith, *Adam Smith's Theory of Society*,
https://doi.org/10.1007/978-3-031-68494-4_36

> single moment, or even for a short period of time; but, by their continual solicitations, they often mislead us into many weaknesses which we have afterwards much reason to be ashamed of. The former set of passions often may be said to drive, the latter to seduce, us from our duty. The command of the former was, by the ancient moralists above alluded to, denominated fortitude, manhood, and strength of mind; that of the latter, temperance, decency, modesty, and moderation.
> The command of [i.e., control over] each of those two sets of passions…according to the dictates of prudence, of justice, and of proper benevolence, has a beauty of its own, and seems to deserve, for its own sake, a certain degree of esteem and admiration. In the one case, the strength and greatness of the exertion excites some degree of that esteem and admiration; in the other, the uniformity, the equality, and unremitting steadiness, of that exertion. (*TMS*, pp. 349–350)

Perfect knowledge of the rules of beneficence and justice is insufficient for choosing the perfectly virtuous right actions. We must also have perfect self-command. How are fear and anger expressed in the modern world wherein popular political policies intervene in attempts to redistribute income from the haves to the have nots, as defined for example by, and in contradiction to, the Parable of the Talents (Matthew 25:14–30; KJV)? Hence, fear is driven by the ancient feeling that one has not been given their due, in comparison with others who have received their due, perhaps even in excess; a feeling that can arise from envy, but that modern's always express as being "unfair" since people are uniformly allergic to the idea that their attitude toward others might be in any way envious. A central source of disharmony, it was directly addressed in the Lord's Prayer…"And forgive us our trespasses, as we forgive them that trespass against us." (Matthew 6:12; NMB).

Our respect and admiration for the virtue of self-command is revealed, Smith believes, in our sense of its beauty as a stand-alone virtue and expressed in the next entry.

We greatly admire those who, facing unusual danger and death, maintain their composure and act with heroism and sacrifice.

> The man who, in danger, in torture, upon the approach of death, preserves his tranquillity unaltered, and suffers no word, no gesture, to escape him which does not perfectly accord with the feelings of the most indifferent spectator, necessarily commands a very high degree of admiration. If he

> suffers in the cause of liberty and justice, for the sake of humanity and the love of his country, the most tender compassion for his sufferings, the strongest indignation against the injustice of his persecutors, the warmest sympathetic gratitude for his beneficent intentions, the highest sense of his merit, all join and mix themselves with the admiration of his magnanimity, and often inflame that sentiment into the most enthusiastic and rapturous veneration. The heroes of ancient and modern history, who are remembered with the most peculiar favour and affection, are many of them those who, in the cause of truth, liberty, and justice, have perished upon the scaffold, and who behaved there with that ease and dignity which became them. Had the enemies of Socrates suffered him to die quietly in his bed, the glory even of that great philosopher might possibly never have acquired that dazzling splendour in which it has been beheld in all succeeding ages. In the English history, when we look over the illustrious heads which have been engraven by Vertue and Howbraken, there is scarce any body, I imagine, who does not feel that the axe, the emblem of having been beheaded, which is engraved under some of the most illustrious of them—under those of the Sir Thomas Mores, of the Raleighs, the Russels, the Sydneys, &c.—sheds a real dignity and interestingness over the characters to which it is affixed, much superior to what they can derive from all the futile ornaments of heraldry with which they are sometimes accompanied. Nor does this magnanimity give lustre only to the characters of innocent and virtuous men. It draws some degree of favourable regard even upon those of the greatest criminals; and when a robber or highwayman is brought to the scaffold, and behaves there with decency and firmness, though we perfectly approve of his punishment, we often cannot help regretting that a man who possessed such great and noble powers should have been capable of such mean enormities. (*TMS*, pp. 350–351).

Inordinately admired are the heroes of truth, liberty, and justice, who died on the scaffold yielding no quarter for the enemies of these virtues. Smith was keen on the heroes who were instrumental in overturning Britain's long history of suppression. What eventually ruled was the idea, once implanted, *that there was a higher power than the king that resided in the people*. This idea is expressed in the American constitution in Amendment IX: "The enumeration in the constitution of certain rights shall not be construed to deny or disparage others retained by the people." This amendment effectively declares that the constitution is an open document subject to the formal recognition of new rights that emerge in the practices of the people. Historically, these have included the explicit recognition of the rights of blacks, women, gays, and the LGBT +. *TMS* was important in articulating the case for liberty, which Smith followed-on so magnificently in *WN* with his theorems on the foundation of wealth creation and human betterment which his Mercantile cronies so badly misunderstood.

From the great school of war we learn that death, the king of terrors, can be overcome.

> War is the great school both for acquiring and exercising this species of magnanimity. Death, as we say, is the king of terrors; and the man who has conquered the fear of death is not likely to lose his presence of mind at the approach of any other natural evil. In war, men become familiar with death, and are thereby necessarily cured of that superstitious horror with which it is viewed by the weak and unexperienced. They consider it merely as the loss of life, and as no further the object of aversion than as life happen to be that of desire: they learn from experience, too, that many seemingly great dangers are not so great as they appear; and that with courage, activity, and presence of mind, there is often a good probability of extricating themselves, with honour, from situations where at first they could see no hope. The dread of death is thus greatly diminished, and the confidence or hope of escaping it augmented. They learn to expose themselves to danger with less reluctance; they are less anxious to get out of it, and less apt to lose their presence of mind while they are in it. It is this habitual contempt of danger and death which ennobles the profession of a soldier, and bestows upon it, in the natural apprehensions of mankind, a rank and dignity superior to that of any other profession. The skilful and successful exercise of this profession in the service of their country seems to have constituted the most distinguishing feature in the character of the favourite heroes of all ages.
>
> A great warlike exploit, though undertaken contrary to every principle of justice, and carried on without any regard to humanity, sometimes interests us, and commands even some degree of a certain sort of esteem for the very worthless characters which conduct it. We are interested even in the exploits of the Buccaneers, and read with some sort of esteem and admiration the history of the most worth less men, who, in pursuit of the most criminal purposes, endured greater hardships, surmounted greater difficulties, and encountered greater dangers, than perhaps any which the ordinary course of history gives an account of. (*TMS*, pp. 351–352)

Thus, do we make heroes of the ruffian lawbreaker—Robin Hood of Norwood—who satisfies out thirst for vigilante justice against those we fancy as too nimble for prosecutorial justice, with friends enough in high places, and revealed ever more in theater, screen, and the TV serial. And if all else fails we have faith that in death they who do real evil will find punishment, while they who do real good will find reward.

Anger is at least as important as fear in providing motivation and may properly express just indignation. Otherwise, anger is disagreeable.

> The command of anger appears, upon many occasions, not less generous and noble than that of fear. The proper expression of just indignation composes many of the most splendid and admired passages both of ancient and modern eloquence. The Philippics of Demosthenes, the Catilinarians of Cicero, derive their whole beauty from the noble propriety with which this passion is expressed. But this just indignation is nothing but anger restrained and properly attempered to what the impartial spectator can enter into. The blustering and noisy passion which goes beyond this is always odious and offensive, and interests us, not for the angry man, but for the man with whom he is angry. The nobleness of pardoning appears, upon many occasions, superior even to the most perfect propriety of resenting. When either proper acknowledgments have been made by the offending party, or, even without any such acknowledgments, when the public interest requires that the most mortal enemies should unite for the discharge of some important duty, the man who can cast away all animosity, and act with confidence and cordiality towards the person who had most grievously offended him, seems justly to merit our highest admiration.
>
> The command of anger, however, does not always appear in such splendid colours. Fear is contrary to anger, and is often the motive which restrains it; and, in such cases, the meanness of the motive takes away all the nobleness of the restraint. Anger prompts to attack, and the indulgence of it seems sometimes to shew a sort of courage and superiority to fear. The indulgence of anger is sometimes an object of vanity; that of fear never is. Vain and weak men, among their inferiors, or those who dare not resist them, often affect to be ostentatiously passionate, and fancy that they shew what is called spirit in being so. A bully tells many stories of his own insolence, which are not true, and imagines that he thereby renders himself, if not more amiable and respectable, at least more formidable to his audience. Modern manners which, by favouring the practice of dueling, may be said in some cases to encourage private revenge, contribute, perhaps, a good deal to render, in modern times, the restraint of anger by fear still more contemptible than it might otherwise appear to be. There is always

> something dignified in the command of fear, whatever may be the motive upon which it is founded. It is not so with the command of anger; unless it is founded altogether in the sense of decency, of dignity, and propriety, it never is perfectly agreeable. (*TMS*, pp. 352–354)

Anger sometimes may be no less noble than fear—for just indignation can find its expression in anger.

Just indignation may manifest simply as anger restrained.

Fear is contrary to anger, and often the motive which restrains it, but the meanness of the motive takes away all the nobleness of the restraint.

The indulgence of anger is sometimes an object of vanity; that of fear never is.

Something that isn't mentioned in *TMS* is that anger badly needs control if it is not to become part of an irreversible escalation in negative reciprocity.

Action governed by prudent self-command in cool deliberation of justice and beneficence is to act most expeditiously and completely in the interest of society.

> To act according to the dictates of prudence, of justice, and proper beneficence, seems to have no great merit where there is no temptation to do otherwise. But to act with cool deliberation in the midst of the greatest dangers and difficulties; to observe religiously the sacred rules of justice, in spite both of the greatest interests which might tempt and the greatest injuries which might provoke us to violate them; never to suffer the benevolence of our temper to be damped or discouraged by the malignity and ingratitude of the individuals towards whom it have been exercised, is the character of the most exalted wisdom and virtue. Self-command is not only itself a great virtue, but from it all the other virtues seem to derive their principal lustre.
>
> The command of fear, the command of anger, are always great and noble powers. When they are directed by justice and benevolence, they are not only great virtues, but increase the splendour of those other virtues. They, however, sometimes may be directed by very different motives; and in this case, though still great and respectable, they may be excessively dangerous. The most intrepid valour may be employed in the cause of the greatest injustice. Amidst great provocations, apparent tranquillity and good-humour sometimes conceal the most determined and cruel resolution to revenge. The strength of mind requisite for such dissimulation, though always and necessarily contaminated by the baseness of

falsehood, has, however, been often much admired by many people of no contemptible judgment.... When law has become...impotent, when the most perfect innocence cannot alone insure safety, regard to self-defence obliges the greater part of men to have recourse to dexterity, to address, and to apparent accommodation to whatever happens to be at the moment the prevailing party. This false character, too, is frequently accompanied with the coolest and most determined courage. The proper exercise of it imposes that courage, as death is commonly the certain consequence of detection. It may be employed indifferently, either to exasperate or to allay those furious animosities of adverse factions which impose the necessity of assuming it; and though it sometimes may be useful, it is at least equally liable to be excessively pernicious. (*TMS*, pp. 354–355)

The commands of fear and anger may be great and noble powers but become virtues only when they are directed by justice and benevolence, which in turn depend upon self-command for proper implementation.

It is from the unremitting steadiness of the gentler virtues of temperance, decency, modesty, and moderation that self-command enables these virtues to avoid misdirection and abuse.

The command of the less violent and turbulent passions seems much less liable to be abused to any pernicious purpose. Temperance, decency, modesty, and moderation, are always amiable, and can seldom be directed to any bad end. It is from the unremitting steadiness of those gentler exertions of self-command that the amiable virtue of chastity, that the respectable virtues of industry and frugality, derive all that sober lustre which attends them. The conduct of all those who are contented to walk in the humble paths of private and peaceable life, derives from the same principle the greater part of the beauty and grace which belong to it; a beauty and grace which, though much less dazzling, is not always less pleasing than those which accompany the more splendid actions of the hero, the statesman, or the legislator. (*TMS*, pp. 355–356)

The conduct of all those who are content to walk in the humble paths of the private, peaceable life, derive a beauty and grace from that content that they will find no less pleasing than the more dazzling actions of the hero, statesman, or legislator.

Again, notice that these amiable passions constitute the dominion of ordinary people. Society may produce elites and paragons of virtue, but its substance is in the ordinary because that is where life is experienced.

Propriety is defined by the intensity or "degree" of expressed passion which may be excessive or deficient. For propriety, pleasant and agreeable passions allow higher intensities of passion than unpleasant and disagreeable passions.

> [T]he point of propriety, the degree of any passion which the impartial spectator approves of, is differently situated in different passions…It may be laid down as a general rule, that the passions which the spectator is most disposed to sympathize with, and in which, upon that account, the point of propriety may be said to stand high, are those of which the immediate feeling or sensation is more or less agreeable to the person principally concerned; and that, on the contrary, the passions which the spectator is least disposed to sympathize with, and in which, upon that account, the point of propriety may be said to stand low, are those of which the immediate feeling or sensation is more or less disagreeable, or even painful, to the person principally concerned. This general rule, so far as I have been able to observe, admits not of a single exception. A few examples will at once both sufficiently explain it and demonstrate the truth of it.
>
> The disposition to the affections which tend to unite men in society, to humanity, kindness, natural affection, friendship, esteem, may sometimes be excessive. Even the excess of this disposition, however, renders a man interesting to every body. Though we blame it, we still regard it with compassion, and even with kindness, and never with dislike. We are more sorry for it than angry at it. To the person himself, the indulgence even of such excessive affections is, upon many occasions, not only agreeable but delicious. Upon some occasions, indeed, especially when directed, as is too often the case, towards unworthy objects, it exposes him to much real and heartfelt distress. Even upon such occasions, however, a well-disposed mind regards him with the most exquisite pity, and feels the highest indignation against those who affect to despise him for his weakness and imprudence. The defect of this disposition, on the contrary, what is called hardness of heart, while it renders a man insensible to the feelings and distresses of other people, renders other people equally insensible to his; and, by excluding him from the friendship of all the world, excludes him from the best and most comfortable of all social enjoyments.
>
> The disposition to the affections which drive men from one another, and which tend, as it were, to break the bands of human society; the disposition to anger, hatred, envy, malice, revenge, is, on the contrary, much more apt to offend by its excess than by its defect. The excess renders a man wretched and miserable in his own mind, and the object of hatred, and sometimes even of horror, to other people. The defect is very seldom

> complained of. It may, however, be defective. The want of proper indignation is a most essential defect in the manly character, and, upon many occasions, renders a man incapable of protecting either himself or his friends from insult and injustice. Even that principle, in the excess and improper direction of which consists the odious and detestable passion of envy, may be defective. Envy is that passion which views with malignant dislike the superiority of those who are really entitled to all the superiority they possess. The man, however, who, in matters of consequence, tamely suffers other people, who are entitled to no such superiority, to rise above him or get before him, is justly condemned as mean-spirited. This weakness is commonly founded in indolence, sometimes in good-nature, in an aversion to opposition, to bustle and solicitation, and sometimes, too, in a sort of ill-judged magnanimity, which fancies that it can always continue to despise the advantage which it then despises, and therefore so easily gives up. Such weakness, however, is commonly followed by much regret and repentance; and what had some appearance of magnanimity in the beginning, frequently gives place to a most malignant envy in the end, and to a hatred of that superiority which those who have once attained it often become really entitled to, by the very circumstance of having attained it. In order to live comfortably in the world, it is upon all occasions as necessary to defend our dignity and rank, as it is to defend our life or our fortune. (*TMS*, pp. 356–358)

The intensity of the passion that people express in given circumstances may be judged excessive, deficient, or neither, by the impartial spectator. The level of expression of a passion and its associated action, where the passion is pleasant and agreeable to those affected, raises the level which is in proper propriety, while unpleasant and disagreeable passion lower the accepted standard for what is considered in proper propriety.

As evidence Smith cites our tendency to tolerate excesses in the affections that unite people in society to the virtues of humanity, kindness, natural affection, friendship, and esteem. Though we find blame in its excesses, "we still regard it with compassion, and even with kindness, and never with dislike." Oppositely, "The affections of anger, hatred, envy, malice, revenge, are, contrastingly, much more likely to offend by its excess than by its defect."

TMS has much to say about envy, a much-avoided topic today which invites us to a study in contrasts in candor. In *TMS*, envy views with malignant dislike the superiority of those who are really entitled to all the superiority they possess. Envy may be an emotion that accounts for persistent concerns for the disparity between rich and poor, described euphemistically as "unfair," although poverty has been enormously reduced by growth and innovation in free societies. A lingering but persistent belief is that somehow the poor are poor because there are rich people, a proposition that has far more credibility in authoritarian than in free societies. But the complaint finds a hearing in the latter, outright rejection in the former. I think most world-aware people would much prefer being born, even if in disadvantaged circumstances, into a free society than into any of the authoritarian others. The evidence is in the Berlin wall to keep people in, and Trump's proposed wall to keep people out. Republicans want no discussion of liberalizing immigration until the wall is finished; Democrats want no wall to be finished in fear that it would preclude liberalizing immigration.

People's sensitivity to personal danger and distress is much more likely to offend by its excess than its defect. We admire as "masculine" the facing of danger with tranquility, and possible death with composure and intrepidity.

> Our sensibility to personal danger and distress, like that to personal provocation, is much more apt to offend by its excess than by its defect. No character is more contemptible than that of a coward—no character is more admired than that of the man who faces death with intrepidity, and maintains his tranquillity and presence of mind amidst the most dreadful dangers. We esteem the man who supports pain and even torture with manhood and firmness; and we can have little regard for him who sinks under them, and abandons himself to useless outcries and womanish lamentations. A fretful temper, which feels with too much sensibility every little cross accident, renders a man miserable in himself and offensive to other people. A calm one, which does not allow its tranquillity to be disturbed, either by the small injuries or by the little disasters incident to the usual course of human affairs, but which, amidst the natural and moral evils infesting the world, lays its account and is contented to suffer a little from both, is a blessing to the man himself, and gives ease and security to all his companions. (*TMS*, pp. 358–359)

The expression of excess sensibility to fear and danger is displeasing to us—none admires a coward. Nor the fretful who complains of every small discomfort. The opposite, wherein danger is met with composure and even heroism, is universally admired and honored. Calmness begets calmness in a world with more than enough evil to go around.

This powerful proposition in *TMS*—despising cowardice and complaining about matters of small consequence—still has legs in contemporary society which is under attack. The popularity of no-one-is-better-then-anyone-else WOC-doctrine of guilt-attacks on people whose ancestors were obviously racist or sexist bears witness to the urge to feel better by demeaning everybody and seeking credibility by dumping manure on yourself as well as all others. What most have seen as markers of persistent progress in the face of only a few voices of small complaints is now elevated to proof of a corrupt and corrupting society. How ironic that the exact same theme in *TMS*, wherein we "humble the arrogance of our self-love to bring it down" to what others will go along with, is the foundation of human sociality and stable orderly society. In Smith the process emerges bottom-up, based on self-command, and defines the voluntary norms that make us free. The "WOC" proposes to determine policies that impose new top-down norms on all citizens through the universities, teachers in the primary and secondary schools, as well as government—a cultural takeover in the culture war.

It is unlikely to last, because it has no foundation in a self-sustaining bottom-up rule making and following process. Liberalism's slow transformation process is claimed to be proof of its failure and the need for revolutionary replacement with a new order. This is a standard populist attack on certain consequences of the expansion of freedom, recurrent throughout our history, e.g., southern laws requiring discrimination against blacks after they were emancipated and even began voting for a time after the civil war.

The greatest love, respect, and admiration is reserved for the person within the breast whose self-command properly reflects dignity and propriety of conduct.

> Steady in our sensibility, however, both to our own injuries and to our own misfortunes, though generally too strong, likewise may be too weak. The man who feels little for his own misfortunes must always feel less for those of other people, and may be less disposed to relieve them. The man who has little resentment for the injuries which are done to himself, must always have less for those which are done to other people, and be less disposed either to protect or to avenge them. A stupid insensibility to the events of human life necessarily extinguishes all that keen and earnest attention to the propriety of our own conduct, which constitutes the real essence of virtue. We can feel little anxiety about the propriety of our own

actions when we are indifferent about the events which result from them. The man who feels the full distress of the calamity which has befallen him, who feels the whole baseness of the injustice which has been done to him, but who feels still more strongly what the dignity of his own character requires; who does not abandon himself to the guidance of the undisciplined passions which his situation might naturally inspire; but who governs his whole behaviour and conduct according to those restrained and corrected emotions which the great inmate, the great demigod within the breast prescribes and approves of; is alone the real man of virtue, the only real and proper object of love, respect, and admiration. Insensibility and that noble firmness, that exalted self-command, which is founded in the sense of dignity and propriety, are so far from being altogether the same, that in proportion as the former takes place, the merit of the latter is in many cases entirely taken away. (*TMS*, pp. 358–360)

The person of dignity and propriety of conduct, the person who feels fully the cost of their own calamities, and the injustice done to them, but who still more strongly feel what the dignity of their own character requires, who do not abandon themselves to the undisciplined passions inspired by their immediate circumstances, and whose self-command restrains, filters, and enhances their conduct, constitutes the real person of virtue.

The development of self-command may be challenged by want of sensibility to injury, danger, and distress; also, by an excess. Foreign war and domestic faction are the great spurs to self-command.

[T]hough the total want of sensibility to personal injury, to personal danger and distress, would, in such situations, take away the whole merit of self-command, that sensibility, however, may very easily be too exquisite, and it frequently is so. When the sense of propriety, when the authority of the judge within the breast, can control this extreme sensibility, that authority must no doubt appear very noble and very great. But the exertion of it may be too fatiguing—it may have too much to do. The individual, by a great effort, may behave perfectly well; but the contest between the two principles, the warfare within the breast, may be too violent to be at all consistent with internal tranquillity and happiness. The wise man whom nature has endowed with this too exquisite sensibility, and whose too lively feelings have not been sufficiently blunted and hardened by early education and proper exercise, will avoid, as much as duty and propriety will permit, the situations for which he is not perfectly fitted. The man whose feeble and delicate constitution renders him too sensible to pain, to

> hardship, and to every sort of bodily distress, should not wantonly embrace the profession of a soldier. The man of too much sensibility to injury should not rashly engage in the contests of faction. Though the sense of propriety should be strong enough to command all those sensibilities, the composure of the mind must always be disturbed in the struggle. In this disorder the judgment cannot always maintain its ordinary acuteness and precision; and though he always may mean to act properly, he often may act rashly and imprudently, and in a manner which he himself will, in the succeeding part of his life, be for ever ashamed of. A certain intrepidity, a certain firmness of nerves and hardiness of constitution, whether natural or acquired, are undoubtedly the best preparatives for all the great exertions of self-command. (*TMS*, pp. 360–361)

Those naturally endowed with unusual sensibility, whose too lively feelings have not yet been hardened by trials will avoid situations beyond their fit capacity. Those whose delicate constitution make them too sensible to pain, to hardship, and to every sort of physical distress, should not be professional soldiers, or contest in factions. While the sense of propriety should be strong enough to command all those sensibilities, the mind must always be disturbed by the struggle. In this ordeal, one's precision of judgment may suffer; and though one may intend proper action, rashness of action may be followed by regret. A certain intrepidity, firmness, and hardiness of constitution, whether natural or acquired, are undoubtedly the best preparations for all the great exertions of self-command.

The day of trial must not come prior to the schools of war and faction.

> Though war and faction are certainly the best schools for forming…hardiness and firmness of temper, though they are the best remedies for curing him of the opposite weaknesses, yet if the day of trial should happen to come before he has completely learned his lesson…the consequences might not be agreeable.
>
> Our sensibility to the pleasures…amusements and enjoyments of human life, offend ... either by its excess or by its defect ... [but] the excess seems less disagreeable than the defect…a strong propensity to joy is certainly more pleasing than a dull insensibility to the objects of amusement and diversion…what is chiefly to be found fault with is not so much the strength of the propensity to joy as the weakness of the sense of propriety and duty.. (*TMS*, pp. 361–362)

What is chiefly to be found at fault is not so much the strength of the propensity to joy, but the weakness of the sense of propriety and duty. Proper preparation must precede exposure to real trials. But some trials may be beyond any capacity for preparation. It is hard to imagine how anyone can be prepared for the ravages of today's recognition of wartime post-traumatic stress disorder.

Although it is agreeable to think highly, and disagreeable to think meanly, of ourselves, to others and the fair and impartial spectator, the defect must always be less disagreeable than that for any excess of agreeableness.

> The principle of self-estimation may be too high, and it may likewise be too low. It is so very agreeable to think highly, and so very disagreeable to think meanly, of ourselves, that to the person himself it cannot well be doubted but that some degree of excess must be much less disagreeable than any degree of defect. But to the impartial spectator it may perhaps be thought things must appear quite differently, and that to him the defect must always be less disagreeable than the excess. And in our companions, no doubt, we much more frequently complain of the latter than of the former. When they assume upon us, or set themselves before us, their self-estimation mortifies our own. Our own pride and vanity prompt us to accuse them of pride and vanity, and we cease to be the impartial spectators of their conduct. When the same companions, however, suffer any other man to assume over them a superiority which does not belong to him, we not only blame them, but often despise them as mean-spirited. When, on the contrary, among other people they push themselves a little more forward, and scramble to an elevation disproportioned, as we think, to their merit, though we may not perfectly approve of their conduct, we are often upon the whole diverted with it; and where there is no envy in the case, we are almost always much less displeased with them than we should have been had they suffered themselves to sink below their proper station. (*TMS*, p. 362)

Smith's complexity of conditional and interpersonal opinion here is hard to follow so let me attempt a rephrasing to see if you think I have him right: Some degree of excess in our own vanity is surely less disagreeable to us than a deficiency. But to others and to the impartial spectator, our deficiency must always be less disagreeable and more tolerable than our excess. In our companions, however, we are more likely to complain of an excess than a deficiency in their vanity. But if the same companions allow any other person to assume an unjustified superiority over them, we may blame and even despise them for it. When, on the contrary, among others, such people push themselves above their merit, though we may not entirely approve of their conduct, we are often diverted with it. If there is no envy in the case, we are almost always much less displeased with them than we should have been had they suffered themselves a little less vain in their own self-estimation.

When evaluating our own merit, character, and conduct, there are two standards: one of perfect propriety where we are always deficient, and one relative to the level that others commonly attain in the world where we may exceed or be deficient.

> In estimating our own merit, in judging of our own character and conduct, there are two different standards to which we naturally compare them. The one is the idea of exact propriety and perfection, so far as we are each of us capable of comprehending that idea. The other is that degree of approximation to this idea which is commonly attained in the world, and which the greater part of our friends and companions, of our rivals and competitors, may have actually arrived at. We very seldom (I am disposed to think we never) attempt to judge ourselves without giving more or less attention to both these different standards. But the attention of different men, and even of the same man at different times, is often very unequally divided between them, and is sometimes principally directed toward the one, and sometimes toward the other.
>
> So far as our attention is directed toward the first standard, the wisest and best of us all can, in his own character and conduct, see nothing but weakness and imperfection; can discover no ground for arrogance and presumption, but a great deal for humility, regret, and repentance. So far as our attention is directed toward the second, we may be affected either in the one way or in the other, and feel ourselves either really above or really below the standard to which we compare ourselves.
>
> The wise and virtuous man directs his principal attention to the first standard—the idea of exact propriety and perfection. There exists in the mind of every man an idea of this kind, gradually formed from his observations upon the character and conduct both of himself and of other people. It is the slow, gradual, and progressive work of the great demigod within the breast, the great judge and arbiter of conduct. This idea is in every man more or less accurately drawn, its coloring is more or less just, its outlines are more or less exactly designed, according to the delicacy and acuteness of that sensibility with which those observations were made, and according

> to the care and attention employed in making them. In the wise and virtuous man they have been made with the most acute and delicate sensibility, and the utmost care and attention have been employed in making them. Every day some feature is improved—every day some blemish is corrected. He has studied this idea more than other people; he comprehends it more distinctly; he has formed a much more correct image of it, and is much more deeply enamored of its exquisite and divine beauty: he endeavors as well as he can to assimilate his own character to this archetype of perfection. But he imitates the work of a divine artist, which can never be equalled. He feels the imperfect success of all his best endeavors, and sees, with grief and affliction, in how many different features the mortal copy falls short of the immortal original: he remembers, with concern and humiliation, how often, from want of attention, from want of judgment, from want of temper, he has, both in words and actions, both in conduct and conversation, violated the exact rules of perfect propriety, and has so far departed from that model, according to which he wished to fashion his own character and conduct. When he directs his attention toward the second standard, indeed, that degree of excellence which his friends and acquaintances have commonly arrived at, he may be sensible of his own superiority; but as his principal attention is always directed toward the first standard, he is necessarily much more humbled by the one comparison than he ever can be elevated by the other. He is never so elated as to look down with insolence even upon those who are really below him: he feels so well his own imperfection, he knows so well the difficulty with which he attained his own distant approximation to rectitude, that he cannot regard with contempt the still greater imperfection of other people. Far from insulting over their inferiority, he views it with the most indulgent commiseration, and, by his advice as well as example, is at all times willing to promote their further advancement. If in any particular qualification they happen to be superior to him (for who is so perfect as not to have many superiors in many different qualifications?) far from envying their superiority, he who knows how difficult it is to excel, esteems and honours their excellence, and never fails to bestow upon it the full measure of applause which it deserves. His whole mind, in short, is deeply impressed, his whole behaviour and deportment are distinctly stamped with the character of real modesty; with that of a very moderate estimation of his own merit, and, at the same time, of a full sense of the merit of other people. (*TMS*, pp. 362–365).

In evaluating our own merit, or judging our character, and conduct, we sometimes use an ideal or perfect standard and at other times a practical standard much like that which has been attained by friends and companions. When ranking our character and conduct against the ideal of perfection the wisest and best of us all can imagine only weakness and imperfection finding no basis for arrogance and presumption, and much room for humility, regret, and repentance. When ranking ourselves using practical standards we feel ourselves either above or below that which is commonly attainable.

The wise and virtuous person directs their principal attention to the idea of exact propriety and perfection, an idea that has gradually formed from their observations upon the character and conduct both of themselves and of other people. This ideal is a conception that emerges within the breast as a slow, gradual, and progressive work, of the great judge and arbiter of conduct. This idea in every person is more or less accurately drawn, is more or less just, its outlines are more or less exactly designed, and according to the care and attention employed in making them. In the wise and virtuous person, they reflect the utmost care and attention employed in forming them. Each day a feature is improved, a blemish is corrected. They have studied and comprehended it more distinctly than others and being more enamored of its beauty than others they endeavor to adapt their own character to this archetype of perfection.

When ranking companions with respect to practical standards of attainment of our companions we have a sense of being superior but are much more humbled by their achievements, than we are elevated by their deficiency, and eagerly promote their advancement. If in some respect, another is indeed superior to us, they who know how difficult it is to excel applaud their deserved attainments.

Great liberal artists feel the real imperfection of their own best work; the inferior artist, satisfied with their own performance, compares their work with those below them.

> In all the liberal and ingenious arts, in painting, in poetry, in music, in eloquence, in philosophy, the great artist feels always the real imperfection of his own best works, and is more sensible ... how much they fall short of that ideal perfection of which he has formed some conception, which he imitates as well as he can, but which he despairs of ever equalling. It is the inferior artist only who is ever perfectly satisfied with his own performances...and it is chiefly to the works of other artists, of ... lower order, that he ... compare[s] his own works... The artist sits down to

> his work undisturbed, at leisure, in…all his skill, experience, and knowledge. The wise man must support…the propriety…of his own conduct in health…sickness…success… disappointment, in the hour of fatigue and drowsy indolence, as well as in that of the most awakened attention..The injustice of other people must never provoke him to injustice. The violence of faction must never confound him. All the hardships and hazards of war must never either dishearten or appall him. (*TMS*, pp. 365–366)

Undisturbed, the artist sits down to their work, at leisure in their skill, experience, and knowledge. The wise person supports the propriety of their own conduct in all stages of success and disappointment, and when attention is most focused. Injustice by other people must never provoke them to injustice; faction must never confound them; the hardships and hazards of war must never dishearten or appall them.

People estimating their own merit direct their attention to the ordinary attainment of others but some justly feel themselves above this and are generally acknowledged so. They have little sense of their own weaknesses.

> Of the persons who, in estimating their own merit,…character and conduct, direct by far the greater part of their attention…to that ordinary degree of excellence which is commonly attained by other people, there are some who really and justly feel themselves very much above it, and who, by every intelligent and impartial spectator, are acknowledged to be so. The attention of such persons, however, being always principally directed, not to the standard of ideal, but to that of ordinary, perfection, they have little sense of their own weaknesses and imperfections; they have little modesty; are often assuming, arrogant, and presumptuous; great admirers of themselves, and great contemners of other people. Though their characters are in general much less correct, and their merit much inferior to that of the man of real and modest virtue, yet their excessive presumption, founded upon their own excessive self-admiration, dazzles the multitude, and often imposes even upon those who are much superior to the multitude. The frequent, and often wonderful, success of the most ignorant quacks and impostors, both civil and religious, sufficiently demonstrate how easily the multitude are imposed upon by…extravagant and groundless pretensions. But when those pretensions are supported by a very high degree of real and solid merit, when they are displayed with all the splendour which ostentation can bestow upon them, when they are supported by high rank and great power, when they have often been successfully exerted, and are upon

> that account attended by the loud acclamations of the multitude, even the man of sober judgment often abandons himself to the general admiration. The...foolish acclamations...confound his understanding; and while he sees those great men only at a certain distance, he is often disposed to worship them with a sincere admiration, superior even to that with which they appear to worship themselves. When there is no envy in the case we all take pleasure in admiring, and are...naturally disposed...to render complete and perfect...the characters which, in many respects, are so very worthy of admiration. The excessive self-admiration of those great men is well understood, perhaps, and even seen...with some degree of derision, by those wise men who are much in their familiarity...with reverence, and almost with adoration. Such, however, have been in all ages the greater part of those men who have procured to themselves the most noisy fame, the most extensive reputation—a fame and reputation, too, which have often descended to the remotest posterity. (*TMS*, pp. 366–367)

If there is no envy in the case, we find pleasure in admiring people of great and complete perfection and accomplishment. We understand their excessive self-admiration, and accept the derision expressed toward some of them by people of discernment but who revere and adore them.

The self-important have been in all ages the greater part of those individuals who have procured to themselves the noisiest fame, the most extensive reputation—a fame and reputation that extends to the remotest posterity.

In writing this book, I have come to see myself privileged in finding wisdom in the works of Adam Smith that seem to be not part of the conventional understanding. I believe I have found methodological uniqueness. If that is an unjustified illusion, other scholars will suspect it, come to know it, and my error will be revealed. If it is justified, it will be examined and surely found wanting in some respect.

Self-admiration accompanies great success and authority.

> Great success in the world, great authority...have very seldom been acquired without some degree of this excessive self-admiration. The most splendid characters, the men who have performed the most illustrious actions...in the situations and opinions of mankind; the most successful warriors, the greatest statesmen and legislators, the eloquent founders and leaders of...sects and parties; have many of them been not more distinguished for their very great merit than for a degree of presumption and self-admiration altogether disproportioned..to that...merit. This

> presumption was, perhaps, necessary not only to prompt them to undertakings...(others)...would never have thought of, but to command the submission and obedience of their followers...When crowned with success, accordingly, this presumption has often betrayed them into a vanity that approached almost to insanity and folly. Alexander the Great appears not only to have wished that other people should think him a god, but to have been at least very well disposed to fancy himself such. The sound head of Cæsar was not so perfectly sound as to hinder him from being much pleased with his divine genealogy from the goddess Venus; and...to receive, without rising from his seat, the Roman senate...that...present him with some decrees conferring upon him the most extravagant honours...The religion and manners of modern times give our great men little encouragement to fancy themselves either gods or even prophets. Success, however, joined to great popular favour, has often so far turned the heads of the greatest of them, as to make them ascribe to themselves both an importance and an ability much beyond what they really possessed; and...to precipitate themselves into many rash and sometimes ruinous adventures...(*TMS*, pp. 367–369)

Great success in the world and great authority are seldom acquired without some accompanying measure of self-admiration, which if not a cause, then is a consequence of their success. The egocentricity of the successful helps to drive, or derives from, their accomplishments. "When crowned with success, accordingly, this presumption has often betrayed them into a vanity that approached almost to insanity and folly." One is reminded of so many contemporary politicians and the challenge of how to vote when you have two of them bucking head-to-head and there is no lesser of the two evils that can relieve your quandary.

Great abilities and ambitions encourage individual enterprises that succeed or fail and often colorblinds our respect for them.

> In the humble projects of private life, as well as in the ambitious and proud pursuits of high stations, great abilities and successful enterprise in the beginning, have frequently encouraged to undertakings which necessarily led to bankruptcy and ruin in the end.
>
> The esteem and admiration which every impartial spectator conceives for the real merit of those spirited, magnanimous, and high-minded persons, as it is a just and well-founded sentiment, so it is a steady and permanent one, and altogether independent of their good or bad fortune. It is otherwise

with that admiration which he is apt to conceive for their excessive self-estimation and presumption. While they are successful, indeed, he is often perfectly conquered and overborne by them. Success covers from his eyes, not only the great imprudence, but frequently the great injustice, of their enterprises; and, far from blaming this defective part of their character, he often views it with the most enthusiastic admiration. When they are unfortunate, however, things change their colours and their names. What was before heroic magnanimity, resumes its proper appellation of extravagant rashness and folly...Had Cæsar instead of gaining, lost the battle of Pharsalia, his character would at this hour have ranked a little above that of Catiline, and the weakest man would have viewed his enterprise against the laws of his country in blacker colours than perhaps even Cato...Fortune has...great influence over the moral sentiments of mankind, and, according as she is either favourable or adverse, can render the same character the object either of general love and admiration or of universal hatred and contempt. This great disorder in our moral sentiments is by no means, however, without its utility; and we on this, as well as on many other occasions, admire the wisdom of God, even in the weakness and folly of man. Our admiration of success is founded upon the same principle with our respect for wealth and greatness, and is equally necessary for establishing the distinction of ranks and the order of society. By this admiration of success we are taught to submit more easily to those superiors whom the course of human affairs assign to us; to regard with reverence, and sometimes even with a sort of respectful affection, that fortunate violence which we are no longer capable of resisting; not only the violence of such splendid characters as those of a Cæsar or an Alexander, but often that of the most brutal and savage barbarians, of an Attila, a Gengis, or a Tamerlane. To all such mighty conquerors the great mob of mankind are naturally disposed to look up with a wondering, though no doubt with a very and foolish admiration. By this admiration, however, they are taught to acquiesce with less reluctance under that government which an irresistible force imposes upon them, and from which no reluctance could deliver them. (*TMS*, pp. 369–371)

Fortune influences the moral sentiments of humankind depending upon whether she is favorable or adverse, rendering the same character either loveable or hate-able. Such disorder in our morality is not without its utility in serving to inspire our admiration for the Wisdom of God. We admire success on the same principle that we respect wealth and greatness, and that establishes the distinction of ranks, and the order of society. With such admiration we follow more easily those superiors whom we regard with reverence. We even may be less resistant to the violence they sometimes champion. Mighty conquerors are looked upon by the great mob of humankind with wonder and foolish admiration. By this admiration, unfortunately, they are taught to acquiesce with less reluctance to a government which an irresistible force imposes upon them, and from which no reluctance could deliver them.

Excessive self-estimation viewed at a distance gives perspective favoring the person who rests content in the truth of their own character.

> Though in prosperity...the man of excessive self-estimation sometimes appear to have some advantage over the man of correct and modest virtue; though the applause of the multitude, and of those who see them both only at a distance, is often much louder in favour of the one than...the other; yet, all things fairly computed, the real balance of advantage is perhaps...in favour of the latter and against the former. The man who neither ascribes to himself, nor wishes that other people should ascribe to him, any other merit besides that which really belongs to him, fears no humiliation, dreads no detection, but rests contented and secure upon the genuine truth and solidity of his own character. His admirers may neither be very numerous nor very loud in their applauses; but the wisest man who sees him the nearest, and who knows him the best, admires him the most. To a real wise man, the judicious and well-weighed approbation of a single wise man gives more heartfelt satisfaction than all the noisy applauses of ten thousand ignorant though enthusiastic admirers...(*TMS*, pp. 371–372)

People who neither ascribes to themselves, nor wish that other people should ascribe to them any other merit besides that which really belongs to them, fear no humiliation, dread no detection, and rest peacefully content and secure upon the genuine truth and solidity of their own character. Their admirers may be neither very numerous nor loud in their applause but the wisest person, who sees them the nearest, knows them best, and admires them the most. To receive the judicious approbation of a single wise person gives more heartfelt satisfaction than the noisy applause of ten thousand ignorant but enthusiastic admirers.

Amidst the intoxication of prosperity just esteem is regarded as mere magnanimity and envy.

> The wise men who see ... [the man of excessive self-admiration] the nearest admire him the least. Amidst the intoxication of prosperity, their sober and just esteem falls so far short of the extravagance of his own self-admiration, that he regards it as mere malignity and envy. He suspects his best friends; their company becomes offensive to him; he drives them from his presence; and often rewards their services not only with ingratitude but with cruelty and injustice: he abandons his confidence to flatterers and traitors, who pretend to indolize his vanity and presumption; and that character which in the beginning, though in some respects defective, was upon the whole both amiable and respectable, becomes contemptible and odious in the end. Amidst the intoxication of prosperity Alexander killed Clytus for having preferred the exploits of his father Philip to his own...The humble, admiring, and flattering friends, whom Alexander left in power and authority behind him, divided his empire among themselves, and after having thus robbed his family and kindred of their inheritance, put one after another every single surviving individual of them, whether male or female, to death. (*TMS*, pp. 372–373)

For those of extravagant self-admiration any just and sober evaluation is dismissed as envious. They suspect their best friends, whose company becomes offensive, driving them from their presence, and often reward their services with ingratitude, or even cruelty and injustice, abandoning them in favor of flatterers who appeal to their vanity and presumption.

We easily sympathize with the excessive self-estimation of those who project great superiority.

> We frequently not only pardon but thoroughly enter into and sympathize with the excessive self-estimation of those splendid characters in which we observe a great and distinguished superiority above the common level of mankind. We call them spirited, magnanimous, and high-minded—words which all involve in their meaning a considerable degree of praise and admiration. But we cannot enter into and sympathize with the excessive self-estimation of those characters in which we can discern no such distinguished superiority...We call it pride or vanity—two words of which the latter always, and the former for the most part, involve...blame. (*TMS*, p. 373)

We sympathize with the excessive self-admiration of those who we perceive as successful. Nor can we sympathize with the excessive self-admiration of those we perceive as achieving no superiority of success who are said to indulge their pride and vanity for which we find cause for blame. This accounts for the attitudes of people toward presidents like Trump, Nixon, Johnson, FDR...

Pride differs from vanity although both are expressive of excessive self-admiration.

> Those two vices [pride and vanity], however, though resembling ... modifications of excessive self-estimation, are yet in many respects very different from one another.
> The proud man is sincere, and in the bottom of his heart is convinced of his own superiority; though it sometimes may be difficult to guess upon what that conviction is founded. He wishes you to view him in no other light than that in which, when he places himself in your situation, he really views himself: he demands no more of you than what he thinks justice. If you appear not to respect him as he respects himself, he is more offended than mortified, and feels the same indignant resentment as if he had suffered a real injury. He does not even then...explain the grounds of his own pretensions: he disdains to court your esteem: he affects even to despise it, and endeavours to maintain his assumed station, not so much by making you sensible of his superiority as of your own meanness: he seems to wish not so much to excite your esteem for himself as to mortify that for yourself. (*TMS*, pp. 373–374)

The proud person is sincere, genuinely convinced of their superiority (though you may struggle to figure out why). They wish others to see them as they see themselves and are offended if this is not so. Nor do they then explain themselves, preferring rather to not court the esteem of such people, and attributing any failure to their meanness. They depend and rely upon those enemies.

The person of vanity is not sincere and is seldom convinced of the superiority that they wish others to ascribe to them.

> The vain man is not sincere, and, in the bottom of his heart, is very seldom convinced of that superiority which he wishes you to ascribe to him. He wishes you to view him in much more splendid colours than those in which, when he places himself in your situation, and supposes you to know all that he knows, he can really view himself. When you appear to view him, therefore, in different colours, perhaps in his proper colours, he is much more mortified than offended. The grounds of his claim to that

> character which he wishes you to ascribe to him he takes every opportunity of displaying, both by the most ostentatious and unnecessary exhibition of the good qualities and accomplishments which he possesses in some tolerable degree, and sometimes even by false pretensions to those which he either possesses in no degree, or in so very slender a degree that he well enough may be said to possess them in no degree. Far from despising your esteem, he courts it with the most anxious assiduity. Far from wishing to mortify your self-estimation, he is happy to cherish it, in hopes that in return you will cherish his own. He flatters in order to be flattered: he studies to please, and endeavours to bribe you into a good opinion of him by politeness and complaisance, and sometimes even by real and essential good offices, though often displayed, perhaps, with unnecessary ostentation. (*TMS*, pp. 274–275)

The vain person wishes you to view them in much more splendid colors than those in which, when they place themselves in your situation, and suppose you to know all that they know, they can really view themselves. When you seem to view them in more modest colors, they are much more mortified than offended. Far from despising your esteem, they court it with the most anxious assiduity. Far from wishing to mortify your self-estimation, they are happy to cherish it, hoping that in return you will cherish their own. They flatter in order to be flattered; they study to please, endeavoring to buy your good opinion of them by politeness and complaisance, and, if real, by displaying unnecessary ostentation.

Vain persons seek in their dress, equipage, and way of living a higher attainment of rank and fortune than really belongs to them.

> The vain man sees the respect which is paid to rank and fortune, and wishes to usurp this respect, as well as that for talents and virtues. His dress, his equipage, his way of living, accordingly, all announce both a higher rank and a greater fortune than really belong to him; and in order to support this foolish imposition for a few years in the beginning of his life, he often reduces himself to poverty and distress long before the end of it. As long as he can continue his expense, however, his vanity is delighted with viewing himself, not in the light in which you would view him if you knew all that he knows, but in that in which he imagines he has by his own address induced you actually to view him. Of all the illusions of vanity, this is perhaps the most common. Obscure strangers who visit foreign countries, or who, from a remote province, come to visit for a short time the capital of their own country, most frequently attempt to practise it. The folly

> of the attempt, though always very great, and most unworthy of a man of sense, may not be altogether so great upon such as upon most other occasions. If their stay is short, they escape any disgraceful detection; and, after indulging their vanity for a few months or a few years, they return to their own homes, and repair by future parsimony the waste of their past profusion. (*TMS*, p. 275)

As long as the vain person can maintain the expenses of a high rank and fortune, their vanity is delighted with viewing themselves, not in the light in which you would view them if you knew all that they know, but in that in which they imagine they have by their own address induced you actually to view them. This is surely the most common of all the illusions of vanity.

The proud person can seldom be accused of the folly of the illusions of vanity.

> The proud man can very seldom be accused of this folly. His sense of his own dignity renders him careful to preserve his independency, and, when his fortune happens not to be large, though he wishes to be decent, he studies to be frugal and attentive in all his expenses. The ostentatious expense of the vain man is highly offensive to him. It outshines, perhaps, his own. It provokes his indignation as an insolent assumption of a rank which is by no means due; and he never talks of it without loading it with the harshest and severest reproaches. (*TMS*, pp. 275–276)

The proud person's sense of dignity motivates them to independence. If their fortune is not large, they are frugal, finding offensive the ostentatious expense of the vain person's attempt to attain a rank unjustified by their performance. Pride cannot maintain itself in conjunction with the illusion of vanity.

The proud person feels ill at ease with their equals, still more ill at ease with their superiors, and seeks a humbler company.

> The proud man does not always feel himself at his ease in the company of his equals, and still less in that of his superiors. He cannot lay down his lofty pretensions, and the countenance and conversation of such company overawe him so much that he dare not display them: he has recourse to humbler company, for which he has little respect, which he would not willingly choose, and which is by no means agreeable to him—that of his

> inferiors, his flatterers, and dependants: he seldom visits his superiors, or if he does, it is rather to shew that he is entitled to live in such company than for any real satisfaction that he enjoys in it. It is, as Lord Clarendon says of the Earl of Arundel, that he sometimes went to court because he could there only find a greater man than himself; but that he went very seldom, because he found there a greater man than himself.

The proud person, unable to lay down their lofty pretensions, avoids the company of their superiors, and feeling over-awed by them, seeks humbler inferiors and dependents.

The vain person courts the company of superiors as much as the proud person avoids them.

> It is quite otherwise with the vain man. He courts the company of his superiors as much as the proud man shuns it. Their splendour, he seems to think, reflects a splendour upon those who are much about them. He haunts the courts of kings and the levees of ministers, and gives himself the air of being a candidate for fortune and preferment, when in reality he possesses the much more precious happiness, if he knew how to enjoy it, of not being one: he is fond of being admitted to the tables of the great, and still more fond of magnifying to other people the familiarity with which he is honoured there: he associates himself as much as he can with fashionable people, with those who are supposed to direct the public opinion—with the witty, with the learned, with the popular; and he shuns the company of his best friends, whenever the very uncertain current of public favour happens to run in any respect against them. With the people to whom he wishes to recommend himself he is not always very delicate about the means which he employs for that purpose; unnecessary ostentation, groundless pretensions, constant assentation, frequently flattery, though for the most part a pleasant and a sprightly flattery, and very seldom the gross and fulsome flattery of a parasite. The proud man, on the contrary, never flatters, and is frequently scarce civil to any body. (*TMS*, pp. 376–377)

The vain person haunts the courts of kings and the hangouts of ministers projecting an air of being a candidate of fortune and preferment, when in reality they would possess more precious happiness, if they knew how to enjoy not being one. They are fond of being admitted to the tables of the great and of advertising it widely to others. They seek association with the fashionable, the public opinion makers, the witty, the learned, the popular, and are quick to shun friends if public favor happens to run against those friends. Their flattery is frequent, pleasant, and sprightly, very seldom that of the gross and fulsome parasite.

In contrast the proud person never flatters and indeed is often scarce civil to anybody.

But vanity is almost always sprightly, gay, and a good-natured passion; pride is always a grave, sullen and severe passion.

> Notwithstanding all its groundless pretensions, however, vanity is almost always a sprightly and a gay, and very often a good-natured passion; pride is always a grave, a sullen, and a severe one. Even the falsehoods of the vain man are all innocent falsehoods, meant to raise himself, not to lower other people. To do the proud man justice, he very seldom stoops to the baseness of falsehood. When he does, however, his falsehoods are by no means so innocent. They are all mischievous, and meant to lower other people. He is full of indignation at the unjust superiority, as he thinks it, which is given to them: he views them with malignity and envy, and in talking of them often endeavours as much as he can to extenuate and lessen whatever are the grounds upon which their superiority is supposed to be founded. Whatever tales are circulated to their disadvantage, though he seldom forges them himself, yet he often takes pleasure in believing them, is by no means unwilling to repeat them, and even sometimes with some degree of exaggeration. The worst falsehoods of vanity are all what we call white lies; those of pride, whenever it condescends to falsehood, are all of the opposite complexion. (*TMS*, p. 377)

Even the falsehoods of the vain are innocent falsehoods, intended to raise themselves not denigrate others. In justice to the prideful, they seldom stoop to falsehood and if they do, the falsehoods are not innocent, but mischievous, and meant to lower other people. Pride is indignant at any unjust superiority given to others, and they would strive to lessen it by undermining the grounds for superiority.

Our dislike of pride and vanity disposes us to rank them below others but in this we are frequently wrong.

> Our dislike to pride and vanity generally disposes us to rank the persons whom we accuse of those vices rather below than above the common level. In this judgment, however, I think we are most frequently in the wrong, and that both the proud and the vain man are often (perhaps for the most

part) a good deal above it; though not near so much as either the one really thinks himself, or as the other wishes you to think him. If we compare them with their own pretensions, they appear the just objects of contempt. But when we compare them with what the greater part of their rivals and competitors really are, they appear quite otherwise, and very much above the common level. Where there is this real superiority, pride is frequently attended with many respectable virtues—with truth, with integrity, with a high sense of honour, with cordial and steady friendship, with the most inflexible firmness and resolution; vanity with many amiable ones—with humanity, with politeness, with a desire to oblige in all little matters, and sometimes with a real generosity in great ones—a generosity, however, which it often wishes to display in the most splendid colours that it can. By their rivals and enemies, the French in the last century were accused of vanity; the Spaniards of pride, and foreign nations were disposed to consider the one as the more amiable, the other as the more respectable people. (*TMS*, p. 378)

Smith believes our tendency to dislike the vain and the proud, and to rank them below the desirable personal attributes of others, is a wrongful evaluation. Compared with their own pretensions they are contemptible, the vain rank not nearly so high as they think of themselves, and the proud rank not so high as they wish you to think of them. However, when the proud person is truly superior, the pride is frequently attended with many respectable virtues—truth, integrity, a high sense of honor, with cordial and steady friendship, with the most inflexible firmness and resolution. When vanity is attended with real superiority it is accompanied by humanity, politeness, and a desire to oblige in all little matters, and sometimes with a real generosity.

Vain and vanity are words that always have negative connotations; proud and pride on the contrary are more positive.

The words vain and vanity are never taken in a good sense. We sometimes say of a man, when we are talking of him in good-humour, that he is the better for his vanity, or that his vanity is more diverting than offensive; but we still consider it as a foible and a ridicule in his character.

The words proud and pride, on the contrary, are sometimes taken in a good sense. We frequently say of a man that he is too proud, or that he has too much noble pride, ever to suffer himself to do a mean thing. Pride is in this case confounded with magnanimity. Aristotle, a philosopher who certainly knew the world, in drawing the character of the magnanimous

> man, paints him with many features which, in the two last centuries, were commonly ascribed to the Spanish character; that he was deliberate in all his resolutions; slow and even tardy in all his actions; that his voice was grave, his speech deliberate, his step and motion slow; that he appeared indolent and even slothful, not at all disposed to bustle about little matters, but to act with the most determined and vigorous resolution upon all great and illustrious occasions; that he was not a lover of danger, or forward to expose himself to little dangers, but to great dangers; and that, when he exposed himself to danger, he was altogether regardless of his life. (*TMS*, pp. 378–379)

Contrary to the negativity associated with words like "vain" and "vanity", "proud" and "pride" express nobleness and magnanimity. In qualifying our judgment of the vain person, we may speak of them as the better for their vanity, or that their vanity is more diverting than offensive. But pride is often taken in a good sense. We say of the proud person that they are too prideful to do anything mean. The proud are often among the heroic, willing to expose themselves to great danger.

The proud person feels self-sufficient and beyond improvement. The vain seeks superiority, believing only that they have it before it is due.

> The proud man is commonly too well contented with himself to think that his character requires any amendment. The man who feels himself all-perfect naturally enough despises all further improvement. His self-sufficiency and absurd conceit of his own superiority commonly attend him from his youth to his most advanced age; and he dies, as Hamlet says, with all his sins upon his head, unanointed, unanealed.
>
> It is frequently quite otherwise with the vain man. The desire of the esteem and admiration of other people, when for qualities and talents which are the natural and proper objects of esteem and admiration, is the real love of true glory—a passion which, if not the very best passion of human nature, is certainly one of the best. Vanity is very frequently no more than an attempt prematurely to usurp that glory before it is due. Though your son under five-and-twenty years of age should be but a coxcomb, do not upon that account despair of his becoming before he is forty a very wise and worthy man, and a real proficient in all those talents and virtues to which at present he only may be an ostentatious and empty pretender. The great secret of education is to direct vanity to proper objects. Never suffer him to value himself upon trivial accomplishments; but do not always discourage his pretensions to those that are of real importance. He would not pretend

> to them if he did not earnestly desire to possess them. Encourage this desire; afford him every means to facilitate the acquisition; and do not take take too much offence although he should sometimes assume the air of having attained it a little before the time. (*TMS*, pp. 379–380)

The proud person is so well contented with themselves that any notion of an amendment of character is beyond their consideration. They who feel themselves all-perfect naturally will despise all further improvement. Their self-sufficiency and the absurd conceit of their own superiority often accompanies them from youth to advanced age and, as Shakespeare's Hamlet says, he dies with all his sins upon his head, unanointed, and unannealed. And thus, pride is the greatest and deadliest of the seven sins. And metaphorically it is why the Pontius Pilates' of this world are still washing their hands, and the Judas's still suffer from pain and small ambition—having neither pride, nor vanity.

But it is the desire for the esteem and admiration of other people that is the object of the real love of true glory—a passion which, if not the very best passion of human nature, is certainly one of the best. Vanity is very frequently no more than a premature attempt to usurp that glory before it is due.

Therefore, seek esteem and admiration justified by your own deeds. There will be ample opportunity in ere. Better to make your own mistakes than plagiarize those of others.

But the proud person is often vain, and the vain person is often proud.

> Such, I say, are the distinguishing characteristics of pride and vanity, when each of them acts according to its proper character. But the proud man is often vain; and the vain man is often proud. Nothing can be more natural than that the man who thinks much more highly of himself than he deserves should wish that other people should think still more highly of him; or that the man who wishes that other people should think more highly of him than he thinks of himself should, at the same time, think much more highly of himself than he deserves. Those two vices being frequently blended in the same character, the characteristics of both are necessarily confounded; and we sometimes find the superficial and impertinent ostentation of vanity joined to the most malignant and derisive insolence of pride. We are sometimes upon that account at a loss how

> to rank a particular character, or whether to place it among the proud or among the vain. (*TMS*, p. 380)

Nothing can be more natural than that they who think much more highly of themselves than they deserve should wish that other people should think still more highly of them; or that they who wish that other people should think more highly of themselves than they think themselves should, at the same time, think much more highly of themselves than they deserve.

Thus confounded, we sometimes find the superficial and impertinent ostentation of vanity joined to the most malignant and derisive insolence of pride and are at a loss as to rank a particular character, as either proud or among the vain.

Some people of merit underrate and others overrate themselves; though not very dignified they are far from disagreeable.

> Such characters, though not very dignified, are often in private society far from being disagreeable. His companions all feel themselves much at their ease in the society of a man so perfectly modest and unassuming. If those companions, however, have not both more discernment and more generosity than ordinary, though they have some kindness for him they have seldom much respect; and the warmth of their kindness is very seldom sufficient to compensate the coldness of their respect. Men of no more than ordinary discernment never rate any person higher than he appears to rate himself. He seems doubtful himself, they say, whether he is perfectly fit for such a situation or such an office, and immediately give the preference to some impudent blockhead who entertains no doubt about his own qualifications. Though they should have discernment, yet, if they want generosity, they never fail to take advantage of his simplicity, and to assume over him an impertinent superiority which they are by no means entitled to. His good nature enable him to bear this for some time; but he grows weary at last, and frequently when it is too late, and when that rank which he ought to have assumed is lost irrecoverably, and usurped, in consequence of his own backwardness, by some of his more forward, though much less meritorious, companions. A man of this character must have been very fortunate in the early choice of his companions if, in going through the world, he meets always with fair justice even from those whom, from his own past kindness, he might have some reason to consider as his best friends; and a youth, too unassuming and to unambitious, is frequently

followed by an insignificant, complaining, and discontented old age. (*TMS*, pp. 380–381)

The companions of one who modestly underrates their own performance feel at ease in the society of a person so modest and unassuming. If the person is both more discerning and more generous than ordinary, they seldom earn much respect. People of ordinary discernment never rate any person higher than they appear to rate themselves, saying that such a person seems doubtful for such an office, and immediately give the preference to some impudent blockhead who entertains no doubt about his own qualifications. Though they should have discernment, if they want generosity, they never fail to take advantage of the simplicity of such people, whose good nature enable them to bear this for some time, but weakness sets in, and their proper rank is lost irrecoverably and usurped by some who are much less meritorious—an impudent blockhead who entertains no doubt about his own qualifications.[1]

The lowly rated sometimes rate themselves still lower and sink into idiotism, but idiots often are capable of being educated.

Those unfortunate persons whom nature has formed a good deal below the common level, seem sometimes to rate themselves still more below it than they really are. This humility appears sometimes to sink them into idiotism. Whoever has taken the trouble to examine idiots with attention, will find that in many of them the faculties of the understanding are by no means weaker than in several other people, who, though acknowledged to be dull and stupid, are not by any body accounted idiots. Many idiots, with no more than ordinary education, have been taught to read, write, and account tolerably well. Many persons, never accounted idiots, notwithstanding the most careful education, and notwithstanding that in their advanced age they have had spirit enough to attempt to learn what their early education had not taught them, have never been able to acquire, in any tolerable degree, any one of those three accomplishments. By an instinct of pride, however, they set themselves upon a level with their equals in age and situation, and, with courage and firmness, maintain their proper station among their companions. By an opposite instinct the idiot

[1] Smith surely has in mind his distinguished god-natured friend David Hume whose integrity and skepticism combined to provide opposition to his ever receiving a university appointment (surely made to many a "blockhead" of lesser accomplishments).

> feels himself below every company into which you can introduce him. Ill usage, to which he is extremely liable, is capable of throwing him into the most violent fits of rage and fury. But no good usage, no kindness or indulgence, can ever raise him to converse with you as your equal. If you can bring him to converse with you at all, however, you will frequently find his answers sufficiently pertinent and even sensible. But they are always stamped with a distinct consciousness of his own great inferiority.
> He seems to shrink, and, as it were, to retire from your look and conversation, and to feel when he places himself in your situation, that, notwithstanding your apparent condescension, you cannot help considering him as immensely below you. Some idiots, perhaps the greater part, seem to be so chiefly or altogether, from a certain numbness or torpidity in the faculties of the understanding. But there are others in whom those faculties do not appear more torpid or benumbed than in many other people who are not accounted idiots. But that instinct of pride, necessary to support them upon an equality with their brethren, seems totally wanting in the former, and not in the latter. (*TMS*, pp. 381–382)

According to Smith's observations, many who are accounted idiots are capable of education and can learn to read and write. But the idiot feels himself below every company into which you can introduce him. Ill treatment to which he is extremely liable, can throw him into the most violent fits of rage and fury. But no kindness or indulgence, can ever raise him to converse with you as your equal. If you can bring him to converse with you at all, however, you will frequently find his answers entirely pertinent and even sensible. But they are always stamped with a distinct consciousness of his own great inferiority.

That degree of self-estimation which contributes most to the happiness and contentment of a person seems likewise most agreeable to the impartial spectator.

> That degree of self-estimation, therefore, which contributes most to the happiness and contentment of the person himself, seems likewise most agreeable to the impartial spectator. The man who esteems himself as he ought, and no more than he ought, seldom fails to obtain from other people all the esteem that he himself thinks due. He desires no more than is due to him, and he rests upon it with complete satisfaction.
> The proud and the vain man, on the contrary, are constantly dissatisfied. The one is tormented with indignation at the unjust superiority, as he thinks it, of other people; the other is in continual dread of the

> shame which he foresees would attend upon the detection of his groundless pretensions. Even the extravagant pretensions of the man of real magnanimity, though, when supported by splendid abilities and virtues, and, above all, by good fortune, they impose upon the multitude, whose applauses he little regards, do not impose upon those wise men whose approbation he can only value, and whose esteem he is most anxious to acquire. He feels that they see through, and suspects that they despise, his excessive presumption; and he often suffers the cruel misfortune of becoming, first the jealous and secret, and at last the open, furious, and vindictive enemy of those very persons whose friendship it would have given him the greatest happiness to enjoy with unsuspicious security. (*TMS*, pp. 382–383)

The person who esteems themselves as they ought, and no more than they ought, seldom fails to obtain from other people all the esteem that they think due. They desire no more than is due to them, and they rest upon it with complete satisfaction. The proud and the vain person, on the contrary, are constantly dissatisfied. The one is tormented with indignation at the unjust superiority, as he thinks it, of other people; the other is in continual dread of the shame which he foresees would attend upon the detection of his groundless pretensions.

Though our dislike of the proud and the vain disposes us to rank them below their proper station, we seldom mistreat them.

> Though our dislike to the proud and the vain often disposes us to rank them rather below than above their proper station, yet, unless we are provoked by some particular and personal impertinence, we very seldom venture to use them ill. In common cases we endeavour for our own ease rather to acquiesce, and, as well as we can, to accommodate ourselves to their folly. But, to the man who underrates himself, unless we have both more discernment and more generosity than belong to the greater part of men, we seldom fail to do at least all the injustice which he does to himself, and frequently a great deal more. He is not only more unhappy in his own feelings than either the proud or the vain, but he is much more liable to every sort of ill-usage from other people. In almost all cases it is better to be a little too proud than in any respect too humble; and, in the sentiment of self-estimation, some degree of excess seems, both to the person himself and to the impartial spectator, to be less disagreeable than any degree of defect.

> In this, therefore, as well as in every other emotion, passion and habit, the degree that is most agreeable to the impartial spectator is likewise most agreeable to the person himself; and according as either the excess or the defect is least offensive to the former, so either the one or the other is in proportion least disagreeable to the latter. (*TMS*, pp. 383–384)

In common cases of pride and vanity, we tend to accommodate ourselves to their folly. But, to the person who underrates themselves, unless we have both more discernment and more generosity than most people, we seldom fail to do at least all the injustice which they do to themselves. They are not only more unhappy in their own feelings than either the proud or the vain but are much more liable to every sort of mistreatment from other people. In almost all cases it is better to be a little too proud than in any respect too humble; and, in the sentiment of self-estimation, some degree of excess seems, both to the person themselves and to the impartial spectator, to be less disagreeable than any degree of defect.

In this, therefore, as well as in every other emotion, passion, and habit, the degree that is most agreeable to the impartial spectator is likewise most agreeable to the person themselves; and according as either the excess or the defect is least offensive to the impartial spectator, so either the one or the other is in proportion least disagreeable to the person.

Conclusion of the Sixth Part

The pursuit of our own happiness recommends prudence. Concern for the happiness of others calls for the virtues of justice and beneficence.

> Concern for our own happiness recommends to us the virtue of prudence; concern for that of other people, the virtues of justice and beneficence—of which the one restrains us from hurting, the other prompts us to promote that happiness. Independent of any regard either to what are or to what ought to be, or to what upon a certain condition would be the sentiments of other people, the first of those three virtues is originally recommended to us by our selfish, the other two by our benevolent affections. Regard to the sentiments of other people, however, comes afterwards both to enforce and to direct the practice of all those virtues; and no man, during either the whole course of his life or that of any considerable part of it, ever trod steadily and uniformly in the paths of prudence, of justice, or of proper

> beneficence, whose conduct was not principally directed by a regard to the sentiments of the supposed impartial spectator, of the great inmate of the breast, the great judge and arbiter of conduct. If in the course of the day we have swerved in any respect from the rules which he prescribes to us; if we have either exceeded or relaxed in our frugality: if we have either exceeded or relaxed in our industry; if through passion or inadvertency we have hurt in any respect the interest or happiness of our neighbour; if we have neglected a plain and proper opportunity of promoting that interest and happiness—it is this inmate who in the evening calls us to an account for all those omissions and violations, and his reproaches often make us blush inwardly, both for our folly and inattention to our own happiness, and for our still greater indifference and inattention, perhaps, to that of other people. (*TMS*, p. 385)

No person whose life has been steady in the paths of prudence, justice, and of proper beneficence has failed to be guided by the sentiments of the supposed impartial spectator, the great inmate of the breast, the great judge, and arbiter of conduct. If we have either exceeded or relaxed in our frugality, in our industry; if we have even inadvertently hurt the interest or happiness of our neighbor; if we have neglected a plain and proper opportunity of promoting that interest and happiness—it is this inmate who in the evening twilight calls us to an account for all those omissions and violations of the days of our years. Here then is the heart and soul of the thousands who engage the bottom-up steering wheel of society.

Self-command restrains our actions according to a sense of propriety mediated by the impartial spectator within the breast.

> But though the virtues of prudence, justice, and beneficence, upon different occasions be recommended to us almost equally by two different principles; those of self-command are, upon most occasions, principally and almost entirely recommended to us by one—by the sense of propriety, by regard to the sentiments of the supposed impartial spectator. Without the restraint which this principle imposes, every passion would upon most occasions rush headlong, if I say so, to its own gratification. Anger would follow the suggestions of its own fury—fear those of its own violent agitations. Regard to no time or place would induce vanity to refrain from the loudest and most impertinent ostentation; or voluptuousness from the most open, indecent, and scandalous indulgence. Respect for what are, or for what ought to be, or for what, upon a certain condition, would be the

> sentiments of other people, is the sole principle which upon most occasions overawes all those mutinous and turbulent passions into that tone and temper which the impartial spectator can enter into and sympathize with. (*TMS*, p. 386)

Respect for what are, for what ought to be, or for what in each context would be, the sentiments of other people, is the sole soul-principle which upon most occasions overawes all those mutinous and turbulent passions defining the tone and temper which the impartial spectator can enter and sympathize with.

Sometimes turbulent passions are restrained not so much from a sense of impropriety as by prudent consideration for their bad consequences if indulged.

> Upon some occasions, indeed, those passions are restrained, not so much by a sense of their impropriety as by prudential considerations of the bad consequences which might follow from their indulgence. In such cases, the passions, though restrained, are not always subdued, but often remain lurking in the breast with all their original fury. The man whose anger is restrained by fear does not always lay aside his anger, but only reserves its gratification for a more safe opportunity. But the man who, in relating to some other person the injury which has been done to him, feels at once the fury of his passion cooled and becalmed by sympathy with the more moderate sentiments of his companion, who at once adopts those more moderate sentiments, and comes to view that injury, not in the black and atrocious colours in which he had originally beheld it, but in the much milder and fairer light in which his companion naturally views it; not only restrains, but in some measure subdues his anger. The passion becomes really less than it was before, and less capable of exciting him to the violent and bloody revenge which at first perhaps he might have thought of inflicting. (*TMS*, pp. 386–387)

The restraint of passion to prudently avoid any of its bad consequences, may subdue or not, the passion; if not, it may lurk in the breast with its original fury. The person whose anger is restrained by fear does not always lay aside their anger, but only reserves its gratification for a safer opportunity. But the person who is calmed in explaining their injury to another may be released from the intensity of their immediate feelings, viewing it in the milder light beheld by the companion.

Passions restrained by the sense of propriety are to some degree subdued by it, but those restrained by prudential considerations are frequently inflamed by the restraint.

> Those passions which are restrained by the sense of propriety are all in some degree moderated and subdued by it. But those which are restrained only by prudential considerations of any kind are, on the contrary, frequently inflamed by the restraint, and sometimes (long after the provocation given, and when nobody is thinking about it) burst out absurdly and unexpectedly, and with tenfold fury and violence.
> Anger, however, as well as every other passion, upon many occasions may be very properly restrained by prudential considerations. Some exertion of manhood and self-command is even necessary for this sort of restraint; and the impartial spectator sometimes view it with that sort of cold esteem due to that species of conduct which he considers as a mere matter of vulgar prudence; but never with that affectionate admiration with which he surveys the same passions, when by the sense of propriety, they are moderated and subdued to what he himself can readily enter into. In the former species of restraint he may frequently discern some degree of propriety, and, if you will, even of virtue; but it is a propriety and virtue of a much inferior order to those which he always feels with transport and admiration in the latter. (*TMS*, p. 387)

Smith's discussion of the restraints motivated by prudence may be illustrated by the case in which negative reciprocal actions are in danger of escalating. Thus, one prudently avoids punishing an improper hurtful action because it risks being seen as unjustified. The essence of deterrence by punishment is the existence of an implicit consensus that certain intentional actions—murder, theft, and robbery—are to be discouraged as criminal, and the violation of contractual promises are to be discouraged through civil action to recover damage. Road rage usually illustrates the lack of such a consensus in traffic manners, but many avoid this escalation by prudently accepting actions viewed as of an insulting disrespectful nature. Prudence assures that not every hurtful action requires retaliatory action to discourage it.

Prudence, justice, and beneficence are virtues identified as having agreeable effects recommending them first to the actor, afterward to the impartial spectator.

> The virtues of prudence, justice, and beneficence, have no tendency to produce any but the most agreeable effects. Regard to those effects, as it originally recommends them to the actor, so does it afterwards to the impartial spectator. In our approbation of the character of the prudent man, we feel with peculiar complacency the security which he must enjoy while he walks under the safeguard of that sedate and deliberate virtue. In our approbation of the character of the just man, we feel with equal complacency the security which all those connected with him, whether in neighbourhood, society, or business, must derive from his scrupulous anxiety never either to hurt or offend. In our approbation of the character of the beneficent man, we enter into the gratitude of all those who are within the sphere of his good offices, and conceive with them the highest sense of his merit. In our approbation of all those virtues, our sense of their agreeable effects, of their utility, either to the person who exercises them or to some other persons, joins with our sense of their propriety, and constitutes always a considerable, frequently the greater, part of that approbation. (*TMS*, pp. 387–388)

In our approbation of the prudent person, we feel with complacency the security they must enjoy under the safeguard of that virtue.

In our approbation of the just person, we feel with complacency the security which all those connected with them—in neighborhood, society, or business—must derive from their scrupulous commitment never either to hurt or offend.

In our approbation of the beneficent person, we enter the gratitude of all those who enjoy their good offices and conceive with them the highest sense of their merit.

In our approbation of self-command, the effects may be agreeable or disagreeable.

> But in our approbation of the virtues of self-command, complacency with their effects sometimes constitutes no part, and frequently but a small part, of that approbation. Those effects may sometimes be agreeable, and sometimes disagreeable; and though our approbation is no doubt stronger in the former case, it is by no means altogether destroyed in the latter. The most heroic valour may be employed indifferently in the cause either of justice or of injustice; and though it is no doubt much more loved and admired in the former case, it still appears a great and respectable quality even in the latter. In that, and in all the other virtues of self-command, the

> splendid and dazzling quality seems always to be the greatness and steadiness of the exertion, and the strong sense of propriety which is necessary in order to make and to maintain that exertion. The effects are too often but too little regarded. (*TMS*, p. 388)

The splendid and dazzling quality of self-command resides in the greatness and steadiness of its exertion, and the strong sense of propriety which is necessary to make and to maintain that exertion.

In this passage on self-command in society, Smith has not yet developed his findings in *WN*, based on liberal free societies, that so long as we do not violate the rules of justice, in pursuing our own trading gains in markets, we create wealth by unintentionally increasing specialization, limited only by the extent of markets. And thus, then, as now, we improve a lot of all those myriads of people who we do not, cannot, and need not know, who, since Smith's time, have relentlessly done better generation after generation.

On the socio-economic consequences of free liberal versus authoritarian societies, you have only to compare South Korea, a rich country showering the world with exports, and necessarily enriching themselves with imports, with North Korea, struggling to feed itself.

Of course, today we have many besides North Korea who cannot or will not believe these theorems, whose predicaments are evident in world data sets, and who despair that we are taking insufficient action to intentionally assist the world's poor. Never mind that we provide much such generous assistance but do much more harm than good in sending donations of free goods and money to the poorer nations and thus undercutting the development of their own enterprises for engaging in such productive actions at home. Neither donations nor reparations, as in post WWI Germany, can enrichen people because they undercut industry and destroy work and products in the recipient country.

We in wealthy free countries are the fortunate ones who, thus blessed, began this process early and have created wealth via the same process that the poorer nations must adopt if they are not to become forever our and their own unhappy dependents, falling further and further behind.

Epilogue: Selections from *The Wealth of Nations (WN)*

The following entities are Smith's 1776 *An Inquiry into the Nature and Causes of the Wealth of Nations (WN)*. This edition of Smith's work is based on Edwin Cannan's careful 1904 compilation (Methuen and Co., Ltd) of Smith's fifth edition of the book (1789), the final edition in Smith's lifetime.

I will proceed by turning to some of the key theorems and memorable passages in the *WN* interspersed by occasional related text from *LJ* where Smith expressed many ideas in economics.

"The division of labor" refers to the specialization of labor skills emerging naturally in free societies. As Smith knew, this specialization is indirectly related to capital investment and innovation, extends to other productive inputs (capital and land), and is the first principle in accounting for wealth creation.

Wealth creation is a consequence of labor specialization.

> The greatest improvement in the productive powers of labour, and the greater part of the skill, dexterity, and judgment with which it is any where directed, or applied, seem to have been the effects of the division of labour. (*WN*, Vol. I, p. 5)

> It is in consequence of the division of labour, which occasions, in a well-governed society, that universal opulence which extends itself to the lowest ranks of the people. Every workman has a great quantity of his own work to dispose of beyond what he himself has occasion for; and every other workman being exactly in the same situation, he is enabled to exchange a great quantity of his own goods for a great quantity, or, what comes to the same thing, for the price of a great quantity of theirs. He supplies them abundantly with what they have occasion for, and they accommodate him as amply with what he has occasion for, and a general plenty diffuses itself through all the different ranks of the society. (*WN*, Vol. I, pp. 12–13)

This wealth creating process had its beginning in the century before Smith wrote but began accelerating by 1800 and has continued relentlessly to enrich all those who have embraced its freedom-of-action principles. Smith's qualification "in a well-governed society" was important because the full effects of specialization in private markets can be spoiled or dimmed by state intervention even if well-intentioned. Modern economics and data sources overwhelmingly support this first principle of economics.

The division of labor is an unintended consequence of the human propensity for exchange.

> This division of labour, from which so many advantages are derived, is not originally the effect of any human wisdom, which foresees and intends that general opulence to which it gives occasion: It is the necessary, though very slow and gradual, consequence of a certain propensity in human nature which has in view no such extensive utility; the propensity to truck, barter, and exchange one thing for another." (WN, Vol. I, p. 15)

You can go to school because your parents work in the oil fields or write as a member of The New Yorker editorial board, while others support them by buying gasoline or subscribing to The New Yorker. We all live by taking in each other's laundry so to speak.

Nothing could be simpler than Smith's theorem on the effects of free trade through markets but much of the world is not very rich because they do not have the opportunity to freely engage in this way with others and it is even widely believed, falsely and sadly, that it is not true because others take advantage of us by charging high prices and paying low wages.

We all depend upon each other and each of us get what we want from others by serving their self-love.

> It is not from the benevolence of the butcher, the brewer, or the baker, that we expect our dinner, but from their regard to their own interest. We address ourselves, not to their humanity but to their self-love, and never talk to them of our own necessities but of their advantages. (*WN*, pp. 16)

In *WN*, Adam Smith nowhere sites *TMS*, wherein he states the proposition that…

> Actions of a Beneficent tendency which proceed from proper motives seems alone to require reward; because such alone are the approved objects of gratitude or excite the sympathetic gratitude of the spectator." (*TMS*, p. 112)

In trade, spectators like the butcher, baker, and brewer shower their benevolence on us in return for our own benevolence, each of us willingly, and thus with gratitude, giving to others that which other most wants from us and serving their self-love. We want meat, bread, or beer from others, who want our money from which we are eager to part in return. Just as in *TMS*, where you feel required to reward beneficence, so in an exchange in *WN* we each reward others for benefits freely given to us. In neighborhoods giving and receiving may occur at different points in time. But in a trade the giving and receiving are simultaneous. Even strangers may enter such bargains as familiarity and trust is not a premium when traders each see what they are getting and giving. It is then over and each is on their way.

Why do so many in this world appear to see others as taking from them, not giving to term? Because, I suggest, they see others as taking our money and we focus on that loss, not on what we receive. For every dollar we outlay, we receive more than a dollar's worth of stuff, otherwise we are idiots to have spent that dollar.

The great differences in natural talent is not so much the cause, as the effect of the division of labor.

> The difference of natural talents in different men is, in reality, much less than we are aware of; and the very different genius which appears to distinguish men of different professions, when grown up to maturity, is not upon many occasions so much the cause, as the effect of the division of labour. The difference between the most dissimilar characters, between a philosopher and a common street porter, for example, seems to arise not so much from nature, as from habit, custom, and education. (*WN*, Vol. I, p. 17)

That we are free to choose in liberal societies leads to the development of natural talents, not the other way around. This is why free societies flourish. Authoritarian societies also have the division of labor but it has not been so great a source of wealth creation and human betterment. In Smith's time people were breaking away from a tradition in which you followed in your father's footsteps. Smith's father had been a lawyer and comptroller, and he became a philosopher and professor, then a tutor, and finally a customs officer. James Watt's father was a ship and house builder while he became a great inventor.

The division of labor is limited by the extent of the market.

> As it is the power of exchanging that gives occasion to the division of labour, so the extent of this division must always be limited by the extent

> of that power, or, in other words, by the extent of the market. (*WN*, Vol. I, p. 19)

A street porter as well as a philosopher is unlikely to find employment in a small town; both will be more likely seen in a large city. My grandfather, Charles A. Smith, was a tool dresser in the oil fields and, just as coal miners are only seen where there is coal, tool dressers are only seen in regions where there is an oil strike. But once the wells are drilled, and the oil is flowing, tool dressers were not needed. Being willing to move from one strike to the next, Grandpa earned very high wages, and retired with savings in his fifties after the Eldorado strike brought him to Wichita. Self-made, he proceeded to live off interest and rental income, but ultimately was impoverished by government-made inflation—"ze monster." Except for me, he would have died alone, his nearest remaining issue who could love that wonderful human being some 70 years ago (1955).

Trade is greatly inhibited by barter giving rise to a demand for money.

> The butcher has more meat in his shop than he himself can consume, and the brewer and the baker would each of them be willing to purchase a part of it. But they have nothing to offer in exchange, except the different productions of their respective trades, and the butcher is already provided with all the bread and beer which he has immediate occasion for. No exchange can, in this case, be made between them. He cannot be their merchant, nor they his customers; and they are all of them thus mutually less serviceable to one another. (*WN*, Vol. I, p. 24)

> Commodities that have emerged as a means of payment include oxen, salt, shells, dried cod, tobacco, sugar, and hides. All were durable and desirable but limited in the extent to which they could serve in exchange. Metals were more generally serviceable: "Metals can not only be kept with as little loss as any other commodity, scarce anything being divisible less perishable than they are, but they can likewise, without any loss, be divided into any number of parts, as by fusion those parts can easily be reunited again; a quality which no other equally durable commodities possess, and which more than any other quality renders them fit to be the instruments of commerce and circulations." (*WN*, p. 25).

The main inconvenience concerned the trouble of weighing and assaying them. Transactions costs were high as Ronald Coase teaches us.

Thus arose the institution of coinage which standardized the weight and value of monetary coin.

> The inconveniency and difficulty of weighing those metals with exactness gave occasion to the institution of coins, of which the stamp, covering entirely both sides of the piece and sometimes the edges too, was supposed to ascertain not only the fineness, but the weight of the metal. Such coins, therefore, were received by tale [story or message] as at present, without the trouble of weighing. (*WN*, Vol. I, p. 28)

Through a succession of small steps, we see an evolutionary process whereby a stable means of payment emerged in fits and starts, fueled by government currency monopolies that made possible universal markets in all goods and services and a corresponding vast increase in wealth across individual countries that were predominantly free, while leaving behind most of the authoritarian countries. The voluntary emergence of markets in the convertibility of these currencies into each other enabled this wealth creation to extend to the global economy. In many countries that process generally dwarfed the universal tendency to follow bad economic policies to intervene counter productively incurring unnecessary costs that have generally tended to be small relative to the great private engine of wealth creation. That productive process has extended even to authoritarian countries in the Mideast and Asia to the extent that they have engaged in world import–export markets, thus liberalizing their external trading relationships. Even North Korea can avoid mass starvation by exporting coal, building missiles, and enabling these workers to buy essential food, clothing, and shelter.

Coinage, and the subsequent issue of paper money convertible into coin, established government monopolies over their respective currencies with unsurprising self-dealing consequences.

> The denominations of those coins seem originally to have expressed the weight or quantity of metal contained in them....[Sovereigns everywhere—Rome, French, Scots, and English resisted not the temptation to debase their currencies and to live off the proceeds] For in every country of the world, I believe, the avarice and injustice of princes and sovereign states,

> abusing the confidence of their subjects, have by degrees diminished the real quantity of metal, which had been originally contained in their coins. (*WN*, Vol. I, p. 29)

The universal tendency of governments everywhere to pay their bills by living off the debasement of their protected monopoly currencies is greatly facilitated, but also greatly obscured, today, by the creation of convertible monopoly digital deposit currencies that enable government spending in lieu of taxes. Money today consists of bank deposits which people transfer to others via bank transfers to make payment to the providers of goods and services of which coin and paper dollars are a trivial fraction.

Thus, the US President increased deficit financed spending by trillions of dollars in 2021–2022 during the pandemic shutdown in which ordinary workers could not get to their jobs. Consequently, the economy, far from suffering from inadequate demand, suffered from an inadequate supply caused entirely by external conditions. If workers are sitting at home, not producing any goods and services and you write them checks on deposit money, it does not require some special kind of genius to see that the policy is inflationary. Such a bad policy quickly morphed into the worst in all recent times.

It is important to understand, that Inflation is always, everywhere, and only, the consequence of two conditions: First, government consumption spending that exceeds tax revenue collections; second, the deficit financing of this consumption by means of an expansion in the supply of money by direct action of the central bank. Together, these two conditions produce the modern equivalent of the old-fashioned debasement of the currency. Moreover, these conditions provide guidelines for your thinking that helps you to see in principle how far, and how long, the inflation will persist, and help to anchor your thoughts amidst the confused media-leveraged report of historical happenings, and press releases by the central bank.

The resources needed to supply the real cost of the government's consumption must be provided by the economy, the government not having made such provision through taxation.

The immediate consequence of the inflationary increase in prices is to reduce the real value of all assets in the economy that are denominated in fixed annuity payments. These assets include all bonds—Treasuries, state, corporate, and private issues—and all insurance, lease, and rental contracts.

This economic process is governed by a simple market rule: inflation continues until the real value of asset resources is reduced sufficiently to supply the government's original consumption of goods and services. The resources to pay for that consumption must come from somewhere. The economy finds them through an inflationary reduction in real asset value.

Thus, inflation has a purpose, an economic function that enables you to estimate its extent and end point.

The economy's response is entirely associated with the given original government consumption. If there is new deficit-financed government consumption spending, then this inflationary process is compounded in response to the new initiative.

In the United States, the Federal Reserve authorities, whose actions caused the inflation, are now (c. 2023–2024) cast in their emerging role of rescuing the economy from the consequences of its own actions. The news media, and discussion focus, are on interest rate policy, "designed to slow inflation." The real operational meaning of FR intervention is that (since the economy is already busy inflating assets to pay for the government's consumption), by increasing the interest rate that the FR pays the banks for deposits and thus pays them for not making loans, more of the resource cost of the government's consumption spending can be shifted from the asset market generally to reduced private new investment and consumption spending.

When the Biden Administration announced that some 3 trillion dollars would be provided to individuals and businesses as "stimulus" to help people pay their living expenses and to keep them on the worker payrolls, government bond market prices fell in anticipation of the new offering by Treasury. The Federal Reserve acted immediately with open market purchases from the selling bondholders, and maintained prices, in accord with their normal responsibility in helping to assure an "orderly market for Treasuries." FR open market purchases of bonds enabled all the new deficit bond sales to be offered and financed by a corresponding increase in the supply of money. Inherently, this was inflationary, although the purchases were partially "neutralized" via a clever device in which the FR buys bonds, not for its own account which would enable an increase in private bank loans causing even more inflation, but for the account of Treasury. In real terms, and "in truth," the FR is accommodating government consumption by simply creating money in whatever amount is needed to make the promised government payments. Notice, however, that this means that the government is not budget restrained but rather is assured that the spending will be fully financed from new money creation. Although thereby rendered costless to the government, the resulting predictable inflation has the important economic function of reducing the market value of all assets denominated in fixed annuity payments to release the resources to provide for the government's original consumption.

So, the government's spending is costless to the government, but it is not costless to the economy or to its citizens who pay for it out of a corresponding inflation-caused reduction in wealth. FR increases in interest rates merely exert some measure of influence by shifting more of the asset market cost into reduced new investment—a minor uninteresting twist on the fundamental asset value-reduction economic process.

I am not enough of an insider to have an intelligent opinion on how this economic process is perceived by Treasury and FR officials. Their public statements suggest much fumbling and stumbling through a delayed focus on the here and now of "inflation targeting," unguided by a coherent economic model. Inflation is first "viewed," or claimed, by the FR as uncertain, then recognized, but will be controlled through interest rate policy. Rates may have to be raised again, etc. This is a "Steering Wheel" model that connects higher interest rates with the lowering of inflation, which means relative to the asset market forces already at play.

Because the process, as it plays out sequentially in the news, appears and indeed is complex, indirect, and unpredictable, citizens gain no insight into what is being done to, as well as for, them; they have not a clue as to how they are victims, and not mere passive beneficiaries. Indeed, Chairman Powell of the FR, is represented as having saved us from the inflation that he earlier had unceremoniously created in cooperation with the sitting president.

How can the above narrative of FR policy—first, be a cause of the inflation, second be the instrument of saving us from that inflation—come about? I think it is a straightforward consequence of how the FR sees its role. First, their job is to act in financial service (as fiduciary agent) to the government by assuring "an orderly market for Treasuries." That means that when the government increases its spending above tax revenue, the FR buys enough Treasuries in the open market to assure that the public will buy and hold the new Treasuries to be issued. Everybody seems, apparently, to see this as good service to all by the FR—certainly, we do not see the media raising a stink about it. Some surely would, so I must conclude that they do not understand the true process at work. Second, when the unpredicted, and uncertain inflation, arrives, the FR job is to raise interest rates thereby purposefully "targeting" (note the precision of words) a reduction in inflation. Everybody seems to see this as good service to all by the FR. As Adam Smith said, half the world's troubles are caused by self-deceit and here it is in full dress.

My narrative above simply places these events in sequence as part of an economic whole and portrays that whole as a bad service to all in financing the government's relentless growth. No American Democratic politician would see this as good service to all. They want to use government to help the poor but do not want to cause inflation. Loyal American Republican politicians see the importance of scaling back the growth of government. What they do not see is their instrumentality in that growth in supporting FR "good thing" actions. Otherwise, they would want to abolish the FR. The fundamental theorem is that bad things are always done in the name of the good. It is self-deceit (or -deception) and is the cause of much deliberate yet unintended misery.

Universal debasement practices were routinely practiced by all sovereigns which have defied policy correction over the centuries because their currencies also made possible enormous private sector wealth creation.

> By means of those [debasement] operations the princes and sovereign states which performed them were enabled, in appearance, to pay their debts and to fulfil their engagements with a smaller quantity of silver than would otherwise have been requisite. It was indeed in appearance only; for their creditors were really defrauded of a part of what was due to them. All other debtors in the state were allowed the same privilege, and might pay with the same nominal sum of the new and debased coin whatever they had borrowed in the old. Such operations, therefore, have always proved favourable to the debtor, and ruinous to the creditor, and have sometimes produced a greater and more universal revolution in the fortunes of private persons, than could have been occasioned by a very great public calamity. It is in this manner that money has become in all civilized nations the instrument of commerce, by the intervention of which goods of all kinds are bought and sold, or exchanged for one another. (*WN*, Vol. I, pp. 29–30)

And thus, the vast increase in wealth creation, made possible by using money in private commerce, has easily outpaced the uncontrolled issuance of monopoly money by governments to pay their bills. This free-riding corruption will increase unabated in the form of politics as usual. But the increase in wealth will also continue and we have no assurance that government will not thereby grow at ever faster rates.

Smith was good at seeing both the deceptions and the basic harms done by Mercantilist (cozy government-business) doctrines and that the harms were covered up the more powerful deep force of wealth creation.

He was also good at understanding price discovery and the revelation of hidden information in the market process. I claim that this was because he understood auctions as a buyer price revelation process, which he generalized (in his thought process) to two-sided supply and demand markets, and thence to multiple markets, with both buyers and sellers active. Smith never stated this as an explicit proposition, but it underlies his market narratives of price formation. His detailed model even predicts asymmetries in price formation discovered in my first experimental markets, a fact that I only realized some sixty years later. That lesson taught me that I had not read his work carefully enough.

One meaning of value is "value on use" or an item's utility; the other is its "value in exchange" in trade for other goods.

> The word VALUE, it is to be observed, has two different meanings, and sometimes expresses the utility of some particular object, and or value in exchange, sometimes the power of purchasing other goods which the possession of that object conveys. The one may be called "value in use ;" the other, "value in exchange." The things which have the greatest value in use have frequently little or no value in exchange; and on the contrary., those which have the greatest value in exchange have frequently little or no value in use. Nothing is more useful than water: but it will purchase scarce any thing; scarce any thing can be had in exchange for it. A diamond, on the contrary, has scarce any value in use; but a very great quantity of other goods may frequently be had in exchange for it. (*WN*, Vol. I, p. 44)

Later marginal utilitarians criticized this passage arguing that Smith did not distinguish the total utility of water or diamonds from their marginal utility and that price depended on the marginal utility of a unit. But as we shall see Smith well understood the role of scarcity in price determination/explanation. Thus, although water was cheap and ordinarily could be "had for the lifting" we have the example of a single cruise of water exchanging for 10,000 crowns in the Arabian desert. Smith did not have the modern language but he had the modern understanding.

Labor measures the real value of commodities at different times and places better than money because it provides a measure of the ever-present toil and trouble of acquiring a unit of the commodity.

> Every man is rich or poor according to the degree in which he can afford to enjoy the necessaries, conveniencies, and amusements of human life. But after the division of labour has once thoroughly taken place, it is but a very small part of these with which a man's own labour can supply him. The far greater part of them he must derive from the labour of other people, and he must be rich or poor according to the quantity of that labour which he can command, or which he can afford to purchase. The value of any commodity, therefore, to the person who possesses it, and who means not to use or consume it himself, but to exchange it for other commodities, is equal to the quantity of labour which it enables him to purchase or command. Labour, therefore, is the real measure of the exchangeable value of all commodities. The real price of every thing, what every thing really costs to the man who wants to acquire it, is the toil and trouble of acquiring it. (*WN*, Vol. I, p. 64)

Smith recognized that the value of money varies over time and space and does not provide as satisfactory a measure of that expenditure per unit of a commodity as the equivalent labor it takes to earn the price of purchasing a unit. Thus, the felt or real cost of anything is the toil and trouble of obtaining it. A measure of how much better off you are today than 50 years ago is to compare how long you would have to work to earn a car 50 years ago versus now. For example, a car might cost you 50% more of your income 50 years ago. Observe, that he is NOT saying that labor is the source of all value, he is simply saying that a meaningful personal indication of how much better off you are today than yesterday is to ask how long you would have to work to buy something yesterday versus today. Many scholars have confused these two things and unintentionally debased Smith's great contributions to fundamental economics. He makes this transparently clear in the next entry.

The exchange value of commodities depends only on their labor cost prior to the accumulation of capital and the appropriation of land.

> In that early and rude state of society which precedes both the accumulation of stock and the appropriation of land, the proportion between the quantities of labour necessary for acquiring different objects seems to be the only circumstance which can afford any rule for exchanging them for one another.
> In this state of things, the whole produce of labour belongs to the labourer; and the quantity of labour commonly employed in acquiring or producing any commodity, is the only circumstance which can regulate the quantity of labour which it ought commonly to purchase, command, or exchange for. (*WN*, Vol. I, p. 65)

Smith was sometimes incorrectly thought to have embraced the labor theory of value wherein all goods are valued in terms of the labor cost of making them. In this passage we see that he did not make this error. As above, we see that he believed that labor could serve as a useful standard for measuring the comparative value of commodities, but that did not place him among those like Ricardo and Marx who advocated the labor theory of value.

Smith goes on to argue that, with the accumulation of capital and the appropriation of land, commodity production generally requires labor, land, and capital and if the demand is sufficient, the price must cover the total unit cost or the sum of wages, rent, and profit. Hence, the true resource cost of anything is the sum of its costs across the resources of labor, land, and capital each with its own return that must be paid to call forth its employment in producing product.

In the next three entries, Smith articulates his conception of the role of scarcity and his conception of demand as buyer "willingness to pay" for a unit of a good out of wealth given up. Also, he describes the dynamic process whereby prices form, or are discovered, in a market through the interactive "higgling and bargaining" of the buyers and sellers who come to market to buy or sell units of a commodity. His focus is entirely on buyer and seller actions, motivations, circumstances, and consequent prices in a market. This constitutes a full narrative account of the elements that convert the private valuations of individuals into the public price information that accounts for specialization and wealth creation. Markets thus have the important economy function of generating public prices from private hidden values. In this, Smith had the fundamental Hayekian idea that market prices constitute and information system. He lacked only the modern language of information theory.

The market price of a good is regulated by the demand for it, its abundance in proportion to this demand, and the wealth of the demanders.

> The market price…is regulated by 1stly, the demand or need for it, 2ndly, the abundance of it in proportion to this demand; and 3rdly, the wealth of the … demanders. Ist, a thing of no use, as [a] lump of clay, brought into the market will give no price, as no one demands it. If it be useful the price will be regulated according to the demand, as this use is general or not, and the plenty there is to supply it. A thing which is hardly of any use, yet if the quantity be not sufficient to supply the demand, will give a high price; hence the great price of diamonds… Abundance on the other hand such as does more than supply all possible demands, renders water of no price at all and other things of a price the next thing to nothing. The scarcity on the other hand raises the price immoderately—This also depends on the other circumstance, viz the riches or poverty of the demand. We are told that a merchant and a traveler … meeting in the desarts of Arabia, the merchant, in want of water, gave the traveler 10,000 crowns for one cruise of water. This price, however necessitated, he could not have given had he had only 100 crowns about him. If there is less than is sufficient to supply the demand, the parties contend who shall have it. The case is here the very same as at an auction. If there be two persons equally in fancy with any thing and equally earnest to have it, they will bid equally according to their abilities…The richest however will always get it as he is best able to bid highest. (*LJ*, p. 358)

In this *Lectures on Jurisprudence* (*LJ*) passage, Smith clearly understands how buyer demand, based on the use value (utility) and wealth (means of payment), combine with scarcity to determine price. Below, in *WN*, he will supplement this with a more general treatment of supply. Conceptionally, he understands that the highest bidder wins at auction, that the amount bid for an item depends on utilitarian use value, on wealth as the means of payment, and that the item is unique and thus scarce. He has a modern understanding of auction markets and generalizes it to the operation of supply and demand markets. That quite qualifies as good rigorous economics.

Buyer and price response when sellers bring too little to the market and price begins too low.

> When the quantity of any commodity which is brought to market falls short of the effectual demand, all those who are willing to pay the whole value of the rent, wages, and profit, which must be paid in order to bring it thither, cannot be supplied with the quantity which they want. Rather than want it altogether, some of them will be willing to give more. A competition will immediately begin among them, and the market price will rise more or less above the natural price, according as either the greatness of the deficiency, or the wealth and wanton luxury of the competitors, happen to animate more or less the eagerness of the competition. Among competitors of equal wealth and luxury the same deficiency will generally occasion a more or less eager competition, according as the acquisition of the commodity happens to be of more or less importance to them. Hence the exorbitant price of the necessaries of life during the blockade of a town or in a famine. (*WN*, Vol. I, pp. 58–59)

Every word counts here, as Smith postulates the case in which the quantity supplied of a commodity is inadequate to allow the effective demanders to buy it—all those willing to pay (at least) the whole value of the wages, profits, and rents required to bring it thither. Buyers, rather than failing to buy, compete to bid up the price depending on how great the deficiency is, and how great their wealth is. Demand is defined, given the quantity desired, quite generally as the willingness to pay (WTP) by an individual or (WTP) by the collection of all buyers going to market, for example at an auction.

Implicitly, Smith is thinking of commodities as discrete units, which is entirely satisfactory and general in retail shopping markets. Think about what is in your shopping basket at the supermarket: 1lb bacon, one small jar olives, 1lb butter, one quart of milk, one medium box of Wheaties, etc. Look in your neighbor's basket: 1lb bacon, one large jar of olives, one half gallon of milk, one large box of Corn Flakes. All buy one package of each item, including 6-, 12-, or 24-pack batches of water bottles. The market solves consumer inventory problems by packaging everything in batches appropriate to, and depending upon, your family size, how large your pantry is, and how often you shop.

A few sizes fit all.

During the early covid pandemic, people realized they would be stuck in their homes, would shop less frequently, and needed larger-than-normal inventories of paper products, and other non-perishable food and convenience items, and hence emptied the store shelves to supply the new home inventory requirements. Simultaneously, people were eating out less, and restaurant required inventories fell sharply. The economy redistributed inventories in response to changing consumer demand.

Seller and price response when sellers bring too much to market and price begins too high.

> When the quantity brought to market exceeds the effectual demand, it cannot be all sold to those who are willing to pay the whole value of the rent, wages and profit, which must be paid in order to bring it thither. Some part must be sold to those who are willing to pay less, and the low price which they give for it must reduce the price of the whole. The market price will sink more or less below the natural price, according as the greatness of the excess increases more or less the competition of the sellers, or according as it happens to be more or less important to them to get immediately rid of the commodity. The same excess in the importation of perishable, will occasion a much greater competition than in that of durable commodities; in the importation of oranges, for example, than in that of old iron. (*WN*, Vol. I, p. 74)

Sellers, each bringing units to the market, supply more goods in total than there are buyers willing to pay the full costs of the sellers that is necessary to sustain that supply, and some part of it must be sold for less. Hence, the market price will sink below the full cost, or "natural" price. How much it falls below this cost depends upon how much the excess induces competition among the sellers and how important it is to them to get immediately rid of the commodity. For perishables like imported oranges, it will occasion more competition than durables like old (scrap) iron.

Notice that Smith has a general theory of market price, not a theory, or only a theory, of "long-run" price sufficient to pay the full costs of the sellers. Perishables induce eager immediate price cutting by sellers, durables to less price cutting as sellers try to dribble excess units out more slowly and in pace with the flow of demand.

Also carefully note that in the previous entry, when sellers offer too little to the market, price rises above their supply costs, because of the competitive actions of buyers. It is the buyers, not the sellers, who realize that supply is short, know what they are willing to pay, and proceed to reveal such information to sellers in their interactions with each other. Sellers, however content to be paid their full costs, learn from buyers that they can do even better.

Now, in his second example, with sellers offering too much to the market, price falls below their supply cost, because of the competitive action of sellers! Discovering that demand is inadequate and sales slow, they scramble to cut prices and avoid failing to earn some sales revenue.

Hence, Smith's model of market price adjustment in response to shortages, or to surpluses, offers very precise predictions concerning the behavior of buyers versus sellers.

Moreover, his model is more general than implied by framing it only as shortages or surpluses based on what sellers bring to market. Thus, sellers may be in the market for goods or services made-to-order after they know the price. In markets for hamburgers, haircuts, and plumbers, prices are determined, or negotiated, before they deliver the product or service. So, the model is really about the cases in which initial prices begin too low, and rise, because of the actions of buyers, or begin too high, and decline because of the actions of sellers. The model predicts differential behavioral responses by buyers and sellers and its testability is thereby enhanced because of the detailed specification of initial conditions and who initiates action.

Impressively, Smith's behavioral predictive model of buyer and seller price formation in markets was confirmed in the first market experiments, which unintentionally and unknowingly tested his model (Smith, 1962, 1964).[2] In retrospect, the predictions were confirmed using two-sided, oral outcry auctions: When prices start low, buyers are more active than sellers in raising their bid prices; when prices start high, sellers are more active in lowering their asking prices.

We have no comparable such precision from neoclassical price theory starting in the 1870s and proceeding down to modern theory. The dominant price adjustment mechanism was, and is, based on a conjecture by Leon Walras, wherein a fictionally given theoretical trial price yields positive or negative excess demand, which then causes price to rise or fall, without specific reference to buyer or seller actions. In contrast with Walras's idea of a given price, Adam Smith understood that there could be no prices given by anybody until they had been discovered jointly by buyers and sellers, and that was his object and motivation in modeling.

[2] Smith, Vernon L. (1962) "An Experimental Study of Competitive Market Behavior," *Journal of Political Economy*, 70(2), 111–137.

Smith, Vernon L. (1964) "Effect of Market Organization on Competitive Equilibrium," *Quarterly Journal of Economics*, 78(2), 181–201.

Naturally occurring conspiracies in restraint of trade, or to raise prices, however desirable to prevent, are impossible to prevent by means consistent with liberty and justice; nor should the government do anything to facilitate such private arrangements, e.g., by requiring registration.

> People of the same trade seldom meet together, even for merriment, but the conversation ends in a conspiracy against the public, or in some contrivance to raise prices. *It is impossible indeed to prevent such meetings, by any law which either could be executed, or would be consistent with liberty and justice.* But though the law cannot hinder people of the same trade from sometimes assembling together, it ought to do nothing to facilitate such assemblies; much less to render them necessary. A regulation which obliges all those of the same trade in a particular town to enter their names and places of abode in a public register, facilitates such assemblies. (*WN*, Vol. I, p. 145; italics added)

The state, ever desiring to effectuate and extend its control, requires registration, and in this, as in many ordinary circumstances, is the unwitting agent of action that may be inimical to the public interest.

Recall, that 2000 odd years ago, a state census registration is why there were no rooms available in the Inns of Bethlehem, why it was feared in high places that a kingly threat had been born that might well be beyond the state's reach, and why, thirty odd years later, Pontius Pilot acted so shamelessly and uncourageously as to feel that he had to ceremoniously wash his hands after having found a man innocent but convicted by a populist mob.

Being consumers, everyone remembers what Smith said here about businesspersons hardly able to meet even for merriment without scheming to raise prices, and wanting the state to intervene to neutralize and fight that process, while forgetting that this is scarce ever possible in a manner consistent with liberty and freedom, Though the state ought not do this, the state surely ought not also to do anything to facilitate that restraining process. Businesses everywhere, however, are motivated to seek assistance by political intervention to aid their case in marketing products to consumers. But consumers are much more numerous than businesses and can vote down such political interventions.

Usury ceilings on interest charged for loans should be fixed at just above the lowest market rate to avoid tempting lenders to simply

charge higher rates for riskier loans thereby contributing to market instability. loan markets cannot clear based on interest rate charges alone.

> The legal rate, it is to be observed, though it ought to be somewhat above, ought not to be much above the lowest market rate. If the greater part of loans in Great Britain, for example, was fixed so high as eight or ten per cent, the greater part of the money...would be lent to prodigals and projectors, who alone would be willing to give this high interest. Sober people, who will give for the use of money no more than a part of what they are likely to make by the use of it, would not venture into the competition. A great part of the capital of the country would thus be kept out of the hands which were most likely to make a profitable and advantageous use of it, and thrown into those which were most likely to waste and destroy it. Where the legal rate of interest, on the contrary, is fixed but a very little above the lowest market rate, sober people are universally preferred, as borrowers, to prodigals and projeetors. (*WN*, Vol. I, pp. 338–339)

Thus, in modern America, did State usury interest law ceilings do incentive work in encouraging lenders to focus on borrower risk-of-default evaluation, rationing their loan allocations, and thus avoiding simplistically charging riskier borrower's higher interest rates. Ignoring any such notion that State usury laws might exist for sound reasons, the federal Depository Institutions Deregulation and Monetary Control Act (1980) abolished interest ceilings for primary mortgages on residences. This opened a market, doomed to become unstable, for risky subprime loans in which the higher risks were not borne by the mortgage originators, who simply substituted higher interest charges for an increase in the equity stake of the borrower. The prior incredible success of transportation deregulation, by opening the industry to entry and price competition, was inappropriately extended to the mortgage loan market where the interest price alone is not sufficient to control borrower demand; you must also raise the equity stake of the riskier borrowers to limit the risk of default on the loan. But transportation is a consumer product bought for use, not bought for reselling. Houses and financial instruments, however, have both a use or holding value, and a resale market value, in which resale price expectations may diverge from use value, accounting for their far greater instability. While the deregulation of transportation service was a resounding success under President Carter, his deregulation of financial markets, carried still further by President

Reagan, was coupled with a bad public housing mortgage policy, causing a household balance sheet crisis.

Every person, in intending only their own gain, is led by an invisible hand so to direct industry that its product will be of the greatest value.

> [T]he annual revenue of every society is always precisely equal to the exchangeable value of the whole annual produce of its industry…As every individual, therefore, endeavours as much as he can both to employ his capital in the support of domestic industry, and so to direct that industry that its produce be of the greatest value ; every individual necessarily labours to render the annual revenue of the society as great as he can. He generally, indeed, neither intends to promote the public interest, nor knows how much he is promoting it. By preferring the support of domestic to that of foreign industry, he intends only his own security; and by directing that industry in such a manner as its produce be of the greatest value, he intends only his own gain, and he is in this…led by an invisible hand to promote an end which was no part of his intention. Nor is it always the worse for the society that it was no part of it. By pursuing his own interest he frequently promotes that of the society more effectually than when he really intends to promote it. I have never known much good done by those who affected to trade for the public good. It is an affectation, indeed, not very common among merchants…(*WN*, Vol. I, p. 421)

And thus did Smith articulate his best-known theorem in *WN* stating the bottom-up process of unintentional wealth creation in free societies.

Much earlier, in his lectures on jurisprudence, he had expressed his view that commercial and industrial enterprise were important in promoting the independence and integrity of the labor force.

Commerce and manufactures promote independency—the Best police for preventing crimes and raising wages. the paris nobility have more servants per family than those of england, and disgruntled paris servants account for the higher paris crime rate. dependency leads to indigency and corrupts honesty.

> The nobility in Paris keeps far more menial servants than ours, who are often turned-out on their own account or through the caprice of their masters, and, being in the most indigent circumstances, are forced to commit the most dreadful crimes. In Glasgow, where almost no body has

> more than one servant, there are fewer capital crimes than in Edinburgh. In Glasgow there is not one in several years, but not a year passes in Edinburgh without some such disorders. Upon this principle, therefore, it is not so much the police that prevent the commission of crimes as the having as few persons as possible to live upon others. Nothing tends so much to corrupt mankind as dependency, while independency increases the honesty of the people. The establishment of commerce and manufactures, which brings about this independency, is the best police for preventing crimes. The common people have better wages in this way than in any other, and in consequence of this a general probity of manners takes place through the whole country. Nobody will be so mad as to expose himself upon the highway, [as a robber] when he can make better bread in an honest and industrious manner. The nobility of Paris and London are no doubt much upon a level, but the common people of the former, being much more dependent are not to be compared with these of the latter and for the same reason the commonality in Scotland differ from these in England, though the nobility too, are much upon a [same] level. (*LJ*, pp. 486–487)

For Smith nobility stood for privilege, for sheltered protection from having to earn one's way by merit. In a letter to a friend, he said "That in every profession the fortune of every individual should depend as much as possible upon his merit, and as little as possible upon his privilege, is certainly for the interest of the public" (Mosner, E. C., and I. S. (eds), 1978, *The Correspondence of Adam Smith*, Oxford University Press, Liberty Fund Edition, Letter 143, p. 178).

Two principles account for people's willingness to enter civil society and ultimately to obey a civil magistrate: authority and utility.

> There are two principles which induce men to enter into a civil society...the principles of authority and utility. At the head of every small society or association of men we find a person of superior abilities: in a warlike society the is a man of superiour strength, and in a polished one of superior mental capacity. Age and a long possession of power have also a tendencey to strengthen authority. Age is naturally in our imagination connected with wisdom and experience; and a continuance in power bestows a kind of right to the exercise of it. But superior wealth still more than any of these qualities contributes to confer authority. This proceeds not from any dependance that the poor have upon the rich, for in general the poor are independent, and support themselves by their labour, yet tho' they expect no benefit from them they have a strong propensity to pay

> them respect...Among the great, as superior abilities of body and mind are not so easily judged of by others, it is more convenient, as it is more common, to give the preference to riches. It is evident that an old family, that is, one which has been long distinguished, by it's wealth has more authority than any other....Superiour age, superior abilities of body and of mind, ancient family, and superiour wealth seem to be the four things that give one man authority over another. (*LJ*, pp. 401–402)

Strong, powerful families predominate in the first forms of civil order that emerge out of foraging societies. Superior ability, strength, age and long possession of power, and wealth confer authority. These features tend to emerge in pastoral and late foraging and hunting societies. Wealth in nineteenth century native American tribes consisted of horses which provided mobility, hunting prowess, and victory in war. The wealth in French and Spanish Basque families was carried in sheep providing an abundance of meat, milk, cheese, and wool. In Papua New Guinea, wealth was measured in pigs.

On the principle of utility in accounting for a people's willingness to obey a civil magistrate.

> The second principle which induces men to obey the civil magistrate is utility. Everyone is sensible of the necessity of this principle to preserve justice and peace in the society. By civil institutions, the poorest may get redress of injuries from the wealthiest and most powerful, and tho' there may be some irregularities in particular cases...yet we submit to them to avoid greater evils. It is the sense of public utility, more than of private, which influences men to obedience...If government has been of a long standing in a country and if it be supported by proper revenues, and be at the same time in the hands of a man of great abilities, authority is then in perfection.
>
> In all governments both these principles take place in some degree, but in a monarchy the principle of authority prevails, and in a democracy that of utility. In Britain, which is a mixed government, the faction's formed some time ago under the names of Whig and Tory were influenced by these principles; the former submitted to government on account of its utility and the advantages which they derived from it, while the latter pretended that it was of divine institution, and to offend against it was equally criminal as for a child to rebel against its parent. Men in general follow these principles according to their natural dispositions. In a man of a bold, daring, and bustling turn the principle of utility is predominant, and a peaceable,

> easy turn of mind usually is pleased with a tame submission to superiority. (*LJ*, p. 402)

The public utility services provided by the government through a civil magistrate are particularly enabling of justice as security from injury by one citizen toward another, and peace in providing security from invasion by foreigners. Monarchies rely more strongly on authority, democracies on utility. In Britain the eighteenth century factions contesting for the power to organize the government were the Whigs and Torys, both influenced by these principles; the Whigs submitted to government because of utility and the advantages which they derived from it. The Torys depended more on authority, pretending that they had received divine inspiration in support of its authority.

Three duties of the government in a society of natural liberty: protect citizens from the violence or suppression of foreign societies; protect citizens from the injustice of other citizens; provide public works and institutions beyond the scope of individuals to provide.

> According to the system of natural liberty, the sovereign has only three duties to attend to; three duties of great importance, indeed, but plain and intelligible to common understandings: first, the duty of protecting the society from the violence and invasion of other independent societies ; secondly, the duty of protecting, as far as possible, every member of the society from the injustice or oppression of every other member of it, or the duty of establishing an exact administration of justice; and, thirdly, the duty of erecting and maintaining certain public works and certain public institutions, which it can never be for the interest of any individual, or small number of individuals, to erect and maintain... (*WN*, Vol. II, pp. 184–185)

The proper function of the state in a society of natural liberty is to enforce the ancient rules of justice to provide security from injury; that is, to secure its citizens from injury by foreign nationals, and from injury to each other. And finally, to erect and maintain public works that the private sector is believed incapable of supplying through natural incentives. Modern economists, however, have learned that "public works" need not require government ownership. Pipelines, national power systems, bridges, and highways can be provided by private sector initiatives and sustained by charges for their use. Lighthouses were once built by businesses that contracted with port authorities to collect fees from passing ships when they docked in ports. Port authorities had an incentive to avoid overcharging which would limit transport. Highways, bridges, and tunnels can be supported by tolls, and structured by rules assuring alternative competitive routes between points. Pipelines and national power systems can be structured by competitively ruled private joint ventures with multiple owners, just as competing morning and evening newspapers in large cities once co-owned the specialized type press facilities needed to print their papers. Thus, have private institutional structures emerged that can provide public works, but they require government support for their implementation. Indeed, practice has shown that such institutions sometimes fail and are not a universal mechanism for structuring all such public projects.

Smith's third "duty of erecting and maintaining certain public works and certain public institutions, which it can never be for the interest of any individual, or small number of individuals, to erect and maintain" has been extended to include the redistribution of tax revenue to the support of the indigent, women, children, social security, universal health, and others deemed unable to earn sufficient income to support themselves. In effect new classes of "privilege" have been defined and supported by transfers from those whose merit has led to abundant earnings to those whose merit has led to earnings deemed inadequate. The latter are seen as "victims" of unintended relative hurt who deserve compensation. By thus redefining terms Smith's system of rule-governed conduct can be used to justify modern forms of direct political intervention. But it seems clear that Smtih would disapprove because these interpretations violate his central principle that all such beneficent actions must be voluntary, uncoerced, and therefore are endogenously sustainable.

Adam smith was sympathetic to the cause of the american colonies, believing that they should be fully represented in sharing the cost of their administration, and expressed these dissenting views as a loyal british citizen and advisor to the british government: dissent was a responsibility of loyalty.

> If the colonies, notwithstanding their refusal to submit to British taxes, are still to be considered as provinces of the British empire, their defence in some future war cost Great Britain as great an expence as it ever has

done in any former war. The rulers of Great Britain have, for more than a century past, amused the people with the imagination that they possessed a great empire on the west side of the Atlantic. This empire, however, has hitherto existed in imagination only. It has hitherto been, not an empire, but the project of an empire...a project which has cost, which continues to cost, and which, if pursued in the same way as it has been hitherto, is likely to cost, immense expence, without being likely to bring any profit; for the effects of the monopoly of the colony trade, it has been shewn, are, to the great body of the people, mere loss instead of profit. It is surely now time that our rulers should either realize this golden dream, in which they have been indulging themselves, perhaps, as well as the people; or, that they should awake from it themselves, and endeavour to awaken the people. If the project cannot be completed, it ought to be given up. If any of the provinces of the British empire cannot be made to contribute towards the support of the whole empire, it is surely time that Great Britain should free herself from the expenee of defending those provinces in time of war, and of' supporting any part of their civil or military establishments in time of peace, and endeavour to accommodate her future views and designs to the real mediocrity of her circumstances. (*WN*, Vol. II, pp. 232–233)

Index

Vernon L. Smith, *Adam Smith's Theory of Society*,
https://doi.org/10.1007/978-3-031-68494-4

Q

R